THE TRUTH IS ALWAYS GREY

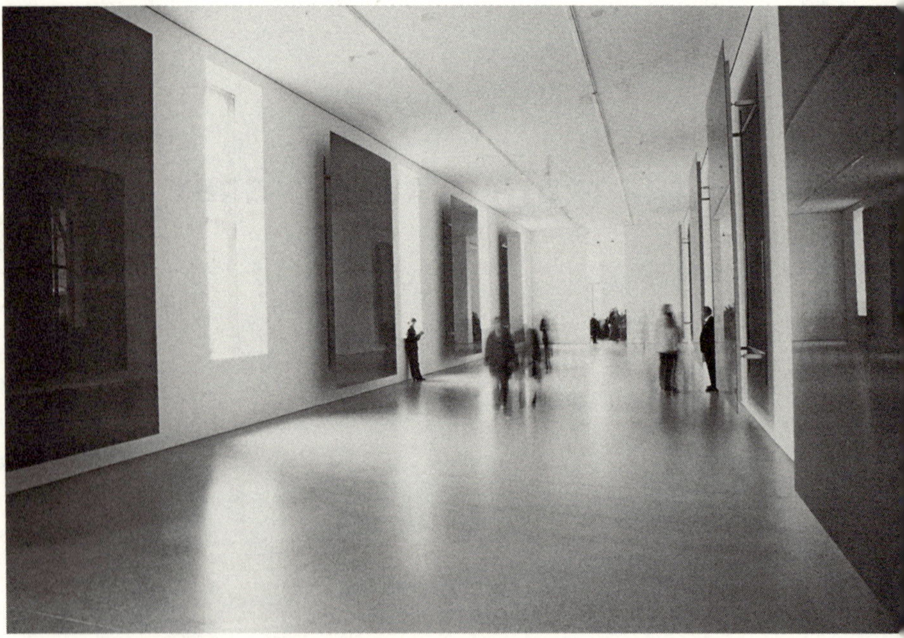

THE TRUTH IS ALWAYS GREY

A HISTORY OF MODERNIST PAINTING

FRANCES GUERIN

University of Minnesota Press
Minneapolis
London

Frontispiece: Gerhard Richter, *Eight Grey*, 500 × 270 × 50 cm each. Deutsche Guggenheim, Berlin. Installation view, 10 November 2002–3 January 2003. Enameled glass and steel photograph by Mathias Schormann. Copyright Deutsche Guggenheim, Berlin and the Solomon R. Guggenheim Museum, New York.

MM Publication of this book has been aided by a grant from the Millard Meiss Publication Fund of the College Art Association.

A portion of chapter 4 was previously published in "Searching in Grey: Cy Twombly's Untitled Paintings," in *Die Farbe Grau*, ed. Magdalena Bushart and Gregor Wedekind (Berlin: Walter de Gruyter, 2016).

Published by the University of Minnesota Press
111 Third Avenue South, Suite 290
Minneapolis, MN 55401-2520
http://www.upress.umn.edu

ISBN 978-1-5179-0044-1 (hc)
ISBN 978-1-5179-0045-8 (pb)

A Cataloging-in-Publication record for this book is available from the Library of Congress.

Printed in the United States of America on acid-free paper

23 22 21 20 19 18 9 8 7 6 5 4 3 2 1

In memory
Georgia Fee (1951–2012)

You cannot say that it is light or dark. It is a color or non-color that I identify with. I don't believe in absolutes. The truth is always gray.

—**Anselm Kiefer,** *Anselm Kiefer: Heaven and Earth*

CONTENTS

INTRODUCTION

THE COLOR GREY

> Whether all grow black, or all grow bright, or all remain grey, it is grey we need, to begin with, because of what it is, and of what it can do, made of bright and black, able to shed the former, or the latter, and be the latter or the former alone. But perhaps I am the prey, on the subject of grey, in the grey, to delusions.
>
> —**Samuel Beckett**, *The Unnamable*

IN AUGUST 1888 Vincent van Gogh wrote a letter to his brother Theo from Arles in which he described the café where he was sitting through a rainbow of colors. The brilliance in his description mirrors his excitement for his environment. He is particularly enthralled by the seemingly infinite palette of greys in which the scene before him is painted. It is, he pronounces, "pure Velásquez." He takes care to communicate the exact hue of grey of the walls; they are grey all over:

> The floor is of grey bitumen like a street pavement, grey paper on the walls, green blinds always drawn, a big green curtain in front of the door which is always open, to stop the dust coming in. So it already has a Velásquez grey—like in the "Spinning Women"—and even the very narrow, very fierce ray of sunlight through a blind, like the one that slants across Velásquez's picture, is not wanting. Little tables of course, with white cloths. And behind this room in Velásquez grey you see the old kitchen, as clean as a

> Dutch kitchen, with floor of bright red bricks, green vegetables, oak chest, the kitchen range with shining brass things and blue and white tiles, and the big fire a clear orange. And then there are two women waitresses, both in grey, a little like that picture of Prevost's you have in your place—you could compare it point for point.
>
> In the kitchen, an old woman and a short, fat servant also in grey, black, white. I don't know if I describe it clearly enough for you, but it's here, and it's pure Velásquez.[1]

Van Gogh is inspired by this scene and he starts painting. The array of greys and their complement to what are usually referred to as chromatic colors—red, orange, green—does not conform to the conventional image in and of grey. There is nothing somber or melancholy or drab about this café in Arles. On the contrary, grey gives the scene its energy, and Van Gogh the inspiration to paint, via his reminder of the masterpieces of Velázquez, and, further on in the letter, those of Vermeer. Subsequently, Van Gogh opens out this scene in grey, suggesting a use of grey in painting to represent the simplicity, comfort, and warmth of his life in the provincial town. Simultaneously, Van Gogh's description suggests that painting or painted representation is the only way to describe the infinite array of greys that otherwise escapes our attention when we look at the world with the naked eye. Language does not have the breadth or precision to describe the nuances in grey that are so effortlessly envisioned in painting.

Van Gogh expresses through discussion of Velázquez's *Las hilanderas / The Spinners* (ca. 1657) what for him is the familiarity and warmth of grey. Van Gogh's enthusiasm for a world painted in grey reveals his engagement with and exploration of a color that has not only been a preferred medium and color for centuries of artists but likewise is the reiterated preoccupation of some of the most highly regarded twentieth-century modernist and postmodernist painters. These include artists such as Alberto Giacometti, Pablo Picasso, René Magritte, Vilhelm Hammershøi, and, in the postwar period, Agnes Martin, Jasper Johns, Cy Twombly, Mark Rothko, or their European counterparts such as Anselm Kiefer, Luc Tuymans, and Gerhard Richter. These artists don't quote Van Gogh, or even Velázquez, as influences. Nevertheless, their grey paintings are connected to a tradition of works that have privileged grey as the medium for exploration and expression of the concerns of painting over centuries.

Perhaps the most interesting aspect of Van Gogh's image is his disregard for and eventual inversion of conventional assumptions about grey. Even more striking is the fact that this same repudiation is everywhere present in the grey paintings of the twentieth century, as well as those of earlier centuries. Van Gogh's successful attempt not only to put colors into words, but also to use textual translations of color to paint the scene, to capture its tone, and its temperature in writing for his brother, is to be acknowledged. For Van Gogh has a confidence in grey, and, in turn, its translation into words that goes against the grain of conventional philosophical wisdom about color in general and grey in particular. I argue that the same confidence that radiates from Van Gogh's letter to his brother infuses nineteenth-century painting and plays a key role in the articulation of the painted aesthetic of early modernism. This fascination with and exploration of grey continues into the early decades of the twentieth century, particularly in the modernist shift toward abstraction in analytical cubism. In turn, it reaches its most vivid depiction in postwar modernist abstraction in the United States.

For Van Gogh, grey is a color. Grey is legitimate, it is provocative, and it has the capacity to generate warmth, excitement, and creativity. Van Gogh was not the only one in his historical moment to espouse the aesthetic qualities of grey. Forty years earlier, Charles Baudelaire celebrated the grey of a Delacroix painting at the Salon of 1845: "The painting is grey . . . grey like nature, grey like the summer air when the sunlight at dusk falls trembling on each object."[2] For Baudelaire, the delicacy, luminescence, and lightness of the air as it is rendered in paint are made possible by the fact that Delacroix's palette is grey. According to Baudelaire, Delacroix was one of the great painters, in a league with Leonardo and Michelangelo, and his painting was in the vanguard because it was on the cusp between Renaissance and modernist painting. After the Salon of 1845, numerous paintings continued to express the inspiration Van Gogh experienced in the café in Arles and the excitement Baudelaire found in the shimmer of Delacroix's grey palette.

What happened to change the critical reception and, more broadly, the public perception of grey? Gradually, throughout the late nineteenth century and into the twentieth, grey loses its appeal. Until, in the aftermath of World War II, a writer such as Theodor Adorno condemns the color. For Adorno, grey is the boredom of the capitalist world; it is in need of negation and color through music, for example.[3] Most interesting, for Adorno, grey is one-dimensional and superficial, in keeping with his vision of capitalist commodification and his newly industrialized world. When he says grey must be negated, this is because he understands grey to feed the false idealism of a world without thought and substantive meaning. This, for Adorno, is the ultimate rejection.[4]

Adorno is not alone in this searing critique of grey among writers and thinkers of his generation, particularly those who come of age or reach their most profound insights around the time of World War II. And yet, against this background of pessimism for grey, artists nevertheless continue to paint in grey. They indulge in grey, and in so doing, they continue to celebrate grey as the color most appropriate to their pursuit of painting. Moreover, their work reveals a conception and use of grey that is central to the development of modernist painting.

In a landmark (for grey) exhibition at the Menil Collection in Houston, Dominique de Menil mounted *Gray Is the Color* in 1974, an exhibition that inspired the color of the complex of buildings that houses the Menil Collection. A historian, collector, and curator, de Menil was among the first to grant grey painting legitimacy within the art museum.[5] In America, it took another thirty years before the Art Institute of Chicago and the Metropolitan Museum of Art's exhibition *Jasper Johns: Gray* cast the spotlight on the grey works of one of America's most important postwar painters. With this exhibition in 2007, grey was somewhat cautiously reintroduced to an American public as being significant. I use the word "cautiously" because even though the exhibition put grey on center stage, there was an underlying ambivalence or superficiality in its attitude to grey. Even though the Art Institute and the Metropolitan Museum of Art devoted a whole exhibition to Johns's grey paintings, the critics and reviewers were distracted from the form and significance of grey. It is true that there is much discussion of the grey paintings themselves in the catalog and reviews of *Jasper Johns: Gray*. There is, however, minimal engagement with the grey that dominates his oeuvre and this exhibition in particular.[6] That is, there is no analysis of grey as a color, no sustained critical or philosophical discourse on what grey enables Johns to do, what Johns does with grey, or how it reflects back on the rest of his oeuvre and the history of modern art more generally. In short, the question of why the exhibition focused on Johns's use of grey and not another color is never addressed.[7]

The Truth Is Always Grey begins from this history of a dramatic falling out of favor of the color grey between the mid-nineteenth and mid-twentieth centuries.[8] When the history of writing and criticism on grey—both as a color and in painting—is juxtaposed with the actual use of the color grey in the development of a modernist aesthetic, the color's changing critical fortune is even more remarkable. There is an overwhelming inconsistency between the immense experimentation with grey for the definition of modernist painting and the attention given to the color by critics and commentators. In the same period of one hundred years in which grey plummets toward critical disrepute, it becomes increasingly present, increasingly complex in its use, and increasingly dense in its meaning on the canvases of some of the most prominent modernist painters. The attitude of respect toward, even celebration of, grey witnessed by Baudelaire and later van Gogh is never jettisoned by subsequent painters. On the contrary, grey is so often the means and materiality for their exploration of what it is to paint, and what painting is in the twentieth century.

Baudelaire's applause for Delacroix's grey painting coincides with the increased use of the color grey to explore the possibilities of painting, and is expressed on the eve of the gathering momentum toward modernism. *The Truth Is Always Grey* is devoted to this same intersection of grey as a color and the development of a modernist aesthetic. Grey is often the chosen color for explorations in painting as it pushes closer and closer toward (and then away from) abstraction in the twentieth century.

Broadly speaking, then, *The Truth Is Always Grey* argues for the "symbolic substance" of grey, a color that is apposite to rethinking the value and trajectory of modernist painting and its insights. To make this argument, I foreground five key characteristics of grey.

First, grey painting has a history that hitherto has been undervalued. Some of the most significant and radical transgressions of European modernist art were made in grey at the turn of the nineteenth into the twentieth century. That is, grey comes into its own at the height of the second industrial revolution, and gathers force as Europe moves toward two world wars. Vanguard experiments in, for example, symbolism, postimpressionism, and analytical cubism all underline the link between grey painting and industrial modernity, that is, between modernist painting and the historical world in which it is conceived. To make this argument, I explore the shattered images of Picasso and Braque's analytical cubism, Giacometti's portraits of the isolated anonymous souls of modern life, and from an even earlier period, Whistler's pollution-drenched London air in the *Nocturnes*. In the same way that the grey in these paintings has a long history, it also provides the stepping-stone to a discussion of postwar modernist paintings that use grey. In turn, the aesthetic and value of these postwar modernist paintings in grey become the primary focus of this book.

I argue that moments of historical transgression and disturbance often give context to the creative potential of grey. That is, while grey has been used in painting for centuries, at least as far back as the Middle Ages, the works of early modernism in the nineteenth century make overt a form and structure for the painted grey surface at times of historical upheaval. In addition, the same form and structure of grey are then taken up and pushed beyond their limits in the postwar years. Included in my notion of moments of historical change or upheaval to which painters respond in grey is the development of new forms of representation. For example, early European modernists often use grey as the color that best connects painting to the new art forms of photography in the nineteenth and cinema in the early twentieth century. This, of course, is in keeping with the search for a modernist aesthetic of painting, a search that takes place alongside the development of the new art forms at times of historical transformation.

Second, I argue that grey is a color. Like all colors, grey has varying temperatures, tones, rhythms, and meanings. As a color, grey is shown to be unique when painters choose it to strip their representations of all external concerns. They are able to interrogate the substance and meaning of painting without the distraction, assumptions, weight, and hermeneutic baggage of red, blue, or green, for example. *The Truth Is Always Grey* shows that grey is the ideal color for the modernist pursuit of painting. Grey is flexible, malleable; it can be pushed and pulled in different directions, worked and reworked into new, unanticipated materiality and meaning. Grey is not fixed: it both reflects and absorbs light, and it extends the spectrum between black and white, between the extremes of all other colors. Grey has the capacity to move its viewer beyond the materiality of paint. Contrary to Wassily Kandinsky's claim that it is "depressing," "toneless," "immobile," grey is always in motion, always shifting and constantly evasive.[9] Modernist painters use these qualities of grey in their pursuit of the concerns of painting as representation.

Third, due to these unique characteristics, grey paint is used by prominent mid- and late twentieth-century artists, particularly in the United States, to pursue the questions that preoccupy painting. Thus, to give one example, in grey, Andy Warhol produced multiple screen-painted versions of Liz Taylor, Elvis, electric chairs, car crashes, and race riots in works that challenge the viewer's numbness to the representation of death and disaster as it is splattered across the contemporary press. The same paintings question the role of painting at a given historical moment: Do they amount to just another series of mass-produced images? Are they seen as such? Or do they need to imitate mass-mediated images if we are to attend to them? In the twentieth century, a number of artists explore questions regarding the resonance and relevance of painting in an age of mass media through using grey. Picasso's use of a multitude of greys in *Guernica* (1937), as if in revolt against the drama and destruction of the ravages of war, is often cited as the inspiration for these representations.

As I demonstrate in a discussion of *Guernica,* like no other color and no other medium, grey is a medium with which painters engage with the urgent matter of what is painting in this world. *Guernica* is just one of many grey paintings that assume the responsibility of painting to envision the identity of twentieth-century European history, filled as it is with wars and disasters that demand reflection, memorial, and simultaneous illustration. Of course, the use of grey to represent and thereby engage with history is different from the history of grey as a medium, although the two are necessarily entwined on these canvases. A distinction must be made between the history of grey as a medium for representation (though it is often used toward abstraction) and the history of the events represented in grey.

For this reason, an interaction with the historical world around it is the fourth characteristic I attribute to grey painting. In particular, grey in the twentieth century is the most appropriate color for the examination of the role of painting in a world in which industry and industrialization have changed the color of life to a multitude of greys. Grey has repeatedly and consistently been used not only for formal and aesthetic reasons but also because it has a historical resonance and identity with the industrial advances that take place all around it. Grey is the color that best describes this perspective on the twentieth century, the metals in which it is built, the factories in which it is produced, the cities in which it is lived.

Through these four characteristics of grey, I demonstrate how prominent twentieth-century artists reimagine the centrality of the color to the development of the history of art, and engage its traits for depiction—however abstract—of their historical moment. This history of modernist art through the lens of grey sees painting reinvented, propelled forward, and always in search of the question of what is painting in the twentieth and twenty-first centuries. Because these centuries are framed by industrial revolutions, the development of capitalism, world wars, the Cold War, and eventually the digital revolution, painting takes up the color of the machines that made all of this possible: grey.

The fifth characteristic of grey is revealed when I place my argument within the terms of Adorno's claim for grey. *The Truth Is Always Grey* demonstrates that, in contradistinction to his dismal vision, grey holds within it the very complexity and contradiction that Adorno believes only music can provide. Of course, Adorno mentions grey in passing, and then, it's another way to pose his theory of negation. Thus he colors his theory of capitalist commodification grey for polemical as well as philosophical reasons. Nevertheless, his citation can be used as a springboard to more nuanced visions of grey. Although grey may not start the revolutions Adorno was hoping for, it does provoke, it is open, and it thus points beyond itself, often to possibilities yet to come thanks to the viewing experience it invites. Like the music Adorno celebrated, *The Truth Is Always Grey* argues that grey painting has the capacity to play with absence and presence, seducing its viewer by way of its material surface toward an experience of immateriality, trafficking between the steel grey of its palette and the light that it attracts as well as becomes. Thus, the first four characteristics of grey are the scaffolding that supports the fifth: a unique experience of modernist painting had by viewers of grey painting.

Grey as a medium crosses historical boundaries; it continually challenges the categories of art historical formulation. As such, grey enables us, or implores us, to question the assumptions of a historically determined modernism. This task of reconsidering art history necessarily begins from an awareness of grey as itself the exemplary modernist color, even as it can be identified in earlier centuries.[10] Accordingly, because of its fluidity, its contradictions and possibilities, grey is not simply a common bond between paintings across centuries. Rather, grey invites a broader claim about painting per se. A study of grey enables recognition that painting has always been interested in its own physicality; it has always seen this physicality manifest on its surface, even when a realist perspectival picture space claimed to be the image that covered that surface. At the same time, because of its proximity to and dependence on light, grey also leads to a nonobjective experience of seeing and knowing the world.

Applause for Grey

It is true that not all writers and commentators on modern art have denigrated or ignored the visions of and in grey painting. Indeed, the absence of discussion becomes surprising only when we consider the discrepancy between the widespread use of grey in the twentieth century—to an intense degree at key moments in the development of certain artists—and the parallel textualization of these works.

There are other examples of the serious critical attention paid to grey. In chapter 1, I detail Leon Battista Alberti's respect for grey in his well-known discussion of color and light. Similarly, more contemporary critics have made instructive comments on grey. For example, Philip Ball applauds Rembrandt's masterful use of a "restricted palette" and observes that it lends a "certain sincerity and honesty" as well as reflects the artist's "ruinous, impoverished end."[11] Specifically, of the dark-grey palette used for the background of *Portrait of Margaretha de Geer* (ca. 1661), Ball says it "has left an incredible subtlety of pigmentation lavished on it."[12] Ball does not pay a lot of attention to grey in his book, but in these glimpses, he readily acknowledges the importance of grey to the painterly effects in certain artists' work, as well as the development of color theories such as that of the influential German chemist Friedrich Wilhelm Ostwald.[13] Ball's acknowledgment is typical of the interest shown by critics who applaud the use of grey painting: even though they are interested in its possibilities, the interest remains limited to a few, often indirect, observations.[14]

Once modernism gathers momentum in the early twentieth century, artists themselves continue the applause for grey painting begun by Alberti and taken up by Baudelaire four centuries later. In what might be understood as an affirmation of Van Gogh's belief that after red, yellow, and blue, all colors are an endless variation of grey, I argue in the coming chapters that the palettes of painters from Picasso and Braque, through Giacometti to American postwar modernists as diverse as Warhol, Johns, Martin, Twombly, and Brice Marden, engage the significance of painting through the infinitely differentiated hues, meanings, and uses of grey.[15]

Modernist Grey

J. M. W. Turner's paintings are my springboard to early modernist uses of grey. His waterscapes are an inspiration because they coincide with the invention of photography and repeatedly appear in grey. In addition, many of the concerns of Turner's storms, beaches, and skies about to explode—with rain or with sun—are further explored in twentieth-century abstract grey painting. In some ways, the placement of Turner's paintings is arbitrary, because, as I demonstrate in chapter 1, the history of grey as a medium begins well before Turner. Nevertheless, I use Turner's waterscapes to show how grey can provide structure, aesthetic, and a potential significance for twentieth-century modernist painting. In turn, the history of grey painting from its earliest coincidence with industrial modernity on Turner's canvases offers a new perspective on modernist grey painting. This perspective sees and understands modernism as a set of ideas that move between different art forms and across historical periods. Thus, the singular focus on grey as a proposition for modernist painting demonstrates that even as painting searches to redefine itself in the twentieth century, its most acute insights and visual conceptions come at the interface with other art forms and media (in grey), and in its connection to the historical world. I give this argument legitimacy by placing it side by side with the work of critics closely associated with existing histories of modernist art—from Johannes Itten and Josef Albers, through Clement Greenberg and Michael Fried, to Rosalind Krauss, T. J. Clark, and Briony Fer.

The continuity between what is usually understood as early and late modernism, the undeniable resonance between bodies of work across periods and nations, is the first, and perhaps the most important, revelation of grey. A focus on grey painting leaves us with no choice but to rethink the periodized organization of modernism, particularly as it is understood and responded to by painting. The themes and concerns of modernist grey abstract painting are identifiable in grey works over centuries. Along these same lines, the identification of modernist characteristics and principles in the work discussed here is a way to approach its concerns even though the appellation will not always accord with accepted definitions.

To give one example, Gerhard Richter would protest the label of modernist being applied to his work. And yet, I argue that the modernist preoccupation with grey, the concerns, themes, and compositional explorations in grey, finds its best example on his canvases. I am not attached to a circumscription of Richter's painting as modernist, postmodernist, or any other designation. Rather, my designation functions more as a means to conceptual clarity. To this end, I argue that his search for the meaning and ultimate perpetuation of the problem of painting in the postwar moment is a continuation of, as well as an evident departure from, the modernist aesthetic and historical development. Richter says that he begins from the void of grey, but his paintings continue to use grey to interrogate possibilities and to reimagine painting as a form, medium, and material at the end of the twentieth century and into the twenty-first.[16] Grey may be a void, but it is an incredibly generative void within Richter's oeuvre. Unlike any other artist, Richter has continued to reinvent and thus to push the identity of painting beyond its apparent end point, again and again, even when he produces tapestries or exhibits photocopies of his paintings.[17] Moreover, Richter's grey is an example of the use of the color to meet the sociopolitical and historical ends that I identify as characteristic of modernist painting. Thus, it does not matter that his grey works span fifty years and might, more conventionally, be variably identified as neoexpressionist, photorealist, or postmodernist. What matters is that they engage with the five characteristics of grey, all of which contribute to an innovative reconception of modernist painting.

The Death of Painting and the Rise of Monochrome: The Russians, the New Yorkers, and Grey Painting

The monochrome, allover abstract color-field canvas born at the beginning of the twentieth century, is integral to the life of grey painting as I understand it. While I argue that none of the postwar grey canvases are monochrome, the history of monochrome within modernist painting nevertheless influences the aesthetic, rationale, and impact of grey abstract painting. The kinship of the monochrome and grey abstract painting is based on the fact that, within my history, they have both been used to address questions and problems of painting within the project of modernism.

Again and again, painting in grey defies all that is said about the supposed modernist erasure of the painted gesture, about death and mourning, about modernism, and about the end of painting.[18] At least, if modernism is reconsidered in postwar American and European grey paintings and in prewar monochromatic painting, then the complexity and double edge of modernism, as well as grey painting's defiance of traditional conceptions of modernism, are exposed. Kazimir Malevich declared the end of painting in 1918 with his famous *White on White,* "a declaration" that introduced nonrepresentational, objectless painting to the world.[19] He set in motion a new narrative in the history of art, a narrative that was quickly taken up by others such as Piet Mondrian and, most radically, by Marcel Duchamp. The Duchamp readymades are now accepted as a derisive expression toward painting. They claim painting is no more than retinal stimulation that needed to be done away with in preference to artworks not produced by artists, that is, not the descendants of the romantic movement.[20] The readymade proclaimed the end of painting, once again. How to address this crisis of painting stirred up by Duchamp? The answer for painters was, of course, the monochrome canvas.[21] Monochrome painting was the response to a call to dissolve the urge to represent, to search for the immateriality of painting, for painting that would be without dimensions, without specific associative ideas, and without psychological burden.

In the postwar period in the United States, artists such as Frank Stella, Carl André, and Ad Reinhardt led a generation concerned to reduce painting to its most fundamental form, and strategy, its constitutive elements of space and color. While Donald Judd condemned painting for its inability to leave illusionism behind and made the radical move to sculpture, he did not ignite the revolution as is often claimed.[22] But painting was reduced to color, light, and surface well before Stella, André, and Reinhardt removed the object of representation. To be sure, these radical shifts in painting were taking place well before World War I, even before Duchamp's readymades, and prior to Malevich's and Alexander Rodchenko's monochromes. Indeed, they can be traced back to the work of Édouard Manet and Claude Monet in the nineteenth century. While Manet challenged the invisible line between painted representation and world, between image and spectator, and thus destroyed the illusory wholeness of the represented world, Monet took strides away from figuration toward abstraction with the execution of his famous water lilies. Similarly, in 1909, before Duchamp, Picasso, and the analytical cubists were already committed to breaking up the picture plane in full disregard of its otherwise illusion of coherence. Moreover, Picasso's revolution was envisioned in grey. And because Picasso, early modernist artists such as Manet and, later, Giacometti, and symbolists such as Hammershøi have extended periods in their oeuvres when they paint solely in grey, I understand their work as key stepping-stones in the trajectory toward the realization of the radical abstractions in grey of postwar American painting.

Following Duchamp's daring and radical rejection of representation altogether at the time of World War I, the discussion about the dethroning of painting was (re)ignited in earnest.[23] It was then, after this war, that painting of a single color, a so-called pure color, could possibly become the only object in question.[24] Like much of the impetus for radical shifts in representation in the first decade of the twentieth century, it was political and social turmoil that drove the displacement of the represented object by color in painting. In Revolutionary Russia, Malevich believed materialism would give way to transcendence through spiritualism. Accordingly, the white square on a white square was destined to reflect "the supremacy of pure feeling or perception in the pictorial arts."[25] Malevich's suprematist colorfields displaced the object once and for all, in the ultimate realization of what Kandinsky described as he looked at Monet's haystack:

> Previously I only knew realistic art . . . and suddenly for the first time I saw a picture. It was the catalog that told me that that was a haystack. I numbly felt that the object was missing in this picture. Painting received a fabulous power and magnificence. Unconsciously, the object was also discredited as the inevitable element of the picture.[26]

Rodchenko's monochromes were, at the time, the ultimate iconoclastic gesture. He too announced the end of painting in September 1921: "I reduced painting to its logical conclusion and exhibited three canvases: red, blue, and yellow." And he would later write, "I affirmed: It's all over. Basic colors. Every plane is a plane, and there is to be no more representation."[27] As we shall see, Picasso takes up the so-called monochromatic palette to represent social turmoil and, eventually, war. And the color he chooses is grey.

Modernist painting's relationship to the monochrome has no ostensible connection to grey as it is conceived in the critical and historical literature. Even with the usual focus on Picasso and analytical cubism's immersion in a brown-and-grey palette, grey is not mentioned as being in any way important to this narrative. This lacuna is the focus of *The Truth Is Always Grey*. I shall demonstrate the significance of grey to the working through of the questions of painting toward and beyond modernist abstraction, particularly as they center on the discourses raised by monochromatic painting. While I insist throughout that the greys found in modernist painting are not monochrome, the critical questions attached to monochrome painting are the concern of grey. By tracing the importance of grey paint to the development of modernist abstraction, I recast this history and, with it, the relationship between painting and the world beyond the frame. Thus, in my narrative, modernism is also a historically influenced phenomenon.

The early postwar American high modernists, such as Robert Ryman, Martin, and minimalists such as Judd, Robert Morris, Stella, artists working in a so-called monochromatic palette, were keen to cut off painting's relationship to the world as a way of moving away from the illusionism of painting. However, the history I offer of grey modernist painting, and the development of painting that parallels this history, are always influenced by industrialization, by war, by certain strands of capitalism. As I demonstrate, painting cannot be separated from the world in which it is produced. Further, when this history is traced, it is not a trajectory that is immediately familiar: it is a history of modernist and postmodernist art that does not draw connections between two world wars, Duchamp, and abstract expressionism. My focus is not the continuity of pre- or postwar painting. On the contrary, I am concerned with the way in which grey carves out its own historical trajectory. Nevertheless, the particularity of the history forged by grey painting happens to unfold simultaneously with a history that sees postwar painting as a continued pursuit of the questions and themes of modernism.

Following a chapter on grey and its use in premodern paintings in ways that show traces of the characteristics of modernist abstraction, I devote chapter 2 to nineteenth-century paintings influenced by photography. Paintings by Turner, John Constable, and James McNeill Whistler, the American in London, show how the grey of photographic reproduction, the grey of cities filled with smog, and the grey of post-Enlightenment social transformation, all come to define the painted aesthetic in this era. In an extension of this, at the end of the nineteenth century, grey paintings by artists such as Manet, Monet, and in Northern Europe, Hammershøi—works considered to give birth to modernist painting—move ever closer to high modernist abstraction. In addition, with the rise of industrialization, and nineteenth-century developments in chemistry, dye colors had a strong impact on the manufacture of pigments. In the late nineteenth century, synthetic dyes worked together with industry to change the fabrication of pigments as they became stable for the first time.[28] As a result, the rainbow of greys on the palette of Van Gogh's mind became a reality.

In the twentieth century, hand in hand with the burgeoning of second waves of industrialization across Europe, grey paint is used in new and exciting ways that depart from its use and application in the nineteenth century. Chapters 3 and 4 are devoted to the American postwar painters. For the first time, grey becomes fully abstracted, without figurative reference, in the early 1950s. In turn, the historical and social import of paintings in the postwar period is transferred to the relationship between grey and other colors, the relationships between paint and other media, between the painted grey canvas and the artist and observer.

There are numerous abstract grey paintings from this period of American art, many of which I do not discuss. I focus instead on paintings by artists who either use a grey palette throughout their career, such as Johns and Marden, or who have a significant period in their aesthetic development when they choose grey, such as Twombly and Martin. That said, I also discuss paintings by artists who paint key works in grey that illustrate the thematic concerns of modernism in grey, such as Warhol and Rothko.

One of the primary arguments of *The Truth Is Always Grey* is that in the twentieth century, grey is a color both produced by, and productively used to represent and interpret, the world we inhabit. If lapis lazuli was an expression of the wealth of the patron and his socially elevated station in the fifteenth century, in the twentieth century, grey paint is chosen to reflect, influence, and engage the undulations of industrial modernity, war, and the changing face of representation.[29] Grey is brought to life in the twentieth century as it intersects with so many historical phenomena in its midst.[30] I have already mentioned photography, and could add the cinema, the printed press, all of which are colored grey. The blank screens of other media—television and computers—are grey, as are key objects integral to the progress of industry and capitalism, such as factories and the bitumen on the roads. Twentieth-century grey painting explores all of these phenomena when it inquires into its own status and examines its relationship to the world.

In traumatized postwar Europe, grey assumes a real responsibility to the world outside the frame. Grey on the European postwar canvas reflects, remembers, and represents the Holocaust, civil war, and the revolution that begins in the press. Popular media—the press, photography, cinema—spawn the production of Picasso's *Guernica*, contribute to the development of the isolated, deformed grey figures in Francis Bacon's paintings, for example, and end up in the provocative works of Luc Tuymans in the early twenty-first century. I reference these European paintings, but I do not give them designated attention because *The Truth Is Always Grey* explores the questions of modernist painting as they reach toward abstraction in the United States. There are, of course, European painters who are committed to abstraction, but because of the commitment to history, their search often has different motivations and meanings that would make inclusion here a distraction. That said, I devote the final chapter, chapter 5, to the enormous output in grey of German artist Gerhard Richter. Richter is one of a handful of European artists whose grey paintings engage with the questions of abstract modernism as well as historical representation. I would argue that Richter envisions in grey all that can be said and imagined for modernist painting and its aftermath, as well as for the possibilities in grey painting in a postwar world.

Richter engages with grey across his career; he takes time out in other colors, and turns back to grey for further reflection on all of the questions that concern painting in the second half of the twentieth century and the beginning of the twenty-first. In addition, his paintings offer the most complex, most ambiguous, and thus most challenging, responses to the resolution of these questions. However, in spite of Richter's status as one of the most prominent painters of his generation, he is not working in a vacuum. Not only is Richter consciously indebted to the history of art as it is often envisioned on his canvases, he also is involved in his historical moment as well as surrounded by other artists working in grey paint. Thus, it is important to acknowledge that his grey paintings only have the impact they do thanks to the context of the artworks that give them meaning, such as those discussed in the first four chapters.

The Irony of Grey

This book's title, *The Truth Is Always Grey*, comes from a statement made by Anselm Kiefer in which he describes his use of lead as a symbolic material: "You cannot say that it is light or dark. It is a color or non-color that I identify with. I don't believe in absolutes. The truth is always gray."[31] In lead (and grey), Kiefer identifies the inherent contradictions that underlie an asserted absolutism in twentieth-century politics, culture, and artistic meaning. For Kiefer, lead is the material and grey is the color of German history, in particular the Holocaust. Lead and grey are death, trauma, disaster, and loss. There is apparently nothing alive in Kiefer's dense grey worlds strewn with lead books.[32] Grey, however, is also enigma, instability, uncertainty, and contradiction. And, I would argue, this transience and ambiguity of lead, as well as of grey, are what give it possibility; they are a glimmer of light in a lead sky. Fields of dead, grey lead always end up in a thin red line on the horizon of Kiefer's world. In Kiefer's vision, death can never be separated from life; destruction is only the inverse of incompletion. Fire and energy have not fully passed through Kiefer's nevertheless ashen landscapes. Kiefer is a romantic after all, and his insistence on grey and lead, their fluidity and ambiguity, is not accidental. Grey and lead both embody the possibility of change, of a truth, however distorted, that is never absolute or clear. My use of his quotation as the title of this book is a conscious appropriation of Kiefer's ironic use of grey as well as his notion of truth as it is visualized in grey lead.

My focus on grey paintings in *The Truth Is Always Grey* is also a gesture of irony, an irony that I hope breeds openness and possibility like the trace of red on Kiefer's horizons. The simultaneous art historical and the broader historical context enable revelation of the ambiguities of painting in the modern period as they are explored in grey. These ambiguities may not be immediate, but they always become apparent to those who stand before the paintings for a length of time. Typical of grey, and a characteristic enthusiastically embraced by grey painting, is the tendency toward uncertainty and contradiction.

Anselm Kiefer's bold announcement that "the truth is always gray" may not reflect a widely held belief regarding the possibility of truth, or the accepted wisdom about grey. But as the following chapters demonstrate, the modernist grey canvas lives and breathes in a space of uncertainty. It has a form and an effect that hover over, at times indulge in, the impossibilities and contradictions of representation way beyond its own lifetime, the hesitant identity of the modernist artist, and most profoundly, the power to challenge its viewer to confront her own insecure identity in its presence. And these inconsistencies, contradictions, challenges as the defining characteristics of a certain strain of modernist abstract painting, are the revelation of the grey canvases here discussed. In every way, on every level, these works in grey confirm that their truth—the truth of painting, our truth, and the truth of the relationship between us and them—is always grey.

1

WHAT IS GREY PAINTING?

TRACING A HISTORICAL TRAJECTORY

When we're asked "What do the words 'red,' 'blue,' 'black,' 'white,' mean?" we can, of course, immediately point to things which have these colors,—but our ability to explain the meanings of these words goes no further! For the rest, we have either no idea at all of their use, or a very rough and to some extent false one.

Ludwig Wittgenstein, *Remarks on Colour*

In gray there is no possibility of movement because gray consists of two colors that have no active force, for they stand the one in motionless discord, the other in motionless negation, even of discord, like an endless wall, a bottomless pit.

Wassily Kandinsky, *Concerning the Spiritual in Art*

TO MAKE A CLAIM for the variability and significance of grey paint, and for grey's identity as a color is, at face value, to contradict the way artists have discussed and conceived of it, particularly with respect to nineteenth- and twentieth-century modernism. Kandinsky summarizes the negativity toward grey articulated by many: grey is the arrest of all movement, the ultimate void, "an endless wall, a bottomless pit." Kandinsky's opinion is a common one. He says grey is the moment when everything stands still, when there is nothing, no sound, just immobility and a feeling of desolation.[1] Indeed, for a painter grey is the most difficult color to work with: it is apparently lifeless, without subtlety, nuance, and, to use Kandinsky's words, without "active force." And yet, this negativity contradicts the painted output of many significant twentieth-century artists. Once the color grey is introduced onto a canvas, worked over by the brush, mixed with white, perhaps with other colors, it is vibrant and filled with possibilities that Kandinsky does not recognize. Indeed, artists repeatedly return to the use of grey paint, often with surprising consequences, to challenge the obstacles posed by grey as a color.

In this chapter, I lay the groundwork for the image analyses in the following chapters. First, because grey is nebulous and elusive, this chapter presents an introduction to the question of how to articulate what is grey. I do this through a presentation of historical writings on grey, especially as they discuss its use in painting, but also in the world. Second, I outline the generally accepted—though not always useful—assumptions regarding the visual and emotional associations of grey. Third, having put forward ways of thinking about grey, I turn to a brief discussion of paintings by a selection of artists from the early Renaissance to the early modern period, from Giotto to Goya, all of whom use grey in ways that predate its use in modernism. These analyses illustrate how to write about grey, as well as demonstrate that the concerns of grey painting as far back as fourteenth-century Europe laid the foundation for the developments in modernist abstract painting. Finally, I close by enumerating the concerns and themes that are brought to life in twentieth-century postwar American grey painting. I show that all of these concerns are a development of those explored in grey over centuries.

Writers and philosophers, theorists and critics all agree on the discrepancy between color and language. The two are so independent that the one cannot hope to account for the other. In his grey *Untitled* paintings, Cy Twombly goes so far as to visualize this incongruity. In the *Untitled* grey-ground paintings, especially from the 1960s and 1970s, white line and grey ground never agree; they are in permanent struggle, each resolutely committed to its own form, its own mode of expression, its own "language." The uneven grey ground is always in paint, house paint, industrial paint, or oil paint, while the white lines are wax crayon, pencil, or chalk, the one painted, the other "written." Nevertheless, we must not be deterred by the incompatibility Twombly discovered and explored. If we are to understand the importance of grey painting to the history of art, and especially for its centrality to the continued rearticulation of modernist painting, then in spite of the difficulty of translating color into words, an attempt to do so must be made.

Modern and contemporary grey paintings, taken seriously, actually refute the commonly held assumption that grey has no identity. Thus, the questions arise: What is grey? How can the color be transformed into language? On what basis is it a noncolor? And, equally as important, how does grey refute the claim that it is a noncolor? On what basis can grey be called a color? Wittgenstein is one of a number of philosophers who point to the difficulty of translating colors into words when he wrestles with the discordance between images—both of the mind and of the sensuous kind—and words through discussion of photographs. For Wittgenstein, the photograph is the most objective form of visual representation. But even with the apparent objectivity of the photograph, there is always an inconsistency in visual recognition: one person knows what yellow and blue are when she sees them, for example, but perhaps the next does not share the recognition when she looks at the same colors.[2] While the reasons for this might be cultural, for Wittgenstein, they are not easily explained. Color takes place in the interaction between the color of the thing, the material in which it is fabricated, and the viewer who sees it.

To complicate this already variable relationship, different cultures have different relationships to color, relationships that are formed both in language and in the appearance of objects in the world.[3] Thus, in a given culture, the primary colors are not necessarily blue, red, and yellow. Or the same culture may have no word for brown, simply referring to it as reddish-grey. However, underlying these discordances, as well as those produced by the discrepancy between language and image, is the absence of a fixed materiality of color.[4] As Wittgenstein says, because color has no materiality in and of itself, it eludes language, no matter the cultural context.

Because paint gives color a materiality, particularly when it is applied to a canvas or any other support, paintings in grey are, strictly speaking, a different entity from the color grey. And yet, simultaneously, as representation, a painting can assume the nonmateriality of color. The obvious example here is Monet's use of color as light: white, blue, green across the spectrum are no more than the reflection of the sun, sky, trees, and the clouds in the air as they float across the surface of both the pond and Monet's canvas. The same could be said of the layers of grey paint that form a veneer across Richter's massive abstract works: in painted form, layers of color become emptied of physical substance in their function as abstract qualities of light, movement, surface. It is my contention that in the twentieth century, this paradox of color as paint, of painting as the materialization as well as representation in and of color, is elevated to a primary concern of modernist painting. I think here, in addition to the works of Russian artists mentioned in the introduction, of works by Josef Albers and, later, Mark Rothko, Ellsworth Kelly, and Robert Ryman. These artists consciously and repeatedly focus on color as the substance of their works. In a variety of different ways, all of them are committed to explore the ever-elusive, ever-contradictory properties and behavior of color made material in paint as well as paintings, the representation of color. In keeping with the proliferation of works that focus on the problems of and in painting as color, according to Wittgenstein, the only meaning of any color and the only way to understand color as a phenomenon is in the way it is used. More specifically, its context produces the language for its articulation.[5] If we are to believe Wittgenstein, then it is a legitimate activity to turn to grey painting as a possible place to understand the color grey, even if only for a transitory understanding because of the ambiguous status of painting as representation. Similarly, grey itself is the most obvious color for this investigation because the paradox of the absence and presence, the materiality and immateriality of color as light becomes visualized and, by extension, thematized in abstract grey paintings. The materiality of paint and the immateriality of color as light are most vividly imagined in grey because of the qualities of grey as a color.

If we suspend the slipperiness of the relationship between paint and color, the next question becomes: In Western culture, according to painting, what is grey? Is it all of those colors that lie between black and white? Is it produced through mixing red, yellow, blue, or any other two complementary colors? This latter is the privileged description of grey because black and white are not usually understood as colors. James Rondeau expresses a commonly held opinion in his informative introduction to Johns's exhibition of grey paintings at the Art Institute of Chicago:

> Gray will always appear to be tinged with the complement of an adjacent color. For example, next to red, it looks greenish gray; next to green, that same gray would look reddish gray, and so forth.... A saturated color can be diluted by mixing into it blacks and whites together to produce a tonal range of grayed colors.[6]

Well before Rondeau, Johann Wolfgang von Goethe made a similar assertion about grey: "If all the colours are mixed together they retain their general character as shade, and as they are no longer seen next [to] each other, no completeness, no harmony, is experienced; the result is grey."[7] Goethe goes on to clarify how grey can be mixed: "This grey may be produced in various ways. By mixing yellow and blue to an emerald green, and then adding pure red, till all three neutralize each other; or, by placing the primitive and intermediate colours next [to] each other in a certain proportion, and afterwards mixing them."[8] Goethe and, today, critics such as Rondeau offer the most traditional definition of grey: always dependent on the mixing of at least two other colors. Similarly, Goethe often places grey in the background to examine the behavior of what he calls "bright colours"; grey is the "uncoloured" (neutral) element against which the persistence of vision of other colors is played out and able to be observed.[9] Again, grey has no independence; it is only useful for what it reveals about other colors.

Despite this common tendency to dismiss grey as "uncoloured," there are always nuanced differences in conceptions of grey. Thus, "uncoloured" can take on a number of different shades and hues. For example, notwithstanding his assumption of grey as no more than a background for observation of the behavior of other colors and the tendencies of human vision, Goethe inadvertently gives grey an identity of its own: grey "like apparent colour, always appears somewhat darker than white, and somewhat lighter than black."[10] It is never one or the other. For Rondeau, however, grey has absolutely no life of its own, occupying a nebulous, interstitial space that renders it a nonentity; it has no independent identity. Wittgenstein, for example, also confirms this gloomy picture of grey. He opines that colors illume, but black and grey do no such thing. Therefore, he argues, because they are never luminous, grey and black are not colors. This is in distinction to the role of grey in Goethe's discourse to reveal the persistence of vision, the life of afterimages, and other illusory effects of color on the retina.[11] That is, Goethe believes in grey as light. This equation between grey and light, the coexistence of grey and light has, over the centuries, been both accepted and definitively rejected.[12] That said, it is worth noting that I am isolating fleeting moments of a nuanced argument in Goethe's writings. Because even for Goethe, who accords some depth and identity to grey, its qualities and behavior are ultimately never as interesting as those of other colors in their interaction with each other. Nevertheless, Goethe unawares points to the contradiction that is the creative impetus of grey: it is both opaque and luminous.

Goethe's ultimate goal was to understand color as an expression of the soul, or precisely, the artist's emotional state. Thus, his *Theory of Colours* is an early treatise on how color is physically perceived, as a gateway to its psychological and emotional significance, both for the artist and the viewer. According to Goethe, "A colour that no one looks at, does not exist," and thus, he asks, is a "red dress still red when no one is looking at it?"[13] With this human interaction as the basis of the existence of color, for Goethe, grey holds a unique place. "Grey brings together all other colours," but ultimately, because "colour presently announces itself" when "the artist abandons himself to his feeling," grey is colorless, it is without feeling, before the emotions have stirred.[14] Thus, grey is colorless; that is, it does not exist, even when it is before the eye. Grey is always absent. And yet, in distinction from Newton's scientific theory of colors, Goethe believed that when the color spectrum is recomposed through a second refraction, the colors do not, as Newton claimed, resynthesize as white, but as grey.[15] And the intensity of the grey depends on the darkness or lightness of the colors that were mixed in the first place. Thus, in spite of his naming of grey as colorless, one could argue that for Goethe, grey fluctuates in importance: it is special because it is the color that eventuates on the other side of the prism of refraction. Without overstating the significance of grey for Goethe, even though he places its effects as negligible for the eye on the color spectrum, the internal nuances of his discourse reveal that grey occupies a unique place in *Theory of Colours.*

Late twentieth-century paintings visualize this physical behavior of light in grey paint. In the paintings of Johns, Twombly, Martin, Richter, and others discussed in the following chapters, grey struggles for an identity; it rails against the nonidentity that has been given to grey. In these paintings, grey challenges the assumption that it is only created through mixing other colors, as well as illumining and obscuring these same colors. Nevertheless, contrary to Goethe's claims for the psychological and emotional noneffect of grey, late twentieth-century abstract grey paintings solicit a whole range of emotions, associations, and responses that are rarely melancholic and never static. By bringing grey into the foreground and making it both subject and medium of the artwork, in the paintings I discuss, grey is complex, has an identity, is at times warm and colorful, at others steel cold, but never static. Some of the late twentieth century's most prominent artists repeatedly used grey to express movement, gesture, and depth, to absorb and reflect light, to engage with the questions that define the ambiguous and contradictory terrain of modernist art. Thus, if we remain sensitive to the gradations, intensities, and viscosities of grey paint, these works can be appropriated as the basis of a discourse that challenges, or extends, the work of philosophers such as Wittgenstein who interrogate the question of color.

Even common sense tells us that Wittgenstein's belief does not stand up very well in reality. If we accept that grey is only ever the result of mixing two or more colors, and that it can therefore never be a color itself, surely green as the mixture of blue and yellow can never be a color. When red is added to blue, is it to be called grey, not purple? It appears that the "noncolor" of grey is merely a convenient way to deal with the uncomfortable space between the visual and the linguistic designation of colors. That is, to call grey a "noncolor" is perhaps an unimaginative way of describing the constant ineffability of grey. Or alternatively, the designation of grey as a noncolor might be a convenient repository for a much larger unknown. Namely, is the indeterminacy of all colors inadvertently, or otherwise, projected onto the nebulousness of grey?

Wittgenstein would agree that we always know what a color is;

we recognize it because of the material it forms and the cultural context in which it appears. However, the difficulty is always to find a common language for what we see. If painting is approached as a material, if painting can have the status of an object—as it did for Baudelaire and Van Gogh—grey paint in its materialization on canvas in late twentieth-century abstract painting can form the basis of an attempt to articulate a language for the color grey.

Moreover, to add another layer to the contradiction of grey, in painting we find a tension between its materiality and the immateriality of color. This tension, or what is realized as an oscillation often in the viewing experience, is always left unresolved by twentieth-century grey paintings. In turn, this irresolution in and of grey painting is returned to and forms the basis of the aesthetic experience that describes modernist painting. This experience of material presence and absence created through abstraction is thus another, deeper level of significance that gives grey an identity as a color and supports its repeated use in the experiments of modernist painting.

Josef Albers was committed to the study and instruction of color.[16] While ultimately, his project was no different from that of other philosophers—to create a language for the attributes and behavior of color—the particulars of Albers's claims are sustained by the introduction of colored pieces of paper into the classroom at Black Mountain College.[17] All his findings about color were underscored by the pieces of paper as visual evidence. Albers's use of color as pedagogical tool brings clarification to my understanding of the aesthetic experience of abstract grey painting. Given the behavior of grey paper, the students were encouraged to measure their convictions and conclusions about colors more generally. Although all colors have their own internal logic, Albers writes that the way we perceive color is dependent on the form, size, quality, placement, and what he calls the "pronouncement" of that color.[18] Thus, in a now familiar argument, according to Albers, perception of all colors depends on what sits next to them, their intensity, the measure of their amount and shape, how they connect to other colors. All colors are always "deceptive," relative, and unstable, because they change according to their context. Albers's contribution to this argument, however, is that uncertainty and ambiguity are not only the curse of grey. Given this unpredictability, Albers's task as a teacher was to train his students' eyes to the variables of color as well as to give them a language with which to articulate the multiple illusions generated. He was so convinced of his belief that he refrained from offering a theory of color as this would have prescribed what the students saw, and thus, dulled sensitivity to the unpredictable behavior of color. Instead, he insisted on placing students' perception and experience of color as primary evidence.

Albers used grey for these lessons. He taught and demonstrated the principles of color gradation through the use of grey paper, particularly reproductions from magazines and newspapers. He asked students to "produce so-called grey steps, grey scales, grey ladders" with their grey paper pieces.[19] Albers emphasized that these reproductions show how photographs register the gradations between light and dark very differently from the retina. He could not have demonstrated the same principle by using color reproductions because the perception of colors other than black, white, and grey is subjective, thus unreliable. Again and again, Albers turned to varying greys in reproduction to train the eye to discern how it registers light, dark, and everything in between. This use of grey for compositional and structural, as well as hermeneutic purposes is echoed in abstract painting throughout the twentieth century. Albers's exercises in grey and their resultant impact on the retina produce real-life experiences that have parity in the viewer's experience of grey painting. The viewer of painting perceives its tones and hues on the grey scale and is led to possibilities of grey in its engagement with varying degrees of light. I would argue that this is possible in grey because it is spared the apparent "subjectivity" of other colors as Albers describes them, a subjectivity that gives them emotional meanings and attachments. In grey's freedom from solicitation of viewer emotion, it is the purest, most abstract, color.

Besides the aesthetic relevance of Albers's pedagogical exercises, his teachings also have a concrete impact on grey modernist painting. As was the fate of all at the Bauhaus, Albers was forced to leave Germany when the Nazis came to power, and he took his lessons on color interaction and behavior to the famous Black Mountain College in North Carolina.[20] Among his students at Black Mountain College were Robert Rauschenberg and Cy Twombly, both of whom continued the exploration of color, and also the use of grey, throughout their careers. It is not surprising that the deceptions and unpredictable behavior of color as Albers laid them out, together with his refutations of conventional thought about color, came to dominate the work of Rauschenberg and Twombly. Inded, Twombly's grey grounds show all of the sophisticated arguments made possible by this otherwise critically neglected color. In the same way that Albers used grey photographic reproductions to teach the behavior of color, so Twombly constantly engages with photography when he privileges grey for his exploration of the processes and dynamics of painting, drawing, representing. Similarly, Twombly's grey grounds masterfully span the spectrum between light and dark, warm and cool, opaque and transparent, just as Albers taught.

Lastly, Albers's pedagogical uses of grey, together with its description in his writings and use by his students, would strongly suggest that grey has unique properties and an identity of its own. Even if that identity is marked by change and uncertainty, it is not dependent on any other color for its definition or description. Grey may bleed into others and become unstable and unreliable when mixed, and it may end up as symbolic of the behavior of all other colors. Even if Albers didn't say as much, however, we can confidently conclude that given its specific and multiple uses, grey has an identity of its own.

We remember that Albers's reliance on grey in the classroom, particularly in the study of the properties of color such as light, intensity and hue, was dependent on the properties of black-and-white photographic reproductions:

> We study gradation by producing so-called grey steps, grey scales, grey ladders. These demonstrate a gradual stepping up or down between white and black, between lighter and darker.
>
> For such exercises, we first collect as many greys in paper as possible, and preferably independent of commercial grey sets, which usually offer a too limited choice, or, worse, unequal steps. Rich sources for many paper greys are black-and-white reproductions from popular magazines.[21]

Following Albers, we can argue that it is only thanks to the industrial reproduction of images that the specific uses and, in turn, unique value of grey are recognized. This coincidence of photography and grey painting as it is exploited by Albers in the classroom chimes with my claim that the many dimensions of grey painting as a medium accrue meaning in the age of industrial modernity. Similarly, the status of grey as it is given by Albers is always in motion, and, together with the importance of mass-mediated reproduction to the growing prominence of grey, these qualities of motion and fluidity are used for the definition of the formal exploration of modernist abstract painting. Something special happens to and in grey in the age of industrial modernity.

To summarize, following Albers's arguments in *Interaction of Colour,* grey paint can be seen as a discrete color to be applied to the canvas and identified by the viewer. And at the very same time, in these painted representations, grey never stands still; it always bleeds into, is tainted by, formed by, and becomes other colors. Grey, like any color, is identifiable and always in motion; it is viscous and permeable, always in a state of temporal and spatial transience. In the same way that Albers used grey paper to convince his students of the characteristics and behavior of other colors, so grey painting can be seen to encapsulate all there is to ask, to know, to understand about the work of abstract modernist painting.

The Unique Possibilities of Grey

Leon Battista Alberti's writings on color offer an approach to the innovation possible in grey in the modern era. In one of the most forward-thinking discourses on color, Alberti is also one of only a handful of writers who acknowledges the significance of grey. In his radical alteration to the understanding of black and white and their relationship to chromatic colors, Alberti shows that chromatic colors are not made through mixing more or less black and white. In addition, he places black, multiple intensities of grey, and white on a color scale of their own. As Alan Shapiro notes, this distinction of grey as unique underlies the understanding of color from the eighteenth century onward.[22] Alberti elevates grey to the color through which all others pass, the color that gives coherence to composition in the same way that his notion of perspective gave spatial coherence to painted representation. Alberti is guided by nature, and thus grey, or ash as he calls it, is the color of the earth, a mixture of black and white. According to Alberti, all colors are composed of grey, because all colors must be made darker or lighter, brighter or duller through the application of grey:

> There is fire-colour, which they call red, and the colour of air which is said to be blue-grey, and the green of water, and the earth is ash-coloured. We see that all the other colours, like jasper and porphyry stone, are made from a mixture. So, there are four kinds of colours, of which there are countless species according to the admixture of white and black.[24]

Alberti also recognizes that grey has the capacity to reflect and absorb, to create darkness and light in painting. Alberti is a rare critic who acknowledges this quality of grey. Similar to his notions of the creation of color hues, appropriate degrees of black or white—and, by extension, grey—are always added to pigments to create the effect of light and shade.[25] Painters have visualized this observation across the twentieth century, even if it is done in ways that are different from the examples of Alberti's time. In addition, it is not only the principle on which black-and-white photography is made possible, but when applied to paint, the capacity of grey to absorb and reflect light, to hold all colors of the spectrum within it pace Baudelaire, gives it a fluidity to which no other color can lay claim.[26] Moreover, this fluidity is what makes grey the most appropriate color for envisioning the dilemmas and contradictions of the modernist aesthetic, and in turn, for the experience of this aesthetic.

Keeping in mind Alberti's confidence in grey, we go back and see that even those writers and thinkers who do not overtly privilege the possibilities of grey, do so by default. Wittgenstein, for example, might approach the question of grey's behavior in light differently, but he nevertheless discusses it as being in interaction with light when he writes that the difference between white and grey is dependent on the intensity of the environmental light.[27] Although he does not say so directly, the implication here is that grey, unlike other colors, can become the barometer of the world around it. Once again, it is the proximity to, even the equation with, light that makes grey a unique color.

The Cultural Significance of Grey

The definitions of all colors, including grey, are only ever culturally determined. The cultural context of grey as it appears in modernist abstract painting and, in turn, its identity as a unique color are given by the rise of industrial modernity and capitalism in the late eighteenth and early nineteenth centuries. Industrial modernity, the production and use of grey paint, and the development of modernist painting toward abstraction cannot be separated. Put another way, to understand the significance of grey on the modernist canvas, we must understand it within this context. In a unique interdependence, the relationship between grey and industrial modernity, and later, postindustrial capitalism, also coincides with the substance, that is, the materiality of grey as a color made for artists. In the nineteenth century, grey became available as a ready-made pigment.[28] Prior to this, various metals, most notably titanium, lead, and iron, were ground to make white. Thus, unlike many other colors—including black and white—prior to the mid-eighteenth century, grey had to be mixed on the palette.[29] With the advent of the industrial revolution, the synthetic manufacture of iron oxides became cheaper; they were made in greater quantities and were more easily purified to ensure they were nonhazardous. Grey became available as a ready-fabricated oil-based pigment.[30] Although it was technically possible to manufacture grey pigment earlier, it only reached the market at the same time as industrial manufacturing grew and artists were looking for a greater range of pigments. I shall elaborate on this parallel development of the color grey as it is used in modernist painting and the development of industrial modernity when I turn to the image analyses. At this point, however, it's worth nothing that the connection is rarely mentioned in cultural histories of color. More usually discussed are the cultural, linguistic, and social uses of grey.

For example, in his writings on the mystery and meaning of color in different cultures, anthropologist Michael Taussig mentions grey only as a muted color equated with brown, green, and beige. This oversight comes despite the fact that he identifies the diametric opposition of color to black and white in philosophical discourse.[31] That is, he recognizes the significance of black and white, but not grey. Even if he believes it to be a noncolor, one would expect more attention to grey in a book on the social and cultural significance of color. According to Taussig, color, like capital, is always double-edged, always powered by a dialectical interaction with its opposite.[32] In addition to highlighting the use of various colors in literature, art, the theoretical discourses of writers from Goethe through Walter Benjamin to William Burroughs, Taussig mines the role of color in rituals for an array of cultures. He argues that color is not to be trusted, that it is deceptive, an illusion designed to deceive. He calls color a mask for the truth. Color in general, and every individual color, is always duplicitous. In contrast, Taussig echoes Roland Barthes when he argues that black and white hide nothing but rather present the truth.[33] He believes, along with theorists, artists, writers, and philosophers, as well as the cultures he studies, that the authenticity of color animates, excites, and attracts; it stirs passions and even has mystical and magical qualities. Black and white, however, engage no emotion or desire. Taussig demonstrates that color has been instrumental in the rituals of old and new cultures, and it has been the creative inspiration and motivation of artists and writers, particularly in the post-Enlightenment period. But the most vibrant and seductive of colors belong to the colonial world, to the "exotic" places far from the Western world. The West has chosen to promote the colors of industry and capitalism: brown, beige, grey, muted greens, and blues. The irony of the West's preference for the muted tones of industrial modernity is made salient through Taussig's narrative. Even though he doesn't remark on the irony, it's not difficult to notice that these apparently dull and nondescript colors are also the most duplicitous of all.

Taussig's overall argument insists that color and our interactions with it are contradictory, no matter our cultural context. In his work more generally, Taussig demonstrates that every color is tainted with ambiguity, with oppositional meanings that reflect the dialectic of modernity. Color is both deceptive and the bearer of truth; it is fixed and fluid, credited with rational and mythical dimensions. And when he examines color through reference to Van Gogh, Sergei Eisenstein, and of course, Albers, Taussig shows how twentieth-century images recast the cultural history of color as real and lived. Even though he does not discuss it, grey painting can be held up as exemplary of this dialectic because it mimics the behavior of color per se as Taussig describes it in post-Enlightenment. Grey, like the contours of industrial capitalism, is mercurial, always ambiguous, provocative, and unresolved. In the same way that Taussig describes capital, so grey holds within itself the logic of dialectical oppositions that are, ultimately, instrumental to the forward motion of social process. In the case of grey, this "social process" can be equated with the continued reinvention of painting. And for the viewer of grey painting, it's the doubt and challenge to accepted and expected perception of the world that it generates.

Taussig demonstrates the general contradictory and dialectical significance of color as a transcultural, transhistorical phenomenon, and simultaneously, he details the culturally specific visions and uses of individual colors. The fact that he pays little attention to grey is probably in keeping with his own vision of the modern world. For Taussig, it is a colored world, filled with artificial brightness for the purposes of advertisements that ignite and reinforce a belief in the intoxication of the commodity.[34] I agree with Taussig's characterization, but I also want to extend it. He briefly acknowledges that this vision of multicolor is in dialectical opposition to brown and beige, thus grey, but does not overtly address the dialectical opposition within grey. I insist that grey be included in the "colors of capitalism" and furthermore, that it is sine qua non, the color of capitalism. Grey embraces truth and deception, excites as well as deadens the emotions, comes to symbolize life as well as death. Grey, like capital, can never be pinned down. Through its use within modernist painting for the exploration of certain themes and concerns, the quality and substance of grey as a historically and culturally specific phenomenon (or event) are persistently elusive.

As an extension of their contextualized understandings of color, other writers also point toward the historical significance of grey. Wittgenstein, for example, like Albers, often repeats that his arguments about the perception and understanding of color are made in the age of photographic reproduction. In a well-known example, Wittgenstein takes a black-and-white photograph of a man, a boy, and a lathe; he proceeds to convince that even though the objects in the photograph are black and white, we still see the boy's hair as blond, the grating as zinc-colored.[35] Thus, Wittgenstein's claims about our recognition of color, even when it is not visible, make sense within an age of black-and-white photography. Moreover, once again, the growing prominence of grey on the painted canvas happens side by side with developments in photography in the mid-nineteenth century, and more specifically, about fifty years later, photography in black and white.

Accordingly, we need to extend both the context and the meaning of color as Taussig discusses them if we are to embrace the variability of grey. Modernity has another side to the bright and colorful world that captivates Taussig. Modernity is usually defined as an era of industrial manufacture, of machines, work, and rationalization. Typically, this world is represented as grey, because grey best encapsulates the routinization of modern life. Again, even though grey is the color most appropriate in the age of industry and modern life, this does not have to be a negative ascription of grey, and nor is it fixed within this context. Throughout this period, especially the late nineteenth and early twentieth centuries, when modern painting comes into its own, grey continues to evolve and transform. Grey is given depth through its reference to the cultural and historical context that surrounds its development on the canvas. Moreover, this important relationship between paintings and their contexts is two-way. Grey is used again and again as a medium with which to interrogate the relationship between painting and the world around it.

The more recent writings of Michel Pastoureau assist with the articulation of this characteristic of grey modernist painting. If modernist abstraction is defined in relationship to the world around it, what is the grey color that becomes the medium of painting? Pastoureau addresses the historical and cultural specificity of the conception and use of color.[36] He discusses how the meanings we attach to various colors have changed over time, and varied from place to place, culture to culture, and at times, within a given culture, from person to person. Characteristically, grey does not stay still long enough to allow for a definition to be formulated, even to identify its use within any single historical period or cultural context. There is evidence to suggest, however, that the notion that grey as a color on a spectrum between black and white is an entirely modern one. According to Pastoureau, in the medieval sensibility, the color we now refer to as grey was in fact red.[37] Grey at this time, however, evoked the idea of stains, spots, discolorations, or animals flecked and dappled with grey hairs.[38] What we see and what we articulate as grey today seem to be entirely historically and culturally determined.

Even within a single culture there can be multiple and conflicting conceptions of and symbolic values attributed to grey. For example, while Pastoureau claims that capitalism is colored grey, to reiterate, for Taussig, capitalism can also be conceived as filled with garish, bright colors. Likewise, grey is the color of life, the color often seen and thought of as describing life behind the Iron Curtain, in socialist East Germany during the Cold War. In support of his argument that modernity is grey, Pastoureau gives the examples of Hammershøi's painted interiors and a Manet portrait such as *La chanteuse de rue / The Street Singer* (ca. 1862).[39] Once again, however, the identification and definition of grey are fluid, as Pastoureau also includes Picasso's *Guernica* in a discussion of black, and Goya's *Tres de mayo / Third of May* (1814) in a chapter on yellow, whereas in chapter 2, I refer to all of these paintings for their creative, variant uses of grey.[40]

Pastoureau explains that at the end of the Middle Ages, grey was attributed with richness, hope, light, and social status. While culturally, up until this time, grey had represented the color of peasants and the austerity of monks, by the fifteenth century it came to symbolize hope, joy, and life. Pastoureau quotes the example of a poem by Charles d'Orléans (1394–1465) to argue that grey is the sign of hope and good humor in the Middle Ages. D'Orléans's poetry contains passages such as this:

> He lives in good hope
> Because he is dressed in grey
> That he will have, his opinion
> And his desire
> How many there are outside of France
> This side of Mount Senis
> He lives, etc.
>
> Until he, etc.

Has lost his countenance
And all his joy and his laughter
He gains the worth of paradise
By the power of patience
He lives, etc.[41]

Thus, as long as the protagonist of the poem is in grey, he lives in hope and joy. While there are many such examples of grey as lively and representing optimism in the Middle Ages, this period of enthusiasm for grey was short lived: very quickly the spark was extinguished and grey returned to signify melancholia, boredom, sadness, old age.[42]

Then, once again, in the Romantic period, particularly in the eighteenth century, the creativity of grey returned to the forefront of the social and symbolic imagination.[43] The paintings of the German Romantics fit nicely into Pastoureau's history of grey. The most obvious examples are Casper David Friedrich's works, which are usually filled with a luminescent silver sky that absorbs the light of the setting sun, or emits the first rays of daybreak. Here, grey is the color of hope, the time of day, the space of life when liberation, spiritual transcendence, and fulfillment will be most profoundly experienced. Grey in the German Romantic painterly tradition is the color of possibility, the color of opposites merged together in paintings that represent the fusion of light and darkness in the interstice that emerges as day turns into night. Grey is the space and the color within which the solitary wanderers of Novalis and Joseph Freiherr von Eichendorff are graced with insight and vision.[44] In twentieth-century grey painting, the Romantics' symbolic use of grey as an articulation, as well as inhabitation, of the interstitial is revivified. In the age of industrialization and its products, such as photographic-based representation, grey painting captures the contradictions of the world around it.

Grey in the World

Pastoureau reiterates that grey is the color of industry and can be used to describe capitalism, a color description that began in the mid-eighteenth century and continues today in the West. His is a one-dimensional view of grey and of capitalism, however. For Pastoureau, the grey suit, the attire of contemporary capitalism, reflects the sobriety of the Protestant Anglo-Saxon moral belief system.[45] Pastoureau understands this use of grey to reflect social mores in the context of the "war on color" that began in the Middle Ages around the same time as religious iconoclasm. As he explains, Protestantism was entirely constructed around a black, grey, and white axis. Its chronoclastic beliefs mirrored the all-pervasive iconoclastic traditions of Western religious institutions in the sixteenth century, and were thus played out through representations, or images, in grey. As Douglas Druick states in his historical contextualization of Johns's career-long output in grey, "Protestant Reformers purged churches of both images and color, deeming them offensive to the senses and corrupt thanks to their association with Catholic liturgy."[46] Evidence of the purging of color can be found in the use of grisaille altar cloths in the medieval Protestant church.[47] It must not be assumed, however, that the medieval church interpreted grey as we do today. From today's perspective, within the history of religion, grey is the color of asceticism, deprivation, and prohibition. But in earlier centuries, grey was the color of high moral fiber, sobriety of mind, and religious fortitude. Grey was also the color of old age in the Middle Ages, a time when old age was not looked down on but characterized by "wisdom, fullness, knowledge." Intelligence was also colored in grey.

Pastoureau believes that the sobriety of modern capitalism as it developed in the late nineteenth century has its roots in these medieval, as opposed to Reformation, beliefs about grey and the privilege of the black-grey-white axis. The shifting significance of grey continues over the centuries, and it always depends on historical inventions and transformations. In keeping with this trajectory, as I argue in the following chapters, grey continues to change its role in the world thanks to the influence of black-and-white photography, the connection to the cinema and other media of industrialization, the devastation of World War II, and the technological revolution of the late twentieth century.

Beyond ecclesiastical life, and beyond the Middle Ages, culture in general was also influenced by and represented in grey. At the beginning of the sixteenth century, with the birth of the printed document and the engraved image, culture and imagination became dominated by black, white, and grey. Culture, clothes, housing, art, and business were all carried out in black and grey. Because it was impossible to reproduce colored images on a printing press, every image on the printed page was black or grey against a white background. According to Pastoureau, the black print on white pages of books, as well as somber clothes—black and grey suits, white shirts, and black blazers—are the inheritance of the Protestant war on images, and by extension, color. Moreover, the dominance of at best, black-and-white image reproductions in books, and at worst, no images, has been handed down from the earliest days of the mass production of words by the printing press. This "deprivation" of color has come hand in hand with the astringent values and conservative mores of Western capitalism.[48]

Of course, this is only one side of the contradiction of capitalism. Marx himself maintained that capitalism was a vital force; driven by the logic of its mode of production, it was filled with creativity and color. Marx's is the same world that Taussig extends into the vibrant colors of advertising and artificial brightness. Thus, to be sure, while capitalism produces homogeneity, the side of it that Pastoureau identifies as grey represents only one side of the contradiction. Similarly, it represents only one of numerous characteristics of grey.[49]

In addition to Pastoureau's discussion of clothes, one of the most obvious sites of contemporary cultural expression in grey can be found in the steel and iron constructions in industrial and postindustrial urban centers. These constructions are everywhere present in the paintings, walls, surfaces—of the canvas and elsewhere—in modernist and postmodernist painting of the twentieth century. This engagement with and reflection of the historical context can give abstract paintings historical significance and, at times, even social meaning. This intimate relationship with the historical context is what underlies the use of grey for more than just formal or medium-specific concerns. And yet, paradoxically, the medium and materiality of grey are never definitively historically bound. As I demonstrate, abstract painting in the twentieth century simultaneously resists historical limitation through its continuity with the use of grey across centuries.

Photographed and Painted Grey

Concomitant with the development of abstract painting's gradual shift to grey, silver nitrate processing is invented and put into widespread use. The process was not used for the earliest photographs—they were sepia—but was for the production of those at the turn of the twentieth century. These so-called black-and-white photographs are the first significant invention of mechanically produced images in grey. More impressively, the infinite breadth and depth of grey come alive on the "silver screen" of the silent cinema. Dreams, not dirges, fantasies, not the mundane realities of daily life, are brought to life in the magical and colorful greys of the movies in the heyday of classical cinema production.[50] With the advent of the Hollywood studio system in the late 1920s, grey has a raison d'être that not only lifts its audience into a new realm of experience but also gives viewers moving silhouettes that take representation to a new dimension, and give images a new life in the first half of the twentieth century. The image literally begins to move along an ever-increasing spectrum of grey. For the first time we are plunged into darkness, seated in silence, and before our eyes and to our ears the illusion of life in light and conversation is projected on the movie screen. It is an illusion brought to life in the most vibrant and colorful of greys.

These technological inventions, developments and social transformations coincide with the moment in twentieth-century painting that grey takes on a momentum of its own. Grey paint is also transformed into new forms, to create new kinds of affect, and to give a whole new set of meanings. In keeping with the flourishing of grey in everyday life in the age of industrialization, and the burgeoning production of moving images, the color grey becomes independent as art and representation move on a parallel path toward abstraction. As painting and artistic representation move toward a sustained self-reflexive engagement with their own materiality, as they move away from narrative and figurative urges, toward the use of paint to express emotion, the ambiguity of life, and the impossibility of representation, so too grey takes an increasingly central role in the history of art. Grey comes to cover the canvases of postwar paintings in Germany, other European countries, and the United

States especially as artists struggle with the forces of industrialization, technologization, and the isolation of modern life.

Grey in Art History

Over centuries, grey has had a crucial role in the history of art: it has been used to challenge and complicate traditions and norms, along the way proving wrong every negative assumption made about the color. Grey has been used variously since the Middle Ages, to sketch, to paint narratives, to study fabrics and their fall, to investigate the interface between painting and sculpture, and always to take painting in new directions. Even in premodern times when grey was used for more conventional reasons, this was often in order to challenge the same conventions. In grey the same themes have been explored throughout the centuries, if in a different visual language.

In a catalog entry for an exhibition from 2008, *Pas la couleur, Rien que la nuance,* Axel Hémery offers a gloss on the changing definition and role of grisaille across centuries and schools in Western Europe.[51] In spite of the fact that Hémery's history of grey, or what he calls grisaille, is somewhat schematic and by no means exhaustive, it is a useful overview for guiding discussion of the centuries of tradition in grey paint. Hémery's summary does not address the ambiguities and multiple statuses of grisaille in any one epoch, a choice that effectively highlights the changeability of grisaille as color, technique, medium, and form across centuries. A selection of his examples demonstrates the longevity of applications of grey in art history for similar, but not identical, technical, formal, aesthetic, and thematic uses as those found on postwar American modernist canvases.

I have already mentioned *Las hilanderas,* Velázquez's painting to which Van Gogh refers in his letters. Here, grey is the background against which the Greek myth about the rape of Europa is played out. The tapestry in the alcove at the back of the space inside the painting is bathed in light, itself a depiction in grey, and the two—grey and light—come together to create a stage. The illumination that striates this stage in the recess of the painting brings the scene to life such that the mythical characters appear to spill out of the tapestry and onto the stage before it. As a result, it is impossible to say if the warrior who comes to rescue Europa is woven into the tapestry or if he stands on the stage itself. This provocative use of grey to blur the line between reality and representation, and inside this, between two- and three-dimensional representations, is reiterated in the modernist search for the purpose, status, and value of painting.

Then there is the grey of the walls that surround the spinners. It is a darker grey, allowing for the intensity of the red that reflects on the face of the old spinner, the brilliant red of the curtain as it is pulled back by the girl who might be mistaken for an angel. Velázquez's greys serve multiple functions. All at once, they illuminate, ground, and enable the fusion of setting and action, of representation and reality, of the three different spaces of the painting: tapestry, the stage of the alcove on which the myth is played out, and the spinners in the foreground. Such uses of grey paint might be seen as ancestral to modern painting's exploration of related issues of representation as it becomes confused with the reality that surrounds it. And the ambiguities of grey, its ability to confuse and confront, make it appropriate to the search for an identity of painting that had not yet been determined at the time Velázquez was painting.

GIOTTO IN PADUA

Well before Velázquez, in one of the earliest examples of grey painting, or grisaille as it was known at the time, around 1305 Giotto painted a fresco cycle for the Scrovegni Chapel—also known as the Arena Chapel—a chapel that sits on the edge of the city of Padua. The cycle represents the life of the Virgin Mary and the life of Christ, on three vertical levels, reaching up to a barrel vault ceiling covered in a starry, blue-colored sky. Along the bottom of the walls, beneath the main scenes, at dado level, seven Virtues and Vices confidently stand, sit, or step out of their painted illusory recesses. The seven Virtues on one side, the seven Vices on the other are punctuated by pillars painted to resemble marble. The seven Virtues and their antithetical Vices are painted as marble tablets, given a dimensionality and a motion that remind the modern-day viewer of the static silent cinema figure who is brought alive by the motion of film.[52]

Giotto's dado cycle engages in a number of themes that resonate through centuries of grey painting. First, in their relationship to sculpture and cinema, typical of narrative devices in grey, Giotto's figures negotiate the interstice between art forms: they draw attention to the relationship between sculpture and painting, cinema and painting. Grey is a common color choice for negotiation of the interface of painting and other media. Similarly, Giotto uses grey for compositional as well as thematic purposes that will recur across the centuries to come. He uses the capacities of grey to interact with light as a way to challenge perception. And lastly, in the dado of the Scrovegni Chapel, Giotto uses grey on the margins, at the edges of the main commission, thus drawing attention to the place and possibility of experimentation in and through grey painting. Let us look carefully at each of these uses of grey.

The frescoes of Virtues and Vices are among the first works that critics, both from Giotto's time and today, cite in discussions of how grey paint can be used to "imitate sculpture." However, as Alexander Markschies remarks, the distribution of light and shadow in the articulation of the allegorical figures is unique: white paint, and various other forms of shading, outline, and definition are not in the imitation of marble sculptures, but rather, are used to realize the allegorical significance of the figure.[53] He says, for example, of Envy: "The figure seems almost to radiate a brightness of its own, which subverts its haptic qualities."[54] Added to Markschies's observation is the striking fall of the figures' garments, for example. Thus, Hope, represented as a sylphlike angel figure, flying up and out of her framed recess on her way to heaven where she will receive a crown, held by an angel that awaits her in the corner of the frame, wears a dress that is light and flowing, giving her movement and definition. By contrast, the robe of Desperation, who has hanged herself, falls to the ground, weighted by the severity of her actions. Similarly, Foolishness wears a bizarre dress, and with his thick foreshortened legs, is going nowhere. In one of the most dramatic, almost deafening gestures communicated through the handling of grey cloth, Anger is caught in the act of ripping open her dress to bare her smooth white skin to the heavens. Thus, Giotto extends his signature handling of light and color to create billowing, softly blowing, or heavy falling grey fabrics to fill these allegorical figures with meaning, emotion, and narrative agency. Through these qualities, they not only motion toward sculpture but also converse with the cinema. The stance, dress, and placement of the figure inside, outside, or moving across the precipice of his or her framed recess indicate that none are mere sculpted representations. These are figures in motion. They are like film characters in the process of performing their allegorical meaning.

The sight lines and perspective of the figures also mean their dimensionality and placement in relationship to their frame are skewed. Not just the foreshortened legs of Foolishness, but the perspectival execution of all the figures is unusual. The Scrovegni Chapel was split into sections, each of which had a separate entrance. The smaller front section was reserved for the family of Enrico Scrovegni, the wealthy banker who commissioned the chapel and its frescoes.[55] The longer main section was open to the public on various ceremonial occasions. The Virtues and Vices adorn the walls of this main section, the one open to the public and accessed from the back of the chapel. Thus, when the family entered by the left apse door, they would not have seen the Virtues and Vices. Halfway down the aisle toward the altar, today's visitor and the fourteenth-century congregation are followed by the bodies, but not watched by the eyes of Foolishness, Inconstancy, Anger on one side and the corresponding virtues of Prudence, Fortitude, Temperance on the other. As the visitor stands parallel to Injustice on the left and Justice on the right, exactly in the center of the main part of the chapel, she is watched and faced by the two largest and most regal of the figures. Injustice and Justice sit on thrones, adorned with the symbols of their significance. Their figures and recesses are of larger dimensions for several reasons. Not only because of their allegorical function, but also again in keeping with the expression of Giotto's mastery, the dimensions of the figures are determined so that they have a naturalistic appearance when their audience stands directly in front of them, at midpoint in the chapel.

We will remember that when Michelangelo sculpted *David* (1501–4), showing David just prior to the struggle with Goliath, and placed it in competition in Florence, David's overarticulated feet, and the motion of the sculpture toward a diminished perspective were rendered with the promise that the figure would be seen from below in the square outside Santa Croce, in Florence. This articulation for perspectival viewing was radical and unheard of at the time—two hundred years after Giotto had completed his commission for the Scrovegni Chapel in Padua. Thus, even though such visual harmony as it is experienced from the central point of the Scrovegni Chapel was being practiced in painting and sculpture in 1500s Italy, Giotto's perspectival manipulation was so far ahead of its time that the figures stepping out of their recesses must have appeared spectacular to the people of Padua.[56] In keeping with the depiction of the figures in the main fresco cycle, Giotto painted the Virtues and Vices to capture the vivacity and essence of their allegorical meaning. They are animated, in motion, filled with looks and perspectives that are also dependent on their spatial location around the chapel. None of this seems to be done in the interests of representing sculpted figures.

The figures of the Virtues and Vices are three dimensional, but they are not made to mimic the three-dimensional world of reality. Like Velázquez's spinners, they confuse the line between representation and reality. In addition, as can be inferred from the comments of Giotto's most astute critics, they are executed in grey to separate them from the biblical narrative painted on the vault above.[57] Typically, from the tenth century onward in Italy, the dado was used to represent secular narratives, in contrast to the ecclesiastical depictions above. In the series of Virtues and Vices, Giotto is able to reflect on, or better, magnify, the ethical and moral values that are in existence, but not drawn out in the narratives above.[58] This placement of grey on the margins, both literally and figuratively, becomes a defining characteristic of the use of grey in art for centuries to come. The figures are, as critics and commentators agree, allegorical. They are Virtues and Vices, personifications of moral beings that have been read variously to highlight moral moments within the upper frescoes, or as independent moral instructions to be apprehended by the local congregation.[59] Thus, they are neither mimicking sculpture nor are they particularly concerned to represent any sort of real world, even if they confront their audience with the moral choices of the present. They are representations like the rape of Europa, illusions that nevertheless engage with real life in their midst. Given the placement and narrative context of the figures, it seems more likely that Giotto painted them for didactic purposes. The Virtues and Vices were a lesson for the congregation, announcing, "This is who you are, and this is who you can become if you do not pay your taxes, treat your wife with respect, take care of your desires, and so on." As Giuseppe Basile points out, with the Virtues on the right side of the chapel, and the Vices on the left, the congregation was given a choice as to which path it will follow: heaven or hell.[60]

In addition, it may have been that, because they were not visible to the Scrovegni family or the officiating clergy, the Virtues and Vices were experiments for Giotto. The patron was not usually interested in the illustrations on the edges marked by the dado or the predella in Renaissance churches. Therefore, these spaces allowed for more flexibility and experimentation.[61] The dado was often painted by assistants from the workshop, suggesting less constraint in the commission and freedom to explore, including, as Giotto begins to do in the representations of the Virtues and Vices in Padua, the trompe l'oeil effects.[62] The experimentation that is pursued in the spatial margins of the Scrovegni Chapel, and later in Northern Renaissance religious painting, is intriguing. Given that grey colors the literal and conceptual margins of painting in the twentieth century, Giotto might be understood to preface this tendency with his use of the marginal spaces of the chapel.

There are periods in their development when artists take time to reflect. So often, as I will discuss, in these times out of the spotlight, when artists question the purpose and intent of painting, they choose to visualize their pursuit in grey paint. Typically, the works produced in these periods do not attract the same attention as those executed in other colors. While it is overreaching to claim that the experiment and risk of the Virtues and Vices in the Arena Chapel cycle influence twentieth-century grey painting, it is possible to trace connections in grey painting back through the centuries.[63]

Lastly, and again, this important characteristic is found in grey painting from Giotto onward: the Virtues and Vices are not entirely grey. Not only are the Virtues and their correpsponding Vices backgrounded by a different color—blue, red, dark grey, green, purple—but their robes, which are central to the definition of their allegorical meaning, are defined through the dark shading and outlined in that same background color.[64] For example, the clinging, yet full and swinging robe of Inconstancy as she tries to balance on a sphere that rolls down a sloping marbled surface, itself executed in reds, browns, and oranges, is achieved through the dark purple of her background.

Her motion is articulated through a use of white highlights. Envy, an ugly old woman, her hand clenched tight around a bag of gold, her tongue transformed into a protruding angry serpent, her other hand grasping for more and extending well beyond the space of her frame, stands in the orange, red, and white highlighted flames that devour her from below. This use of different colors to emphasize certain motifs and moments in grey painting continues until the present day.

Giotto uses grey as a formal strategy to create images that challenge our perception. As a result, grey drives the undoing of conventional conceptions of the relationship between representation and reality, and the relationship between figure and ground. Likewise, we may want to argue that Giotto uses grey to bring alive the relationship between painting and the sculptural quality of three-dimensional representation, or painting and the cinema that has not yet been invented. Moreover, this reach for sculptural articulation in painting is not simply an imitation of sculpture. Rather, artists like Giotto explore the relation to sculpture as a way of achieving something uniquely painterly. With their embrace of questions of perception, reality, dimensionality, movement, color, and emotion, the grey Virtues and Vices are one of the most powerful early examples of multidimensional possibilities of grey painting as a medium.

ANDREA DEL SARTO IN FLORENCE AND RENAISSANCE GREY

In one of the Renaissance's most treasured uses of grisaille for technical, formal, and narrative purposes, Andrea del Sarto's fresco for the Chiostro dello Scalzo in Florence, painted between 1509 and 1526, pictures the life of John the Baptist (Plate 1). Del Sarto's frescoes are among the strongest evidence that grey paint has historically served complex compositional and narrative purposes. While figures and events in grey do tell John the Baptist's life story, the color is also central to the technical and painterly concerns of the artist. Grey in the cloister creates a painted series that is both unique and pivotal to the history of the medium that, looking back, lays a foundation for grey modernist abstraction. The frescoes are said to be painted in grey because the confraternity (founded in 1376), as the patron and occupier of the cloister, was made up of poor and humble people.[65] The name of the cloister (Lo Scalzo) tells of the leader's wont to proceed through the city barefoot as a sign of his patience and humility.[66] Vasari also writes in *The Lives of the Artists*:

> The men of that company in Florence which is called the Company of the Scalzo used to assemble at the head of the Via Larga, above the houses of the Magnificent Ottaviano de' Medici, and opposite to the garden of S. Marco, in a building dedicated to S. John the Baptist, which had been built in those days by a number of Florentine craftsmen, who had made there, among other things, an entrance-court of masonry with a loggia which rested on some columns of no great size. And some of them, perceiving that Andrea was on the way to becoming known as an excellent painter, and being richer in spirit than in pocket, determined that he should paint round that cloister twelve pictures in chiaroscuro that is to say, in fresco with terretta containing twelve scenes from the life of S. John the Baptist.[67]

Like Giotto's frescoes in Padua, and in keeping with the use of grey paint in the Renaissance, del Sarto's paintings are inseparable from their relationship to light. The interaction between grey and light drives the narrative on the walls of this Florentine cloister. The white used for the highlights still shines today, five hundred years after the cycle was executed. Similarly, as we stand in the center of the cloister, we note that the frescoes are uneven in color, in the intensity of the paint, and in line that define the figures. Notably, *Preaching of the Baptist to the Multitude* (1515) and *Baptism of the Multitude* (1517) on the south wall of the cloister, which was once the atrium of the confraternity's chapel, are heavier, darker, and, as Vasari points out, filled with intense emotion and "burning desire."[68]

As the sun comes up and over the atrium—today covered by a glass roof—when afternoon approaches, it shines directly on the west corner of the intimate space. The intensity of the light demands that the images in the west corner be darker than the others in order to withstand the glare and reflection of afternoon sunlight. When visitors sit in the space for a period of time, they will note the changing colors of the cycle. It is not only that the frescoes are painted around the four walls in anticipation of the direct sunlight at different times of day, but the paintings also shift from an orangey brown through to steel grey as the sun moves across the atrium. In turn, these shifts announce the dramatic highpoints in the life of John the Baptist. Everything leads to the capture and execution as the figures on the south wall at its west-facing end come alive when the sun is at its brightest. Thus, del Sarto's frescoes show the impossibility of making definitive claims about the color grey. Because when these paintings are seen in the space for which they are created, the tone, temperature, density, and hue of the grey colors change according to the time of day, changes that in turn create the narrative across that day. Still today, five hundred years later, the full meaning of the events depicted is dependent on the movement of the sun.

Inside the narratives, at the level of composition, the folds in John the Baptist's robes as he preaches, baptizes the masses, and again when he is in prison, are given life and energy by a use of grey. At these most important moments in his life, the robes are dramatically "lit" by a white-grey. The more dramatic the events, the stronger the chiaroscuro of their depiction. The heightened emotion of these events is further emphasized by their placement on the southwestern walls, to ensure they are lit by the sun when its rays are at their strongest. The muscles of the men who attend the baptism, as well as those of John the Baptist, and the robes that cover their lower bodies, are also delicately executed through the use of white on grey. The blade of the executioner's sword is colored silver to reflect the light of the sun at midday. Such aspects of the frescoes also show the skill of the artist as he works with grisaille, especially given that, as is often pointed out, del Sarto worked quickly to give his figures and draperies a natural fluidity.[69] In these moments, he is more interested in the telling of the narrative than he is in interpreting the personalities of the figures. And the undulations of the narrative are realized in the relationship between grey paint and sunlight.

As pointed out in a catalog of his work from 1989, it is common for del Sarto to interchange the figures and faces of Christ and John the Baptist, biblical figures and allegorical figures, even figures from other cycles in a given fresco.[70] Del Sarto is not interested in the details of the depiction of reality; he is interested in the sweep of light, the creation of relief through a two-dimensional image, the multidimensional story that he tells as a way of creating drama, emphasis, and impact. Historians from Vasari onward point out that the most forceful of the twelve images in the cloisters are heavily influenced by Michelangelo, Albrecht Dürer, and a host of other painters contemporary with del Sarto.[71] For example, the powerful and clearly defined naked human figures in the latter part of John's life lend a vivid immediacy to the images we know from Michelangelo's ceiling in the Sistine Chapel. Similarly, he uses a common Renaissance strategy of stressing the narrative importance through fashioning dense folds of the fabrics to mark the most intense moments in John the Baptist's life.[72] None of his contemporaries, however, painted a biblical cycle in grey. Del Sarto may have been influenced, but the cloisters are one of the most unique examples of grisaille in the High Renaissance. These frescoes witness a rich and creative palette of greys put in the service of a dimensionality that goes well beyond its use in single panels.

In techniques and forms taken up from still earlier centuries, especially in Italy, the sixteenth-century cycle in Florence—like del Sarto's *Portrait of a Young Man* (1517–18) in the National Gallery in London—indulges in the representation of sumptuous grey textures of different fabrics and surfaces in discourses on value as well as on the inner qualities of the paintings' human subjects. This may not be unique to del Sarto's frescoes, but it is brought to the fore thanks to their execution entirely in grey paint. In addition, representations of fabrics, surfaces, and other grey cloths are carried through to the twentieth century. To name one example, in Johns's paintings, grey fabric becomes the entire canvas; grey is expanded to the technique, medium, subject, and object of painting. In still other panels of the cloister cycle, we see del Sarto's dynamic use of grey in its interaction with light to create surface, a strategy implemented by Gerhard Richter in his large abstract paintings.

There are many paintings in Renaissance Italy that use grey, some more famous than others. Luca Signorelli, for example, in his most mature artistic period painted a panel in grisaille, *Allegory of Fecundity and Abundance* (1500–1502), now in the Uffizi Gallery Museum in Florence. It is an image that probably belonged to a bedstead in a nuptial bedchamber. The background is black, and the figures are not realistic, with white being used to emphasize the breasts, muscles, and the abundance and eroticism of the body. Grey in Signorelli's panel is used to meet unusual ends: to represent the body as sensuous, in respect of the wedding it celebrates. Similarly, the use of grey for fabric that announces the social and cultural value of its wearer in a portrait was common at the time in Italy. From a painting such as Signorelli's *Allegory of Fecundity and Abundance* we learn two things. First, we cannot make assumptions about the history and significance of grey; the uses to which it is put are not predictable, conventional, or consistent. Second, these uses can nevertheless be found to resonate and recur across centuries and often find profound realizations in twentieth-century modernist abstraction.

In another example, Titian painted portraits in grey; in the same room as del Sarto's *Portrait of a Young Man* in the National Gallery in London is *Man with a Blue Sleeve* (1512). Titian's painting is exhibited in London under its alternate title, *Man with a Quilted Sleeve.* The title confounds in more ways than one. For, unusually, it is not the identity of the man that is important here, but the sleeve of his dress. The billowing, voluptuous grey satin consumes nearly half the surface of the canvas, and even more radically, through an optical illusion, it transgresses the space of the painting, appearing to encroach on ours. The sleeve is all that matters. On reflection, this emphasis on the richness of a man's cloth as the measure of his identity is often the case in portraiture.[73] The sleeve that dominates the painting takes over as the subject of this image. And the sleeve is painted in grey, despite being called blue. Perhaps, in Titian's world, blue was called grey, a possibility that unsettles our preconceptions of both grey and blue.[74] Similarly, the fabric is intimate and erotic; its delicate stitching laid bare in a way that neither grey nor sleeves are supposed to be. It is not true that grey is reserved for the depressing and the gloomy. This man is arrogant, self-assured, yet with a pleasant look on his face, and thanks to the luminescent color of his opulent dress, we are alerted to his vanity.[75]

The first question that occurs when standing before Titian's *Male Portrait: The Sick Man* (1514) in the Uffizi is, why is the man all in grey? Is it because he is sick? Like the sleeve in the *Man with a Quilted Sleeve,* the fur collar on the sick man's coat is luxurious, and grey. The red hem of his shirtsleeve, visible as a line between his gloved hand and his coat sleeve, is the only other color in the painting. Even his skin is grey, pallid, the life lost from his cheeks. The meticulous detail of the portrait is its most compelling characteristic. The painted surface is sensuous, delicate, as is the figure of the sick man; his beauty and the intimacy of his underclothes express a tenderness made possible in grey. Titian's portrait of a sick man with the oversized grey collar on his coat is also realistic: the detail of each individual fiber of the collar is so fine that one can be distinguished from the next. When standing before the painting, it is as though photography had been invented 350 years too early. The realism is so precise we could be looking at a photograph. In another characteristic that can be seen to foreshadow the use of grey in later centuries, the coat, the left shoulder, the left side of his face bleed into the grey background. This tendency of merging the figure with the background becomes characteristic of the portraits of those who occupy the streets in Manet's paintings at the end of the nineteenth century. Furthermore, the blurring of figure and ground becomes a defining quality in the development of the modernist aesthetic, into the twentieth century.

PIETER BRUEGHEL THE ELDER

Fascinating examples of grey are also found in the Renaissance paintings of Northern Europe. Greys were often used for the backside of altar panels—another marginal space for painting—and in other ways to bring new insights.[76] Pieter Brueghel's *Christ and the Woman Taken in Adultery* (1565), a panel held at the Courtauld Institute of Art in London, indicates the differences between Netherlandish and Italian Renaissance works in grisaille. I mention this painting because we could be forgiven for mistaking it as ahead of its time, an error easily made because of Brueghel's introduction of everyday peasants into a religious narrative. In Brueghel's small painting we see grey used to depict a world that lies somewhere between secular and religious, the real and the illusory. But it is a quiet, reflective world. It is not simply Brueghel's style, a style that refuses to distinguish saints and religious figures from mortals, that makes the wood panel ahead of its time. Rather, the texture of the robes, and the momentum that ignites the nevertheless stone-cold figures on a chilling stage, make it unusual. The numerous Pharisees who are the audience within the painting are either captivated by Christ's words in the sand—"He that is without sin among you, let him first cast a stone at her"—or they dissolve into the dark background. Brueghel's interpretation of a scene from the Gospel according to John is like a still from a moving image, caught to accentuate this moment of high tension. It is also a story played on a stage, the floor of which is Christ's page as he writes the rhetorically triumphant directive to a deeply political and righteous audience.

In its exposure of the duplicity of the world that ruthlessly judges without social conscience or self-consciousness, Brueghel's painting in every way looks forward to the work of Goya three centuries later. It is a scene that might be found in the Inquisition chambers in nineteenth-century Spain, just as it might be found in *The Third of May 1808.* The intimate folds of grey fabric as a subject matter might just as easily fall across Manet's canvas in his echo of Goya's image, in *L'exécution de Maximilian / The Execution of Maximilian* (1867–69). The power and politics of Brueghel's representation of the Gospel of Saint John as an allegory of an unforgiving society give it a charge that is echoed in political paintings hundreds of years later. Once again, the use of the soft range of greys to emphasize the chilling nature of the scene before us is less intended to imitate sculpture than it is to create an effect of naturalism: it is as though the Pharisees, even Christ, are peasants toiling in a field outside Brueghel's door. Similar to earlier uses of grey, the Flemish master also uses it to ignite the painting with intense light. The light falls dramatically on the back of Christ and bathes the protagonists in the scene. There is also an intensity to the brushstroke that is ahead of its time, a brushstroke that is free and fluid, set loose from the stringent requirements of patronage and religious painting. Up close, we can see the strokes as they have been made by the artist's hand. We would be surprised to find a brushstroke like Brueghel's on a nineteenth-century canvas and thus, on a Renaissance wood panel it is astounding.

Breughel might be said to be one of the first artists to use grey to meet political ends, but this does not detract from the technique and Breughel's use of color. In an article from 1952, Fritz Grossmann remarks that the painting is an exploration of shade, tone, and hue, resulting in anything but a flat, monochrome painting.[77] Grossmann elaborates on the painting's embrace of warmth and coolness, for example, in the depiction of the man on the right whose robes and beard are tinged with red as opposed to the cold grey of the Pharisees and scribes, who are all but lost in the blackness of their surroundings.[78] The stark contrast, together with the softness of the white used to illuminate the woman's round face, her pregnant belly, and delicate shoulders, a woman familiar from Brueghel's village and country landscapes, is potentially the artist's way of gathering sympathy for her adulterous acts. Her charming, fully lit, gentle, and classical appearance sets her apart from the onlookers. She is both stylistically and emotionally distinct from her judges. This has much to do with the fact that she is also in the light, giving her face a warmth that is nowhere to be seen on the surprised faces of the Pharisees. Brueghel uses the grey palette in an unusual way: to delicately nuance the robes and light that falls on each figure. In turn, this is designed to solicit his viewer's sympathy for the woman. That is, Brueghel uses grey to engage his viewer emotionally, with the ultimate goal of conveying his social convictions.

The warmth he expresses through nuances in grey invites us to stand on the "stage" with the woman, in the heat of the light that bathes the scene. This placement of the painting's viewer not with the Pharisees, but rather at the side of the woman, sets us apart from the audience within the painting; it asks us to identify with her, not them. When the Pharisees have all turned away as they do in the gospels, we will be left to surround the woman before Christ instructs her to leave. This place is opened up for us on the stage as a light that shines and waits for us. It is a light created in grey. This painting from the Northern Renaissance may capture the coldness of the scene through its deft use of grey paint, but it also uses grey for exactly the opposite reason. Grey thus becomes the vehicle of this narrative, a narrative that reaches out to embrace us.

FRANCISCO GOYA

As painting progressed toward the modern period, grey increasingly came to dominate the canvas. Similarly, with the approach of industrial modernity, grey became used more often for a range of political, historical, and thematic concerns. For example, Goya's *The Tribunal of the Inquisition* (ca. 1814–16) is a delicate work, executed in grey to create a secret underground world. This dark and menacing vision is haunted by grey walls, an insolence expressed by grey costumes, even the grey skin of the judges. However, while the subject matter narrates injustice, oppression, and public humiliation, the darkness in grey that surrounds the action is a compositional technique that strengthens the illumination of the performance. Grey is the stage on which the drama of Goya's embittered view of humanity is played out. Grey hovers around the inquisition as if the London fog that creeps through the opening pages of Dickens's *Bleak House* had spread uncontrollably to fill the underground chambers in Madrid, especially toward the back of the gallery in the painting.[79] And yet, if this vision is ominous, the threat does not come from the intense grey walls, or the grey costumes and faces of the prosecution. Rather, grey enables the clarity of vision marked by the facial expressions, bodily poses, and gestures of the lawyers, judges, and court officials, and the stooped postures of the "guilty" and faceless defendants.[80] The infinite array of greys that color the monastic habits and the faces of the oppressors give the painting its substance, and are used as a typology for the humans. The costumes of the performers promote, for example, the arrogance of a lawyer and the powerlessness of the defendant. Clearly, it would be misleading to claim that the dramatic uses of grey in this intense and eerie scene are the manifestations of a noncolor, or of a color that is no more than a depiction of pessimism and the repressiveness of the Church. Goya's scene might be ominous, but it is also somewhat fantastic in its reversal of the traditional representation of the Spanish Inquisition. The scene is replete with emotions that are typically seen in red, black, and blue. If for no other reason than that Goya paints space in grey, as the material realization of a literal and psychological clandestine, the subject matter of this image is far from the void that philosophers of color often claim to be demarcated by grey. Thanks to these enigmatic uses of grey, the focus on surfaces, textures, and the specific use of grey to illuminate the scene, Goya's nuanced, atmospheric grey underground world might be understood as ancestral to a modernist use of grey paint to meet related ends.[81]

Goya the premodern master further envisioned the representational possibilities and limitations of twentieth-century painting when he decorated the walls of his house on the outskirts of Madrid in the final years of his life. On these walls, grey took on a whole new dimension. In these paintings, posthumously labeled *The Black Paintings* (1819–23), transferred to canvas in 1874, and moved to the Prado Museum some years later, without realizing it Goya anticipated the coming of cinema. That is, on the static canvas he created images moving through time and space in a narrative energized by light. The fourteen paintings designed as redecorations are not easy to talk about as a group. They are diverse and thus can be inexplicable when seen as a series. There are continuities, however. For example, most of them use chiaroscuro to create the dramatic action of a story in motion. This is especially obvious in *The Saint Isidore Pilgrimage* in which the procession made by people from all walks of life toward San Isidore's Hermitage in Madrid is constructed through manipulating a palette of varying greys. Those in the background are darker, smaller, depicted through broader brushstrokes. They are in the distance, on faraway hills moving through time and space, just as they would if they were shown through a cinematic camera, complete with night lighting.

Anne Hollander discusses Goya's love of light as a medium most clearly identifiable in the graphite sketches. She argues that the privilege given to light and its sculpting through darkness enables Goya's sketches to be seen as a preface to the cinematic tendency that stresses the immediacy of subjective vision.[82] Other art critics offer balance to this reading by pointing to the reportage of the larger, public scenes in Goya's oeuvre, of which *The Saint Isidore Pilgrimage* would be one, even if it is designed for display on the walls of his own private house. It is true that the uniqueness of Goya's images, his articulation of the fantasy, the sordidness, the forbidden, and the horrifying, is enabled through a skillful handling of light and darkness in this series. However, in the so-called black paintings, color or paint is light, and all of these visions are rendered along the spectrum of grey paint. In *The Saint Isidore Pilgrimage,* perspective, movement, and the secrecy of the drama are also performed in grey, while paint as light sets the stage for the drama.

Paintings such as *The Witches' Sabbath, Reading, Two Men and a Woman,* and *Judith and Holofernes* in the same series also boast a use of grey that creates an atmosphere of secrecy. In the black paintings, and again, as we will see in the nighttime depiction of *The Third of May,* Goya's grey is a vehicle for light. The light of these paintings is bright, beckoning us into the worlds of his figures. Likewise, the opposite is also true: the penetration of the light into our world, even as no more than a possibility, is achieved through grey, the product of grey on Goya's walls, and when they are moved to the Prado, on the canvas. Thus, all of these paintings are dark only in composition, suggesting that grey is anything but morbid and bleak. Grey facilitates depictions of light, a passage through time and space, change, motion, and drama on Goya's walls and canvases. When understood in this way, Goya's use of grey paint is not only a preface to the black-and-white cinematic narratives of the early twentieth century, but it also prepares the way for the later, modernist uses of grey paint.

There are more examples of the varied use of grey paint in the history of art, however; at this stage paintings by Velázquez, Giotto, del Sarto, Titian, Brueghel, and Goya demonstrate that while the color grey has been misjudged, generalized, dismissed, and even ignored by critics and historians, it has been used with force and energy to compose and express in painting itself. Similarly, in all of these paintings, grey is used to create possibilities of testing the limits of painting, blurring its definition through reference to other art forms and media, some of which had not been invented. Retrospectively, as early as the sixteenth century, grey challenges the lines between reality and representation, between painting and other media, between light and darkness, and critiques the actions and motivations of those in power.

In most discussions of paintings by Velázquez, Titian, and Goya, there is scarce mention of the use of grey to create luminescence, or its conscious use in the depiction of tense public dramas. When critics discuss Goya's black paintings, for example, they routinely mention that the series is dark, that both individually and together, these paintings represent Goya's decreasing faith in humanity, his own spiral into deafness and insanity at the end of his life.[83] Similarly, the cycle is understood to anticipate surrealism and other aspects of a twentieth-century modernist aesthetic. The grey palette, even in its lighter tones in *The Dog* (1823) or *Leocadia* (1819–23) is not discussed.[84] The same is true of the critical commentary on Titian's *Man with a Blue Sleeve,* or *Man with a Quilted Sleeve* as it is known in London: interest focuses on whether the man is Titian himself. Alternatively, critics ask, what does the portrait say of the unknown Renaissance man? Is it Titian's lover? How can Titian's sexuality be identified in the softness and delicacy of the portrait?[85] Very little attention is given to the color of the sleeve. It is apparently unimportant.

Themes of the Modernist and the Abstract in Grey

When grey became the vehicle for solving the problem or paradox that motivated modernist abstraction in the postwar period on both sides of the Atlantic, its use was complicated. Unlike Malevich's white or black, and perhaps more like Yves Klein's blue, in the postwar years, grey became vividly connected to materiality. In the twentieth century, art developed a preference for grey as the color in which to explore the questions of painting. World War II ended, and the need for spiritual transcendence and the loss of self in the immateriality of painting as a higher form of consciousness were no longer the required in art. As Adam Lowe claims, grey became a color that was often used to show

> how images are made and what it is to be an artist. The materials condition everything. An understanding of their physicality adds yet another layer. The pigments, dyes, gums, resins, varnishes, gessoes, gelatines, milk and egg products, oils, bristles, chemicals all have their own stories and histories.[86]

From the 1950s onward, grey became about the physical substance of paint and the act of painting. Grey was also used to reflect on the return of dimensionality, to admit that history and temporality, space and geography were always the inevitability of modernist painting. If Klein's blue engages the narrative of money, wealth, and privilege, grey engaged with another strand of capitalism and its social consequences. Grey was also used in a reflection of and on the relationship of painting to the industrial, the postindustrial, and their impact in the wake of World War II.

In the aftermath of tumultuous wartime events, as well as the development of new visual media within modernity, and the consequently shifting role of representation in relationship to history, artists and critics reassessed the identity and impetus of painting in the second half of the twentieth century. The result was a shift toward abstraction. In the introduction I suggested that Rodchenko's iteration of the end of painting may in fact be a reiteration. Legend now has it that Paul Delaroche was the first to proclaim the end of painting in 1839 on first seeing the daguerreotype. He announced: "From today painting is dead."[87] Whether or not the wisdom can be attributed to the French painter, we can be sure that the particular realism of the photographic image both put pressure on the status of visual representation and initiated a self-consciousness of painting. Painting increasingly became defined in relationship to photography. What the end meant for Delaroche in the mid-1800s was quite different from its meaning for Rodchenko, or later, Ad Reinhardt who declared that he was "just making the last paintings which anyone can make."[88] However, while painting had once thought itself safe in its distinction from sculpture, after 1839 it was pushed to distinguish itself from photography. This was to become the obsession of the modernist aesthetic: to look at the way the new medium of photography had an impact on painting, and to explore the interface between the two. The photograph was everywhere present in the lives of those who were attempting to find a place for visual representation in the turmoil of Europe in the early twentieth century. Photography gave painters new ways of seeing the world as well as set new limits for the possibilities of realism, for example. Thus, the influence of photography on the transformation of painting in its midst is variegated and often multidimensional. In chapter 2, I explore the space occupied by photography in the conception and practice of painting in the nineteenth century. Ultimately, I demonstrate that photography was the concern of painting from the mid-nineteenth century onward. It is true that even if the technological inventions were not yet available, painters were already thinking and seeing the visual possibilities of the photographic image as far back as the fourteenth century. Nevertheless, it was only when the photographic image was invented that painting saw the need to assert its distinction.

In addition to photography, there are other twentieth-century art forms against which painting distinguishes itself in modernity. For example, the depictions of the violin, the mandolin, and the harp in cubism remind us that painting is inspired by sound and music. When it is juxtaposed with aural media, the visuality of painting is emphasized. Post–World War II, the articulation of painting as distinct from and yet always in conversation with other art forms and media becomes increasingly sophisticated and is given depth. Painting is defined alongside and in contrast to theater, music, performance, sculpture, photography, and the cinema. This interface with other media in conversations about the identity of painting is often colored in grey. The paradoxes and ironies that come of its relationship to other art forms are pivotal to modernist articulations of painting. Grey, with all its own paradoxes and ironies, is the most appropriate color in which to explore this relationship. Moreover, and more importantly, grey paint becomes a medium in which distinctions between different media will eventually no longer be possible.

To give one example, in Richter's grey paintings from the 1960s onward, the lines between painting and photography become erased, redrawn, and re-erased such that painting can no longer be defined through recourse to understanding its distinction from another medium. Richter was not the first to make such a claim: such ideas are already identifiable in the grey paintings of Johns or Twombly in the 1950s and early 1960s. Even earlier, Francis Bacon, for example, in the 1940s not only explored the interface of painting and photography through a repeated turn to the use of grey paint, but his works also imagined the spaces where painting and theater, painting and photography, painting and cinema, painting and politics intersect. The intersection always happens in a nebulous grey zone. This is the first of the five themes that structure my analyses of paintings, namely, how grey is used in the search for a definition of painting through juxtaposition with other media. The five themes enable the reconsideration of the history of modernist painting specifically, and twentieth-century art history more generally, as they are seen in grey.

The second theme is that of changing notions of vision and seeing that coincide with the growing use of grey for abstract painting. T. J. Clark interrogates the lines, planes, angles, edges, and ironies of Picasso's analytical cubist paintings through the lens of a photograph of the same paintings. The photograph is taken of the paintings together at the front door of the villa the artist rented at Sorgues. In this article, Clark asserts that Picasso's paintings were "a summer's effort at sustained visual articulacy," made to engage a viewer and to challenge that viewer's relationship to vision and the visual.[89] These challenges to perception and vision realized in grey painting at the turn of the century came to characterize modernist abstraction. Clark says of Picasso's *Man with a Guitar* (1912–13) and other works as they are depicted in the Sorgues photograph:

> It [the photograph] means to insist on the paintings' consistency and density, on the look they have of sharing a language and pressing that language on to new and more difficult discriminations; and it imagines a viewer able and willing to tune into the least particulars of the articulation, trying on readings and discarding them with real Nietzschean gaiety.[90]

According to Clark and those critics writing in the journal *October*, cubism is the fulcrum around which modernism turns.[91] As such, the challenges to vision are offered when cubist painting confronts the viewer with his own expectations of and desire for a coherent world within the frame, as the mirror of his own independent reality. The sometimes shocking confrontations of cubism are carried out repeatedly in the modernist breaking apart of classical perspective, creating a painted surface that departs from coherent and seamless worlds. Again, while a continuity between viewing experiences in prewar Sorgues and postwar New York City, for example, must be approached with caution, in the grey paintings discussed in chapters 3–5, the confrontation with human vision and transformations in visual perception continue to be realized in the forcing of new visual relationships between viewer and painting across the twentieth century.

The third theme to guide my analysis is a consideration of the historical and social value of grey painting. The zeal to articulate painting as painting, and the urgency to find its place in the world, began at the turn of the nineteenth into the twentieth century as a response to the approach of political and social unrest, and finally, war in the mid-1910s. Throughout the art historical and critical literature, one can trace the ongoing discussion of whether or not painting is idealist, whether or not painting should be idealist in order to fulfill its function as painting, that is, as art.[92] Or is painting a medium, an expression that is given meaning through its reference to the world?

Does painting carry the responsibility to engage with the history that unfolds beyond the frame? And if so, how does this happen when painting is always moving toward radical abstraction, flatness, and self-referentiality? Or, as Robert Ryman would have it, is painting rescued from idealism thanks to the very materiality of paint as an object, irrespective of whether it is figurative or abstract?[93]

These questions are asked by art historians, largely in retrospect. The role of modern painting and its relationship to the world, its references beyond the frame, are seen in the postwar period as the constant concern of early twentieth-century European abstract painters. And in American art criticism and theory, they become tantamount to the definition and identity of modernist painting. Greenberg was adamant that modern paintings refer to their own material form and process in a program of self-examination rather than create "images" of the world.[94] Ever since, this self-referential position has had a place within the definition of modernist art, not least because monochrome and color-field painting, with their apparent reference to nothing other than their own materiality, reinforce it. As others have argued, this is only one side of the contradiction that defines modernism.[95] Nevertheless, what remains unique about grey and the grey paintings of the postwar period in particular is that, together with their exploration of the form and process of painting, they engage with the world in unique ways.

I argue that the relationship with a viewer gives the materiality of abstract grey painting another form of social charge. The specificity of grey's interaction with and dependence on light for definition enables an experience that is different from that ordinarily had with painting. The tension between the painted object and the shift to illumination that is often visualized in the tension between surface and depth, grey and other colors, or, for example, in the case of Johns's encaustics, between the body of the artwork and that of the artist. This shift gives us insight, a new experience, that is, a level of awareness that potentially generates new ways of seeing and thinking. Thus, in its relationship with a viewer, abstract modernist grey painting has an unforeseen social potential. To qualify this potential: it is based on engagement with a viewer in a process of uncertainty, an uncertainty that is in itself provocative.

The fourth theme is that of the ongoing debate regarding the relationship between the artist and his or her art, a debate that reached a crescendo in the modern period with the search to remove all gesture and trace from the painted surface. Modernism characteristically searches to resolve the tension between the ambiguous role of the artist and his relationship to painting. That is, on the one hand, the modernist canvas often pushes toward anonymity or collectivity and abstraction, away from figuration, in an apparent claim for the "democracy" of abstract painting. The Russian suprematist painters characteristically depicted blocks of color, red, black, white, and later focused on design, photomontage, and typography in the interest of socialist progress. This movement, begun by Malevich's so-called monochromatic paintings, provides many obvious examples. And yet, on the other hand, the inevitable individualism of each artist's signature, whether it be recognizable as style or, at the turn of the twentieth century, as the trace of the painted gesture, even the individual hanging of work within a space of exhibition, was a stamp of the painter as artist. While this paradox was, of course, most pressing in the revolutionary climate of 1920s Russia, it is everywhere alive on the cubist, futurist, and even postimpressionist canvases in Western Europe at the same time.

The role of the artist as the privileged (social) visionary is thematized on the canvases of all but a few postwar painters who are searching for the identity of painting in their time, in grey. To use Richter again as an example: he instantiates his presence on the canvas only to erase it, over and over again. Endless repetition of assertion is folded into the gesture of his own effacement, which, in itself, becomes a highly controlled gesture of self-elevation and simultaneous deposing of the artist as authority of painting. By extension, the assertion of his authority as artist becomes a reinforcement of Richter's conception of painting specifically and, as he continues to reinvent through assertion and effacement, the role of painting more generally at this moment in the history of art. Richter is not the first nor the only one to complicate his control of the canvas, even if his way of doing it is unique. His is, like those of other artists of his generation, a simultaneous continuation of and departure from the modernist pursuit to identify the relationship. Ultimately, it is in this relationship of simultaneous affirmation through repetition and critique of the role of the painter as individual visionary at every level that grey painting, as I understand it, throughout the twentieth century is productively understood in relationship to a specific history of modernism.

Lastly, the fifth theme I explore shows how the color grey itself is connected to the material world through an embrace of industrialization. More profoundly, grey is the color of annihilation, as well as memorial and memory of the atrocities of war; grey is the color of the screens on which the world is experienced at the end of the twentieth century. Grey is used by various painters to engage with this rapidly redefined world, even when it is used for abstract and apparently self-contained, or self-referential, painting. The relationship between painting and industrialization is begun well before the advent of industrially fueled warfare in the twentieth century. The grey that engaged with the historical world by virtue of its very qualities and characteristics is a post-Enlightenment phenomenon. Even as artists refer back to earlier centuries, the phenomenon begins in the eighteenth and nineteenth centuries, when it is seen on the canvases of Turner and Whistler in Britain, and Friedrich in Germany.[96] In the paintings of Turner and Friedrich, grey is a color well suited to the painted depiction of nature as a refuge from the earliest manifestations of industrialization. And as I elaborate in the next chapter, for Whistler, grey is the color of encroaching industrialization along the Thames.

In Europe, the relationship to industrialization is different again. Superficially, we might say that painting in Europe has a figurative element that does not exist in American postwar painting. This is, to reiterate, largely thanks to the impact of two world wars and the responsibility of artists to engage with that impact, its aftereffect, and its memory for the future. Nevertheless, this doesn't mean that painting in America is not in historical relationship and, at times, given a political significance. Moreover, this significance is not of the type that claims abstract expressionism was an American art movement used as propaganda, enabled by federal intervention and designed to undergird the fight against communism.[97] The politics of grey has a specific meaning. Grey is used to engage with everyday life, with the mass media, and more generally to negotiate the very charged interface with illusionism against which representation defines itself. Grey, unlike any other color, engages with the spread of industrialization and the technological revolution of the twentieth century, particularly as both are played out in representation.

Finally, to cast all this from another perspective: if the traces of grey for the continued pursuit of the questions of modernist painting can be found as far back as Giotto, Velázquez, Titian, Brueghel, Goya, and even earlier, I must reiterate that in the late nineteenth and early twentieth centuries, the uses and meanings of grey paint are not identical to those of the fourteenth through sixteenth centuries. Grey, its application and appearance on a canvas, its dominance of the pictorial plane, its summation of all that painting can and intends to do, is also the result of the color's history, the way it is produced in natural pigments and later, in oils and acrylics, its resonance with the developments and transformations brought by the industrial and technological revolutions. Thus, if abstract painters of the twentieth century breathe an energy and excitement into the use of grey, if they push it in directions it has not previously explored, this has to do with the world that produces that paint and the impact of this same world on those who use it.

2

VISUALIZING MODERN LIFE

PHOTOGRAPHY'S INFLUENCE ON NINETEENTH-CENTURY GREY PAINTING

IN THE NINETEENTH CENTURY, the birth of photography changed everything. On the one hand, reality could be reproduced in images of unprecedented likeness, and on the other, these wondrous visions were marked as representation by their sepia tones, and not long afterward, so-called black and white. More accurately, these apparent "windows onto the world" were mechanically generated images that reproduced the world along a spectrum of grey.[1] Photography brought with it the conundrum of a new medium, the transformation of the relationship between reality and representation, new perspectives from which to see the world, and new opportunities to see it. At the very same moment in Europe and America, the effects of the Industrial Revolution set in. Colored dyes and pigments began to be synthetically produced. No longer was white mixed with black and other colors to create the spectrum of greys. Grey was manufactured as its very own color.[2] Simultaneously, in art, from the mid-nineteenth century onward, the changes that took place thanks to industrialization set the stage for abstract twentieth-century grey painting. In particular, photography and cinema and their discoveries resonate across twentieth-century painting. Works painted in the midst of the development of photography by artists such as Whistler, Manet, Hammershøi, and later, Giacometti, are key historical precedents to abstract grey painting in the postwar years.

Others have identified the birth of modernist abstraction in the rising smoke given off by Monet's trains in the *Gare Saint Lazare / Saint Lazare Station* (1877).[3] We could say that the motion and ambiguity of grey in modernism begins with this smoke. These wisps represent the painterliness of Monet's oeuvre, the moment when paint and object become separated. The paint, the smoke, the grey, are all ephemeral, and yet, they coalesce to envision the density, coldness, and energy of the comings and goings at the Saint Lazare station in the late nineteenth century. The separation of paint as color from the objectlessness of smoke imagines a more caustic alienation: that of modern life. As T. J. Clark would have us notice, the grey blur, also found in the left-hand corner of Manet's *Vue de l'exposition universelle de Paris / View of the Paris Universal Exposition* (1867), represents the moment of uncertainty, or ambiguity, that best visualizes the confusion of modern life in nineteenth-century Paris.[4] Again, Clark notices the steam that so fascinates the young girl as the metaphor of modernity in Manet's *Le chemin de fer / The Railway Line* (1873) for the same reasons: it is the appearance of the transitory, a reflection of the instability that constitutes the historical moment of industrial modernity.[5] Like Manet, Monet imitates this moment in his use of a white that becomes dirty, blue, grey, luminous as the trains pull into the station in 1877. It is not simply the blur on the edges of the canvas that convey confusion, but the clouded confusion of industrial life that is so perfectly captured in these paintings. Painting, modernity, and industrialization come together in grey, in the moment that smoke becomes white and spills into blue, grey, brown, and the grit of the painted air.[6]

In this chapter, I consider the concomitance of the developing photographic aesthetic, the development of industrial and social modernity, and the growing dominance of the color grey in the shifts toward modernism. In particular, I focus on paintings by Manet, and before him, Whistler and Turner, because the works of all three are profoundly influenced by the invention of photography and cinema. These artists also engage with the aesthetic and themes that are central to the identity of modernist abstract painting. I also consider the fragmented spaces and objects of analytical cubism as the paintings from the prewar period that most forcefully use a grey palette to engage the connections between depictions of space, the surface of the canvas and painting as an object. The painted interrogations of analytical cubism respond to the development of photography, cinema, and other modern media, as well as contemporary historical forces. I examine how the shifting role of the artist as a creative genius and apparent visionary begins to push toward the anonymity that results from the abstraction of analytical cubism, and is taken in a different direction by Giacometti before, during, and after World War II. In postwar Europe, Giacometti works with a grey palette in portraits that move closer to both abstraction and anonymity; grey is a vehicle to interrogate his own uncertain identity on the canvas. And lastly, I examine Picasso's political murals for their occupation of the intersection of grey, industrial modernity, modernist aesthetics, and war and violence. Picasso's *Guernica* (1937) and other paintings are outstanding evidence of grey as a color used to engage with politics in the twentieth century.

Édouard Manet on the Streets of the Modern City

Of all the artists working in the mid- to late nineteenth century, Manet is one of the most prominent whose process and aesthetic were influenced by new inventions.[7] Interestingly, Manet's palette is predominantly grey. Again and again throughout his career, Manet painted portraits, usually of street people and those in his circles, portraits in which both background and dress are grey. As Carol Armstrong notes, in many of these portraits, the figures eventually begin to fade into their background. In tandem with the verge on indeterminacy of figure and ground, for Armstrong, "white color saturation and virtual absence of color begin to lose their difference, and framing edge, literal surface, and painted illusion begin to lose theirs."[8] Others articulate this confusion in terms of Manet's representation of space, particularly in its foreshortening and flattening out: the apparent artificiality of the grey background becomes like a screen against which characters are portrayed in close-up. Manet does not paint a perspectival recession to the scene that defines these figures. As Armstrong notes, the composition can be considered photographic: Manet's best-known portraits show figures against indeterminate grey backgrounds. It is as if they are posing in a photographer's studio before a grey screen.[9] Likewise, as if in respect of its function as an otherwise nondescript background to a figure that is usually in the midst of an activity, the image has the appearance of being cropped like a photograph, bringing the figure into close-up. In paintings such as *La chanteuse de rue* and *Les bulles de savon / Boy Blowing Bubbles* (1869), *Le philosophe / The Philosopher* (1869), *Le portrait de Suzanne Manet / Portrait of Suzanne Manet* (1870), and *Berthe Morisot au bouquet de violettes / Berthe Morisot with Violets* (1872), grey is the medium through which Manet chooses to confound, dissolve and render ambiguous the distinction between realism and illusionism. This blurring of distinction is the unstable premise of modernist art. Critics of photography may not comment on the erosion or confusion of the distinction between realism and illusionism, but it is cast into relief by the development of photographic representation at the same time as Manet is painting. At this historical moment, photography promises a window onto the everyday world while never hiding its own blurred, indistinct edges, that is, its status as a representation.[10] Manet is not alone in embracing this possibility and radicality of photography on his canvases, but he is the painter of the 1860s and 1870s who repeatedly realizes these visions in grey.

Why has Manet's grey palette not been the topic of more focused discussion in all that has been written about his paintings? Critic after critic remarks that Manet was the painter of his time when they link various aspects of his oeuvre to the social and cultural developments of the 1860s and '70s. Whether it is representation of modern life in *Olympia*'s sexuality for sale that flaunts all formal and ideological codes,[11] amorphous faces that no longer reveal an inwardness or self-reflection and establish a new relationship between painting and its observer,[12] the flatness and realism of the aesthetic and subject matter, or the speed and ephemerality of his painterly process,[13] since Émile Zola's review of the Salon of 1867, Manet continues to be heralded for ushering in a new era in painting.[14] And, as a reflection of the contemporaneity of Manet's painting, he paints his time in grey. Grey is the color of industrial modernity taking place within and beyond Manet's frame in the 1860s and 1870s.

Armstrong is one of the few critics to explore the use of color on Manet's canvases, and she convincingly demonstrates Manet's elaboration of Baudelaire's comments on the indeterminacy of color in modern life as represented by Delacroix's paintings.[15] But even Armstrong does not mine the richness of grey to the extent she could in support of her argument. Rather, she identifies the indeterminacy of the violets, pinks, reds, the "game of colors" played on Manet's canvases, as what drives their visualization of modernism.[16] Strands of Armstrong's argument, namely, those connected to Baudelaire's writing, demand discussion of the other colors in these well-known paintings. Nevertheless, for the discourses of indeterminacy and confusion, Armstrong could have looked no further than the multitude of greys that bring both Manet's modern world and his modernist canvases alive. Significantly, figure and ground melt into one another as the grey feathers of the owl in *Jeune femme en 1866 / Young Woman in 1866* (1866) dissolve into the grey background and are simultaneously rendered flat on the painting's surface by the lack of distinction between the figure and the space that surrounds it. Or, in other examples, the grey costumes of Manet's single figures facilitate all of the confusion and instability of the individual and his or her relationship to the modern world. In *La chanteuse de rue* or *Portrait de Théodore Duret / Portrait of Théodore Duret* (1868) and *Un bon verre de bière / A Good Glass of Beer* (1873), the dress becomes continuous with the pavement in the first painting and the wall behind the solitary figures in the other two. When figure and ground merge into grey, the painted canvas pushes toward the flatness that characterizes modernist representation.

In addition to his grey challenge to classical perspective and portraiture, Manet is rightly identified as the painter of modern life because in these grey worlds we see the fragmentation of the image, often ill-defined faces in close-up, and the breech of a form of representation that nevertheless reaches toward realism. On Manet's canvas, consistently, all of these formal traits of modernist painting are executed in varying shades of grey. In *Les bulles de savon* we see modernity caught in the transparent bubble at the end of the boy's straw. Like Jean Siméon Chardin's better-known portrait of the same title from 1734, Manet's engages with the transience of life, and the ephemerality of the image in modernity, as it is captured in a photograph, reflected on the shimmering surface of the soap bubble and later brought to life by the cinema.[17] Unlike Chardin's image, but in keeping with many of Manet's portraits, the boy is alone against a grey background, performing for an audience that might be on the other side of the wall that separates him from it as well as from us. The grey palette, which articulates luminosity, energy, and ephemerality, together with the realist gesture of the depiction gives us further evidence that Manet's paintings are sibling to the photographic images being developed contemporaneously.

In addition, like *Les bulles de savon,* a number of the portraits and scenes of modern life, such as *Portrait de Eva Gonzalès / Portrait of Eva Gonzalès* (1870), or *La serveuse de bocks / The Waitress* (1879), and better-known examples such as *La chanteuse de rue* or *Un bar aux Folies Bergère / A Bar at the Folies-Bergère* (1882), are not simply representations of modern life; they reinforce the performance of life as representation. That is, on Manet's canvases, painting itself becomes the performance. Painting is a performance, a representation that is mirrored in the gesture toward the absent audience of the boy blowing bubbles, or three lonely figures on *Le balcon / The Balcony* (1868–69), figures who themselves are the audience of a spectacle we do not see. Perhaps they watch the (absent) spectacle of modern life below their balcony.

Before these paintings, we are struck by the looseness and the speed of Manet's brushstroke, again revealing a vivacity often coupled with the energy of modern life. Even Manet's most revered masterpieces are painted with a very fast and loose brush, resulting in a thin layer of paint. There are moments when the technique is so extreme that he makes paint look like a sketch, or alternatively, allows it to verge into abstraction. This resultant gesture of ephemerality is typically coupled with the influence of photography on painting. A number of writers have commented on Manet's dependence on photographs in his artistic process. However, photography's influence on Manet's aesthetic, composition, form, and color runs far deeper than a strategy for technical development.[18] For Manet, the photograph as a representational aesthetic and logic is everywhere reflected in his grey spaces, places, portraits, and the activities of everyday modern life. It is not just the speed of photography, but the color it replicates, namely, grey, that connects Manet's painted characters to the new medium.[19]

Un bar aux Folies Bergère is often held up as Manet's modernist statement par excellence. The painting captures the élan of modern life, as well as the melancholy, sadness, and loneliness of a girl on her own in a bar. The unsettling use of reflection, of a mirror that does not produce a mirror image, the curious appearance of the acrobat's legs along the top of the painting, the distorted reflections of the man and the woman through the use of a mirror image, have been written about repeatedly.[20] I would argue that the isolation created through the ambiguity and uncertainty of grey paint does the same. The intense melancholy that overwhelms the painting and the roughness of the crowd begin with the same mottled grey counter on which the woman leans. It is a counter in grey that might be borrowed from Velázquez and later lent to a painting by Jasper Johns. The grey counter is reflected in the mirror, separating the woman from the crowd. The bottles behind her, which may also be a reflection, sit on a grey table, further confusing the viewer. Which is the reflection of the counter on which the woman leans? And the light given off by the chandeliers that may also be a reflection is a smoky grey, infusing the air with a staleness that weighs upon her already forlorn look. These qualities, together with the single woman in a public space, as well as the activities pursued around her, give *Un bar aux Folies Bergère* both its tone and emotion. In addition, the loose grey strokes that form the table, the light, and dull the woman's dress rhyme with the wisps of smoke identified by Clark. The grey is the uncertainty, the ambiguity of life pictured at the Folies Bergère in 1882.

The City

Modern life, photography, cinema, and grey are all intimately related to the growth of the city as the focus of industry in the late nineteenth century. Before Manet painted city life, British Romantic artists such as Turner and Constable painted landscapes in paintings that marveled at the energy and motion of the natural world. The landscapes often represent natural worlds on the precipice of storms, allegorically read as the storm of the industrial era on the horizon. In the use of grey paint to express the tumult of both literal and metaphorical impending storms, these artworks establish precedents to the reflections of modernity in grey on Manet's canvases. Certainly, in Turner's *The Thames above Waterloo Bridge* (ca. 1830–35), every detail that makes this well-known stretch of water recognizable is removed, erased by the fog and the mist that hang over the city of London, like a strange creature, living, breathing as it creeps down the river. The fog is painted in grey.

Likewise, Manet's contemporary James McNeill Whistler painted images of London and the Thames in his most renowned series of *Nocturnes* in the 1870s.[21] These thirty-two paintings in variations of grey, green, and blue begin to blur the horizon line, in the indeterminate moment of day turning into night. They transform London's dark smog-filled air into a delicate translucent grey-blue. Whistler's blurred horizon line, a blur achieved through a spectrum of greys, is his contribution to the approach of abstraction in twentieth-century grey painting. Even in their thematic concerns—the shadows in play at the heart of industrial life, seen from a boat on a river—these works resonate throughout the twentieth century's depictions of modern life in grey painting. It could be argued that Whistler's images have nothing to do with industrialism and modernity, but when we look at an image such as *Nocturne, Grey and Gold, Westminster Bridge* (ca. 1871–74), it's difficult to see through the smog and the pollution as it hangs in the London sky over the Thames at the end of the day. The cranes on the distant shoreline, the lights gently striating the river as daylight disappears, all imagine a London that has been hard at work in factories filled with the machines that have colored its air.

As if the image of London cloaked in the refuse of the industrial day is not enough, Whistler paints the *Nocturne* series in a paint so thin and so fluid that it gives the impression of being transparent, even unfinished. When the paint is denser, the brushstrokes still disappear into the weave of a highly absorbent canvas, as though they are subsumed by the thick air that hangs over London. The indulgence in hue and tone dominates the canvas in harmony with the pollution of the London skies by industrial waste. Thus, the opaque air forms a transparent image that makes subject matter ambiguous and thereby captures the signature of grey—to absorb and reflect light, to be tactile and optical, transparent and opaque. The coming together of these qualities, the transparency of the paint, the dismal grey air, the push toward abstraction in the representation of the city of London, were the reason why Whistler's *Nocturne* paintings were so fiercely debated at the time of their exhibition. They were too new, too different, too radically modern in their reflection and absorption of the modern industrial world outside Whistler's studio in Chelsea, for the conservative critics to accept, let alone applaud.[22]

In one of the most mysterious of the thirty-two paintings, *Nocturne: Blue and Silver—Battersea Reach* (1870–75), the factories, cranes, and ship masts are like specters in the smog-filled air that is, nevertheless, bathed in moonlight. For Whistler, this is akin to the London outside his studio window as we see it in his vision of Westminster Bridge or the tiny *Nocturne: Blue and Silver—Chelsea* (1871). The multiplicity of grey-blues that make up these tranquil dusk scenes are the perfect material for Whistler's fascination with tone, hue, and industrial working life at various times of the day and night. Similarly, because his primary interest is to represent light, first and foremost, water is the perfect subject matter. Water, like grey paint, mirrors the light that shines on its surface. As the medium of paint takes over as the subject, the *Nocturnes* don't simply glisten in the light that defines their scenes at dusk; they also anticipate the revelations of modernism's realization of abstraction. They are exquisite. And yet, when the two *Nocturnes* on display at Tate Britain are seen in context, it's not difficult to imagine why they caused such a ruckus at the time of their exhibition. Not only do they represent a more "distasteful" or unattractive side of London—the everyday of industrial England.[23] Their grey approach to abstraction is a long way ahead of the nymphets, naked ladies, and idyllic countrysides with which they keep company at Tate Britain today in a room filled with paintings from the 1840s.[24]

Whistler represents a world in transition in paintings that hover at the edges of the art world. These visions are not popular, they are revolutionary in their execution, and they are of a world that no one really wants to see at the time that they are painted.[25] Whistler's is a world in which the Romantic landscape has moved to the city, and the clarity of the wanderer's vision has become clouded by the fog and the pollution that envelops him in London. There is no transcendence of this world, no place from which to reach clarity of insight, no glistening light on the horizon of Whistler's London. Because for Whistler there is no escape from the horizontality of the cityscape: motion is only possible along the lateral plane, and there is no vanishing point in the background for the eye to fall into. Our eye rests on the surface of the canvas, a canvas that replicates the industrial world. By the time of analytical cubism in the twentieth century, this tension between foreground and background, the full flattening out of the surface, the foreshortening of perspective put into motion by painters such as Whistler, becomes one of the defining principles of modernist painting. More importantly, all of the radicality of the *Nocturnes* is enabled in and by grey. And simultaneously, the *Nocturnes* extend the vocabulary of what gets realized in grey paint.

Whistler was not the only one in his time painting the city in grey, influenced by photography and industrialization. For example, Paul Maitland, a follower of Whistler, was a British painter who appropriated the grey London sky and thick London air for his images of industry along the Thames. In contrast to the stillness of the river in Whistler's depictions, and more in the vein of Turner's and Constable's before him, Maitland's brushstrokes are thick and always in motion, as if searching for a materiality that will echo the commotion in the world created by industrialization. Maitland's paintings are interesting because they realize the pollution and stirring up of the world created by industry at full throttle, the same industry that is hinted at in the natural worlds of Turner's work and that Whistler made the focus of his representations of London. That said, Maitland's industry is depicted in a very different guise. Maitland brings industry and pollution to the fore; he makes them real and begins to depict openly the secrets of this dismal world. Even the Thames, in a painting such as *Cheyne Walk West, Afternoon* (ca. 1883–84), is filled with the debris of the day's activities, churned up by what the river has witnessed. Thus, on Maitland's canvases, grey is not used as the engine of an oscillation between transparency and opacity. For Maitland, grey is thick and tactile, like the dirt on the streets.

It is difficult not to see the influence of photography, not only in the variations of grey in paintings such as Maitland's *Barges, Chelsea Riverside, the "Eighties"* (ca. 1885–90), or the lateral sweep of *Riverside Industries* (ca. 1889). Photography gives these paintings and probably Whistler's the opportunity to represent a different reality, an image that keeps the viewer squarely focused on the present, on the reality of an unfinished world, a world that continues beyond the limits of the frame. For Maitland this world is sensuous, pungent, and tainted by a realism that makes the scene less than appealing. This is in distinction to the landscapes of a pre-photographic era in which an illusion of completion and wholeness is given through the perspectival rendering of illusory spaces, in idyllic times, in clear blues, greens, yellows. Grey enables the painted world of the industrial moment; grey is used to mirror the unseemly reality of London at the turn of the century.

In paintings that differ on many levels from those of the French and British examples, the interiors of the Danish painter Vilhelm Hammershøi are among the most striking examples of the impact of photography and a photographic way of seeing the world on grey painting. Hammershøi's paintings simultaneously enlarge the possibilities of what grey can achieve, particularly as an expression of city life. They are consumed by firmly shut doors and windows that appear to exist solely for the light that shines through them. Hammershøi depicts a world that might be understood as the opposite of the commonly held image of modernity and of modernism. Hammershøi's world is private, intimate, silent. His depictions are everywhere influenced by photography, but unlike Manet's, the challenge to the distinction between realism and illusionism is achieved through the unsettling perspectives created in geometrically precise empty interiors. While Manet's men and women on the streets become merged with their backgrounds, Hammershøi's figures are clearly defined against sparse grey walls but are nevertheless lost in their own reveries, visually independent from their environment, and yet, always at home in empty rooms. Grey is the medium for these unsettling visions.

Hammershøi's images and their aesthetic reveal another side of modernity, and modern life, but one nevertheless defined by the urban industrialization that devours the air in Whistler's and, even more so, Maitland's London. The isolated figures in perspectivally skewed spaces show the penetration of the exterior commotion into the domestic space, creating isolated interiors that offer neither warmth nor escape. Hammershøi uses grey as the engine of these representations and their consequent meaning. His painted interiors rely on the inventions of photography and silent cinema for their grey palette as well as their composition, the quality, atmosphere, and meaning of a realism that is touched by illusionism. Grey represents the uncertainty of worlds in transition. Grey is the appropriate medium for the representation of the interface between photography and painting, reality and illusion, and the penetration of inside domestic spaces by the transformation of industrial modernity on the outside.

In paintings such as *Sunbeams or Sunshine. Dust Motes Dancing in the Sunbeams* (1900), light is made palpable as it falls through paned windows onto an interior floor (Plate 2). The glass is partly opaque and there seems to be little to see on the other side of the window. Hammershøi's windows are always a compromised interface between inside and outside, and while open doors can be used to extend physical space within the painting, the windows remain closed and opaque. And yet, the window is the structure through which light is able to pass, into the room. In this and other images such as *Study in the Sunlight* (1906), windows are devices to draw attention to the presence of an "off-frame," a world outside, beyond that in the image, without its being visibly present.[26] Or rather, the off-frame is made present only through the light that enters the space. Even though it is still in the steel grey colors of the walls and floors, the light is always bright. The skewed light always illuminates as it falls on walls and floors, and because that illumination is often the only form in the image, like the beam of light that is the only trace of an object in the cinema, the light is the event itself in these Hammershøi paintings. The light is an intruder into the spare, cold interior depicted within the frame. Light in Hammershøi's paintings has the capacity to bring warmth and intimacy to the cold spaces, in a way that human figures have done in the art of past centuries. Indeed, the light shares the same qualities of tenderness, reflection, and warmth that Hammershøi gives to the woman in the *Interior, Strandgade 30* paintings. Thus, the sunlight that falls through windows that may or may not be in the frame animates the painted space and the painting itself. Against the empty grey walls and floors, across the shut doors of Hammershøi's grey world, the brightness of the sun can be glaring.

When asked about his use of grey paint in an interview, Hammershøi is quoted as saying that grey enables one to see chromatic color more brightly. "I am intimately convinced that the less a painting is colored, the more it succeeds from the point of view of chromatism."[27] In an extension to this way of seeing, we might argue that Hammershøi's representations of empty and silent interiors envision modernity and modern urban life from the other side of the door.

They reflect the opposite, and thus, emphasize the noise and activities that make the world on the other side of the opaque windows alienating. This contrast between interior and exterior spaces, a contrast explored and envisioned in light, was the preoccupation of the silent cinema at this very same time in Denmark and other Northern European countries.[28] Thus, Hammershøi might be understood to appropriate the aesthetic, form, and significance of cinema and art photography as they were being developed in his time. It is an appropriation that only makes sense in a palette of sumptuous greys.

Similar to, but strikingly different from, the material light of Whistler's *Nocturnes,* Hammershøi's light is palpable, realist, and always attached to the window whose frame it casts as shadow. And although it may create hope and warmth in otherwise sparse, cold worlds, because of the realist depiction of interior spaces, there is no invitation to transcendence, no apparent spiritual or philosophical significance to the light. In addition, because it is in direct contrast to the tone and temperature of the bare room, the light shines ever more brightly. If the light, and the space it animates as well as defines, is the subject, if only through its skewing of this space, then even in images such as *Interior with Easel and Punch Bowl* (1907), light is as mysterious as the thoughts of the solitary woman with whom it shares the space but rarely interacts.

The spaces are unsettling because of the lines that structure the paintings' compositions: cornices, doors, and window frames are geometrical, but they are never fully at right angles, never squarely depicted. It is as though when we look at one of Hammershøi's interior spaces, we see the product of a camera that has been held at a canted angle, but where and how the camera was placed in relationship to the resulting image is difficult, if not impossible, to say. The unusualness of the angle created in conjunction with the fall of the light underlies an uncertainty within the frame, just as it does when we can't fully grasp the relationship to reality of the representation. So it's a different kind of disturbance to the status quo from that usually identified on modernist canvases, a disturbance that comes from the absence of a single, even an optimal, viewing position. It is, however, a skewing that can be identified in postwar grey abstract paintings. The always just-out-of-frame spaces create this disturbance that is underlined by a use of grey. For example, in *Soleil dans le salon*

/ *Sunshine in the Living Room* (1903), the reflection of light on the wall comes at an angle such that it is impossible to tell where the window is placed in relationship to the room. The light falls on a wall with receding perspective, but not toward a vanishing point in the background. We become preoccupied with placing the light in relationship to the cornices and the rest of the space. The pursuit is always a failed one, we are forever uncertain of the logic of the space. It is a quiet space thus becomes filled with anxiety and uncertainty.

Hammershøi works in relationship to the Dutch tradition of paintings that represent light falling into interior spaces. The influence of Vermeer is obvious, as is the work of Pieter Janssens Elinga, Emanuel de Witte, and others from the seventeenth century. In juxtaposition with their works, the modernity of Hammershøi's becomes exaggerated. The spaces in Hammershøi's paintings are urban spaces, usually that of his own apartment in Copenhagen. They are private interiors that are supposed to be, or that we imagine to be, havens of peace and privacy, secure from the outside urban world. The greys are cool, alienating, the color of urbanization. This is in contrast to the Dutch seventeenth-century interiors that are vibrant, multicolored, and, even when sparsely furnished, rich with emotion. Hammershøi depicts empty scenes or spaces of domesticity that are only animated by the light that shines through obscure windows. He then makes the space strange by casting this mysterious light on walls at skewed angles. The spaces are rarely inviting because they are sparse, silent, too extreme in their relief from the chaos of urban life. Despite their apparent clinicality, they are intimate spaces that we are not invited into; it's as though the isolation, stillness, and silence are a way of shutting us (and the outside world) out, rather than of keeping the inhabitants in. The very same ray of light that makes the spaces intimate and private also makes them impenetrable. This contradiction, enabled in and by the nuances of a grey palette, in turn, points to the modernist contradiction, here established between interior and exterior spaces. Thus, grey is extended by Hammershøi to depict the penetration of the inside by the outside, of privacy by the public world of modernity.

In keeping with its use in previous centuries, grey is never monochromatic or one-dimensional in Hammershøi's paintings. Grey is filled with a rainbow of other colors. Grey also always moves through a spectrum of tones and temperatures from warm to cool, light to dark, opacity to transparency. These qualities lend brilliance and depth to grey, and the greys are also ephemeral. The range of colors is also critical to an understanding of grey as always in motion, and its maintenance of ambiguity, fluidity, and flexibility allows it to be the field for experimentation and daring, in a world where nothing sits still, where new technologies are developing rapidly, making life uncertain.

It makes sense that these European artists would paint their urban environment in grey as it overwhelmingly colors the transformation to daily life.[29] London, as Dickens so confidently convinced us simultaneous with the birth of black-and-white photography, is the city that most eloquently captures the density, texture, and gamut of grey. Of course, Manet paints Paris, a city in which the air is not imagined to be filled with industrial waste and the mist is characteristically luminescent, not heavy and dark. Even the one-legged man in *Rue Mosnier* is in the light and brightness of a Paris day (*Rue Mosnier aux drapeaux / Rue Mosnier Decorated with Flags* [1878]). And we will remember, in Gustave Caillebote's *Rue de Paris, temps de pluie / Paris Street, Rainy Day* (1877), that even in the rain, Paris glows in the light. And yet, as Baudelaire told us in his writings of the city, the secrets of Paris were characterized by the people of modernity who did not always bask in this same light: prostitutes, walkers, philosophers. It is these people who fittingly articulate the Paris seen by the painters of modernity. Manet's grey world is of people. In short, the city presents artists of the nineteenth century with the opportunity to envision the present, the here and now of modern life. And photography gives them an aesthetic through which to imagine these depictions, an aesthetic that befits the changing characteristics that come thanks to industrialization. In turn, this thematization in grey is their contribution to the development of grey as a medium and genre of painting.

On the Grey Surface

The walls depicted and spaces defined by Manet and, for example, Hammershøi preface the shift to abstraction in postwar twentieth-century painting and, in particular, its focus on the surface of grey painting. Foucault discusses Manet's use of walls in paintings such as *Le bal masqué à l'Opéra / The Masked Ball at the Opera* (1873–74) and *L'exécution de Maximilian* to close down space in a way that amounts to a disruption of classical representation. In these works, as well as in *Un bar aux Folies-Bergère,* for example, Manet erects a grey painted wall that both foreshortens the space of the painted world and repeats the canvas itself, creating a two-dimensional horizontal, fractured space, as opposed to a three-dimensional world.[30] This notion of the wall transposed to the canvas as an object, painted by Manet and expounded by Foucault, is illustrated in other Manet images such as *La serveuse de bocks* and *Gare Saint Lazare*.[31] In all these paintings, the scene depicts figures gazing at "spectacles" that are nevertheless hidden from us, the viewers of Manet's paintings. In *Gare Saint Lazare,* for example, the child gazes at an event we do not see, and the mother watches us as we view the painting and the scene therein. As such, this has been said to represent nothing more than the recto and verso of the canvas: the gazes draw our attention to what is before and behind, to the side of the picture at which we look, itself acting as a wall between the absent foreground and background. The real "spectacle" or event of the painting is elsewhere. Manet's painting is thus argued to be no more than a two-dimensional representation of the absence of the events.[32] As described earlier, Hammershøi uses the inside walls as a screen for the real event—the behavior of light—taking place in his living room.

Manet also includes real walls in his paintings. Viewers are drawn, for example, to the grey wall behind the slain emperor in *L'exécution de Maximilian.* That wall against which the scene unfolds, and over which the painted spectators ogle, with its array of greys, might be understood as a template for all of the grey painted surfaces on and as the abstract canvas of the late twentieth century. Such walls show the moment when painting and color come together to create a surface that stands in for the entirety of painting, even in its incomplete form—in the case of Manet's fragmented canvas—in postwar modernist abstract painting.

To elaborate: From Leonardo onward, the use of grey paint has always been tied to materials, surfaces, veils, and drapery. In the spirit of Leonardo, the depiction of fabrics has both further complicated the conception of the canvas as surface through the effect of doubling. Manet continued this preoccupation with fabrics found on the canvases of previous centuries. In addition to using clothes to melt the single figures into intense grey backgrounds in his portraits, in *L'exécution de Maximilian,* Manet instantly draws our eye to the folds and the fabric of the executioners' grey uniforms as they stand, rifles raised, in the act of murder. We do not need to see their faces because the nonchalant fall of the creases of their grey pants says everything that needs to be said about them. The riflemen are doing their job.

As we know, the grey backgrounds, surfaces on surfaces, of twentieth-century painting did not begin on Manet's canvases. Manet reinterprets Goya's *Tres de mayo,* and as I have demonstrated, Goya's work is key to the history of grey. Like the subject matter itself, the dramatic grey of the sky in Manet's painting is inspired by Goya. In *Tres de mayo,* night has fallen. The fabric of the soldiers' coats is striking for its folds as they are articulated through light. The light source is in front of the soldiers; indeed, what looks to be a portable light claims to be the sole source of the painting's illumination. And yet, the soldier closest to us on the end is lit from behind. How can that be? Where is the light that illuminates him? This manipulation of light is typical of Goya throughout his career. In painting after painting of Goya's we recognize that the play of light is, in the portraits, the war paintings, and *The Black Paintings,* alike, only made possible by the rich, textured greys of his palette: grey which is the stage on and the screen against which his human dramas are painted. It is common for Goya's figures to emanate light against a dense grey background. I think here of *La condesa de Chinchón / The Countess of Chinchón* (1800) with her porcelain skin, her exquisitely luminescent pearl dress, her beauty made stunning by the grey against which she is painted. But in *Tres de mayo,* the relationship between light and grey is more complicated. In this painting, light is made visible through the modulations in the different colored greys of the soldiers' coats. In *Tres de mayo,* grey forms the background that will enable the focus, via the action and lighting, on the man in yellow surrounded by bloodied corpses. Grey also is the measure of the light that shines on the soldiers, as well as the shadows they cast. Grey is both the stage of this frightening drama and the costumes of those taking part. Again, after Goya, grey is by no means a shadow cast over this tortuous vision. Rather, the violence is rendered with power and intensity through the light that places the man in the focus, the same light that glints off the rifles of the soldiers and illuminates the expressions of the men who cover their eyes at the horror. The same light bathes the blood of the already slain as they lie sprawled on the mound in the foreground. It's a grey world, but the doom is expressed through gestures in light, not through grey paint. Grey enables the secrecy; it sets the stage for everything that comes alive on this canvas, in the early hours of the third of May 1808.

Thus, Manet gathers inspiration from Goya's dramatic uses of grey and light, a painter who was working before the advent of photography and cinema. Goya's early nineteenth-century depictions are nevertheless a precedent to all that can be said about the impact of photography and cinema on grey painting. Not only is Goya's palette the color of the media still to be invented, but also his dramatic images use walls and color as light to illuminate and define them well before Manet. Goya also uses grey to depict the dynamism and motion of narrative scenes that emphasize the violence and injustice of war.

Fabrics, skin, and all manner of surfaces become of utmost importance at the turn of the twentieth century to underscore the flattening out of perspective, thus accentuating the surface of the modernist painting as an illusory representation of the world, or as a self-referential object. Moreover, through Manet's use of grey fabrics and walls in his political paintings, the color grey is used as a screen against which to play out the violence and anger of war. Such screens mimic those placed behind the subject being photographed from the earliest days of photography. Quoting Jacques Rivière's 1912 writings, Clark argues for the contradiction of the modernist painting's relationship to the surface. He says, after cubism, "from now on, everything in the picture will admit to the picture being flat. The object-world will offer itself in the form of juxtaposition, not silhouette. But painting, insofar as it is representation at all, will always have depth as its object."[33] This internal struggle, integral to the continued understanding of the conditions of painting, is taken up in grey from the turn of the twentieth century onward when artists explore fabrics, canvases, screens, walls, and other surfaces as metaphors of painting itself. Eventually the surface and painting become one to produce an abstract grey image. This grey image, in turn, bears the traces of the impact of photography and cinema on the ever-changing identity of painting.

With the introduction of machines and mechanical reproduction of images that see the world from different angles, different perspectives, through the lens of the photographic and later the cinematic camera, painting was forced to turn inward and reflect on its own status in the world. Due to the advent of the photographic and cinematic in particular, the two-dimensional plane of all pictures became imagined differently. The self-reflection of painting was realized in myriad ways through and on the surface of painted representation. Moreover, by the close of the nineteenth century, photography was growing in influence as a way of seeing the world, thus spawning theoretical texts on its ontology, effects, and meaning of as a new medium.[34] When painters were not directly translating formal photographic properties onto their canvases as surface, they were being influenced by the new ways of seeing the world.[35]

I want to say that grey animates the modernist imagination's exploration of the painted surface because of its properties. Grey is not distracting; it is to the point and always the reduction or elevation of paint to its purest form. Grey is a color on which we (and the artist) can focus, without being distracted by the emotional resonance and psychological implications of other colors. Other reasons for the centrality of grey to abstract modernism will become apparent as I go on, but first, to continue the discussion of grey surfaces.

The cubist surfaces of Picasso's paintings from his analytical period, 1908–12, and also Braque's works from the same years are among the most obvious examples of modernist explorations of the surface. Likewise, these paintings illustrate the paradoxical nature of the relations between light, color, space, the form of painting, and the resultant relationship with the viewer. Always muddy, grey paintings such as *La femme à la mandolin / Woman Playing the Mandolin* (1909), *Portrait of Daniel-Henry Kahnweiler* (1910), or the somber *Portrait of Wilhelm Uhde* (1910) by Picasso and *Violin et bougie / Violin and Candle* (1910) or *Nature morte avec harpe et violin / Still Life with Harp and Violin* (1912) by Braque are repeated attempts to shatter the coherent two-dimensional plane of the picture surface. These fragmented worlds mark a sustained exploration in and of grey, as well as groundbreaking, conscious attempts to fragment what had always been the coherence of the picture plane. In this phase in the development of cubism, Picasso and Braque are preoccupied with exploring the radical possibility of rearticulating the painted surface, and they pursue this preoccupation in grey.

Much has been written about Picasso's rose and blue periods. They have been held in awe, under the microscope, analyzed, historicized, criticized. Until the Guggenheim's 2012 exhibition *Picasso: Black and White,* Picasso's consistent fascination with grey, however, had not captured scholars' and historians' attention.[36] Even then, in spite of the dominance and complexity of grey in the paintings, curiously the color grey does not feature in the exhibition title. Before this exhibition, when relevant paintings are the focus of investigation, grey is not given prominence. Witness the discussions of paintings such as *Ma jolie / My Pretty Girl* (1911–12), *Femme au guitar / Woman with Guitar* (1911), *L'homme au violin / Man with a Violin* (1912), or the war paintings.[37] What matters is the representational content: the creation of distinct planes on the two-dimensional surface of the canvas, the geometricality of objects, the dissolution of the human body, the radical invention of a new form of art that foregrounds the creation of irresolvable tensions between painting and the world outside the frame. In the later black-and-white paintings, if Picasso's color palette is noted, it is done so primarily in the interests of a discussion of the impact of photography and the press on the representation of war and violence.[38]

That said, in his discussion of analytical cubism as the metaphor of modernist painting, and a handful of Picasso's paintings as the metonym of cubism, Clark explains Picasso's grey palette as an insistence on the artifice of painting.[39] That is, the muted greys and browns of, for example, *Piano l'accordéoniste / The Accordionist* (1911), describe the illusory, and ultimately, failed attempt of painting to produce a likeness of the world. Grey, like the black-and-white photography in his environs, is Picasso's visual indication that painting is an imitation of the object world. The grey is also Picasso's indication that, during these years, painting is being taken "back to the drawing board," its defining characteristics scrutinized. It is the sign of the process of inquiry in which Picasso is engaged between 1909 and

1911.[40] While Clark's interpretation of Picasso's use of the so-called grey monochromatic palette is convincing, it is only one aspect of the repeated and insistent choice of grey in these paintings.

As Picasso and Braque launch their intense fragmentation of the modern world through dynamism on the canvas, how can it not be significant that this is a world in which capitalism has turned everything grey? Grey is the color of the suit worn by Anton Vollard in Picasso's portrait of 1910 because he is a modern man. And grey is the unrecognizable face in *Daniel-Henry Kahnweiler*, pragmatic businessman, art connoisseur, and collector. Kahnweiler was a man behind the scenes; like those on the backside of a Northern altarpiece—of the sort that was once done in grisaille—he laid the ground for what would come to be modern capitalism. It makes sense, then, that Kahnweiler must be painted in grey.

Picasso and Braque are rarely cited as the predecessors of abstract expressionism or the European neo-avant-garde. Why would they be, especially when both are adamant that their work is of a different heritage? Picasso and Braque choose grey for a reason. And it is not simply because Cézanne before them had painted the portraits of those who crossed his path in grey suits. Cézanne distorted the picture plane and set the human body free from its enslavement to a background for definition. But this is not the only connection between his portraits and those of Picasso and Braque in the analytical period. They all use grey, the color of photography, the color that will not distract from the expression of the world around them through line, form, shape, and dynamic: the world they paint is fragmented, chaotic, confusing, qualities that are emphasized in grey. Olivier Berggruen notes in his essay for the Guggenheim exhibition catalog:

> The strictly tonal range of black-and-white photography allowed for greater pictorial clarity, which Picasso pursued through much of his work. The clear distribution of light and shade became a guiding principle during Picasso's Cubist years. Color, which was seen as purely decorative, was abandoned, and textures, densities, and variations of gray and other colors helped achieve a sustained sense of depth and coherence.[41]

For pictorial and compositional as well as cultural reasons, Picasso, Braque, and Cézanne before them used grey to visualize the energetic pulse and overall impression of their era: the modern world. While Clark plays down the correspondence between cubism and the world it represents, we will note that this is necessary for his argument regarding the failure of painting to imitate that world.[42] The project to draw attention to painting as an object of its own reference, a project that began—arguably—with analytical cubism, can still be colored by that same world.

Accordingly, among the representational issues at stake at the turn of the nineteenth into the twentieth century is the return of the patterns and rhythms of modern life to the pictorial surface. To achieve this, to visualize the fragmentation of modern life, Picasso and Braque stripped away other issues from the picture plane: their paintings are emptied of the colorful distractions of modern life. The works are line and form executed in grey. And then, when Picasso began to put things back together again, in the years of synthetic cubism, other colors returned to the canvas. While we find moments of grey in Picasso's paintings after 1912, especially around 1926 with images such as *Atelier de la modiste / Workshop of the Milliner* (1926), *Figure* (1927), and *Minotaure* (1928), his palette again turns completely grey in the late 1920s and early 1930s when he paints the arabesque forms of women for which he is best known in this period. All of the women are painted in grey before, after, or during their creation in other colors.

After images of seated women, and self-portraits with women, in 1937 Picasso paints his masterpiece *Guernica.* With *Guernica* and the preparatory works, the form of the figure, and particularly the female figure, changes dramatically. It no longer has the soft, curvaceous arabesque form that shows gentility, femininity, and emotion. The figures scream, enraged by the violence and rape that has been done to them, their children, and the world they are forced to endure. In response to the end of World War II, the women of *The Charnel House* (1944–45), and *Las meninas (After Velázquez)* in 1957, cry out their anger even louder. With the postwar paintings in particular, form becomes secondary to the confusion, the turmoil of a world ripped apart. I return to these paintings later when I discuss the use of grey as a political strategy. For the moment, it is sufficient to say that the stripping away of all but the texture, speed, and chaos of the surface in grey equates with Picasso's (and Braque's) use of grey paint as a medium for the communication of other ideas. In grey, Picasso sets out to explore each new turn in the development of his ideas about painting. To put it another way: When Picasso takes painting "back to the drawing board" to discover its ability to represent, he takes it back to grey. Grey is the color in which he finds out how painting can represent, especially when its task is to communicate the extreme trauma of World War II. That is, grey is the color he uses when painting takes on its most serious task: to represent the horrors of war and the violence of men.

After Picasso, exploration of the surface of the painting takes many different forms and techniques. From abstract expressionism, and Pollock's dynamic interaction with the surface, through color-field painters' reiteration of the surface, the thick buildup of paint in works like those of Rauschenberg, to Marden's sleek, flat, and apparently flawless surfaces, there is no single use of paint to mark the surface in the late twentieth century. But always, there is a concern for the characteristics of paint on the surface, and the use of paint to draw attention to this surface. What happens on the grey surface is unique. In the works in grey of artists from Newman and Rothko to Richter in Europe, even when they are concerned with figuration, the representational aspects of painting fall away to allow an image of light, dark, color, motion, and texture to mark the canvas as a painted and repainted surface.

Of Figuration, Abstraction, and the Sea Between

Grey is intertwined with the expansion of social modernity, the photographic image, and a developing abstraction in the emergent modernist aesthetic. In grey, color in its purest form has the resonance of representation, and at times, even when abstract, color bleeds into figuration. Kirk Varnedoe draws on William Hazlitt in his observation of this fundamental contradiction of abstract art. Abstract art is always about nothing, and simultaneously, has a likeness or is a figuration of something.[43] The experience of standing before a picture of nothing and having something gradually be revealed is familiar in the presence of modernist abstraction. Moreover, as Varnedoe confirms, abstraction is never a void, never without representation or figuration, even if only in a gesture that takes shape in the viewer's mind. This tension between abstraction and figuration is perhaps nowhere more vividly realized in grey paint than it is in representations of the sea.

The sea is most often acknowledged to best represent the modernist tug-of-war between figuration and abstraction, and especially when the horizon line becomes blurred, when sea, sky, and sand merge into one amorphous stretch of grey. Together with the city, the sea is both a perfect vehicle for an exploration of the vast and unpredictable medium of painting itself, as well as the entire spectrum of grey and its capacity to capture ambiguity, and to obscure distinctions. If only because grey can be dark or light, absorb or reflect light, be warm or cold, like the nebulous and ephemeral state of the sea, the sky, and the air in between, grey is the ideal color to capture the sea.

The ineffable mark of the line where the sea meets the sky, and again where it departs from the ground we stand on at the shore, is also the line at which the distinction between figuration and abstraction becomes ambiguous.[44] The lines of horizon and shore as they are transposed to painting are the most perfect opportunity for the representation of what always eludes representation, the infinity of nature, and by extension, the verge into abstraction. In the twentieth century, it is in Piet Mondrian's paintings of the sea that abstraction, figuration, the influence of photography, and eventually the cinema begin to come together. Ironically, this merging of phenomena and forces is attained through a removal of the horizon altogether.

The sea is also the natural phenomenon to which photographers from the earliest days of their medium are drawn. When photographers celebrated the new possibilities of vision through the mechanical lens in the late nineteenth and early twentieth centuries, the sea was a favorite subject. Photographers such as Henri Cartier-Bresson, Alfred Stieglitz, and André Kertész saw the sea from different angles; they saw it through their photographic lenses from above, from the shoreline, from boats, and from deep below its surface. Similarly, the development of shipping as a new mode of transport, across oceans for leisure, immigration, and the transport of goods, meant that the sea too became tied to the innovations of the Industrial Revolution.

Photographers joined these journeys and took spectacular images of their progress across oceans as well as of the vessels that carried them.[45] In motion pictures, early filmmakers were fascinated by the sea, by its restless movement, its mystery, the play of light, the reflection of emotion in its crashing waves.[46] The sea was all about movement, and even in the worst conditions, early filmmakers were compelled to capture it in moving images. Contemporary with these images, painters such as Mondrian also began to envision the sea in exciting new ways. Painting and photography joined forces in the move away from pictorialism at the turn of the nineteenth into the twentieth century. Inspired by the perspectives enabled by photography's aerial, canted, and abstracted perspectives, painters appropriated its visual vocabulary and also depicted the sea from all angles.[47] Against this background, Mondrian's visions of the sea were radical: the sea in his paintings is represented vertically, placing the viewer either on high looking down, or perpendicular to the horizon—it is not always possible to tell which. Because of its own confusion and uncertainty, grey was the perfect color to represent the transformations to aesthetics and representation as they were envisioned by Mondrian's seas.

In paintings such as *The Sea* (1914), or *Composition No. 10—Pier and Ocean* (1915), Mondrian introduces the sea as a grid-like formation held within the oval frame of the painting's background. The sea here is bounded, flat, without a horizon line to mirror our own finitude in the face of all that we cannot see, cannot know, cannot grasp. This "composition" expresses Mondrian's attempt to rationalize, order, and know scientifically the mysterious and emotional turmoil of the sea. Mondrian's lifetime exploration of such patterns of verticality and horizontality, in the end, reveal that his attempt is always in contradiction to a goal that is never attainable. The form is only "grid-like"; it does not and cannot replicate the tight, intractable structure.

As it was theorized by its earliest critics, and reflected in early modernist painting, photography offered the opportunity to freeze the world in a moment in time, and consequently, the possibility of placing the human eye as all-seeing and omnipotent, looking down on and in command of the world below.[48] Mondrian captures the attempt at rationalization made by the photographic camera when he paints the sea from the unique perspective of above. He sees the sea as photographers saw the city: a form at which, thanks to technology, it was possible to look at from above. From this perspective, the sea is endless. Thus, Mondrian turns nature into an abstract image, seen in painting from the perspective of the photographic camera, thereby admitting the struggle between the natural and the technological or mechanical that takes place in representation. Thus Mondrian transposes the struggle of technology and nature to painting. All of this is realized, not only through paring down the composition to the line between abstraction and figuration, to the order that is found in the unfathomable space of the sea, but also through the use of a grey palette. It is no surprise that he represents the sea in grey paint, the color of the photographic image, the color that has often been used to mark the ineffability and unpredictability of the sea.[49] Grey carries within it, thus repeats, the clouding and uncertainty that hover over the ill-defined horizon line, the tension between a merged figure and ground, the collapse of distinction between representation and abstraction, between nature and its mechanically produced image. All of these aesthetic concerns are appropriated from Mondrian and pushed to new limits in postwar abstract grey painting.

Krauss discusses the characteristically modernist figure of the grid as a form of stasis: it is "a paradigm or model for the anti-developmental, the anti-narrative, the anti-historical."[50] The grid resists change, in Mondrian's paintings; the grid is the sign of uncertainty, the attempt to fix time and space, where really, this is not possible. Through the oval frame device that surrounds the grid of Mondrian's grey oceans seen from above, it is as though we are looking through a closed window at the infinite phenomenon of the sea. If indeed we look down on a grid, then it doesn't accord with Krauss's observations. In Mondrian's paintings, the grid is only ever an attempt to tame and circumscribe the sea, to frame it within a frame. It is a failed attempt, always. Because as we look down on, or out at the sea in *Composition II* (1913), for example, the forces of nature continue to extend and vibrate behind the grid; their rhythms and resonances continue to be expressed. They may lose definition toward the edges, but we do not mistake the limit of the framing device to be final.

In a quintessentially modernist strategy, Mondrian is also interested in challenging the distinction between figure and ground. So perhaps these are not grids after all? Surely a grid implies the distinction between structure and content, figure and ground. The exchange of figure and ground in Mondrian's painting results in blocks of color and lines, usually in black, initially vying for precedence on the canvas. In his later work, the color and lines are neither and both figure and ground. They are interchangeable. In his compositions of the sea, Mondrian still has a figure—the sea—that is ultimately inside a frame, becoming no more than a surface illusion. Thus, in his paintings the sea again points to the eventuality of abstract painting. In 1913, however, it is still too early for the distinction between figure and ground to be removed altogether. It is significant that Mondrian pursues the possibility of abstraction in his representations of the sea in grey. That is, he reduces painting to line, to a contest between figure and ground, to the relationship between the space of painting and its frame—which we see also in a painting such as *Grey Tree* (1911)—the relationship between line and movement. Appropriately, these dynamic and shifting relationships are forged in grey.

In *Grey Tree,* Mondrian removes the distraction of color and concentrates on the brushstroke: thick, defined, and defiant bare boughs that vibrate in the still, cold air that surrounds them. The boughs become lines, depending on our perspective, in tension with the air that is really a series of staccato, emphatic horizontal white to grey strokes. Line and color are always engaged in a struggle with each other, even if that color happens to be somewhere on the spectrum between white and dark grey. Mondrian's depictions of the natural world bring into focus the struggle between rationalization and nature, between the finitude of thought and knowledge and the infinity of nature. What Krauss calls the grid is surely the attempt to rationalize, to know and control, the unpredictability of nature. Conversely, for Mondrian, rationality is not possible; it is always unfinished, like the lines that never reach the edge of the canvas. Mondrian's aesthetic reflects and repeats in grey, the many struggles that collapse into abstraction in postwar American paintings in grey. These struggles that ultimately define modernist painting are most vividly depicted in grey.

Seeing Differently in Grey

At the same time that Mondrian is painting, in Paris, Picasso and Braque are making cubist works that depart radically from all that comes before them. The paintings represent the disintegration of a coherent, seamless world. The represented object or person is seen from multiple angles and perspectives, all at once, its pieces as if in motion, ricocheting around the canvas. There is no way to cohere the vision of the violins, vessels, and figures, to access the object, instrument, or person in its entirety. Rather, the viewer is called on to shift her eye around the canvas, also in motion across and around fragmented spaces. For Picasso and Braque, the breaking apart of the image and our visual expectations must be, and are always, in grey.

Before analytical cubism shattered the otherwise coherent surface of the picture plane in the early twentieth century, painters of the German Romanticism and very early modernists in Britain challenged the accustomed perception in painting, thus the vision of the world. They broke apart the principles of classical perspective in a different way. Again, in the nineteenth century these artists began to explore the surface of the canvas to draw its dimensionality closer to flatness than depth. It is true that artists such as Turner and Whistler painted in a variety of colors, not just in grey, but their landscapes, especially those involving water depicted at the interstitial moments of daybreak and dusk, always reach toward grey, even when they are identified as green or purple. In grey these artists direct their attention, and that of their viewers, away from the object or figure of representation, which is, at this time, receding in importance as the subject of painting. In the nineteenth century, the push toward abstraction was, in turn, the basis of the challenge to the depth of the image; it was already critical to the depiction of transformations to perception in and of painting.

As indicated earlier, where a horizon exists in the paintings of Turner, Whistler, or even Monet, it always blurs its beginning and end, as if to confuse our sense of the world, to distort the marker and measure of our own humanity. Knowledge of the world through vision is no longer reliable. At the time of their execution, these works were radical. Whistler's *Nocturne: Blue and Gold—Southampton Water* (1872) is a strong case in point (Plate 3). He places the shipping vessels along the water at Southampton to mark the horizon line. And so the horizon is recognizable, if in disguise. Nevertheless, in this study of night that is really a study in light, Whistler also flattens the perspective with a sky that is the mirror image of the water. This *Nocturne*, like others, is, to use a vocabulary that is not yet known to Whistler, a horizontal pan. The horizontality of the image in a pre-cinematic culture is astounding because it reduces the shapes on the land to shadows; they are subtle, ghostlike forms that push both water and sky outward, away from a depth of field, gesturing toward pure abstraction, gesturing toward the cinema and the twentieth century.

The flatness of the perspective in some of the *Nocturnes* draws on the photographic aesthetic. In addition, the narrative of light and darkness taking place in the London air is interested in tonal harmonies, in composition, in the vibrations of shadow in the softly appearing moonlight, all of which are the concerns of photography. Ultimately, these depictions encourage us to see painting and life on the Thames from a different perspective. As we know from his best-known painting, *Arrangement in Grey and Black No. 1* (1871), most usually and incorrectly referred to as *Whistler's Mother*, the artist chose the grey palette to complement his exploration of form and compositional elements over any temptation the viewer may have to focus on narrative. Like *Arrangement in Grey and Black No. 1*, the narrative is not the point of the Southampton or even the Westminster Bridge *Nocturne.* The viewer is encouraged to engage with knowledge of a different kind. What is important is the movement and transparency of fading light, its reflection on water, the ethereality of darkness, the confusion of land and water, of the natural elements in transition. For Whistler, it appears that the same importance should be given to the uncertainty of painting, an uncertainty as it is echoed here in grey. Before these *Nocturnes,* the viewer is led to forgo the notion of painting as a depiction of something, and to see it as something that is, in itself, a unique way of seeing and knowing. In 1870 this vision of painting was unheard of.

Even if Whistler does not repeat the realism of the photographic medium, the *Nocturnes* have much about them that is photographic. Not just the flatness of the perspective but also the speed with which they are painted, the commonplace, everydayness of the industrial world are all present to the surface of the paintings. Whistler's particular application of paint encourages the viewer's eye to stay on the surface. Indeed, there is no alternative: reverie and reflection are not possible before the *Nocturnes.* Rather, we are forced to recognize light and darkness as the subject and substance of these painted depictions, the same qualities, though differently represented, found in photography. Whistler's other works are also heavily influenced by photographic vision—they are often sepia in palette, emphasizing composition above all else, fascinated by tonal quality, and set in the everyday. The *Nocturnes* are timeless; there is a stagnation in the air, even though at this historical moment everything is in transition.

As the twentieth century unfolds, the uncertainty of the viewer's role before the painting is constantly challenged, thus transformed. My point here, however, is that thanks to the coming of photography, and later, the advent of the cinema, the possibilities of vision and perception were multiplied. The impact of these new ways of seeing the world on painting is seen from the earliest days of photography's invention. From these beginnings, the shifts in perception were bound together with the pursuit and meaning of painting as representation. In addition, from the early nineteenth century, these discoveries were being made in grey paint.

Artists on the Verge of Anonymity

Early twentieth-century modernism is often defined by the shifting status of the artist that resulted from changes to the cultural role of art at this time. Aesthetically, with the development of a self-conscious art, as we see in analytical cubism, artists began to theorize their presence in painting in different ways. In prewar European painting, we see what becomes another contradiction in terms: the presence of painters on a canvas from which they simultaneously complicate, displace, fragment, even erase themselves and the traces of their existence as visionary creative geniuses. Indeed, Greenberg who, as early as the 1940s, was among the first to theorize the transience of the artist on and ambivalence toward the canvas, remarked on this ephemerality as the epitome of modernism, even if he rejected it.[51] In keeping with his characteristic blurring of the distinction between figure and ground through a melting of grey forms, Manet's rare self-portrait of 1879, *Autoportrait à la palette / Self-Portrait with Palette,* painted when he was already ill, captures the artist out of focus. The vulnerability of the figure is found on the left side of the face, the shadow cast by his bowler hat and a beard that disappears into the deep grey background. Grey here is the unfinished jacket, the ghostlike face, a hand not yet fully formed. Both man and medium are still to be realized, or perhaps, they are in the process of disappearance.

Alternatively, we find the same dissolution of identity in Picasso's collages in grey. In those examples, discussed earlier, it is all but impossible to distinguish Picasso's creations from Braque's.[52] The same multi-perspectival grey-and-brown palette, and the same geometrical forms cover the paintings of both artists. Modern art was obsessed with the erasure of individual consciousness from the artwork. For fear of imposing a privileged bourgeois (monocular) vision onto a world in which everything is meant to be equal, in which art needs to be on a continuum with the reality of daily life, for the citizen of a democratic world, art had to challenge the institutions that perpetuate injustice and oppression. The artist could not be seen to engage with such inequalities, and therefore, he was to remove his signature from his artwork, thus his identity as unique and superior to the masses. The quest for this anonymity and equality, which is more like a deflection or self-effacement, resulted in some of modern art's most blatant, productive contradictions.

At least this is how it was theorized by early twentieth-century painters who turned to film for the collective, apparently democratic authorship of their vision in this new medium.[53] Again, these artists' attraction to photography, and more important, the cinematic image, was that these media do not carry the trace of the author's presence in the materiality of their image. The photographically reproduced image is, or was conceived to be, anonymous.[54] Of course, the reproduced image can reveal signature styles and gestures that, by the 1960s, came to be understood as the trademark of an artistic visionary.[55] In the prewar period, however, painting's concern was in the trace of the artist on the surface of the canvas through the demarcation of the application of paint with a brush. That said, the presence of the artist as individual author in early twentieth-century painting is not identified by the manipulation of the brushstroke. Even into the postwar years, in European painting the effacement of identity through retreat from an indulgence on the surface never eventuates. The reduction of the surface is a preoccupation predominantly found in the work of American postwar painting.

In one of the most spirited, one might even say obsessive, European examples of the vision of his own contradictory status as the great modern artist, perhaps the most modern of all in this sense, Giacometti paints everyone in his world, and rarely himself. Giacometti paints much later than the turn of the century, at a time when photography is well and truly established as a medium of artistic and documentary production. Nevertheless, his work can be considered as a culmination of the effects of photography and other forms of mechanical representation on painting. He paints portraits of Henri Matisse, his wife, Annette—sitting, walking, standing—his brother Diego, anonymous nudes, heads, busts, and all of them always drowning in a sea of grey. The figures are grey, the background is grey, the frames are always grey. The greys are infinite and varied, in their shades, hues, and tones, textures and densities. But the figures are not. They are all approximately the same. Annette could be mistaken for an anonymous sitter; the head of a man in *Dark Head* (ca. 1957–59) might be different, but it is not distinguishable from the head of *Caroline* (1965). Everyone looks the same; even though the painted figures are named, they are interchangeable, anonymous. The figures have distinct characteristics and yet are simultaneously, unidentifiable. They merge together in grey. Ultimately, the identity of the sitter is not at stake in any of these works, and none of the paintings create subjectivity for the painted. Because, I would argue, they are all about Giacometti, and not about the sitters of their titles.

In a typical gesture for a modernist painter, Giacometti paints the same portraits over and over again, even if the titles identify each as representing a different sitter. Imitations, copies, series of portraits show the potential for mimetic reproduction. In turn, this is the hallmark of an age characterized by industrial techniques and, specifically, the industrialization of image making in the form of photography.[56] In turn, seriality finds its way onto the canvases of the era's most regarded painters, including Giacometti. He paints figures in the same pose, seen from the same frontal point of view, occasionally in profile, the same compositional characteristics, weighed upon by the same grey world over and over again. The proportions and placement of the figure in the frame seem to be the only variable. Thus, Giacometti too is in search of resolution to a problem, so to speak, of painting. But for Giacometti, the problem is how to represent the human individual in paint and, through its relationship to space, its oppression in the alienating grey world that surrounds it. As such, Giacometti's vision of modern life in grey, not the individuals he paints, is the subject of his modernist paintings.

Giacometti's painted figures are caged, boxed, caught in a confusing field of grey. Inside their boxes, they are pressed to the bottom of the frame, sometimes apparently falling out of the frame. Mostly, they shyly consume less than half of the available canvas, the rest being given over to grey, to the frame within the frame, to the wall behind them. They are grey paintings of figures confined—faces trapped within frames within frames. They sit apologetically at the base of the canvas, their eyes dark, penetrating, and otherwise their facial expressions are obscured by the uniformity of Giacometti's vision, at the mercy of his brush, the victims of his black line, and the somber yet hurried grey painted world that surrounds them. They are trapped, not by a simultaneously symbolic and material base that both supports and restrains them, as are his sculptures, but within the frame the artist has given them, and then another that is the edge of the canvas, and another that is the frame that borders them as paintings. Moreover, as if in a *mise-en-abîme* of entrapment, the portraits adhere to a wall behind them, the museum to which the walls belong, the politics of that museum as a cultural center. When they were exhibited in the 2009 retrospective at the Centre Pompidou, the frames continued to replicate, outward to the changing face of the city of Paris, the city that defined their creator during his most productive years. And again, to their status as objects to be marveled at, ogled by infinite tourists and Parisians alike, years later. Some might say the frames of Giacometti's portraits give the images a structure, a logic, or that the frames hold the figures at bay. The frames can also be said, however, to isolate the figures, from the painted world around them and from us fifty years later. And so, these characters, personalities, some famous already, others made famous by Giacometti, elude the artist and the painting, and as a result embody the entrapment and dislocation (as they fall out of the frame) at the heart of the experience and identity of modern subjectivity. The figures in grey, surrounded by grey, produce layer upon layer of anonymity.

John Berger reads the final photograph of Giacometti before he died, a photograph in which he crosses a Paris street, his eyes on the ground, huddled in his coat as armor against the rain.[57] For Berger, the photograph speaks the entirety of Giacometti's lifework: it mimics his self-identification as the trapped, isolated, alienated figure of modern life, looking forward to his own death. According to Berger, in this final photograph the artist not only embodies but also enacts the purpose of his paintings. In the same way, the figures in the portraits perform the purpose of his search. They are representations of the world that entraps and isolates him (and them), rather than explorations of the inner, suffering self. And so, Giacometti is a portraitist in whose paintings the portrait is the material form given to his search. The identity of the figure itself is not important, which is why it is erased, scratched out, rethought, gestures that, by extension, see Giacometti the painter continually and furiously wiping away, rethinking his place on the canvas.

While portraits are usually in search of identity, in the twentieth century, Giacometti's serial grey portraits of the 1950s and 1960s reflect the modernist concern with his own search for meaning, his own existential crisis, the meaning of painting and its relationship to life, his life, modern life. The equilibrium of the figures, the clearly structured axes along which they walk, sit, or stand, reveal Giacometti's pursuit—obsessively so—of the science of painting. It's difficult to imagine such an historical search painted in a color other than grey. How would that look? None of these concerns that are the real content of the portraits would make sense in anything but the muted, carefully nuanced, yet vibrant shades of grey. Grey is the color of industrialization, modernity, and the contradictions of modern life. Grey is the color of the black-and-white photography that effectively renders anonymous the man behind the camera, inside the coat. Grey is the color best equipped to reflect his concern, as Berger would have it, "with the process of life as seen by a man whose own mortality supplied the only perspective in which he could trust."[58]

How to interpret all of this hesitation? Giacometti's reluctance to insert his own figure into the portraits, his apparent absence from the images, together with the sketched nature of many of them, surely reflects the hesitation and uncertainty of his vision, his authority over the only "perspective in which he could trust." The constant reworking, erasure, scraping away, overpainting, and ultimate obliteration of the painted surface that defines Giacometti's process of painting mark the failure of his own vision, the obsession of a pursuit never realized, even if it was a vision in which he believed. The canvas is physically distressed, made fragile and weak, as are the human forms by the struggle of thick impasto, the heavy, layered buildup of the surface. In contrast, the alacrity of the grey paint that surrounds the figures stays consistent in its vibrant, incremental layers, which means it is not subject to the same processes of eradication. In fact, the indication of Giacometti's virtuosity comes in the grey: when the grey background is layered, for example, in *Dark Head*, the many different greys bleed into one another, but they do not cancel each other out. And the greys can be tainted with the most vibrant of colors—violet in *Bust of a Man* (1951), taupe and green in *Head of a Man Face On* (ca. 1956–57), red in the version of *Annette* (1961) at the Hirshhorn Museum in Washington. It is as though, in the grey walls against which the first two ghostlike figures are pinned, and in contrast with Annette's red jacket in the last work, Giacometti finds the truth he is looking for. Thus, it's a truth he pursues in the skeletal figures, and finds elsewhere. Here he is able to express his own vulnerability, his own social isolation, among Europe's late bourgeois intelligentsia. He says as much:

> When I see everything in gray and in this gray all the colors I experience and thus want to reproduce, then why should I use any other color? I've tried it, because I never intended to paint only . . . with gray. As I was working . . . one color after the other dropped out, and what remained? Gray! Gray! Gray! My experience is that the color that I feel, that I see, that I want to reproduce . . . means life itself to me.[59]

The portraits are sometimes sketches in paint, preparations often for the sculptures, if also discrete works in and of themselves. To see them as sketches enhances their tentativeness, the uncertainty and vulnerability that are already confirmed through the dominance of the grey. Similarly, it suggests that the identity of the sitter, thus that of the artist, is always under erasure, always in the throes of destruction. Valerie Fletcher notes how the constant reworking and burial of image upon image beneath the thick buildup of oil paint at times create a convexity to the center of the canvas.[60] In other images, especially those on paper, we see that the support is worn thin, at times, torn away altogether. This fragility is the trace of the image's vulnerability, the ephemerality of the not-quite-finished, where there is no distinction between finished and unfinished.

We will see how these markings connect Giacometti's figures to the pencil scribbles and scrawls on Twombly's canvases, gestures that always signal the artist is never too far away, and yet, simultaneously, indicate that his search to define and identify the representative quality of the line continues elsewhere, not in this painting. Although Giacometti the artist is always somewhere other than on the canvas, at that moment, he is never far away. Perhaps Giacometti is more disillusioned, while Twombly accepts, is even inspired by, the impossibility of his search. Irrespective of the emotions it arouses in the artist, works of the two painters demonstrate the ambivalent relationship of the artist to his representation, to his authority.[61] Alternatively, if he is in command of his vision, then the world on which he reflects in his representation is a source of uncertainty.

Francis Bacon, from Photography to Cinema

Even the most cursory viewing of Francis Bacon's early work reveals the striking resonance with Giacometti's work. In the late 1950s and early 1960s, Bacon painted portraits trapped within transparent cages, or perhaps the paintings only depict the frames of cages? Irrespective of whether the figures are inside or simply framed by white painted lines, they are isolated, distorted, in grey. However, there is a difference between Bacon's and Giacometti's figures, a difference that opens Bacon's works to an entirely different vision of modernity. Even in his most deformed and disabled figures, such as *Head I, Head II, Head III* (1947–48), the sitter is in motion. The heads may be trapped in a transparent box, what Bacon refers to as "the visual machine," their eyes may be erased or forgotten altogether with the mouth as the focus of an erotic desire, but the figure is always in motion. At the very least, the figure is always in transition from one state to another, one space to another, in the process of screaming, as in *Study for Portrait* (1949), or melting under a traumatic erasure—for example, *Three Studies of the Human Head* (1953). While Giacometti's figures sit still, cemented within their grey world, it is often unclear whether Bacon's are inside or outside the box that frames them. Before a painting such as *Study for a Portrait* (1952) in Tate Modern, the screaming figure with a monocle becomes merged with the octagonal glass cage such that his head appears to support it, as if it were a headdress.

If Giacometti's figures in grey worlds demonstrate the influence of photography on painting, embracing the anonymity of the mechanically reproduced static image to depict individuals who are the inhabitants of modernity, Bacon's step forward to embody individuals at the interface of photography and the cinema. In addition to Bacon's appropriation of the figures of the cinema—the most obvious being the screaming nurse whose monocle is shattered in the Odessa Steps sequence in Sergei Eisenstein's *Battleship Potemkin* (1925)—his bodies are always caught by the image in a moment taken from a narrative of transition, whether it be physically, emotionally, or psychologically. Bacon's figures are also engaging with the politics of World War II and what have been argued to be the most extreme consequences of the principles of modernity: totalitarian political systems, violence inflicted on the human body, trauma, and entrapment.[62] While these qualities distinguish Bacon's forms from those of Giacometti, they are also reflections of the artist himself. Bacon's own distorted, deformed, sometimes abject body is repeated over and over again, as if in an attempt to discover his own self. As we have seen already, the ongoing process of discovering a disintegrating self on the canvas is always most powerful when painted in grey.

In *Study from the Human Body* (1949), Bacon turns to the work of Eadweard Muybridge, which is renowned for putting the still photograph into motion. Muybridge's images of humans and animals in motion through stop-motion photography were wondrous for viewers and celebrated in their historical moment. They used the available technology as a springboard into what is commonly accepted as the definition of modernity in their midst.[63] It is true that Bacon's human body shows no joy; it is in motion, however, and that is its power. The figure moves—again and again—beyond despair to a state of possibility, through a curtain said to be inspired by Titian's mysterious and delicately half-drawn curtain that obscures the face in *Portrait of Cardinal Filippo Archinto* (1558).[64] Bacon's figure walks into hope if only because it echoes the movement of a female nude in a Muybridge photograph. It borrows from Muybridge the revolutionary transformation of photography into cinema, of the still, frozen image into one of continuous movement.[65] Thus, in grey, Bacon carries on the tradition of the nineteenth-century preoccupation with the photograph and the possibility of representation as it moves from painting to photography, and again from photography into cinema. Lastly, like the repetition of serial photography's denial of the gesture of authority within the image aesthetic, Bacon's own existence in paintings spawned by photographic-based media reveals an artist in simultaneous formation and disintegration in grey. Thus, rather than being trapped within a cycle of frenetic scratching and erasure, although we do not usually think of Bacon's paintings as being infused with hope and possibility, when the early portraits are placed next to those of Giacometti, Bacon's severely deformed figures look forward into a world of transition, motion, and desire.

Once photography is invented, not only does it develop side by side with the transformations of modernity, but unlike any other medium before it, photography encourages its viewer to see this world as fragile and impermanent. For all of the discourse on fixity and death apparently embedded in the photographic medium, there is as much to say about its thwarted desire to find stasis in a permanently shifting environment.[66] Similarly, while modernity is said to be obsessed with systems of preservation and permanence, Bacon's insistence on grey as the color in which his figures are always in a state of transformation depicts the transience of this same world. The imbalances and grotesquery of Bacon's bodies are permeated with the fluidity and ineffability of modernity.[67] This ephemerality is as characteristic of the era as is the intransigence that reflects the alienation of Giacometti's figures. And again, the complexity and embrace of apparent contradictions are otherwise enabled by the fluidity and impermanence of grey. Grey repeats this impermanence through its own ambiguity.

The Politics of Grey

Perhaps the most famous political painting of the twentieth century is painted in grey: Picasso's *Guernica.* Why is *Guernica* painted in grey? The usual answer is that it is an indictment of war, violence, suffering, and death.[68] That is, the assumption is often that grey is used in an expression of the somber nature of the subject matter.[69] The grey fragmented bodies, screaming heads, and distressed animals are stripped of all realism and the potential to romanticize injustice. Grey is the dedramatization of the story of civil war.[70] Grey, black, and white are not weighed down by emotional or narrative directives as the more obvious colors of red and flesh tones might be. The grey also leaves interpretation open. *Guernica* is open to the possibility of many emotions and ideas, to anger and energy, as well as to a searing critique of war.

We remember the grey of Goya's depictions of war, and after him, Manet's *L'exécution de Maximilian,* in particular, the folds of the fabric of the soldiers' clothes made real in grey, and the looming grey clouds, as though they are an extension of the smoke from the rifles of the firing squad. *Guernica* adds something else to Goya's, Manet's, and all previous depictions of violence and war in grey. *Guernica* is painted in grey because it is the color of contemporaneity: the newspaper and the photograph are the two media through which World War II was more commonly depicted and disseminated to the world. In addition, the printing press and photography are the two media through which Picasso learned of the destruction of Guernica when he was living in Paris. There is not an abundance of painted visions of World War II because the photograph was the celebrated medium through which it was seen. The photographic camera was, by this time, in mass distribution and as a result, there was a proliferation of pictures of the battlefield as it had never before been represented.[71]

Picasso draws on the preferred medium of photography through the choice of grey paint. From here, he puts the image in motion. As Olivier Berggruen argues, Picasso uses the palette of greys to create volume and tonal value, giving them cinematic qualities.[72] Everything and everyone in the mural is in motion, filled with energy as figures scream, protest, and rush to escape or to rescue. The intensity of the action, both of the narrative and figures in motion, becomes emphasized through the grey scale of the cinematic image. Picasso exploits the familiar possibility of grey to focus without distraction, and to fragment the image as if it were a tumultuous cinematic narrative.

In turn, the contrasts and tonal variance of the greys in *Guernica* are said to give the painting a depth and profundity that, despite its size, diffuse its monumentality. The colors, like the collection of fragmented bodies across a horizontal picture plane, are, at one and the same time, distinct to create shock, and yet give overall coherence because they exist on a spectrum of grey. Grey has a dexterity that enables it to keep the contradictions of the figures and their narrative in concert but still suspended in ambivalence. Simultaneously, Picasso removes the realism expected from a photographic depiction. For him, the realism of photography is, perhaps for the first time, seen as a betrayal of the horror and the trauma of war. Photography and a reflected realism are not adequate to the enormity of the trauma that is experienced on the battlefield and the home front of World War II. Similarly, *Guernica*'s grey paint reinforces the singularity of the painted image: it is not an image that is infinitely reproduced and distributed en masse, a distribution that belies the singularity of the traumatic events. Picasso's *Guernica* believes in the power of painting to visualize the violence, destruction, and shattered Basque village following its bombing by German and Italian warplanes, a power that, for Picasso, photography does not have. Grey paint is able to bear this burden, to meet this tall order in a way that no other color and no other medium can.

Picasso returns to the color grey in his representation of violence in his memorial to World War II in *The Charnel House* (1944–45). In this work and *Guernica,* Picasso realized his belief that "painting is not done to decorate apartments. It is an instrument of war for attack and defense against the enemy."[73] If *Guernica* is a cacophonous protest against the Spanish nationalist government's murder of sixteen hundred inhabitants of Guernica, then *The Charnel House* is a sober memorial to those who were murdered by the Nazis. This painting cannot work in isolation from its more famous elder sibling: it makes sense in the wake of *Guernica* with all its controversy, its circulation throughout the world in the years following its creation. And appropriately, *The Charnel House* is kept in New York, at the Museum of

Modern Art, where *Guernica* found a home at Picasso's request for the duration of Franco's dictatorship in Spain. The white, grey, and black of what might at first glance appear to be an unfinished painting make a quiet memorial. And it is the repetition of the depiction in painting of an earlier trauma that makes *The Charnel House* so poignant and powerful. Seen as a relation of *Guernica*'s more raucous representation of the Spanish Civil War, *The Charnel House* is imbued with a sense of exasperation. The same horrendous violence, the same assaults on humanity are still with us, Picasso seems to be saying. Still, the gradations of grey paint that lead to the unpainted sections at the top of the canvas, and a hand, feet, a child's forehead, are like a claim on the impossibility of representation to capture the devastation of what was discovered in the concentration camps. It is the reuse of the same palette, together with the same form as *Guernica,* that gives *The Charnel House* meaning, that makes it a political object. The violence of war happened again.[74]

Picasso's two famous paintings are perhaps the most powerful twentieth-century claims to the political agency of grey. The two works were unprecedented at the time, as much because of their grey palette as the experimentation of their formal and representational qualities. This development in Picasso's palette is testimony to the potential of grey, its capacity to enrage audiences, to radicalize painting, to explore the influence of photography and cinema on the life of a painting that continues to have an impact. Grey reaches new levels with Picasso's use of it in *Guernica* to meet political ends. In addition to marking the evolution of grey in Picasso's oeuvre, these works set new ground for the as yet unexplored political value of grey in the postwar period. After Picasso, it cannot be claimed that grey is nothing and void: here it is charged with the responsibility of political outrage. Similarly, grey after *Guernica* can be promoted as painting stripped back to its most essential attributes in the interests of accentuating the expression of outrage.

Painting continues to explore the interface of its relationship with other media after the advent of photography and photographic-based media. Similarly, the definition in relationship to other art forms is not new.[75] Nevertheless, when the invention of photography redefined notions of realism and documentary, grey, or black and white as opposed to sepia, were the colors in which this was achieved. Black, white, and the grey scale enable the formal precision of the photographic image, especially because chromatic color did not transfer accurately before the invention of panchromatic film.[76] And with the invention of photography, the redefinition of painting becomes urgent. It makes sense that the search for what painting might be at this time of cultural and artistic change and uncertainty is performed in grey. And yet, painting does not simply imitate photography because grey is used to fragment and abstract the image, not for realist depiction. Similarly, the use of the grey palette is never about the austerity of the subject matter as long as it is for the representation of the historical world. To be sure, the political value of painting is transformed when artists in America take up questions of representation in the postwar period. As I shall demonstrate, however, the social and cultural resonance of grey retains its impetus as these painters negotiate the relationship between painting and the modern world.

3

GREY ABSTRACTION

FORM AND FUNCTION IN AMERICAN POSTWAR PAINTING

> Nothing could be further from the authentic art of our time than the idea of a rupture of continuity. Art is—among other things—continuity, and unthinkable without it. Lacking the past of art, and the need and compulsion to maintain its standards of excellence, Modernist art would lack both substance and justification.
>
> —**Clement Greenberg**, "Modernist Painting"

IN POSTWAR AMERICA, Mark Rothko, Jackson Pollock, Jasper Johns, and, later, Brice Marden, Agnes Martin, and Cy Twombly, make their most radical departures into abstraction in grey. These artists turn to grey paint as both color and medium to investigate the question: what is painting? At the very same moment that painting is announced to be dead, they persist in asking the question. And they go further with questions such as, what is the role of the artist in this inquiry? What is the relationship between painting and the world? What is the relationship between painting and the body, painting and other media, painting and the other arts? In grey, these painters demonstrate ambiguity and uncertainty, all the time drawing on the uniqueness of its characteristic reflection and absorption, transparency and opacity, at the interface of illusion and reality, unique, and yet, always a combination of all colors, including black and white.

While the artists discussed in this chapter may have nothing other than their use of grey in common, I take this as the starting point to demonstrate that in grey they explore the concerns of modernist painting. To do this, they strip painting to its most essential elements: grey is the medium with which they demonstrate the importance of composition, the creation of form, and importantly, the fundamental distinction between light and dark, the exploration of the surface, the intersection of painting and other media, painted representation and reality, as well as the interrogation of the relationship between artist and artwork. They continue to reinvent painting and through a self-conscious practice, they identify, reflect, and critique the historical moment of painting within industrial and postindustrial modernity.

In this chapter, I take a two-pronged approach to the use of grey in postwar American abstract painting: first, I analyze the themes or questions of modernist painting as they are detailed and explored in chapters 1 and 2. Second, my analysis continues to take an artist-centered approach: I examine these themes as they are pursued in the paintings of Johns, Twombly, Rothko, Martin, and Marden, and referenced in those of others such as those by Pollock, Newman and Sean Scully. In grey, these artists engage with some of the same questions asked in the prewar years, and extend them into abstract painting. In doing so, they add political and historical dimension to the history of twentieth-century grey painting. Particularly, in the years after abstract expressionism, there are a number of artists who use grey paint to search for resolution to the questions that concern *The Truth Is Always Grey*: What is painting? And, what does it mean to paint in a world in which there is, apparently, nothing left for painting to do, nothing left for painting to show, nowhere for painting to go?[1]

Specifically, I examine the tensions played out across the surface of grey paintings by Johns, Rothko, Marden, Martin, and Twombly, demonstrating their range of responses to the possibilities of reimagining this surface of painting more broadly. There is little consistency in their approaches, but each artist engages a transformation of the painted surface that underlies and underlines the shifts made by abstract modernist art. Moreover, on these surfaces I locate the intention and effect of each artist's use of grey. In the second half of the chapter, I return to the sea as the figure through which postwar

American painters negotiate abstraction. In particular, I demonstrate how they continue the preoccupation with the sea and the horizon line begun in the nineteenth century, and taken up by Mondrian, as a way of exploring the definition of painting itself. Given their embrace of grey paint, together with its unique qualities, it is the obvious medium in which to represent the sea and the questions to which it gives rise for painting. And beyond the sea, beyond the horizon line, I examine the surfaces of Johns's grey work and introduce those of Scully to continue the exploration of the use of grey to interrogate the line between abstraction and figuration in American postwar and, eventually, postminimalist painting.

All of the grey paintings I have discussed thus far, from Giotto's decoration of the dado in the Scrovegni Chapel, through Whistler's representations of London and Manet's portraits of street life in turn-of-the-century Paris are, in some way, painted on the margins. That is, they break with tradition, spill over into spaces on the edge of the narrative and the expectations of art in their time. Their nonconformity is realized in grey as the color of transience, fluidity, anonymity, and transition. Grey is a color that assumes its potency on the margins. In this chapter, I argue that grey abstract works in postwar America inhabit the margins as a way of bringing modernism's discomfort with itself, its ambiguities, and the role of the artist in these discourses of discomfort, to the fore. Some paintings even go so far as to question the limits of modernism itself. My discussion of the paintings' relationship to modernism is given context by art historical discourse. In addition, each of the works I interpret has a relationship, whether central or tangential, to the historical moment in which it is produced. This relationship often results in further doubt about painting, about modernism. While their grey works are not painted on the margins of their oeuvres, artists such as Johns, Twombly, Martin, and even Rothko consciously envision the place of painting itself to be on the periphery, always holding within it its own assertions, as well as often, the very opposite of what it claims. Grey is thus a medium for painting's own undoing. The grey paintings always maintain ambiguity, always leave open the possibility of changing their mind. This fluidity and open-endedness reflect the uniqueness of grey. Grey is the only color that has the potential to return its very defining characteristics to the concerns of what takes place on the canvas. Grey is a color that is used to represent painting as a medium.

We all know that Greenberg was mistaken or, at best, myopic in his claims for the importance of the surface of modernist painting. However, even if we set aside his prescription of how this surface should look, postwar abstract paintings in grey have a tendency to illustrate, not refute, his lofty views: they are concerned with the two-dimensionality of painting, its translation of a three-dimensional world, and the relationship between the two.[2] I identify this relationship in the blurred line between figuration and abstraction as it is pursued in grey—a color that traverses borders and sits at the interstice. In turn, this leads to the important discussion of the continued representation of the sea and the horizon line as the figure where the precipice between abstraction and figuration is negotiated. In distinction from the late nineteenth-, early twentieth-century representations of the sea, the postwar American examples are shown to engage with a different historical context, a context in which the themes and concerns raised by painting and representation have also shifted.

We may also want to reject the notion that a modernist shift away from classical perspective brings with it a revocation of the invitation to become lost in a state of transcendent reverie, preferring to identify the wholeness of the spectator before the works of Rothko, Martin, or Twombly, for example. But the transformation of the spatial limits of modernist painting introduces a different kind of spectator, one whom I characterize by her embodiment.[3] This spectator brings a transformed conception of seeing, a seeing from new and different perspectives to the work of art. Because of the interrelationship between the spatial organization of the grey image and changes to vision, I also begin to identify these modernist shifts to vision, perception, and spectatorial positioning in my discussions of the paintings in this chapter. I explore them more fully in the next.

Lastly, I demonstrate in this chapter that the use of grey to articulate the problems and ambiguities of painting in postwar America increases in intensity and profundity across the twentieth century. There is no evidence in the grey painted aesthetic that painting is a medium in disintegration. On the contrary, grey enables a continued exploration of painting by these artists. In American postwar painting, grey is everything from the means and materiality of painting, through the basis of historical and art historical reference, to the vehicle of thematic exploration, an exploration that is, in turn, characterized by a modernist self-reflection. This self-reflection may lead to a modernism in disintegration and an abnegation of painting. But in the face of these claims, grey continues.

On the Grey Surface of Postwar American Painting

JASPER JOHNS

As critics before me have noted, many of the aesthetic and thematic concerns that began on Manet's canvases reappear on Johns's. In one such concern, Johns uses grey cloth and other fabrics in his interrogation of the surface and dimensionality of painting.[4] Johns probes the identity of painting, and of his paintings in particular, through persistent and varied iterations, manipulations, attachments to, and analyses of the surface. Johns builds up the surface through the encaustic process: he attaches objects, devices, serrates the canvas, and everywhere makes windows, doors, drawers, and mirrors of and within the canvas. Moreover, it is the grey canvas as cloth, and the attachment of grey cloth to the canvas, that creates the tightest kinship between the history of painting and postwar American painting. Johns does more than simply suggest the influence of Manet's canvases. His paintings appropriate the trope of Manet's challenge to painting in the late nineteenth century, as I, after Armstrong, have identified it: that place in grey where the dress, the trousers, the hat, the coat become merged with the background against which the soldiers stand. In *Catenary (Manet-Degas)* (1999; see Plate 4), Johns attaches pieces of grey canvas to the painting as if they are the remains of the trousers, as if he had taken the fabric from Manet's *L'exécution de Maximilian*, particularly, from the version reassembled by Degas. It is as though Johns finds the cloth from the missing pieces of Manet's painting, puts them together just as Degas had done before him, transfers them to his painting, and paints them grey. The uneven, encaustic grey work, with a shadow creeping diagonally across the face of the canvas, is a rewoven re-presentation of the history of painting: from Goya, through Manet, in the hands of

Degas, to Johns. The violence and trauma of the firing squad executing the emperor are here transformed into the story of Manet's representation of the same. It is the desecration of painting, and Manet's painting in particular, that is the tragedy of Johns's rendition. The shape and placement of the fragments re-present the pieces of Manet's 1868–69 version of the painting, but the size does not.[5] At 97 cm × 145 cm × 15 cm, Johns's *Catenary (Manet-Degas)* emphasizes the relationship between grey fragments of cloth and the catenary string that binds them, but does not really. Johns is interested not in historical narrative but in the narrative of painting, in grey, across a canvas, between materials.

With their evocation of the most perfect modernist form—the catenary—as well as their constant discovery of new permutations of spatial, and representational possibilities of and on the canvas, Johns's *Catenary* paintings are the prolongation of his earlier artistic concerns.[6] And in the repetition of Manet's fascination with the disappearance of a distinction between surface and depth, figure and ground in the merging of the figures' clothes and the painting's background, a fascination that Manet in turn takes from painters of previous centuries, Johns continues the questions of paintings in grey from one generation to the next, from right to left across the canvas. He uses the grey palette to stitch together the pieces of cloth onto and as the surface of the canvas. This surface is, in turn, the subject of the same canvas on which multiple layers of fabric are united thanks to a piece of string, fused with grey paint. Since the first wave of Johns criticism in the early 1960s, critics usually agree, after Johns's announcement, that the image or the painting as object and the thing it represents are to be understood as one and the same: an object.[7] If this is so, his paintings in which fabrics, veils, cloths, and clothes are the devices attached to the canvas, are surely the ultimate interchange of paintings as and of objects.[8] In *Catenary (Manet-Degas)*, Johns turns to the story of the material of Manet's painting for the color, form, theme, and interpretation of his own painting in particular, and painting in general.

Near the Lagoon (2002) also comprises four blank pieces of canvas that correspond to Degas's reassembly of the surviving fragments of Manet's *L'exécution de Maximilian.* This time Johns preserves the proportions and turns the composition vertically.[9] Grey enables the secrecy, the shadows in which everything comes alive on Goya's canvas before Manet's, in the executions twinned by the history of art. Johns appropriates the shadow that has become the very substance of painting, together with the color and materiality of the paintings of the generation before him. Johns's grey paintings are the shadows cast on Goya's and, later, Manet's canvases. We can likewise insert Johns's brushstrokes into this tradition, as well as the catenary string that, in its imitation of the fall of fabric in *Near the Lagoon,* for example, is a return of the canvas as well as the linen that veils it. Simultaneously, while the catenary string in *Catenary (Manet-Degas)* unites the pieces of cloth on the surface, in *Near the Lagoon,* its function is to fragment further. Johns's method of embedding the string in the encaustic and then removing it creates crevices, thus, further divisions in the dense surface. Keegan and Lister explain Johns's process of layering, of secreting, of creating new surfaces and spaces for painting:

> The canvas was first coated with a layer of unpigmented wax, which like size, would stabilize the canvas and prevent it from soaking up the hot encaustic paint when it was applied and later reheated. A muted, earthy red (iron oxide red mixed with titanium white) was then painted over the entire canvas, functioning as a colored ground. The four patches corresponding to Manet's fragments are of the same linen and are painted the same muted red. Johns roughly outlined the fragments' positions on the reverse in black and ruled off the area with an extensive 5-inch (12.7 cm) grid in blue crayon. The red fragments were then systematically tacked to the stretched canvas with a knotted stitch of waxed thread at each interval where the grid lines intersected, adding extra knots at some edges.[10]

Once the canvas is painted, Johns begins the process of the catenary, the string that creates the perfect curves etched into the surface of the grey encaustic, and is finally attached to the edge of the hinged wooden frame. The catenary string thus adds further layers of fabric, density, movement, and meaning to those envisioned by Manet and Goya before him. The fabric—of fragments, the stretched canvas, the red and blue underpainting, the black lines, the grey paint, the string, and the impress of indentations and further overpainting before it—comprises the many layers of *Near the Lagoon* as well as *Catenary (Manet-Degas)*. Like the windows and doors on Johns's canvases that can never be opened, these layers are as illusory as they are real. As Keegan and Lister point out, *Tennyson* (1958) has even more layers of canvas and of colored paint than *Near the Lagoon.* Layers and surfaces are there to create material texture, illusory depth, and conceptual complexity. For Johns, layers and surfaces proliferate to guard against the intransigence of a resolute material image.

While there is often a rush to criticize Johns's later paintings—those after the *Tantric* paintings of the early 1980s are claimed to be repetitious—the catenary paintings of the early twenty-first century can, alternatively, be seen as a culminating moment in the possibilities of grey painting.[11] In these works, painting as object and the object of painting become one on the surface. There is no longer anything other than the veil, surface upon surface, the medium used to refer to the medium itself, and to create a dialogue with a history of art in which the fall of fabric worn by executioners is the moment of revelation. Johns's catenary works are the vision of his most mature thinking, and might be understood as an abstract instance of the essence of painting. They are also much more. Like the doors and windows and drawers of other paintings I discuss later, the multiple grey fabrics—canvases, colors, strings and their indentations—refer to nothing other than their own existence, the objects and subjects of representation. Simultaneously, the layers of grey reference the history of art, not only Manet and Goya but also the traces of red underneath the grey, the mutability of the colors that make up grey, remind, for example, of the shading in red that creates definition to the otherwise luminescent garments and bodies in Andrea del Sarto's narrative of the life of Saint John the Baptist in Florence.[12] On Johns's canvases, grey is never simply grey. Grey enjoys a complex and dense relationship with history, with art history, with the medium and meaning of painting in the twentieth and twenty-first centuries.

Furthermore, the density of surfaces in paintings such as *Near the Lagoon* and *Catenary (Manet-Degas)* creates images that can almost, but not quite, be seen on the canvas. As we look at the substance of the thick materials, in all their dimensionality, their unevenness, and their motion, we see rugged landscapes, or "smooth glacier fields, craters, rivers, drifting sands, and melting ice flows."[13] This ability to suspend the viewer always on the precipice of seeing something appearing on the surface of the abstract canvas is, once again, played out nowhere but on the grey catenary surface of Johns's painting. In this gesture, Johns reenvisions the possibility of painting in grey, through abstraction.[14]

All this said, while the catenary works apparently refer to the surface of paintings when they are within the context of art history, as already mentioned, the catenary is also the perfect modernist form. Thus the catenary adds a historical dimension: it is the evidence of engineering structures that reach for perfection in their design. The mathematical equation for the catenary curve was derived as early as the seventeenth century. The structure, however, became used in the design and construction of bridges for the use of road traffic in the early nineteenth century.[15] The best-known examples of such engineering feats are the Brooklyn Bridge (John Augustus Roebling, 1883) and the Golden Gate Bridge (Irving Morrow, Charles Alton Ellis, Leon Moisseiff, 1937). The first modern suspension bridge that uses the catenary structure is the James Creek Suspension Bridge in Pennsylvania (James Finley, 1801). All of these bridges are in Johns's world, in North America. However, these bridges are not, strictly speaking, catenary forms because their hyperbolic chain or cable is weighted at the bottom by the road across which traffic will pass. Neither are Johns's strings always perfect drops because they are, at times, attached to the canvas by the grey paint he uses to paint over and embed them.[16] Alternatively, a catenary such as *Catenary (Manet-Degas)* is unfinished. It stops on the upturn, the string left to fall without purpose before it reaches the left edge of the painting. While Johns may not consciously envision a polemic on the relationship between his grey paintings and industrial modernity, his choice of the perfect engineering form, then interrupted, cut short, or lost in paint, in grey, gives this phase of his oeuvre a resonance with modernity. An image such as *Catenary (Manet-Degas)* both heralds the fragmentation and unfinishedness of modernity, as well as reflects the decentered composition of Goya's vision of war. The catenary is a form that is not perfect, neither in life nor in painting, despite its theoretical conception. Painting in the twentieth century might be understood as equally unresolved.

Johns's surface in grey is never one-dimensional. In a characteristic we associate more with Yves Klein's sumptuous, electric International Klein Blue, Johns's grey can be filled with desire. Johns's surface seduces the body of the painter and his viewer alike: sensuousness, eroticism, and tactility find resonance on Johns's most renowned grey canvases, a resonance for which we need look no further than *Painting Bitten by a Man* (1961; Plate 5). The thick buildup of grey paint, like icing on a cake, is tactile and intense. The grey encaustic surface of *Painting Bitten by a Man* is visualized through a sheer density of paint worked with a lathe across the canvas. Ultimately, however, everything erotic, sensual, physical, and unpredictable about *Painting Bitten by a Man* is expressed through the trace of Johns's own teeth, and behind them his tongue, as they have violated and through that violation simultaneously defined the heavily built-up encaustic grey surface. Thus, in direct contrast to Klein's blue monochromes, Johns builds up the grey paint on this canvas with the intention of violating it, such that its unevenness and unpredictability are the points to be emphasized. The movement of the artist's hand across the canvas is visible in the melting, moving surface. The bottom edge of the painting is, characteristically for Johns, left bare, another indication that painting is not finished, never seamless or perfect. He wants that buildup to be tactile, to look just as it is: dense, glutinous, dramatic, and physical, to remind us of the absent body that has left a scar. For Johns, grey makes physicality clearer, where physicality is "the object nature of the materials."[17] Where the blue paint of Klein's velvet rectangular fields is sumptuous, erotic, a fantasy, perfectly smooth, Johns sinks his teeth deep into the paint to create a wound on the canvas. The edges of this wound reinforce the presence of the physical body, whereas on Klein's surface the uninterrupted coherent texture of paint encourages imaginative wandering, leaving the body behind. There is no fantasy or reverie allowed to play across the surface of a Johns canvas, no buildup in the viewer's imagination to mirror the intensity of the paint. On the contrary, these surfaces are infused with desire: Johns's desire. As viewers, we want to reach out and touch the wound. Before Johns's painting, face-to-face with the physical surface of waxed paint, we are tempted to run our fingers around the edge of the wound, to heal the violence done to the paint by the human body, the artist's body. It is for this reason that the surface of *Painting Bitten by a Man* suspends within it the conditions and concerns of modernist art: the surface transforms the optical into the tactile, it invites the viewer to sense the intimate physical relationship between artist and canvas, and it dethrones the apparent privilege of vision when face-to-face with a painting, as well as the vision of painting. We want to touch it. We respond to it as an object in our world, not as an illusory representation of that world.[18] Johns's surface visibly delights in the sensuousness of paint as it is lathered on and pushed and massaged around the canvas, thus reflecting a delight in the dimensionality of the material world through its transposition onto the canvas. And yet, in a gesture that infuses uncertainty, even a threat, into the painted surface, this delight is undone by the violence, simultaneously speaking the oral desire of the artist. At the very same time as the surface of *Painting Bitten by a Man* revels in the physicality of paint, all power and agency are stymied by the body that scars the already uneven surface.

While many around him—for example, Warhol, Lichtenstein, Stella—were focused on a project to reduce the traces of paint on the surface, to move toward flatness, and efface the gestures of the artist from the material surface of the painting, Johns does the very opposite. He uses paint with great virtuosity to build it up into a tactile, three-dimensional, physical form. The Johns canvas is an object in the world; it is sculpted. In distinction even from Rauschenberg, who, it can be asserted, also creates paintings as objects, for Johns, the material object is paint. Critics often refer to Johns's use of encaustic as the optimal medium for his drama of concealment and revelation through paint. Grey is not simply the color of these encaustics, but rather, grey encaustic is the very medium to which they refer. Max Kozloff, for example, quotes Johns in support of his claim that the painting "is a series of cancellations as much as it is a sequence of additions": "As he himself put it: 'I am concerned with a thing's not being what it was, with its becoming something other than what it is, with any moment in which one identifies a thing precisely, and with the slipping away of that moment.' "[19] Painting is always a space of uncertainty and paradox for Johns. And grey, the neither . . . nor, the color of the question mark, becomes the material of this uncertainty on Johns's canvases. Grey is also the shadow, just as painting is the shadow, not the thing that casts the shadow, of representation.

As David Sylvester says, "It is very evidently concerned with disintegration and re-integration. It operates, as Johns does, in the area between question and assertion."[20] Grey leaves Johns's viewer in a state of suspense.

In summary, the veils, drapery, cloths that are said to culminate in the late catenary work *Near the Lagoon* ensure that the canvas cannot be mistaken as anything other than it is: a material surface that shadows the transformation of the world's surfaces into the surface of representation. And yet, in a true Johns evasion of superficiality and fixity, these surfaces have depth, dimensionality, and a complex history. They are, simultaneously, no more and much more than a surface.

Johns's canvases are also replete with secret doors, windows, hinged openings such as we see in *Portrait—Viola Farber* (1961). As they do throughout the history of art, these figures extend the surface of Johns's canvases: they focus attention on the world behind, underneath, beside the painting, beyond the painting. The window, door, trap door, cracks between panels and various other openings in Johns's paintings gesture toward a world we never physically see in the painting but we know to be there, and are curious to see. At the same time, while these tropes and forms are figurative, and thus, open the painting out, they are also abstract, defining a moment where the painting turns in on itself, away from us, into a conversation with its own surface, at best with the history of art. Thus, Johns's windows and doors might be understood as a reduction, or elevation of the definition of space in Hammershøi's interiors, to the entirety, the very identification of painting.

To give one example: when looking at *Drawer* (1957), the viewer imagines opening the drawer, pulling it out to reveal all that cannot be contained on the surface of a painting, all that is inside a drawer. And then, as if in complete contradiction of a painting such as *Drawer*, in *Portrait—Viola Farber*, the trap door opens to reveal that there is nothing behind the hinged door. Having seen the bare white gallery wall behind *Portrait—Viola Farber*, we begin to realize that the drawer in *Drawer* was probably empty all the time—how can it have been anything else? Ultimately, therefore, there is nothing but the surface of the picture, even though the windows, doors, frames, extensions make reference to a somewhere else, a something else obstructed by the gallery wall.

In "Grids," Krauss notes the significance of the window for artists from romanticism to symbolism:

> The window is experienced as simultaneously transparent and opaque. As a transparent vehicle, the window is that which admits light—or spirit—into the initial darkness of the room. But if glass admits, it also reflects. And so the window is experienced by the Symbolists as a mirror as well—something that freezes and locks the self into the space of its own reduplicated being. Flowing and freezing: *glace* in French means glass, mirror, and ice; transparency, opacity, and water.[21]

For Johns, the various openings as both illusory and real, reflect and enable a seeing into; they give life to transparency and close down opportunity through their opacity. But not in a way that is easily identified in Krauss's characterization. They are designed not only to confound their own appearance as openings but also to invert the expectations of windows, doors, and mirrors as we know them to function in the real world. Painting is only ever painting, an object in the world, not an opening, be it a window, a door or any other opening onto the world. Johns's paintings contain within themselves the contradiction of what is on their surface. As long as these works admit that there is nothing other than the painting, they continue to suggest the possibility of something beyond their frames to which they refer. Again, we are reminded that the impossibility of this situation of painting, and of Johns's paintings in particular, is envisioned in the surface tensions, the presence and absence of painting in grey.

The surfaces of Johns's paintings are the color of bitumen. And as much as they slip and slide away from our search to make sense of them, they can feel like gravel as we experience them with our eyes. This is especially the case when we look at the short, staccato gestures in multiple greys of the numbers, targets, maps, and flags, strokes that create, or leave behind them, a rough, incoherent surface of contention. The grey surface is also like bitumen because it is uneven. Bitumen is the surface of the twentieth century. It seals and protects. Johns uses grey paint as if to tar over the roughness and potholes of the canvas, to fill in the crevices created by the catenary strings, and other colors that lie beneath, colors we don't desire and dare not touch.

To give an example, Johns seals the initial colors of *In Memory of My Feelings—Frank O'Hara* (1995) as if to cover over the inconsistencies, the ambiguities and problems of the original painting. Even though it is not depicted, we see the American flag underneath the grey thanks to the explosion of short crosshatched strokes that begin to resemble the stars of fifty-two states. Or perhaps it is the bitter emotions of the title, the breakup of Johns's relationship to O'Hara, that the painting apparently references, a breakup Johns wants to close definitively.[22] In the same vein, as a dirt road is covered in bitumen, Johns seals the unpredictability and clashes of the primary colors, the reds of the flag, and in so doing, he makes the painting safer to look at, the canvas more comfortable, more banal. The hinged panels are prepared in grey for the convoy of viewer eyes that will travel over their surfaces in an attempt to find the "real" Johns, and thus, their own selves in this painted world.[23] Such use of the material to invite the viewer's survey of the surface is a veritably twentieth-century strategy, executed in twentieth-century shades of bitumen grey.[24] That said, there is a hurriedness, a restlessness to the short brushstrokes that might be seen to be in collision, rather than explosion, like the various greys that comprise the panels that are the single work of *In Memory of My Feelings—Frank O'Hara.* As much as the grey covers over, especially in the top left-hand corner where white stars on a blue background, we imagine, were once prominent, it also exposes the uncertainty of the feelings that are supposedly remembered in and beneath this painting. Grey never sits still; grey in this painting might be somber, but it also captures the turmoil of that solemnity, even as it conceals the other emotions being remembered. Moreover, the motion and ineffability of grey are encouraged thanks to its multifariousness, its traffic in the expanse of the spectrum of what might be recognized as the color grey.

LATE ROTHKO

Johns's specific rendering of the relationship between paint and canvas is unique for painters who use grey. Which is not to say that other paintings are not fused with dimensionality and tactility; rather, that other artists use grey for very different reasons, in very different ways, to construct different surfaces. Although at first glance it may appear as unrelated as it is unwise to move from Johns to Rothko, I place the surfaces of Rothko's and, subsequently, Martin's paintings somewhere between the absent surface of a work such as James Turrell's *Laar* (1974) and the dense grey encaustic of Johns's *Painting Bitten by a Man.*

Sean Scully is particularly eloquent in his discussion of Rothko's interrogation of the relationship between light, space, canvas, and grey paint, a discussion that is also, inadvertently, a discussion of Scully's own paintings, many of which are in grey.[25] He writes of how Rothko's heavenly and devastating canvases radiate out into space, lighting it and offering the spectator an arena into which she is invited to step. And, unbelievable though it may seem, this effect is only achieved through a virtuosic working over and over again of paint on a surface that is nevertheless made to look transparent:

> Rothko said that the surfaces in his painting either expanded or contracted, and that between these two poles we can find everything he wants to say. His idea was not to describe but to make a theatrical arena—a space so authentic emotionally and so clear conceptually that it was capable of holding essential human passion. His own high ambition for art was so compelling that he was forced to blur his edges, simplify his forms and complicate his colours so that his paintings would have enough mystery to hang naked in public.[26]

Of Rothko's magnificent *No. 8* (1964), Scully says it is "a vertical canvas of slate grey upon which floats a solitary vertical figure of grey-black. The effect is gravely beautiful and abjectly lonely."[27] Thus, according to Scully, once the "arena" is defined, once the surface of the painting is realized, Rothko uses color to fill it with the depths of human emotion. And, in *No. 8,* that color is grey.

If the continuity between Johns's paintings and the history of art makes sense thanks to the transportation and transformation of the artistic trope of the cloth, of drapery and dresses, Rothko's visualizations across and of the surface of his paintings forge a different history for painting in the twentieth century. Namely, Rothko's belong together with works of artists committed to the exploration of color as light. We have seen this use of grey as early as the frescoes of del Sarto as they would have been vividly brought to life by the movement of the sunlight across the roof of the Chiostro dello Scalzo in Florence. Later in the history of art at the time of the Enlightenment, and before the advent of photography, painters used color as a metaphor for the search for light and luminosity on the canvas, and consequently, for insight and knowledge into metaphysical questions. This was the concern of, most notably, the German Romantic painters.[28] Artists such as Karl Friedrich Schinkel, Jakob Böhme, Ernst Ferdinand Oehme, and, of course, Casper David Friedrich sought to capture the incandescence of the world, the luminescence of nature as a metaphor for the social world through a use of paint. Friedrich tried and, to a certain extent, succeeded. And Rothko complicates these Romantic visions with a surface that is, at one and the same time, both luminescent and opaque. On Rothko's canvases, color reflects, absorbs, diffuses, floats on, obscures, and invites light. This is always achieved through the working up of different colors on the surface of a canvas. And so, Rothko creates surfaces that simultaneously invite us to fall into, and through differing strategies at various points in his career, frustrate or retract the very same invitation to fall. This ambivalence of painted surfaces that are constantly in the process of undoing their assertions places Rothko's works at the heart of a modernist aesthetic. While Rothko's works have been considered more Romantic than modernist because of their apparent mysticism, the tensions played out on the surface simultaneously give them a place within the conception of modernist art. As a result, Rothko's works create contradictory spatial dimensions on their surface that, in turn, give way to appropriately contradictory ways of looking at the canvas. Martin Jay argues in his seminal work on visuality within modernity, that differing, often conflicting, "regimes" are characteristic of modern vision.[29] While, for Jay, the competing forms of vision in modernity are not specifically those identifiable on Rothko's canvas, I draw the connection to Jay to highlight that what is asked of Rothko's viewer is in keeping with the modernist project.

Before examining the representations of space, surface, and consequent processes of looking at his abstract works, the question remains: what does Rothko do differently on the surface of the grey paintings and, in particular, of the series *Untitled (Black on Gray)* (1969) that he does not do in in his earlier works? The tensions created through his unique aesthetic of abstraction are characteristic of the many colored canvases, especially those in which two or more uneven bands or forms hover over a background of a different color, or the same color in a different hue. In all of his paintings, Rothko engages with an oscillation between surface and depth, foreground and background, as well as opacity and transparency. When painting is preoccupied with the role of color as light, it has no dimensions, like light. Color as light for modernist painting reflects a search for purity, for the moment when painting not only ceases to have reference to the material world but also lets go of its materiality in that world.[30] In the late 1940s and early 1950s especially, Rothko's paintings witness the search for the moment when painting has no substance, except in its articulation of a form.[31] Roland Barthes explains this moment thus: color is imperceptible; it is inscribed like "a pinprick in the corner of the eye. . . . It suffices that color lacerate something: that it pass in front of the eye, like an apparition—or a disappearance, for color is like a closing eyelid, a tiny fainting spell."[32]

On Rothko's grey canvases, it is not only that color, a specific color as well as color as a phenomenon, becomes imperceptible. Rather, as color dissolves into light the distinction between the two become imperceptible in these paintings. This inseparability of color and light is brought alive; the goal is realized in Rothko's grey and black paintings in a unique way. On these canvases, color becomes light and reflects the behavior of light and shadow on a canvas. This is made possible because the relationship of grey to the varying qualities of light is unique. Rothko's other canvases do not have this effect.

Centuries ago Alberti noted that grey is the only color to absorb and reflect light, and it is the only pigment that has the capacity to create both light and darkness. Furthermore, every grey painting embraces this unique absorption and reflection of light to different degrees. It is the raison d'être of grey paint. In grey, an artist such as Rothko uses the color to approach the ethereality of paint as light and luminescence, as well as shadow and darkness. Accordingly, while Rothko's yellows and oranges, deep reds and blues are always involved in an approach to this purity of light, it is in the final works, where the grey paint is dramatically juxtaposed with the opacity of black, that the color grey creates a vaporous, ethereal luminosity. This luminosity all but erases the surface of the painting and, simultaneously, moves into the darkness when grey turns into black. Thus, in the final *Black on Gray* paintings the search is realized for paint to capture the existence of light as it is defined by shadow. Even if the grey field is contained by the white border and the black field above it, within the space of grey, wisps of loosely applied paint become assimilated to air to reveal the ultimate possibility that color can be light, and its masking in shadow. Rothko's paintings, and particularly those in grey, may not reach complete ethereality—because they still have substance as rectangular objects on a wall—but they lay the groundwork for the realization of this goal by artists in the late twentieth century.[33]

Walter Benjamin wrote that color is not the void or some kind of emptiness; it is spiritual, akin to music, and only exists in its imaginative perception. Its physical and material "nothingness" is thereby its power and fullness, its very substance.[34] Paint gives color a form, a spatial organization, and is used to create a material surface. Over time spent before the painting, the materiality of Rothko's works will lead to an immateriality, as it is perceived. The painting "dematerializes" to our eye when we look from a fixed vantage point and enters an "eternal moment of disclosed presence."[35] Benjamin is not alone in this belief that only through the energy of painting can color have an existence.[36] He says that children's coloring-in is the purest form of color because it pays no heed to form, shape, or object, and that, in these images, color has a content of its own. In many ways, the same could be said of Rothko's abstract canvases filled with layer upon layer of color, to the point where color as luminosity and obscurity becomes substance of the works, and we accept the invitation to immerse ourselves in reverie.

Nevertheless, there is a difference, because as I say, Rothko's color is still defined on four sides by the frame. Like the template for a child's coloring-in, however, this frame doesn't provide a definitive border, and neither does it stop Rothko from creating depth to an otherwise two-dimensional painted surface. Unlike a classical perspective, Rothko's depth moves forward; it vibrates and does not recede into a vanishing point in the background. The lighter, more transparent colors always vibrate outward, into the space of the viewer. Thus, while on the one hand, we fall into the possibility of color as light in Rothko's paintings, on the other hand, we are embraced by the color as form when it appears to move toward us. Rothko's depth, his use of color as light comes to meet the viewer, to embrace and seduce. The vertical movement of colored form in the viewer's eye is complicated when those colors are variations of grey.

In abstract painting, paint is the light emitted, the light reflected and refracted, the light absorbed. Rothko's works are exemplars of this tendency. Typically, orange or yellow, especially when painted in juxtaposition with a darker background, will emit light, while darker colors absorb the light that shines on them. Rothko creates further luminosity through gentle working over with lighter colors, even white. And the nature of the surface, whether it is matte or oil with lacquer, will determine the degree of reflection or refraction of light. It is common for grey, unlike other colors, to demonstrate all three behaviors in relationship to the viewer of Rothko's canvases. That is, grey in all its variations can move through reflection, refraction, and absorption.

In interaction with the viewer, the motion and variability of *Untitled* (1968), in the National Gallery of Art, Washington, is filled with air and light, translucence and movement, particularly thanks to the soft edges of the two darker-grey panels. The looseness of the brushstroke, the fast and sheer cover of layers of lighter grey, all the way back to white, create depth and the familiar Rothko effect of darker forms that float on an uneven surface. In the more somber, hard-edged numbered series of works (titled *#1–#8*) from 1964, the slow buildup of dark paint, perceived across time with increasing physical awareness on the part of the viewer, sees the image transform from static black to a textured and tonally differentiated spectrum of greys. Likewise, they move from opacity to transparency, from flatness to depth, again over time, only in the presence of the viewer. Such is the immense possibility and potency of grey paint as it is swept across the surfaces of Rothko's canvases.

To create the multifarious grey surface, Rothko's process is complicated: it is worked over and over, as well as sheer enough to create a delicate luminosity. This search for a unique opticality reaches a particular intensity in his final paintings, the *Untitled (Black on Gray)* series from 1969 (Plate 6). In his earlier works, most notably, the *Seagram Murals* (1958–59), Rothko began the painterly process with a tinted wash as primer to the canvas, a primer that invites the transparency of the paint that will be layered on top.[37] On the earlier canvases color is manipulated to produce a beam of light that effloresces both to create the space of the gallery in which it is seen and, simultaneously, to render transparent the material image. This is usually the result of one color layered upon another and another. Take, for example, the Kunsthaus Zürich's *Untitled (White, Blacks, Grays on Maroon)* (1963) in which the grey rectangular forms are outlined in black and modulated with white, bringing them into relief from the canvas, giving them a dimensionality in which the edges are "illuminated." Similarly, the frayed white form at the top of the canvas is shallow, and therefore, in tension with the density of the varying grey shapes stacked vertically beneath it, a density exaggerated by the maroon and black that lie beneath it.

After 1968 Rothko's process of priming changes and with it the quality of light reflected by the grey forms. In addition, the intense and immobile black at the top of the canvas becomes starker.[38] In the *Untitled (Black on Gray)* paintings, the canvas is primed in white, a white that is ever-present in the luminous grey field that comprises the bottom of each canvas.[39] Likewise, the white persists to dilute the black above in the subtlest, most sensitive moments of these forms. Like other of Rothko's works, these paintings are impossible to capture in words. For this reason, each painting is most accessible when approached from the visual experience of the viewer. Before Johns's encaustic paintings, as I argue earlier, we stand but are never invited inside: they are always hidden behind the cloths, hinged doors, panels, and layers of grey, concealed by the unpredictable, bitumen-like surface of grey. Contrarily, a viewer in the presence of Rothko's works, including the final works in grey, is enveloped by the light, drawn toward them, embraced by a surface that only has a dimensionality when she is before them. The forms bend effortlessly toward the viewer, over time, forming a convexity that billows into the space before the canvas. Rothko's *Untitled* works in grey, including the earlier numbered paintings from 1964, depend on the viewer for the completion of the shifting dimensionality of the surface, and thus their meaning. Johns's paintings are already finished before the viewer arrives. They may await the presence of a viewer, they may extend outside of their physical frame, but they are not in search of completion. The need that Rothko's works have for completion is what makes them about light. Paint is rendered transparent or opaque only over time, in the relationship formed with the viewer, as the viewer is caught in the light that emanates from them, in the luminosity they attract.

Surface is everything for Rothko, and as if in the tradition of Friedrich, who creates illuminated surfaces, from certain angles, under certain lighting Rothko's works can give the impression of sitting before a light box. Color, in its carefully mixed and reworked form, is light, even in the *Untitled (Black on Gray)* paintings. The unique (for Rothko) white border around these fields of black and grey, together with the unprecedented definitiveness of a "horizon line" that separates black from grey, has prompted critics to note the difference between these final paintings and those of earlier years in which the edges between colors are blurred, lacking authority.[40] Critics such as Robert Goldwater have claimed these final works are closed, turned inward; he says they "reject participation and withdraw into themselves."[41] Fer, however, demonstrates more convincingly that if the viewer persists with the works, they reveal themselves over time:

> Although initially they appear empty, with time they open onto a different kind of amplitude. Their sparseness—the simple doubling of the surface, the barely stated condition of enframement—is offset by the way the surfaces become capacious as they unfold in the course of looking at them over time. First, the lighter whites and greys more obviously let the light through in patches, the open brushwork often suggesting mini-vortexes or more intricate passages of veils and drips of liquid acrylic.[42]

Or to articulate it with the language I have been using, the surface transforms as the light-grey brushstrokes swell beneath the dense black above. It is this capacity of Rothko's painted surfaces to transform over time in their interaction with the viewer that makes them unique. Similarly, when these surfaces are grey, juxtaposed with or merging into black, the spectrum of possibility to transform paint into gradations of light behaving in multifarious ways is unprecedented.

In the early 1960s, when Rothko painted these works, such transformations had not yet reached any level of success. It is, ironically, this achievement of transparency, the depth and complexity of the color-fields as light, inviting the viewer to immerse herself in the environment created by Rothko's paintings, that apparently places them outside a modernist aesthetic. For it is the so-called Romantic invitation to contemplation outside the reality of the painting as object, the so-called spiritual indeterminacy, that removes the paintings from the criticality of the modernist project. As Barbara Novak and Brian O'Doherty so confidently assert:

> Rothko's tragic sense, which manifested itself as a degree of pathos in his everyday life, had little traffic with the distancing ironies of modernism. The grand irony of existence and its vicissitudes excluded trivialities he felt were beneath one engaged in a program of such high moral seriousness. His ambitions for visual art went beyond its conventional limits.[43]

It is true that with Rothko's manipulation of paint and color, painting reaches new limits in the late 1950s and 1960s, but to say that these works are beyond modernism is to impose an unnecessary limit. While the paintings may move into the realm of the mystical, as I will demonstrate, the viewer is always returned to the materiality of paint from where she commences the process of seeing. And this return to the formal, this refusal on the part of the paintings to stay in the realm of the tragic, reinvents their uncertainty, their contradictions, and their contrary impulse to reject and distance the viewer. I go on to explain the complexity of the viewing process of Rothko's grey work in chapter 4, but for now, I want to suggest that in grey there is no such place for painting to sit comfortably within modernism. For this reason, in Rothko's paintings we get to see a challenge to modernism that leads to a reconception of its aesthetic. This tendency of Rothko's paintings to test the limit of modernism reveals itself, again and again, to be the work of grey. Indeed, the same is true, but envisioned differently, in the work of Marden, a painter whose grey canvases are often cited, unlike Rothko's, for their commitment to the concerns of the modernist painted surface.

BRICE MARDEN

Marden's grey paintings of the 1960s and 1970s sit somewhere between those of Johns and Rothko. Marden was engaged in what, superficially, might seem a similar process to Rothko's layering to create a conversation on the surface of the canvas. Similarly, after Rothko, Marden's intention throughout the 1960s and into the early 1970s was to create the equation between painting, color, and light. Marden is quoted as saying, "Color is a way of arriving at light."[44] But Marden's canvases are very different from Rothko's even if he is in search of a similar intellectual and visual solution. Marden's paint is visibly dense, opaque, and has the shiny finish of acrylic. In well-known paintings such as the five *Grove Group* (1972–73), even as early as *Return I* (1964–65) and *The Dylan Painting* (1966/1986), Marden uses oil and beeswax to prohibit the viewer's desire and resultant attempt to penetrate the surface. Marden admits that the early works were too reflective, too bright, creating what he calls a "hostile" surface, "a painting that people couldn't see."[45] Even though Marden's process resembles the layering of Rothko, as Carol Mancusi-Ungaro demonstrates, the material of Marden's artistic process creates a wholly different surface, more variegated, more tactile, more physically sensuous and flawed, more in the vein of Johns's thick, encaustic canvases, though never that unpredictable. Similarly, unlike Rothko, Marden is driven to find and produce "the weight of color." As Francesco Clemente explains, for Marden, it is only when color has weight that it consumes all and becomes the painting.[46] That said, even though color is the essence of Marden's painting, this does not mean it is substantial. Compared to Johns's and Rothko's paintings, Marden's surfaces are ostensibly the smoothest and slickest, and the distribution of paint the most even, the least variegated; his works come closest to the modernist aesthetic's evocation of emotion, not just thinking, through painting. Marden describes his paintings in this way: he says that each layer is a layer of feeling, feelings upon feelings in interaction with each other, building up the complexity and the constant unfathomability of modern life as it is experienced through sensation.[47] And within these layers, the feelings are encapsulated in light: a luminescence is somehow caught between the dense layers of paint. Thus, light and emotion are held by the materiality of acrylic paint, placing Marden's surfaces in grey somewhere between the ethereality of Rothko's and the tactility of Johns's.

The complexity of modernist art, and its ambiguity as it is expressed across the surface of a grey painting, are envisioned with clarity by Marden. Indeed, he does this in a way that reminds of Mondrian, and the troubling moments on Manet's canvases. It is at the edges, most notably along the unfinished bottom edge of his paintings, in distinction to the hard, definitive division between greys within the paintings, and in the incompletion of the surface, that Marden's grey works make their most significant contribution to the use of grey paint as a medium to explore the concerns of painting. It is as though the lines and patterns that do not reach the frame of Mondrian's abstract *Compositions,* or the frayed hem on the dress in Manet's *La chanteuse de rue* have found their way to the bottom of Marden's paintings. Similar to the unfinished bottom edge of some of Johns's most celebrated works, Marden's otherwise apparently seamlessly covered expanses of canvas are made vulnerable, ambiguous, and troubling along the bottom edge.

Because the surfaces of Marden's paintings are so even, and apparently flawless—even though up close they are not—together with the certainty of the distinction between different greys in, for example, *The Dylan Painting,* and others such as *Sea Painting I* (1973–74), the vulnerability of the unfinished lower edge is exaggerated and becomes even more disquieting. That said, the "unfinished" bottom edge is Marden's signature, the place on the canvas that reassures the viewer, its moment of predictability. Thus, a tension arises along the bottom; it is a place where familiarity and unpredictability collide. The same can be said of the space between the four panels of *The Seasons* (1974–75) in the Menil Collection, as Marden intended them to be hung. The three spaces between varied grey canvases create the field where breath happens, where thoughts and feelings can grow, and the movement from one color field to the next evolves. This space of uncertainty is created by the presence of a grey canvas on either side. When *The Seasons* were first hung in Houston, they were unfinished. The bottom edge was left suspended.[48] Nevertheless, even when Marden finished *The Seasons,* the space between each perfect canvas left open the possibility of continuation, for imagination in the mind of the viewer (Plate 7). The space between holds within it the moment that Marden walks away from the paintings. Even when this space is preconceived and controlled by the artist, it invites the viewer to enter into the unknown rhythms of nature, the flow of light as it moves into dark. The space gives the paintings dimensionality, paintings that might otherwise be hermetically sealed; slick grey surfaces embrace an element of unpredictability.

Yves-Alain Bois identifies the space created in Marden's post-1986 paintings covered in calligraphic writing for breath, for the body, for a wandering on the part of the spectator, as "Marden's doubt."[49] I wonder if the same "circulation of air between discrete elements," a similar invitation to breathe, might be identified in the possibility and spaces opened up at the bottom of the canvas in the earlier paintings.[50] That said, the smooth, hermetically sealed surface of Marden's canvases, captures a quiet disarray at and beyond the edges. Marden's even surface has only been arrived at through constant reworking, rubbing out of mistakes, and revising the texture of the paint. The space between the paintings, and the unfinished bottom edge, are the moments when Marden reveals the indecision or hesitation in an otherwise methodical suppression of gestures, gestures that Giacometti made explicit through the traces of his presence to the portrait.[51] Similarly, Marden's evasiveness, the ability of his surface to shift imperceptibly between density, transparency, and a presence marked by the buildup of paint in the pre-mid-1980s works, is enabled through the particularity of his use of grey. David Anfam also places Marden's color and process side by side with Rothko's, to demonstrate similarities and differences:

> Chiming with Rothko, as it were, we will recall that Marden spoke of color losing identities, becoming color. Just as it is impossible to pinpoint the exact hues in Rothko's *Untitled,* which resemble those seen when we close our eyelids, so Marden expresses his interest in "the strangest gray I have ever made" and in "putting on a gray [. . .] that under certain conditions shows up green, so you aren't sure about the color at all." For both painters, color shifts subliminally between the noumenal and the phenomenal, presence and erasure.[52]

Marden is an artist who has always chosen grey for the exploration of his relationship to paint, the relationship between color and light, between painting and emotion, between painting and viewer. Marden uses grey in all its various possibilities (and impossibilities) to demonstrate the allusiveness of paint, and the elusiveness of color, of emotion. Grey has the capacity to shift across multiple registers, not just the intellectual and emotional or "incredible," as Anfam would have it.

Even in the 1980s, after a decade of works that begin with the inspiration of Greece and continue its bright chromatic scale, Marden returns to grey with his *Cold Mountain* (1989–91) series. At this point in his career, Marden's signature ribbons begin to cover the grey painted surface. Anfam, after the 1950s art historian Walter Friedlander, argues that Marden is a latter-day Ingres, claiming that, like the French neoclassical painter, Marden uses color for reasons other than color. For Friedlander, Marden uses color because it contains within it a sensuousness that can bring atmosphere. It is as if the viewer begins to sense the perfect skin of Ingres's bathers become one with Marden's grey color field.[53] In his use of grey, we can also say that Marden's work is intimately connected, if only in the shimmering light of the paintings' surface, to the walls of the Chiostro dello Scalzo in Florence. As much as he may want to arouse intimacy in the viewer through a connection with the smooth surface, like del Sarto, Marden is a painter who also wants to eschew all distraction from his path toward color as light. In this apparent contradiction in grey, Marden effectively continues the task of other painters to explore the question of what is grey. The repetition of canvas after canvas in grey, and about grey, each the same, but always different, asks, among other questions, "what is this color?," "what is grey paint?" Moreover, in his unique approach to the color, for Marden, grey is all at once tactile and erotic, ephemeral and unreliable.

Marden neither attaches nor represents objects on the grey surface as Johns does. Neither does he explore color as light through manipulating the relationship between foreground and background, through layering different colors as Rothko does. Rather, as Anfam quoting Marden explains, the artist creates variegation and ineffability through approaching a use of grey as sublime. Marden's palette is always grey. Grey is taken through its spectrum from silver to green to yellow, to purple, and red, from chilling coldness to warmth, from light to dark, from density to transparency, through verticality and horizontality. And, to reiterate Marden, he always merges grey with these other colors, never pitting them against each other as does Johns, and even Rothko in the relationship the latter establishes between grey and black. In turn, Marden's fusion of grey with other colors creates his version of the uncertainty of grey, of color itself, and of the viewer's perception of grey on his canvases. Grey is neither safe nor certain even when it is sublime in a Marden painting.

Marden's task in painting is always to transform what lies before him, whether it is a natural landscape or a painting by Goya or Velázquez, into a slab of grey. Grey has the capacity to do all these things, to move through the questions of painting, to transform materiality into color as light, to approach this interesting question of the relationship between painting and the natural world. Through all of these effects, Marden's paintings continue the search to resolve the internal questions of painting itself: what is it in form, materiality, density, even the surface, process, and effect, and how are these concerns transformed across time? These questions are asked and resolved through an interrogation of the surface of grey painting.

AGNES MARTIN

In a completely different vein, Martin's paintings approach and treat the surface of the canvas as an invitation to engage in a mystery. They tempt or arouse a temptation to leave behind the reality of daily life, but they also retract the invitation. Like Rothko's color fields, so much of the meaning of Martin's works takes place on the surface. Unlike Rothko's, it's almost impossible to find the depth within or behind Martin's surfaces. Her critics have noted on more than one occasion what they identify as "the grids," carefully laid out by hand, usually in graphite pencil. They remark on the paintings' repetition of the weave of the canvas onto which the color underneath is painted.[54] Graphite is a medium so perfectly suited to the weft and warp of the canvas because it is contradictory: it is both tactile and awaiting erasure. This simultaneous presence and promise of absence, achieved through graphite or lead pencil can be thought of as a repetition—albeit with difference—of the canvas itself, which is, in turn, a material that has the sole purpose of being concealed. The graphite anticipates erasure, the canvas awaits its own invisibility. Martin draws with a pencil as a way of merging the weave of the canvas, the background wash, and the pencil. In grey, the distinction between graphite and paint, canvas and its concealment, is not simply blurred. In grey bands and color fields, paint takes over the role of graphite; the two become merged. As we stand before Martin's paintings, there's no telling what we are looking at: Is it the ground or the color? Is it line or form? And as the grey becomes uneven across some paintings (perhaps because of the graphite), there's no telling if we are looking at the variegations of grey paint, or if the light has caught the reflective surface of the painted canvas. In grey, the unending enigma of Martin's paintings reaches its apotheosis. In grey the picture surface becomes a field of possibility, a grey material, or fabric made of canvas, a canvas that becomes one with the paint and pencil on its surface. In another variation of those already discussed, it is as though the curtains and linens represented on the surface of Johns's paintings become the very support awaiting the application of paint on Martin's. And yet, they are already painted. On Martin's grey canvases, especially those from the late 1960s and early 1970s, this ambiguity makes painting impenetrable. Whereas for Rothko, Marden, and Johns, the shifting function of grey gives over to a perception marked by fluidity and motion, before Martin's grey canvases we are left isolated and excluded by the contradictions that hold the paintings' own private secrets.

Kasha Linville, Krauss, and most recently, Fer, all nod toward the transformation of the surface of Martin's canvas from a tactile space that enables a haptic vision to an immaterial meditative space of possibility and revelation.[55] These critics follow the artist's claims about her work and variously align Martin's work with that of the Egyptians, classicists, and Romantics. While it is true that Martin consciously continues the work of the past, the provenance of this meditative, transformative space in Martin's work is not her only concern. Indeed, its very existence is not always obvious. Whether it is medieval, classical, or Romantic, what seduces about the surfaces of these paintings is the transformation of paint into the canvas itself in the creation of "beauty." That is, the paintings create a space in which the medium becomes the support, and in turn the ground is the figure, and paint and graphite become so completely fused that there is no longer any hope to know which comes first, which does what.

In grey works such as *Untitled* (1962) and *Untitled* (1969) in oil or acrylic in pencil or graphite, the image recalls the pre- and early-Renaissance grey paper on which metalpoint and charcoal drawings were executed. Thus, when we look at these untitled works, or *White Flower* (1960), *A Grey Stone* (1963), *The Tree* (1964), and *Leaves* (1966), we no longer see paint on a canvas as we do before Johns's encaustics or even Rothko's color forms. Rather, we see a grey surface that pulsates in the light. All of these works softly vibrate, the light moving around the canvas unpredictably, but poetically as we stand before it. In the moment that we come face-to-face with Martin's paintings, it no longer matters where in the history of art they belong. According to Martin, what matters is that we are moved to happiness and joy, that we experience perfection and beauty in our physical reality as it is influenced by the paintings. More often, before the grey paintings, we experience confusion. As soon as we recognize that the titles are arbitrary, that the same title reappears on paintings that have no apparent connection, at very different points in her oeuvre, we move to the next painting in the hope that it will give access where the previous one did not.

Today, the discussion about where Martin's work fits into the history of art continues. While most critics place her work alongside minimalism, and she liked her work to be considered together with abstract expressionism, as Lynne Cooke points out, Martin also saw it in the tradition of the ancients: "Egyptians, Greeks, Copts, and Chinese."[56] It is possible to place Martin's subdued works covered with hand-drawn lines and painted bands in a number of art historical contexts, or none at all. They can even be placed in the vast infinity of the New Mexico desert, where she lived an ascetic existence for most of her working life. The correspondence to nature and the inconceivable expanse of its possibility are central to her canvases. Yet, as her close friend and gallerist Arne Glimcher reminds us, the paintings are not about the New Mexico desert; the desert is simply the place they are painted.[57] As Martin says often in her correspondences and reflections on art, the goal is always the same: perfection. For her, this goal is what her own paintings are about.[58] Thus, if we follow Martin, the desert is only ever an attempt to find an object to describe these abstractions.

The paintings engage the viewer in a constant process of reversal, inversion, undoing of expectations, and establishment of polar opposites. In short, ambiguity is achieved through paint, ink, graphite, and canvas to create a tension between illusion and materiality. Perfection may be the goal, but it is never achieved. This tension on the painted surface is widespread in postwar American painting, though in the case of Martin's paintings from the 1960s and 1970s, like the anonymity given her by the desert that surrounded her, the works embrace a unique form of abstraction that is not recognizable in the work of her contemporaries.[59]

If we consider Martin's work within postwar American modernism, its uniqueness is instructive. For most viewers, the obvious references in her abstract canvases are to those of Robert Ryman, Ad Reinhardt, and perhaps most consistently, Barnett Newman. Their aesthetic and concern sit comfortably with the works of these artists. But Martin's paintings, like their creator in the New Mexico desert, are isolated. The paintings are self-sufficient; they comprise a movement all their own. And yet, I would argue that in their uniqueness, they look at and reflect on the project of modernism and offer a critical opinion. This is most intriguingly seen on the grey works from the late 1980s and early 1990s. Here, we find a radicality that has been repeatedly overlooked by critics who are so keen to slot the paintings into comprehensibility.

In the late 1980s, Martin painted a number of grey canvases to be exhibited in the Pace Gallery on Greene Street, New York City. They are dark slate grey with the familiar horizontal and vertical bands of varying widths, but they are dense and opaque, rather than transparent and emanating joy. This does not mean that the four 1989 *Untitled* grey paintings do not engage with a complex play of light (Plate 8). Rather, they are more ambiguous than those inspired by the infinite expanse of the desert and the natural world in muted browns, yellows, and the soft pastel colors Martin used increasingly later in life. In the so-called '80s Grey Paintings, Martin reserves her use of grey for her ventures into the complex light of night, and at times, a devotion to death. In addition, even though she denies the presence of the intellectual, of thinking, on her canvases, as others point out, the determined and unrelenting use of the graphite lines is still the compositional definition of the grey paintings. Or is it that the graphite has been transformed into painted grey bands? If so, line and form are one and the same thing. It is the conceptual, as well as the overwhelmingly emotional, use of grey that motivates these late 1980s *Untitled* works.

The graphite and grey paint come together on these late-1980s paintings to create yet another layer of tension between the material and the ethereal as it is already found in postwar American painting. It seems that the very language of modernist painting is made redundant when face-to face with these particular Martin canvases. In these paintings, not only are figure and ground/graphite and paint so confused that they are no longer terms of description, but also the most extreme use of grey moves beyond the limits of modernism. Every one of the images from this period is different, and within each painting, the bands of grey differ—in size, density, and in their relationship to line. Martin uses paint in different ways—sometimes it is transparent, sometimes opaque; sometimes she covers the entire canvas, and at other times, there is a border to contain color. Up close, I wonder if I am looking at the ground, or is it color? Either way, what is the relationship to the line? There is also an enigma in the relationship between the different media, not just what is going on in the frame. All this would suggest that unlike the modernist artist, Martin is not looking to answer the same question or problem of painting throughout her oeuvre. Each canvas might be 72 × 72 inches, and we might see it as colored grey, but again, the singularity of each work denies all claim to repetition. "Repetition," "grid," "monochrome" are all superficial descriptions that don't begin to characterize what is happening on these varied and deeply mysterious canvases.

Martin's grey works thus represent the apotheosis of the use of grey paint for a vision that results in the ultimate dissolution of modernist questions. Martin's grey canvases manage to represent and discard the modernist questions even though she is not always following or pursuing a modernist problem. If the paintings are about the ineffability of color, the fungibility of media, they are the ultimate modernist statement on the use of color as light. But because each painting pursues the questions individually, starting over again with each blank canvas, it would appear that Martin is not even interested in the modernist pursuit. This makes Martin's paintings unthinkable, beyond our ability to articulate them.

To explore another example that lies somewhere in among this outcome of grey on Martin's canvases: standing before *White Flower (1960)*, we await the performance of the event in grey acrylic that it promises (Plate 9). And then, over time, we choose, rather than being forced as we are with Marden's shiny surfaces, to step back. Again, we are unsettled by the difficulty of looking at the canvas. At a distance, the surface density of Martin's painting is transformed. At a distance, the interlocking horizontal and vertical lines dissolve to our vision. The experience is one of a subtle luminescence in a dark field; the canvas becomes as a haze of light, or as Linville describes it in her discussion of a different painting:

> Something very peculiar happens as you move back from this canvas [*Tundra,* 1967]. Because the horizontally brushed, grayish wash on the surface stops near but not against the lines, they seem to have halos around them. These halos actually swallow the lines at middle distance, leaving only their white ghosts.[60]

What Linville doesn't mention is what the viewer experiences before Martin's abstract 72 × 72 inch works: the ultimate unrecognizability resigns the viewer to a state of not-ever-knowing. The two intertwined visual experiences of the same painting, the same surface as both material and illusion, night and day, opacity and luminescence go deeper. The paintings find a transformative space often talked about in discussions of Martin's early paintings in particular. Up until the 1980s, Martin layered the canvas with sheer washes to produce the delicate color of the ground, a delicacy that is crucial to their eventual luminescence and ambiguity. The two responses, of a surface covered with Martin's signature lines and its dissolution at a distance, of the evocation of a darkness inhabited by specters of light, are most articulately rendered in grey.

To put it another way, in grey the canvases represent the coexistence of the modernist, minimalist attachment to structure and the gridded rational order, as well as enabling our acknowledgment of the handcrafted, delicate, variegated surface made uneven and unpredictable by the artist's human hand. Critics refer again and again to the contradiction of Martin's use of the "grid" in the realization of a viewing experience that approaches the sublime.[61] This response is in keeping with Martin's own characterization of her work as reaching for a transcendental perfection, a perfection that is achieved in the natural world, or in classical form.[62] The logic of this argument would be that Martin's surface opens up our experience to a past or future moment of fullness and contemplation, a reverie, a memory, as well as holding us in a present defined by grids, structures and surfaces. Martin's surface creates a space that invites us to fall, unfettered, powerless, into the depths of a world that is beyond language, communication. It is pure visuality. It is sublime.

I want to pose the contradiction differently, however. I believe our eyes are kept occupied, all the time, up close and at a distance. Up close, on the surface, we are engaged in a process of mental mapping and measuring.[63] And, at a distance, we are preoccupied with the movement of the surface colors, the density and luminosity of paint in its unpredictable interaction with graphite. Accordingly, the particular ambivalences, the working through on the surface of Martin's paintings, are placed outside all convenient and very limiting art historical narratives. They do not work out, or resolve for Martin, the same questions of painting, often in grey, that are engaged by those working in the vein of modernist aesthetic. We do not even have to name Martin's painting as modernist, but rather, as I have demonstrated, it is critical to see it in conversation with a generation of grey paintings that are known as such. Its inability to be described thus keeps it isolated, and its viewer intrigued by an ongoing enigma.

CY TWOMBLY

In a final example of a body of work in grey that redefines the intention and substance of modernist painting in postwar America, Cy Twombly's so-called blackboard paintings create surfaces that search for different relationships within and between each canvas, the viewer, and the artist. Typically, critical analysis of Twombly's *Untitled* paintings focuses on the form, linearity, the cursivity, and palimpsestic nature of the white wax crayon, that is, the "chalk" markings. Critics tend to ignore the grey surface. Even Heiner Bastian, the preeminent Twombly critic, historian, and cataloger, is preoccupied with the "archetypal symbols," "ideogrammatic signs," the "metaphorical pictorial language" of the markings and not the canvases they mark.[64] As a result of these discussions, it is assumed that the grey ground is a blank undifferentiated surface awaiting inscription, description, figuration. I shall demonstrate that the relationship between grey and white is more complicated.

As if in a violation of, or an attack on the canvas, the industrial-grey painted surface of a work such as *Panorama* (1955) is built up only to be carved into with a blunt stylus. Like many of Twombly's grey paintings, *Panorama*'s surface is composed of a thin, uneven wash. And then, even before the paint has dried, Twombly attacks the wet surface with a white crayon, carving it with uneven lines, curves, shapes, the elements of what are referred to as his visual language. In *Panorama,* in contradistinction to a sweeping, curving gesture suggested by the painting's title, the white markings are chaotic, indecipherable, and unpredictable. And then, a stylus serrates the grey surface in a determined straight line along the bottom quarter of the painting. The line scars the grey surface. The *Panorama* paintings are not the only early works in which grey paint is carved to spoil the surface, deliberately. Twombly's ultimate violation of these surfaces, as opposed to or as well as drawing on them, is significant. If only because this gesture of destruction is most often practiced on those images grounded in grey. Moreover, the grey is never consistent; it moves from dark, almost black greys to lighter greys, and within the lighter scale, grey can be cold and chilly or it can be light and filled with air. These inconsistences, the fluctuating energy of the grey grounds, mean that the grey is never really desecrated because it never rests. It is not possible to destroy something that remains in perpetual motion.

On or over grey, Twombly does not illustrate the canvas; he spoils it. Thus, grey is never a benign support for something written in white. In an act of scarring, not aestheticization, Twombly cancels out the grey paint, in a gesture that seems related, but not a repetition of Rauschenberg's *Erased de Kooning Drawing* (1953).[65] The two examples are, in fact, quite different: Twombly negates his own painting, whereas Rauschenberg erases someone else's pencil drawing. Twombly's is a gesture of self-desecration of a surface meant to be permanent—industrial paint—whereas Rauschenberg erases a pencil-and-charcoal sketch, an image that has a palimpsestic fate inscribed within its medium and form. And because Twombly's grey is tinted with transience, the gesture of desecration is simultaneously an act of creation.

Krauss discusses Twombly's lines and surface markings, especially in the 1950s, as a kind of graffiti, as a visual language drawn from the streets.[66] In viewing them as graffiti, Krauss understands the lines as violations of the painted surface that, like tagging on a New York City subway car in the 1970s, leave the trace of a criminal presence not only defacing the object being tagged but also engaging in a power struggle with the authorities, asserting identity and command of the urban environment. As she says, it is "always an invasion of a space that is not the marker's own, it takes illegitimate advantage of the surface of inscription, violating it, mauling it, scarring it."[67] While I agree with the apparent violence "performed," as Krauss would have it, on Twombly's canvas, the resonance with urban graffiti does not go far beyond the visual. There is a distinction to Twombly's scratches and doodles that incise and scar grey paint. They may contain a gestural violence, but they are motivated by an altogether different logic. In contrast to urban graffiti, Twombly's white markings are not calligraphic; they are intended to remove or deface identity rather than rewrite the surface with a new, alternative identity as urban graffiti does. Twombly's canvas is a surface distressed, a distress designed to desecrate the painting and all to which it refers. And simultaneously, it is a gesture of possibility.

Unlike urban graffiti, Twombly violates his own grey canvas. Unlike graffiti, Twombly is not interested in reestablishing authority; he does not need to give himself a voice where he previously had none (which is the accepted interpretation of urban graffiti).[68] Twombly questions the authority of painting, his own authority, the status of painting and its representation of the landscape, or even of urban spaces. In paintings such as *Panorama* or, in another of many examples, *Untitled (Bolsena)* (1969), Twombly runs the stylus across a canvas as if to negate the grey ground.[69] (See Plate 10.) To be sure, the uncertainty resulting from this rethinking through violation only happens in the relationship between the white markings and the grey ground. It shares this quality with graffiti: meaning is only possible in relationship to what it marks.

And yet, the rethinking, revision, and uncertainty of the process of painting come well before the stylus or any other white medium is run horizontally across the painted canvas. For the grey ground is, in fact, multiple greys, applied at different times, as if in varied states of wetness. In *Untitled (Bolsena),* the varied greys, always moving, in different directions, across and around the canvas, from right to left, stopping and starting, also cover over the white lines: here at times it is grey that places the white scrawls and markings under erasure. A different grey washes over the other greys and the lines, rethinking the narrative, adding temporality to the story told by the painting. Thus in this example, the variegations of grey are a performance of creativity, not only of destruction. Shadows are cast by the dark greys, and the lightness of air fills areas in the middle of the canvas. It's difficult not to see the lines that dissect this untitled canvas as forming a horizon, especially because in the work's title we look across to the other side of Lake Bolsena in Italy, the lake at which Twombly spent the summer and autumn of 1969, the lake at which he painted this and other *Untitled* works. The greys on either side of the imaginary horizon line are then blown through the wind, caught by the water; drips and flurries of paint come to mimic the natural elements that are always in harmony, and yet, continue to struggle with each other. We don't necessarily see the rich array of grey strokes as representing sky and water on either side of a horizon, but we see the movement of the elements within the strokes. Likewise, standing before *Panorama* we may want to attribute the areas of lighter grey, on the left-hand side of the painting, around the line drawn by Twombly's nondominant hand as it moves across the painting to create the landscape, again in time and motion, to the rubbing out of the chalk markings. But it is not. The lighter color is a rethinking of white by grey, not the other way around. Thus, time spent with these works reveals that Twombly spoils, rethinks, repeats, and creates in grey, as much as he does in white, albeit to meet different ends.

As I will discuss in an analysis of his two *Treatise on the Veil* paintings, the outstanding feature of Twombly's works is that they are always in process. It is as though he uses the grey surface as a canvas across which his thinking in white seeks to solve the problems of painting. They are the traces of his own process of thinking about painting, his own response to what is. In the case of the grey ground paintings, the inquiry is pursued first through the uneven distribution of grey house paint across a canvas, and then in the marking, measuring, inscribing, scratching of that surface as if to negate it. The white markings thus might be seen to give definition to the grey ground, to further describe and incise the grey surface in a philosophical meditation. Accordingly, for Twombly, grey is the canvas, grey is the painting, the ground, and the story of painting as they are all brought to life through a complex relationship to white line in his work.

Thus, in the postwar period, there are many different versions of the re-vision of the painted surface of modern painting. Johns, Rothko, Marden, Martin, and Twombly negotiate the limits of painting through, among other things, the materiality of the painted grey surface, the relationship between artist and painting, between viewer and painting as it is worked through in grey paint. These relationships, as I demonstrate, are filled with contradictions and ambiguities. These moments on the canvas when grey becomes blurred, erased, when it transforms into another color, and when the paintings become vulnerable, are, as Clark says, the moments of curiosity and possibility, moments that I call the "truth" of painting.[70] We could also name them as the moment of the dissolution of painting, the moment when the very existence of modernism is challenged. And yet, it is a challenge that also defines modernism. This contradiction is, by extension, a truth that is characterized by uncertainty, vulnerability, and the commotion of modern life. It is a truth that is always grey.

Figuration and Abstraction

THE SEA

American painting of the postwar period revisits the tension between figuration and abstraction begun in the late nineteenth century through a continued exploration of the sea, and especially, the blur of the painted horizon. Once again, grey is often the color in which to represent the sea and the horizon line. Like grey, the sea and the horizon line are perfect spaces for the exploration of the interstice. As the horizon line is blurred or made obscure in painting, so it indicates the lack of clarity to human vision, and by extension, painted representation. The horizon, where the infinite expanse of sea appears to touch the endlessness of the sky above and the beach beneath is critical to the distinction of representation. Painting horizon lines that are only ever illusions, and yet, simultaneously, appear to human sight in all their concretion, comes to consume the imagination of artists in a new way in the twentieth century. And typically, either the horizon itself or the sky, water, and earth on either side, are rendered in grey. As the Irish-born Scully articulates it, this "elemental coming-together of land and sea, sky and land, of blocks coming together side by side and stacked in horizon lines endlessly beginning and ending . . . their weight, their air, their colour, and the soft uncertain space between them"[71] become synonymous with the possibilities envisioned by painting.

Scully represents seascapes again and again in his familiar blocks of grey and closely colored paint. Marden also makes a direct reference to the sea, where it begins and ends, in two works in grey: *Grove Group IV* (1976) and *Sea Painting* (1973). In both paintings, the natural horizon line of the sea and the lines of the triptych formation also mark the distinctions between different greys. To be sure, the paintings in *Grove Group IV* are not explicit representations of the sea; they are works that reflect or are inspired by what Marden calls the "correctness" of nature as he sees it in the olive groves near his house in Greece.[72] The panels of shifting greys are the colors of the grove, of Greece. Nevertheless, it is difficult to look at *Grove Group IV,* two horizontally attached panels covered in grey encaustic, and not see the sea, especially knowing that the works are inspired by Greece. If the form of Marden's paintings captures the natural world and its enigmas, we can look at the works from the other side: the colors of the sea lend themselves to an elaboration on grey in these paintings. This use of color complements Marden's use of the sea as the "ideal plane," the surface that is a model for that of the painting, especially the grey painting. In addition to the privilege of color, the surface is, as Clemente says, "a surface that is both reflective and absorbent, soft and hard, yin, 'the overcast,' and yang, 'something shone upon.' "[73]

In reality, to the naked eye the line between sea and sky eludes precise location. It is also the only spatial distinction between a green-blue-white sea and a blue-grey sky. As painting replicates the form and "in-forme" of the sea, so the sea mimics the behavior of grey, particularly as it is engaged by American postwar abstract painting.[74] The horizon line can be seen by the naked eye, but is not always articulated: it is where two other forms meet. Like grey, the horizon is both dependent on what surrounds it and has an identity all its own. And yet, it is never static or singular. The same can be said of grey. Grey is the perfect color for representing the nebulous nature of this moment of transition. Thus, artists such as Marden bring together the sea, grey painting, and the interrogation of the space between abstraction and figuration to explore the questions of painting in their work.

Martin also privileges the sea to enable the exploration of abstraction: the painted sea is the recurring figure for all that is captured by the spaces opened up in the imperfect geometry and the infinite, unpredictable expanse of nature in her paintings.[75] In her 2003 painting *The Sea,* Martin's palette has changed, even if it is still grey. In *The Sea,* she covers the familiar square dimensions of her canvas with a dark-grey acrylic paint—or is it a black that is given the appearance of grey by the broken white lines that fragment it? The color sits somewhere between the two. Martin uses grey to create a dark solemnity, or as Crimp would have it, a turmoil that might more closely resemble a storm than it does the luminescent, vaporous elements that appear in her earlier works.[76] The lines that cover the dark-grey ground are rhythmic, but it is as if they are poised to collapse and fall into the deep well of the ocean on which they are suspended. They begin and end somewhere, but it's not clear where. As we look at it, the lines shift thanks to the optical illusion created by their design on the canvas.

Momentarily, standing before Martin's painting, we feel as though we have stepped inside the storm that brews on Constable's horizon line in *Weymouth Bay with Approaching Storm* (1818–19). Or perhaps we are looking down on the sea, from the same bird's-eye perspective of the Netherlands' flatlands in Mondrian's abstract paintings. We recognize, however, that Martin's *The Sea,* in spite of its dark, dense grey, is free of the expressionism of Constable, even the early Mondrian, or Martin's earlier grey washes. The grey here is closer to black, the lines are white, and more distinct than those found in other grey paintings at the end of her life. We inquire of the grey, finally, in a manner that is physical, not intellectual, as we move in and away from the painting. The apparently even distribution of paint, from a distance, and the dense unknown world of grey, with gentle white markings that might resemble the crests of waves, tempt the eye and incite the desire to touch. Viewers also note that in this 2003 painting, Martin removes the horizon line altogether. Thus, although the painting is titled *The Sea,* it does not use the horizon line to examine the interstice between figuration and abstraction. If we imagine the sea in this painting, if it enters the liminal field of uncertainty, it does so because of the title and not the field on the canvas itself, as so often happens with Martin's work. Which means that the painting may have nothing at all to do with the sea. If we choose to be convinced by the title, *The Sea* could be either abstract or representational, depending on the perspective from which we choose to see: perpendicular, from above, beneath—that is, deep under the ocean—or, as if on the shoreline, looking out.

This oscillation between figuration and abstraction seen in Martin's *The Sea* is so often a distinction made in the mind of the viewer, not in the paintings themselves. That is, we may imagine an object, a recognizable material thing in the world when we look at abstract painting. If other artists such as Johns and Richter play overtly with this ambiguity within the image itself, Martin's approach is to create uncertainty and play in the relationship between the title and the image, a play that can be viewed through a similar lens. In the work of artists such as Martin, the line between figuration and abstraction, between sea and sky, between different hues of grey, is not easy to define. Nevertheless, similar oscillations between materiality and ethereality, between figuration and abstraction are ignited if we choose to see the paintings as representations of the sea. In *The Sea,* Martin uses a dense grey acrylic to create a solemn space that we are tempted to touch, but into which we cannot dive. We are only there to look. Maybe, after all, it has nothing to do with the sea?

Even when the painting has no apparent reference to the sea, we look at a bifurcated, color-field canvas, such as Rothko's *Untitled (Black on Gray)* paintings and Martin's *Rain* (1960) or *Untitled* (1959) in which horizontal panels of competing greys are divided by two bands, one of black and one of white. Accordingly, we see a horizon as the structuring principle of the composition. Even Twombly's *Untitled (Bolsena)*, with the line serrating an otherwise chaotic grey painted canvas, prompts recollection of the infinite possibilities of a distant horizon.[77] We want to know there is something to hold on to, even if that something is an illusion and never a reality.

Whereas these artists are ambivalent, Johns directly represents the sea in a painting such as *By the Sea* (1961), introducing a series of questions and concerns that had not been previously explored in 1961. At least, at first glance we might believe in the correspondence between title and painting. *By the Sea* is a stencil painting in which the words "RED" "YELLOW" "BLUE" "YELLOW" reveal (or conceal) layer upon confounding layer of color, seeing and thinking, all of which are caught in the wind like flurry of grey. We want to see and believe that there is some correspondence between the words and the colors that are revealed or concealed underneath, in and around grey. But in the spaces where the stencil must have been, the spaces that spell the words, there is mostly grey. This suggests that grey itself is underneath grey, that grey is the element that binds color. In another image, *Folly Beach* from the following year, 1962, we are deceived into thinking that the color scheme is more straightforward, but it is not. It is impossible to know which comes first, the ground or the color as it is written in stencil text, or the color as it appears on the canvas. Is it the stencil or the grey washed over the top of, or perhaps it is underneath, other colors that are the ground? Or then again, perhaps it is the figure of these paintings? In both paintings, as the expanses of the sea, land, sky become interchangeable, their differences indiscernible, the four panels, the bottom of which is stenciled with the words of all three colors, are blurred. Each word is a rainbow of colors, red, yellow, blue, with grey functioning both as the ground and as what binds them together. We begin to imagine that we are viewing a seaside, as opposed to a representation of the sea, with color and the vibrancy of daylight beaming down. And in the other painting, the clouds have fallen over *Folly Beach*. Once again, we look at these two paintings and imagine the sea, the four panels as the different materials of land, sea, sky and the bottom one where they all merge into one, making it impossible to tell which comes first, how to create order.

The suggestion of distinction, of separation by horizon lines in the upper three panels is then undone in the bottom one. Accordingly, Johns uses the figure of the sea, the seaside, absent horizons, and the turmoil of clouds obscuring all three, as a way to create lack of definition, uncertainty, ambiguity.

For Jeffrey Weiss, a better way to see or to read these two paintings is through their resonance with, but not their equation to, the "fractured, multidirectional, allover chiaroscuro of high Analytic Cubist painting."[78] Accordingly, by extension of Weiss's understanding of the two, it is not the sea that is important here but the merging, once again, of the space of the canvas as object and the sea as what is represented, or better, what we are led to believe is represented. Thus, the chiaroscuro lights, the tonality of grey, the flatness of the surface, the words of the title as objects, and the multiple horizontal panels that comprise the painting, amount to the painting's pictorial reflection of the spaces and infinity of the sea. It is, of course, a spatial possibility that is created through grey in both *By the Sea* and *Folly Beach* as they capture all at once the sea, clouds, waves, the lights as they flicker on the waves of the sea, the beach, and all the activities that take place thereon. Like so many of Johns's other strategies in grey paint, then, the reference to the sea is a means to explore the surface of the canvas, to meld spaces that are both real and an illusion, or rather, suggested and hypothetical. That is, while Johns may be doing something very different in grey from what an artist such as Martin does, the creation of dynamic tensions on the surface of grey painting with reference to the sea continue to pursue the questions that concern his paintings in the 1960s. And, like Martin, it may not even be the sea that is in the paintings. The sea is simply the title given to the line between abstraction and figuration.

Together with the few paintings whose titles name the sea, water, and beach, Johns's paintings everywhere collapse and confuse the line between figuration and abstraction. Johns is interested in painting, in giving visual form to what cannot otherwise be articulated. He does not represent the horizon line, but rather, as illustrated through the preceding discussion of *By the Sea,* there is a sense of becoming lost in a Möbius strip when we attempt to fix form, figure, and subsequently meaning to the paintings. By extension, we might conclude that for Johns, identification of the conventional distinction between figuration and abstraction is ultimately an impossible project in post-war painting. The line between the two is constantly in motion, constantly shifting; like the horizon line, it is never clear to the human eye. It may not even exist.

JASPER JOHNS

I have already discussed how Johns's paintings such as *Drawer* and *Portrait—Viola Farber* turn back on themselves, pass from a representation of something, even if in its suggested absence, to no more than painting, a surface, or perhaps an idea that can only be represented in painting. But the artist's irreverence for clarifying the moment where figuration becomes abstraction and, vice versa, always hovers over a Johns painting. This feature can be found throughout his oeuvre, not only in his representations that reference the sea. A work such as *Voice* (1964–67) is typical of this tendency. A piece of wood leaves behind it the arc of its incomplete motion as it is dragged from the top of the canvas by a characteristic Johns contraption. The wood is a stirring rod attached to a wire, pulled from top to bottom of its half-finished arc by a piece of string, perpendicular to the wire. The same wire is hooked to another that stretches across to the right-hand side of the canvas, which is, in turn, threaded through a small eyelet. Again, this wire is then hooked to another from which a spoon and a fork hang. The shadows of both spoon and fork are hastily represented by a dark grey shape behind them. This concert of greys that become the surface across which the wood is dragged is interrupted halfway down. Up close we see that we are looking not at a single canvas but at two horizontal panels pushed together. The word of the title "VOICE" is stenciled in yet another shade of grey. The piece of wood is either on the brink of erasing the letters, or it is stopped by the letters; we do not know which. The stenciled date, 1964–67, echoes this voice in the bottom left-hand corner, while the artist's name, JOHNS, in letters that are the smallest elements on the canvas, is stenciled in the bottom right-hand corner. Such are the identifiable features of the painting. It is unclear, perhaps not even relevant, what the wires, the spoon, fork, the string, the wood are doing on the canvas. In the Menil Collection in Houston, the intricate contraption attached to the surface of *Voice* speaks of some kind of mechanism, some kind of engineering feat. It is unclear, however, what the use of this technical achievement might be, other than to confuse the relationship between different elements on or attached to the expansive mottled grey surface, or surfaces, on the bifurcated canvas. Maybe they represent the highly complex, finely tuned, perfect resonance of the human voice, the most perfect of instruments? Perhaps the form of these objects is deliberately allusive, made abstract, because they produce an effect that echoes that of the voice: unable to be made visible or represented in any way? Then we must consider the rich, textured, uneven, and mostly unsure-of-themselves multitude of different greys that cover the majority of the canvas. They too render the painting abstract: in their hastily drawn, yet dynamic and resonant, vibration, the greys of the ground might echo the ineffability of the voice. There is also a ragged line beginning about nine inches above the bottom left-hand corner, and ending along the bottom edge maybe twelve inches in from the right-hand corner of this large canvas. It is as though the canvas was torn, and regretting the gesture, Johns decided to paste it back together again. The division of the painting at the center with another such line is different from this more unpredictable feature, if only because at the center of the canvas, the greys are reflected on either side of the bifurcating line. We might be tempted to recognize it as resembling a horizon line, which would make sense because as the greys move away from either side of this line, their resemblance on each side diminishes, just as would the sea and the sky.

I can postulate endlessly on how to interpret *Voice,* but in the tension between halves, between stasis and movement, between objects and their shadows, between different greys, I prefer to see this as a painting that is interested in representation more than it is interested in what is represented. Especially given the title: *Voice,* an instrument that cannot be seen. The human voice, like the horizon line, is ever elusive, and yet, is used to speak, thereby put in the service of the most consistent measure of being human. That said, there is something very delicately balanced about Johns's image, like the human voice, precariously and perfectly pitched, the suspension of objects, controlled by a stray piece of string that makes the painting refer to something that is way beyond painting, an echo of the fine-tuning of something that cannot be seen, but is nevertheless of the everyday: the human voice. Surely, the human voice as the instrument to which all others aspire, but will never attain, sits here on the precipice between abstraction and representation? It is both of the body, the material expression of human identity, and it is, by definition, abstract. The voice is both figure and ground, representation and abstraction, in Johns's *Voice.*

All of this said, there is yet another element that must surely be considered in interpretation of Johns's *Voice.* Newman painted an "all white" field with a thin, off-white zip striating the right-hand side of the canvas in 1950. Johns's *Voice* is both an echo of and a departure from Newman's *The Voice.* The zip on the right-hand side of Newman's canvas is key to understanding the relationship between the two paintings. The zip is like a fence that pulls the viewer back, as she otherwise falls reverently into the expanse of paint—not white, but an intense and undulating array of off-whites in various shades, densities, hues. Viewers cannot get past the fence, the zip; it can't be jumped, broken, moved beyond or even alongside of. Steadfast, and yet somehow uncertain, overwhelming the right-hand side of *The Voice,* despite its complete understatement, the zip works to thrust the viewer's attention back to the center of the painting, pulling her back into the seductive expanse of off-white paint. The Newman zip is the closest thing his paintings have to an object, a materiality, a tactile presence. It is no coincidence that Johns suspends the mundane objects of the fork and spoon on the right-hand side of his *Voice.* It is as though Johns takes the motif of the zip and materializes it on his canvas, makes it the basis of the dense materiality of his painting, its everyday objects that, in turn, leave the grey ground of the painting behind. The realness of the objects, hanging on a painting, makes the grey paint ambiguous, unresolved. The irresolution of all these tensions played out on the surface of *The Voice,* including the gamut of greys that clash as well as resonate, interrupt, and orchestrate, seems to stand in the place of all the contradictory pursuits of twentieth-century American painting in general, and Johns's painting in particular.

SEAN SCULLY

In one last example of the preoccupation of these interstices opened up in the interrogation of the line between abstraction and figuration, created through tensions, particularly as they are explored through representation of the natural world, Scully's proliferation of grey building blocks convinces of the inefficacy of searching to locate the line between the two.[79] There are many discussions of Scully's commitment to painting natural forms and formations, but these forms are not always visible in the paintings.[80] Scully himself reinforces the complex relationship to figuration in his works when he discusses his focus on color, surface, relations—between colors, materials, directions, movements, people, different moments in art history—and the "sense" of the notions he explores.[81]

Despite the apparent visual abstraction of Scully's paintings, the curious and convincing connection between the surfaces, doors, walls, fences, and "visual culture" that he photographed, especially in the 1990s, is more obvious. Scully found that the patterns of his blocks and bricks, stripes and windows exist everywhere, "waiting to be presented in his photographs."[82] His paintings, however, more likely ape the built environment, rather than the natural world. Scully discovered the doors, fences, walls, and facades of Ireland, Mexico, Scotland, and Spain and returns them to the structures and aesthetic energy of his paintings. Similarly, the paintings have consciously reflected the sites and spaces he has seen and experienced. This does not mean that Scully's paintings are realist, and neither are they definitively abstract, as they appear at first glance. Rather, there is an exchange or a connection between the worlds of painting and that of the visual appearance of the human effort to order and domesticate the natural environment. If, for Martin, nature embodies the perfection that painting must emulate, Scully focuses on the way that we attempt to live with nature, using its patterns and logic. The spaces and surfaces that Scully finds, photographs, and eventually translates into painting are always on the precipice of the agrarian and the modern, always somehow anachronistic, never really belonging to the world we see, the material world we inhabit. They are, in effect, neither of nature nor of the built environment. Moreover, in what might be considered a repetition of the impossibility or futility of distinguishing between figuration and abstraction in Scully's paintings, his representations are neither referential nor fully imagined.

Lost Door in Ireland (1999) or the *Walls of Aran* series are images of poor, not always developed, country areas and neighborhoods. Even *A Corner of Barcelona* (1997) apparently depicts a neglected, dilapidated backstreet of an otherwise modern tourist mecca. Like the paintings, Scully's photographs share an attention to surface, to the irregularities in the rational technological world, the softness, the emotional nuances, and the sensuous depths that are not otherwise available to the naked eye, to sensuous perception. Thus, when placed side by side, abstract paintings and figurative photographs are not a representation, or a translation of one medium into another. Side by side, a connection is drawn—or as Scully would have it, their relations are brought to life—made obvious for the viewer on Scully's canvases, between figuration and abstraction. And on reflection, Scully's inhabitation of this curious space between the two is an invitation to see the world in a different way, through different eyes. Grey and brown, as the colors of the rural and forgotten urban environments in Scully's paintings, offer the opportunity to challenge any such distinction between painting and photograph, and, by extension, between abstraction and figuration. Thus, the lines between the two are blurred when the two different media of his work are placed side by side, in relationship with each other, as well as in the paintings themselves, in the representation of the built and the natural environments.

Conclusion

Grey entices exploration of the nebulous line between abstraction and figuration. Grey enables artists to balance precariously on a fence between the two. It works both ways, because these artists' commitment to a suspension or tension between abstraction and figuration is also an invitation to grey. Grey and the world it represents come to coexist. This is the trademark, or a trademark, of modernist art: the line between abstraction and figuration is never apparent. For Johns, Rothko, Marden, Martin, Twombly, and Scully, the color grey, line, and form become inseparable in the search for answers to the problem of how to represent through painting. Whether these paintings reach full abstraction, or stay in debt to the principles of figuration and representation, grey is the interstitial color best suited to the depiction of the ambivalence of the spaces they occupy.

The one thing that binds together these otherwise disparate artworks is the ephemerality and fluidity of their relationship to what art historians have hitherto defined as opposites. The same thing connects them with clarity to grey paintings of the nineteenth and early twentieth centuries. Grey postwar abstract American paintings embrace the material objectness of paint and the ephemerality of a world into which we are invited to step, and simultaneously, from which we are discouraged to enter. They balance on the precipice between abstraction and figuration in what results in an inquiry into representation. Like the color that is chosen to carry out this inquiry, they are always hovering in the in-between, the uncertain, unknown space of transition. This space is made possible by the color grey. Grey also occupies this ill-defined space: it has the potential to be both and neither what is captured by other colors. Grey has the speed and luminosity, as well as all the uncertainty that pervades painting in this era. Grey not only marks the interstice; it also has the capacity to sit either side of the divide. The insights and challenges of modernist abstraction to definitions of the surface of painting are only ever present through the instantiation of or the gesture toward their very opposite. Grey captures these opposites. Grey paint, in its comfort with contradiction, is always in the interstice, offering a space in which the problems of painting can be posed and resolved. Grey, or rather, the multitude of possibilities of grey, is the color best suited to pursue the question of painting in the postwar period. In contradistinction to art historical discourse, far from being dead or complete, the historical trajectory of modernist painting continues, as painting continues to be reinvented in grey. And yet, as I have demonstrated, the very existence of modernism is also discredited.

In their stripping away of the figure, in the merging of paint, support, image, and object, the works of artists such as Johns, Rothko, Marden, Martin, Twombly, and Scully bring abstraction to the fore to explore the identity of painting on their grey canvases. In the next chapter, I show that grey abstract painting in postwar America paves the way for the overt political discourses that come hand in hand with the return to representation in the late twentieth century. This history of modernist painting is one in which the viewer is challenged to explore new modes of vision. Along the way, these late modernist examples shatter aesthetic, historical, and political conventions and expectations. That is, the trajectory of grey paintings—by artists such as Warhol and Mark Tansey—continues to push at the line between abstraction and figuration, ultimately, with a return to figuration.

4

BEYOND MODERNIST ABSTRACTION

THE SOCIAL SIGNIFICANCE OF GREY PAINTING

WHEN GREENBERG INTERVENED in the continuing development of modern art in the 1950s and 1960s, he insisted that painting distinguish itself from all other art forms and, therefore, be "about" nothing other than its own medium and support.[1] To be sure, Stella's painting, and his laconic claim that "what you see is what you see," are testimony to the fact that Greenberg's notion of modernist painting was indeed realized.[2] As most now agree, however, even the formal gestures and questions of American art make references outside the frame. There is no such thing as pure abstraction; there is no such thing as pure opticality.[3] The questions and thematic concerns of abstraction, its emotional resonance, even the relations between forms, strategies, and spaces, all create something more, something beyond what is seen on the canvas. In this chapter I examine some of the different ways that postwar American painting in grey references, engages with, and can be interpreted for its reflection of a modernist art that reaches beyond the frame of self-referentiality. I discuss painting's effacement (and simultaneous reassertion) of artistic authority, the meaning and value of painting as it is determined by, as well as creates, changing modes of perception and vision in the late twentieth century. I also discuss the relationship between painting and other media and art forms, as well as its historical and cultural relevance. I identify the historical, and at times political, significance of grey painting in its relationship to art history as well as to the historical moment when the paintings were made. Once again, in this chapter, the question of grey's contribution to an abstract modernism are addressed through focus on the paintings of selected artists. Thus, my discussion simultaneously reveals new insights into their oeuvres and makes an argument for grey as representative of the concerns of modernist painting. Johns's grey encaustics continue to be central to my analyses, as do the grey paintings of Twombly, Rothko, Martin, and Scully. In addition, I discuss the grey paintings of twentieth-century American painters Philip Guston, and Mark Tansey, and make reference to those of Chuck Close. I also turn to select grey works by Warhol for their key role in the introduction of a political charge to late-modernist American painting.

The Historical Dimension of Postwar American Painting

The engagement of grey painting with the world beyond the frame gives it a historical value, a value that simultaneously extends to a social engagement. In the immediate postwar years in the United States, abstract art took radical turns and was redefined, and reimagined more than once. As critics and commentators of modernism insist and as I have reiterated, the intentions, aesthetic, and impact of modernist painting are often filled with contradiction. The relationship to the external context is no different. Unique to abstract expressionism was the search for a form and material as the subject and substance of painting that would "efface" the social world. In his move to abstraction, Pollock challenged the frames of art as they had been established up to the postwar period, literally, with a process and a context of painting that was previously unheard of. With his "all-over" drip paintings, many of his earliest of which were predominantly grey, Pollock intended to remove the distinction between figure and ground, the space between artist and canvas, to leave the world behind. However, as Clark points out with reference to Cecil Beaton's use of Pollock's early grey paintings in fashion shoots for *Vogue,* when painting has such uses in public and social life, to call it self-referential is paradoxical and not an argument that can be sustained.[4] Irrespective of the intent of the postwar abstract works discussed here, historically, they extend the contradictory landscapes of prewar European modernism through engagement with the historical moment and its social conventions. It is the multidimensionality of this engagement that interests me here.

Before beginning, a word on the theoretical context within which I understand the historical, social, and political layers of these abstract grey paintings. Boris Groys leans on the aesthetic and contextual contradictions to demonstrate the impossibility of radicality in historically defined modernism. For Groys, the political edge is always blunted, and the apparent complicity is always radicalized.[5] In its displacement of passive contemplation and adulation by material forces, the spiritual by materiality, and the triumph of iconoclastic aesthetics, modernism sought to democratize art, to bring it to everyone, irrespective of class, race, social status. From Plato onward, iconoclasts have maintained that mimetic representation is deceptive; it ultimately appeals to the emotions, and therefore seduces, enticing a viewer into reverie and reverence. Social and political democracy depends on truth, immediacy, and a thinking viewer.[6] Thus, the socially and politically conscious artist and critic is led to reject the kind of representation that encouraged reverie. Ultimately, however, Groys demonstrates that this rejection of tradition leads to an iconoclasm that embraces middle-class idealism after World War II. Paradoxically, this idealism—often the result of abstraction—comes in spite of the search for an uncompromising iconoclastic art in postwar America. Drawing on the revolutionary ideas of Mikhail Bakhtin that enjoyed widespread impact on the conception of modernism, Groys argues that in practice, iconoclasm is always ambivalent because every act of creativity is an act of destruction, every act of empowerment must necessarily disable, or disempower, someone, and in the case of art, that someone is usually the viewer.[7] The logic of Groys's argument is that pure abstraction is necessarily a destructive aesthetic. Nevertheless, I would argue, while the search for an art beyond the limits of state control, or in the case of American postwar art, beyond the limits of the art market and the museum, always ends in failure, the implicit critique and intrinsic struggle of abstraction push against and redefine the boundaries of legitimate art and, therefore, social life. Specifically, this redefinition of boundaries is negotiated or experienced by a viewer in his or her perceptual and bodily engagement with the painting as an object. This creative action of the physically present viewer brings meaning and value to the paintings as it opens up to the varying contours of the aesthetic. This experience across time with abstract paintings sees them, in all their complexity, challenge this same viewer's experience of art and of the world. Once again, grey abstract painting has this capacity to describe the viewing experience because of its oscillation between surface and depth, reality and representation, darkness and light. That is, the properties of grey open up to the meaning that results from our perception of abstract modernist art more generally. It is no coincidence that artists such as such as Johns, Twombly, Warhol, and Tansey choose grey to explore the possibility of creating innovative relationships to painting and to their historical world. Because, I would argue, grey is a vessel for contradictions of the same order as those of abstract modernist painting.

The Effacement/Reinstatement of Artistic Authority

Perhaps the most evident shift in the power relations of art and, by extension, the place of the artist in those relations, happened with the shift from a patronage of monarchs and popes in the Renaissance to the rise of modern institutions and the commercial art market as the arbiter of value, particularly in the West. The politics of an artist's work are conventionally measured according to his or her challenge to and negotiation of these institutions. The aesthetic and painterly choices of abstract expressionism in the late 1940s extended the political force of Russian formalism, as well as, in grey, the confrontation of bourgeois viewing expectations as they had been established by nineteenth-century painting. For abstract expressionism, the brushstroke was the "weapon" against social constraint, commodification, and appropriation of American art.[8] When the brushstroke itself became the content of the painted image, all illusion was removed from the canvas. In the wake of abstract expressionism, minimalist, color-field painting witnessed the brushstroke cover the entire canvas. The brushstroke was a depiction of nothing and the simultaneous effacement of all trace of the artist. Abstraction thus became the marker of democracy and signaled an apparent freedom from bourgeois norms. Grey is the color that embodies painting's need both to challenge boundaries and traditions and to explore a viewing experience that leads to a confrontation of all expectations. Similarly, grey is the color that highlights and, at best, challenges the boundaries and traditions of paint as color.

In a continuation of the commitment to challenge the aesthetics and meaning of art, in the 1950s and 1960s, the place of the artist within the creative process, as well as the visibility of his presence on the surface of the canvas, was challenged by American painting. The impulse to dethrone the artist as individual genius and enable the viewer as cocreator of meaning was explored across art forms, accompanied by a critical and philosophical discourse, in the interests of the search for democracy. Thus, apparent effacement of the artist's presence went hand in hand with the rise of postwar consumer culture, the escalating threat of the Cold War, and the migration to America of French thought committed to the dispersion of power and knowledge across class and generational lines.[9]

Within the art world, the role of the artist and the notion of the authenticity of art were radically rethought following the impact of the Duchamp readymade. And as Clark demonstrates in his thoughts on the inextricable relationship between Pollock's abstract canvases and everyday life, "bourgeois consciousness" and the "manufacture" of life are in Pollock's very movement around the canvas, the very drips that cover its surface. How could the creativity of the artist be determined if he had not produced the object? If creativity were measured by use value, surely Pollock and his celebrity status filled this role? How was the authenticity of the painting to be measured if the artist's presence of production could not be identified?[10] American painting of the postwar period relied on the importance of emptying the object of authenticity and replacing it with conceptual spontaneity.[11] Rauschenberg, Johns, and, later, Warhol effaced their presence from the canvas, and in so doing, reinstated it through absence. This contradiction comes to define these paintings. And again, the uncertainty and ambivalence of the artist's presence, this gesture of evasion, erasure, and the inability to be identified, are what keep the work on edge, socially engaged, so to speak. These qualities are what keep abstract paintings in the grey.

Twentieth-century paintings in grey remove authority and individual expression in ways that are unexpected, surprising, ways that also have a profound impact on the spectator who experiences them. Grey opens itself up to the struggle of the artist with his own demise, his own disintegration in the face of the painted canvas. Grey paintings bring the struggle between identity and its effacement that was at the heart of debates around modernist art onto the perceptible surface of the canvas, into the movement of the brush. As is the case with the Rauschenberg Combines, there may still be traces of the painter as author on the canvas, most often in his presence through gesture of the (black) brushstroke, but when we look closely and over time, we see that the artist is always on the way to the loss of his own identity. Just as we see on Rauschenberg's highly charged canvases as objects, they are always in the process of dissolution in the space of their exhibition.

The dissolution of identity as a painter, the erasure of the artist's authority over his material, his expression, all that he knows, and all that he paints, is a visual negotiation in and through grey. Grey carries with it an uncertainty, a fluidity that is the legacy of its composition through the coming together of color and light. This equation of painted color as light never has the stridency, the absoluteness of red, yellow, or blue. Grey is always in motion, always on the verge of a color it is not; it always surprises because it is never what we assume it will be. The mutability and activity of grey paint mean that it is never fully controllable, no one ever owns grey, no one can be fully in command of a work executed in grey. Not the artist, and by extension, not the viewer or the art market. In grey, the messiness of paint that lies behind the rationalization, the abstraction, and the command of modernist painting becomes clear. This loss of an artist's authority when he or she paints in grey, ultimately, repeats the fundamental contradiction of modernist art.

JASPER JOHNS

In Johns's *Fool's House* (1962), the broom that is the center of the painting not only leaves behind traces of its movement on the canvas, it also is later attached to it (Plate 11). In *Device* (1962), rulers cancel out through appearing to have smoothed over those strokes that already exist, perhaps strokes that witnessed the onetime presence of the artist.[12] In *Good Time Charley* (1961), as in *Device*, the instruments through which the paint is applied to and arranged on the canvas have a trajectory over which Johns has no choice, and no control to change. Thus, in the three paintings the autographic stroke as the expression of the artist's personal meaning, insight, and body is challenged, removed from the final composition. Similarly, Johns's application of coat hangers, bits of wood, cutlery, tin cans, and his representation of pop cultural icons and signs such as flags and targets reach to the world of objects that are already in existence. He prefers found objects as the carriers of meaning, rather than having to rely on the creative production of his own vision, his own inventions within the painting. These strategies and gestures are designed to draw attention to the removal of the artistic personality from the work. All of the objects and icons of mass culture affixed to a Johns canvas are now the coauthors of the visual world as seen by the painting.

Despite this self-conscious removal of his authority from the visual field, nowhere would we mistake a Johns flag, a Johns readymade, or a grey encaustic as the work of anyone other than Jasper Johns. These works are always identifiably his. And his use of grey, together with the use of the mass cultural icons, is an attempt to define himself as an artist. Johns's artistic identity is everywhere on display in these works: it is in the "Johns style," Johns's use of encaustic, of stencils, and grey as his chosen color. Even in the specific way that Johns removes his identity from the canvas, he consciously marks each canvas with a signature through the attachment of objects and a use of stencils.

Similarly, Johns continues to rethink his artistic agency across his career. All of his paintings from the 1960s especially—*Fool's House* is a good example—show how Johns engages with the struggle to remove his identity from the canvas, and simultaneously, to explore the role of the artist. Moreover, Johns engages with this paradox through a visual manipulation of grey paint and other objects. In *Fool's House* we see the broom, wiping away the paint underneath it, and the absence of even a stenciled signature, a signature that might identify the fool (Johns?) who once inhabited the house. Thus, Johns's ambivalence and ambiguous relationship to his own authority, his own presence as a part of the painting is performed within the frame. It is performed in grey. If all there is to see and know in the Johns encaustics is on the surface of the paintings, there we see the deep ambivalence and ambiguity of his place and identity in the world of pop cultural icons.[13] We need look no further than the sensuous elements of the painting as an object. Perhaps the most important of these elements is the tactile grey in which he enfolds all the uncertainty and indecision of his place on the canvas.

Most of the time Johns is not so oblique about his presence on the canvas. He leaves traces of his body everywhere. The body, his body, is fragmented; at least in its conception and the visualization of its memory, it is a body that is never left intact.[14] The contortions, distortions, and the inventory of operations made by the traces of Johns's body as that of an artist who sees himself as another object in the world cannot be separated from his exploration of formal issues of painting. The treatment of the body is, for example, evidence of the embrace and simultaneous rejection of both abstraction and figuration. The body is recognizable as an object, and it is always in fragments, hidden behind a curtain or veil, erased by a device, or never more than a body part in the first place.

In a work such as *In the Studio* (1982), Johns paints a self-portrait of sorts. For all the other things going on in this painting—for example, its reflection on the possibility of creating depth of space on a flat canvas, the engagement with questions of representation, perspective, reflection, medium, and framing—*In the Studio* is about the body, Johns's body. The forearm and hand, repeated, in different media, the one an imprint of another (or perhaps not), question the logic of representation and its relationship to reality. Paintings are here seen as objects represented within the painting, *In the Studio,* paintings that are original, not reproductions of those painted earlier, those that might exist as objects in the world. Paintings have the same status as the fragmented body or a piece of wood. Like the paintings here created for the first time, the forearm and hand are in miniature, not real. John Yau argues that for Johns, a work such as *In the Studio* is all about the relationship between reality and painting: this is the very task of the author or artist, to negotiate, examine, and account for the space between the two.[15] In other paintings Johns will invite the viewer to negotiate the space between the two. That is, the process of viewing will repeat the relationship established by the artist between painting and reality. Grey is the perfect color in which to do this, because grey has not yet decided, or arrived at, its conclusions about the relationship between reality and painting. Grey is always in the process of looking for, never having reached the goal of its trajectory. Thus, with grey as our guide, we are invited to negotiate our own relationship to Johns's paintings, the paintings within them, and the studio in which they are represented.

In later works such as the four encaustics in *The Seasons* (1985–87), Johns's presence as artist on the canvas is different again. Here he is present as a shadow, leaving the scene of an image torn asunder. The dissection of these canvases reflects or repeats, unsurprisingly, the schism that exists between the trace of the artist on the canvas and the works he leaves behind. From these brief descriptions of the ambivalent artist on Johns's grey canvases, we begin to see how the complex relationship between the artist and his painting is constantly being rethought. It is a relationship that changes physically as well as conceptually through the presence and absence of his body on the canvas.

Moreover, the rethinking, the continual renegotiation of the artist and his relationship to painting, to his painting, is enabled by grey paint because of its challenge to its own status. The body of the artist and the identity of painting in representation are thrown into question in grey. In 1964 Samuel J. Wagstaff Jr. curated an exhibition at the Wadsworth Atheneum in Hartford, Connecticut. Little documentation of the exhibition exists. Thanks, however, to the inclusion of what are now canonical pieces from the period—Rauschenberg's *Erased de Kooning Drawing* and works by Reinhardt, Johns, Newman, Kelly, Stella—a review in the local Hartford newspaper demonstrates the importance of "no color" to the politics of the exhibition. The reviewer renounces the aesthetic quality of the works, even if they are "unusual" and "witty." She says, "Viewers to this exhibition would do well not to look upon the objects on view as works of art in the accepted sense, but as satirical and witty comments on our mores. These objectives may not have motivated the artists but this is what comes through to the viewer."[16] While she is skeptical of the "nonconventional" substance of the works, the reviewer nevertheless questions the exhibition's curator, who is adamant that because they are grey, the paintings are confrontational. For the reviewer, the works are novel, not conflictual or argumentative. Grey (for Wagstaff, black and white) is the necessary basis of the very challenge delivered by these works. In grey, the comfort and solidity of the viewing experience that would be had before a Titian or a Rembrandt, are replaced with a tentative and dangerous journey across "thin ice."[17] In turn, these different perspectives on the works demonstrate the uncertainty of their significance. As a result, I would add that thanks to the grey, the prominence of the artist is deflated or bracketed to the extent that painting becomes motivated by the relationship of criticality it enlivens in the viewer. Thus, grey is the color that enables a relationship of possibility, a relationship between painting and viewer that opens a space for us to think and see differently.

CY TWOMBLY

In a different relationship to painting and the canvas, Twombly directly refutes the expressive gesture of abstract expressionism. Like much of what takes place in Twombly's works, he often rejects the trace of authorship in a manner quite different from how his critics claim. As I pointed out in the preceding chapter, his scribbles and scrawls, especially from the 1950s and 1960s, have been read as a form of graffiti. The line is said to be a violation of the painted surface that, like tagging on a New York subway car in the 1970s, leaves the trace of a criminal presence not only defacing the object it tags but also removing the artist's presence from the work altogether.[18] However, when we stand before Twombly's paintings, we see him everywhere on their surface. We do not "read" the drawing and writing and scribbling in graphite as defacing the canvas but instead as involved in a struggle with the variegations of thick, colored grey paint. Paint and graphite and sometimes wax are present and argue with each other on the surface, rather than erasing the other's existence. Nevertheless, this does not fully negate Twombly's ultimate authority and neither does it detract from his presence to the painting. In the struggle, the constant conversation, the stopping and starting, the poetic painter in deep reflection can be witnessed on these canvases. And yet, Twombly on the canvas is an artist who has no authority, an artist who is always struggling, an artist whose identity is always under erasure.

Characteristically, Twombly's two large works, *Treatise on the Veil* (1968) and *Treatise on the Veil (Second Version)* (1970), have been interpreted to be about the impossibility of the project he is attempting.[19] (See Plates 12 and 13.) The imperative of the artist to make sense of the world by finding a language with which to articulate and imagine it is writ large across these canvases. The two paintings might be said to display the attempt to rationalize what and how he sees, what he represents. Twombly's work on canvas, akin to Kiefer's dance with the philosophical representation of history, holds within it the seeds of its own dereliction.[20] In Twombly's most haunting canvases, this is played out like a performance in the traces of his own process of thinking as it is witnessed by the surface struggles of the painting. It is not the anonymity of the line itself that effaces Twombly's presence on the canvas. On the contrary, that rolling, fragmented, uncertain line might be seen as the trademark of Twombly's subjective expression. It is in the erasure of those lines, through furious repetition, monotonous movements of the hand, sometimes appearing involuntarily across the canvas, that Twombly questions his own authority over the painting. The fading out of Twombly's patterns and scratches and scribbles, their eventual falling off the edge of the canvas, their stopping and starting all indicate the hesitation and disappointment of the painter who recognizes his own inadequacy. Moreover, these strategies of "effacement" are made possible through the grey on which white is drawn. The grey ground is the material of erasure, the material of uncertainty when it interacts with white lines.

In the many untitled grey paintings, we become witness to Twombly's thinking. Take *Untitled* (1970), for example: cursive lines are drawn in crayon, sometimes haltingly, tentatively, as if with the wrong hand (Plate 14). Moving from left to right three times, we see Twombly create patterns, logic, rhythms, his hand literally moving across the canvas. It is as if we watch him thinking out loud, in crayon on a grey background. At moments, particularly toward the bottom of the huge canvas, it appears he begins to have second thoughts. The white paint that makes the grey background seem lighter, more luminescent, gives the impression of the lines being rubbed out, witnessing a change of mind as the lines head off the grey painting, off the canvas. These movements, and the hesitation of the lines, create an instability to the image that suggests the vulnerability of paint, crayon, and support, all at once. No single one of the painting's elements can contain any other; all come together in this precarious meditation on line, movement, and the mathematics of composition. In the *Untitled* (1968) painting currently owned by the Museum of Modern Art in New York, Twombly deciphers, constructs, measures, and calculates the movement, the trajectory, perhaps the size of the rectangles, and then he rethinks all of those calculations before our eyes, erasing and redrawing what might also be magic carpets as they fly through the grey background, again on the diagonal, but this time, never reaching their destination. This same performance of the artist in process is something we see most often in Twombly's paintings with a grey ground.

In these paintings, we see an artist who continually changes his mind. It is as though Twombly tries to make sense of the magic of movement, but ultimately, the fact that none of the numbers are logical, none of the patterns of motion, none of the rectangles, correspond to any of the others, tells us that the search is probably futile, and at best, still in process. It's this impossibility, this inability of the artist to find what he is looking for in a single representation, his defeated attempt to rationalize, that envisions Twombly's hesitancy as an artist who might otherwise have control over his canvas. This is not to say that Twombly has failed; he has not. Twombly knows from the start that he is searching for an impossible resolution or that the search is the resolution itself. It is a resolution that can only come by way of dissolution, and yet, he continues the search anyway.

MARK ROTHKO

Even for an artist as present to his canvas as Rothko, authority and authenticity are questionable. In his final black-and-grey works, he reaches for grey as the quintessence of all that paint has done for him, and all that grey can do for painting. His authority is being undone as he edges ever closer to his death and the profundity of all that paint can do in the grey moments at the end of his life, in these grey paintings. But this is only one way to see the series, *Untitled (Black on Gray)*.[21] This is an interpretation tied to Rothko's identity as the depressed artist who turns to grey to represent an inner turmoil that will end in suicide. It is also an understanding of grey as dark, pervaded by fear, doom, and negativity. And lastly, it is an interpretation that must ignore the vaporous white ground that illuminates and gives luster to the grey field. Once these paintings are out of Rothko's studio, like any artist, he does not have command over their relationship with the viewer. It is why, I would argue, he so liked to dictate their exhibition, creating the perfect viewing experience, typically one in which the viewer is surrounded by and becomes immersed in the paintings. Surely this only needs to be done in the absence of the artist's control, as a gesture of relinquishing authority. Ultimately, Rothko seems far from the canvases by the time we are with them. He must step aside for us to have an unsettling experience.

Another interpretation of these works begins with the aforementioned blur at the edges of the bands, the blocks of color, and again, the canvas. If we focus on the point where black and grey meet on the canvas, the uncertain dividing line between color fields in all Rothko's paintings, we are led to this alternative interpretation. This line is a telling, provocative moment. It is the moment where the painting loses orientation, becomes vulnerable. This is the moment that pulls the viewer inward so that she can begin to engage with the painting, to understand what happens, the process of layering, the effect it solicits. At least, the line between color bands is the moment when the viewer begins to be pulled forward, to see the work of the painter's mind, close-up. Nevertheless, this is part of the mystery of Rothko's paintings: we can never fully grasp these transitions, let alone identify how they are achieved. As Thomas Crowe recognizes, "The slippages that we find at the margins" defeat us and leave us with nowhere to go but back into the color field, or back away from the canvas.[22] In these moments the confusion and the consequent rewriting of the relationship between paint and the world take place. Because these places on the canvas are filled with uncertainty, anxiety, they are where painting and viewer become most intimate. The edges, whether between colors, or between paint and the canvas underneath as we see in Marden's and Johns's works, are where the artist exposes his vulnerability, his ultimate forgoing of mastery over paint and painting. No matter how controlled and constructed, the edges are the admission of incompletion, imperfection. For this reason, they are the most troubling places on the canvas.

Like Johns's encaustics, there is no mistaking these or any other Rothko paintings for anything but paintings by Mark Rothko. By the 1960s, however, recognition of the artist is not the measure of the painting. The relationship between painter and painting as the focus of meaning changed after Duchamp. As illustrated in the earlier discussion of the viewer's response to the *Untitled (Black on Gray)* series, Rothko is present on the canvases as a mediator for the viewer to open up to him- or herself. The viewer's relationship with Rothko's paintings begins up-close, eighteen inches to be exact, and having surveyed the points of vulnerability on the canvas, we are pushed back and drawn into reverie at the very same moment.[23] This experience of the self is viable only if there is no artist standing between the viewer and the painting. Rothko has left the control of the canvas long ago; meaning is made in the reality of the individual and unique relationship between viewer and painting. The opening out onto the spectator to complete the work, the invitation to step into and become a part of these paintings, undoes the artist's authority, and in its engagement of the viewer for meaning, the painting assumes its authority. There is never the certainty and finitude of the Renaissance, for example, a certainty that comes courtesy of narrative and figurative representation. The invitation to reverie and simultaneous pull to attend to the materiality of paint are the hallmarks of modernist painting, hallmarks that undo didacticism and open the painting to the unexpected. The contradiction that begins between ethereality and materiality, and then leads to different viewing positions, is the foundation of, the impetus for the sociohistorical, at times the political, ramifications of modernist painting. We see the process of oscillation in viewing positions clearly in front of Rothko's final paintings, when we indulge in the relationship between ourselves and the grey-and-black works. Precisely because of the brightness and luminescence of the bottom half of the canvases, the playfulness of the brushstrokes, and the reflection of the density of black, as well as the ambiguity of painting, grey infuses these final Rothko paintings with contradiction and conundrum. Because of the contradictions left unresolved, these are the moments at which Rothko has no control over the reception of the works.

SEAN SCULLY

The undoing of artistic authority continues into the next generation of painters. Scully pays much attention to the blurring of edges in his grey paintings. He also uses this gesture of ambiguity in contrast to and, simultaneously, in concert with the force of the blocks of color—often of browns, blacks, and greys, and always of limited palette—to create irresolution and openness. Scully deliberately resists the finitude of precise edges and boundaries between colors. And while the blocks are intransigent, they are always composed of layers of paint, layers we are reminded of through the visibility of different colors in a single grey block. In this apparent tactility of paint, Scully's blocks are strikingly different from Rothko's layers. The blocks that are otherwise geometrically placed—both vertical and horizontal—give Scully's paintings a rhythm, dynamism, and openness. We see the blocks as they are being painted, what color is used, at any given moment, and its subsequent layering with other colors. This transparency of process is the undoing of Scully as the authoritative master of what he paints; it is the openness to his viewer. Beyond the edges, the awkward laying of horizontal bars on top of verticals that are nevertheless a perfect jigsaw puzzle, also demonstrates openness, to the point of inviting confusion. Even though we detect repetition and order, the order cannot be grasped and it is never the same from one painting to the next. It is an order that cannot be determined by the viewer because there are always elements of chaos to obscure it. Scully might prefer to call it lyrical, but others call it chaotic: for a viewer there is a potential disturbance to the absence of logic in the organization of blocks. *Raphael* (2004) is a good example. The eye of the viewer is drawn immediately to the pair of vertical, nearly square blocks, one in the center on the left, the other along the top edge. Are they the same size? Did the light block begin the same color? Is the one at the top brown on white, the one on the left white on black? Perhaps the one on the top is better paired with the vertical bands directly beneath it? They are the same color after all. There is a circuitous frustration in the search for the logic, or the "right" way to look at the grey blocks. As is often the case with the reception of abstract works, the viewer must move away from logical thinking and begin to envision different patterns in paint. This constant shifting of emphasis, of the form and meaning of the painting, the aleatory events that affect it—for example, where it is hung in relation to other works, or the lighting—leave us in a relationship with the Scully blocks that can never be determined in advance. Full abstraction embraces the chance encounter of the viewing process of these paintings, even when this process is guided and framed. Thus, it is in the turn to abstraction, nonrepresentation, and nonnarrative that the painter is forced to concede his control over, and his authority within, the production of meaning of his work.

Scully is likewise effaced in the repetition that is the basis of this compositional logic. The repetition is multiplied: the repetition of stripes and blocks, one after the other, though always with a difference, whether in size, orientation, the density of the paint, or the combination of colors. There is also a repetition from canvas to canvas, from year to year, across his oeuvre, each repetition being different from the last, but always a repetition of the same image, the same compositional element of the block, ad infinitum. Scully's may be a repetition of something for which he has the copyright, of which his own work is the origin, but it is an act of self-imitation, a fraudulent image of his own copied original. This repetition of fictional originality is a defining paradox of modernist art in the twentieth century.[24] When it is executed in grey, similar to the infinitely reproducible medium of photography, a medium in which the hand of the artist is no longer visible, an image from which the artist as absent begins to emerge.

In their various and unpredictable forms of the artist's self-effacement from the canvas, works in grey by Johns, Twombly, Rothko, and Scully reflect their own status as painters of and in the modern world: grey reflects the contradictions of the modern self in their images. Grey is their undoing on the canvas; grey is the place at which their identity as great artists is challenged. Grey allows the painters to experiment, to challenge their own visions, and to offer those visions to the spectator for a relationship in which they are no longer present. Grey is open to process, experiment, and the possibility of something else. But it is also definite enough to confirm the presence of the artist. Again, the play between absence and presence of the artist creates spaces for the viewer to experience the aesthetic independently, thereby completing works in their moment of indecision.

Perception and Vision

The viewing subject as generator of meaning in modernist art has continued to change place since Manet's *Olympia* first confronted the male gaze. Since 1863 the way a painting is seen has created new layers of effect and meaning. When critics discuss vision and the role of the spectator before the radical modernist artwork they often emphasize disturbance, fragmentation, and the attempt to break routine viewing expectations of an illusory, coherent representation of the world. That is, the goal of painting throughout the twentieth century has consistently been to politicize its viewer through making her an active participant in the creation of meaning. This is one indication of modernist painting's rescinding of the invitation to fall into reverie. Through a constant challenge to the familiarity of viewing practices, modernist painting has kept the questions of painting alive. Rothko, Johns, Martin, and Guston, an artist who painted a handful of key works in grey, challenge the role of the viewer in their abstract grey works. Grey gives these artists the opportunity to strip away other concerns and invite the viewer to focus directly on the movement of the eye, and the self-understanding of the viewing subject that stands before their paintings.

MARK ROTHKO

If we return to Rothko's *Untitled (Black on Gray)* works, painted in acrylic on canvas, the challenge to the viewer's perception becomes clearer. Rothko's untitled series is a mystery, corresponding to the way that, as I demonstrate in chapter 5, Richter's massive grey sheets in *Acht Grau / Eight Grey* (2002) are not. Despite the schizophrenia of Rothko's paintings, paintings split in two by horizon lines that are anything but representations of the natural world, Rothko's *Untitled (Black on Gray)* works invite an experience beyond the physical senses. They stir up feelings, emotions; they seduce, envelop, carry the viewer away to a world where there is nothing but her and the painting, a place where everything else evaporates. In fact, it is not even the body that is left before Rothko's grey painting, but rather, it is some innermost part of the self that connects to the spiritual perfection of the ethereal paintings. At least, this is the experience of Rothko's paintings from a distance.

Up close, the experience is very different: the paintings are experienced as a discovery of the intricate detail on the surface. The drips, flecks, the shifts in tone and density of paint, the fluidity and faltering of the brushstroke attract attention, then fascination. Gradually, over time, as we sit with the paintings, we fall into Rothko's grey—just as we do with the maroon and the black of the *Seagram Murals* (1958–59). This is the drama of Rothko's paintings: the shift from a physical experience of the paintings as a complex surface on the canvas to a meditative space, a space of contemplation in which the paintings must always remain the source of inspiration.

James Elkins discusses being with a Rothko painting as akin to being with someone we love, wanting to draw closer both physically and emotionally.[25] And then, as we move closer, intoxicated with the experience of breathing the same air, we feel our increasing vulnerability. It is not only the painting that is vulnerable, but as we enter into relationship with it, we sense our own unease. In a gesture of self-protection and self-preservation, we step back, into the safety of distance. This is the experience of being with Rothko's paintings. Enticed by the details on the surface, we then fall into the space opened for us by the canvas, and again, by the infinite depths of color upon color. We are rewarded by the variegations and secrets of the surface of Rothko's works if we move up close. And then, again recognizing the discomfort of this intimacy, with nothing between us and the painting, nothing between our own and another's soul, we recoil. According to Elkins, it is here in this falling that the viewer is moved to tears.[26] He explains this as being because Rothko ignites the soul, the inner life, in this process of perception. It is distinct from that had with Richter's paintings that are constantly in a game of attraction and distraction of the physical body, and sensuous perception. As such, for Elkins, Rothko's paintings offer a space of perfect stillness, a space that brings us face-to-face with nothing other than the truth of who we are. These canvases have the potential to show us the stillness, thus the life inside, and it is a stillness so naked that there is nowhere to go but to tears. It is a stillness that is quite opposite of the reflective vision: it is internal; we lose sight of our physical presence before the work, in the world.

The immersion in Rothko's paintings always begins with an intimate relationship to the surface. For it is here that the initial attraction is stirred: in the luminosity, density, transparency, the delicacy of where the brush massages the canvas. We do not, however, fall without warning. We are enticed by the time taken to focus on what we are seeing. The canvas is the same as the previous one. However, as we move around a room of Rothkos, each time we have to refocus, we have to readjust the eye to the nuances of a new painting. Before *Untitled (Black on Gray)* the viewer takes time to see the different shades of grey, to distinguish between the matte and the shiny, the velvet and the woven surfaces. In this way, each of the *Untitled (Black on Gray)* paintings begins on a surface. It might be a flat surface, but it is variegated in other ways, filled with the dynamism of grey brushstrokes, the intensity of black paint; it is filled with marking. The virtuosity of Rothko's painting is seen in the thickness of the paint on the canvas, the working and reworking with different colors, of different thicknesses, using different brushes, in order to create a buildup of paint that nevertheless has the appearance, and the vision, of flatness. The process and the outcome of the surface both issue the invitation to the viewer to fall and, simultaneously, form a barrier that holds us back from losing ourselves completely. At some point, we are pushed back, reminded that there is a price to pay for all that intimacy. With *Untitled (Black on Gray)*, the white border further complicates this movement because it limits our capacity to roam visually around and inside the painting. The white border also acts as a literal fence that stops us from falling too far, too deep: it points our eye back to the center of the canvas. This physical and emotional experience of grey, at the same time, defines the experience of modernist painting.

AGNES MARTIN

Thanks to the presence of similar characteristics in her paintings, it is tempting to agree with Martin's critics and couple her with Rothko, whose spectator oscillates between physicality and transcendence, between a viewer who sees with the eye and one who sees with the soul.[27] However, the physical eye engaged by Rothko is the eye as instrument that gives access to a spiritual engagement. This is quite different from the experience of Martin's paintings that appear determined to keep the viewer at a distance. Before Martin's 72 × 72 inch paintings we are kept in oscillation between different modes of vision, none of which allows any kind of rest or reflection.[28] Martin claims that her paintings all visualize something that cannot be seen, what is known but cannot be articulated: beauty. There is another way of looking at Martin's canvases, namely, a way of seeing in which light is their very substance. When we sit with Martin's paintings, they begin to reach a state where they radiate a light, a light that is created by the effulgence of the so-called gridded fields. In turn, this effulgence is the most articulate claim to power and potential of the painting as both a medium experienced visually and a medium of visuality. In their radiation of light, grey images such as *Leaves* (1966) envision the way that we see, our process of vision as it is generated by modernist painting. We begin on the surface with the pattern made in graphite, often at a distance. We then approach the painting and it becomes no more than material substance, the weave of the canvas, the paint washed over its surface, the graphite, always grey, lines drawn in an effort at representation. Inevitably we move back again—always. Unlike the experience of movement before a Rothko painting, with Martin's images, we are not pushed away. Rather, we move out of a curiosity to see what the canvas looks like from a distance. This process is exacerbated by and in grey paint. When we stand before *Leaves,* we stand before two entirely different pictures: at a distance and up close, one canvas becomes two.[29] We move again, backward, to a third distance, away from the painting. This move to a distance marks the moment when Martin's canvas melts into air, when we become enchanted by its beauty, intimacy, and gentleness. It is the moment when we perceive the shimmer on the surface. This is a beauty that is visually determined; it is not a spiritual or mythical experience. The experience is not one of complete abandon. We are hesitant before *Leaves,* always reminded that there is another perspective of the painting, the one had up close, the perspective that sits side by side with the mesmerizing luminescence experienced at a distance, and still more at different distances. Similarly, as always, there is no way inside *Leaves*; we are ultimately shut out from it, left to admire its surface, never to penetrate its depth with our eye. This bleakness of vision offered the viewer, in spite of the shimmering surface, guarantees the painting's refusal of longing of any description.

Martin's paintings are bounded, and the articulation of limits stops us from falling into abandon as can happen before Rothko's. This is, according to Krauss, because of what she calls the grid on Martin's paintings.[30] Accordingly, viewers are always drawn to the edges, studying that point where the graphite lines meet the background of white, or the white dots meet the grey background in a painting such as *White Flower* (1960). The border becomes an obsession. And so, vision is fixed in the company of Martin's paintings, but only ever temporarily. Inevitably, we move backward again, to find another place from which to see, and again, when clarity is not granted to us at this subsequent distance.

To pick up the earlier discussion of Rothko's *Untitled (Black on Gray),* the edge of modern painting creates a whole new mode of perception. Fer notes that Martin's work always draws attention to the edge, or the border, that is, the limit of the canvas.[31] There is always, without fail, a painted frame inside the wooden one that surrounds Martin's canvas. As Fer also notes, Martin's definition of the limit comes hand in hand with an infinity that is always possible. Because, although the "gridded" pattern does not continue, ad infinitum, beyond the physical limits of the painting, even though it is tightly held by the background onto which it is placed, the infinity is marked by a spiraling inward to the endless vanishing point at its center. Thus, Fer suggests that the edges of Martin's paintings entice us inward. I disagree. Before Martin's canvases there is no guarantee that certainty will be found in the middle, and indeed, we are never able to stay there. The edge, however, offers relative comfort for the viewer, if only temporarily.

The edge is the most important place on the canvas. Pollock, for example, drew our attention to the edges of the canvas by ignoring them: drips, splashes, and splatters redefined the painted field as existing beyond the canvas support.[32] Drips, splashes, and splatters refuse to be curtailed or compromised by the edge of a canvas. Contrary to the experience of the edges between color forms in Rothko's paintings, before a Martin painting we are comfortable to rest at the edges. The edge is not as confrontational because it gives us a place to be with the painting, static, in silence, fixed, and suspended between two worlds. The edge of a Martin canvas is a space that does not tease with ambiguity, as the center does with its motion between the fixity of the "grid" and the dissolution of the same into a sea of infinity. The edge can be marked by anything from unprimed canvas, through a band of acrylic defined by a hand-drawn graphite line, to the demarcation of the wooden frame beneath the canvas. The visual experience of a Martin painting is therefore best described as a physical search and ultimate location of a certainty, a fixed position at which we can rest and assume visual control of the painting. However, the only possibility of this control is found on the edge, that is, at the place where it is not possible to linger.

PHILIP GUSTON

In an example that demonstrates the teasing uncertainty of the modernist viewing subject, Guston painted a series of striking abstract works in grey in the early 1960s. In works such as *Close-Up* (1961), *Head I* (1965), and *Prospects* (1964), Guston anchors a black form in a luminous grey background, or environment. These paintings are the product of a period in his career when Guston was painting in grey as a medium to approach the unpredictable aspects of painting: light, illusion, atmosphere, the body, temperature. Guston explains in an interview:

> Simply black and white or gray and white, gray and black. I did this very deliberately, and I'll tell you why. Painting became more crucial to me. By "crucial" I mean that the only measure now was precisely to see whether it was really possible to achieve—to make this voyage, this adventure and to arrive at this release that we have been talking about without any seductive aids like color, for example. Now I've become involved in images and the location of those images, usually a single form, or a few forms. It becomes more important to me to simply locate the form.... But this form has to emerge, to grow, out of the working of it, so there's a paradox. I like a form against a background—I mean, simply empty space—but the paradox is that the form must emerge from the background. It's not just executed there. You are

> trying to bring your forces, so to speak, to converge all at once into some point.[33]

Although Guston says his works are about anything but color, when standing before them, they are all about color. They are everything grey is supposed not to be; at least, they are everything we imagine grey not to be. While these paintings are known as the artist's "dark paintings," they are, all of them, translucent, warm, filled with tension, movement, and a black, stone-like form that floats above and before the variegated grey background.[34] At one and the same time, the black sculptural form throws the unfinished grey background into relief, emphasizing its shimmering, kaleidoscopic color, creating warmth. Similarly, the black pushes the grey ground off into the yet-to-be defined recesses of the image. Unlike Giacometti's portrait heads that are framed and trapped, Guston's are set free by the lightness of their backgrounds: furthermore, our inability to grasp visually the logic of the layering and the density of the brushstrokes makes them elusive to the viewer. As his fellow modernist Morton Feldman notes when comparing Guston's paintings to music, the moving in and out of focus of the black and white and their relationship to grey, creates a taunt to the viewer who is kept busy, always in the middle of an experience of looking and comprehending the painting.[35]

Guston creates the nebulous space of viewing as a return of the process of painting that, as David Kaufmann points out, "takes the stages of its own composition as subject."[36] In a grey work such as *New Place* (1964), Guston leaves margins unpainted, layers of subtle colors (those that give the paintings their warmth) showing through, or rather, remaining after the insistent erasure Guston has effected through the application of grey. The layers of grey, black, white, the form of shapes and their shadows, the thickness of brushstrokes and traces of color, all of these elements are put into ambiguous relations in Guston's paintings to create the space of motion the viewer is invited to occupy. Grey is the color that emphasizes the space of "in-process" that is at all levels of Guston's paintings from this period. Thus, Guston's grey reduces in order to elevate his art to this specific engagement with a viewer. In grey he creates the space of an enigmatic painting, a painting the eye cannot control. This is becoming the signature vision for the subject of modernist painting.

SEAN SCULLY

Scully's passion for fences, borders, clearly defined, yet always blurred, distinctions between the building blocks that fit together like a jigsaw puzzle in his paintings, offers another mode of vision that is central to the meaning of modernist painting. Scully's works engage the viewer in several different kinds of vision. When looking at a painting such as *Coyote* (2000), optical illusions emerge. The placement of one color next to another, or one shade of grey next to another, teases the eye. What are we seeing? We are constantly being deceived. Some blocks appear to be longer or wider than others, but perhaps they are not. Is the taupe block in the upper left corner wider and shorter than its white echo in the bottom left corner? Do the three grey bands in the center have the same dimensions? The longer we look at the painting, the more difficult it becomes to stabilize the eye, and to answer these questions. The dynamics and rhythms, the relations within and between colors, bring color alive such that their shape and dimensions are constantly shifting. For example, when we stand before *Wall of Light White* (1998), apparently intended to catch the changing light at various times of the year, it is as though we are witness to the movement of the sun across the surfaces of stones.[37] The blocks are in a continual process of transformation; we can never capture them, never objectify the metamorphosis of paint and the natural world it represents. Our persistent attempts to fix the parameters and dimensions of what are, in effect, borders, walls, closed doors designed to hinder the movement of the eye, are defeated thanks to the optical illusions they create. The elusiveness of vision, the inability to control the abstract image, is underlined by the use of grey. Grey is the reflection of all uncertainty. Before abstract painting the desire to rationalize persists. Thus, face-to-face with Scully's blocks of varying shades of grey paint we experience a mobile, ambiguous perception, a visual confusion.

The search to hold on to these slippery objects never ends. Paintings such as the *Wall of Light* series and even *Raphael* create a fascinated viewer, caught up in the layer upon layer of backgrounds and foregrounds, the trafficking between matte and gloss, opacity and transparency of paint, and the speed with which it moves across and up and down the canvas. The movement, viscosity, in effect, the personality of paint are endlessly fascinating on Scully's canvases. Unlike the experience before Rothko's paintings, the fascination of a Scully painting does not take a meditative direction. Rather, the viewer engages in what can be described as a state of being in the process of connection. The eye does not lead into a transcendental reflection because it is kept so busy on the surface of the painting, always trying to scale walls, jump over barriers, and overcome obstacles, rules, limitations, both perceptually and imaginatively.

Involved in this search, tracing the vibrations of paint around the canvas, Scully's viewer is caught up in a world of mystery and, as he would have it, the "alchemy" of painting. These canvases are exhilarating; they offer hope and a sensuous desire to bask in the intense light, in the repetitive structures and rhythms of paintings in which images are reduced to a background with no figure. If Rothko offers an experience of sensuous perception that leads to a sense of falling, and Martin one of incomprehensible mystery, Scully entices us into a process of looking and trying to "figure out," as a ruse that leads to a dream-like, fascination of his paintings. The distinctions of shape and construction between Scully's blocks, Rothko's forms, Martin's lines and forms are distinctions in the technique of grey that, in turn, provide a basis for entirely different experiences of vision with the work of the three artists. Scully gives us no time and no space to reflect and meditate, because of the velocity of the surface, and the intense motion of our eye across it. Nevertheless, in their demand for a viewer in motion, the paintings' incitation of a perceptual motion that searches for meaning and logic amid brushstrokes of uncertainty, demonstrates the sociohistorical turn of modernist painting. The encouragement of an ongoing relationship with their viewer draws the paintings out of self-referentiality, always in search of a way of being together. Grey is the color most appropriate to this search because grey itself is open and looking for what might not have previously been discovered.

JASPER JOHNS

Lastly, Johns realizes a whole different mode of seeing on his canvases. Before a Johns grey canvas, our eyes are constantly in motion, on the surface. It is not a motion that resembles the experience of

Scully's blocks of paint, because the eye is not in a continual search to rationalize the representation, to control the speed of the paint. Johns's canvas is closer to an inverted cinematic vision: in the cinema our eyes remain static, while the images parade past us in imperceptible motion. Before a Johns painting, the eye of the beholder is always in motion, always looking, scanning, discovering the surface of an essentially static image. The multitextured and multifaceted Johns surface actually directs our gaze, instructs us to keep looking, as this movement will, unlike the experience of a Scully painting, ultimately reveal the hermeneutic concern of the image. Once again, the materiality of the dense Johns surface is kept central to the viewing experience.

Before the catenary encaustics, if sensuous perception is not itself experienced, we watch our eyes moving via our imagination. We cannot help but see the catenary string swaying in the wind, the parabolic movement around an imaginary axis, even though the string is firmly attached at its end points to the canvas beneath. In Johns's catenary masterpiece, *Near the Lagoon,* the falling curve appears to slide down the face of the canvas, measuring it against the stenciled lettering along the bottom. The viewer's eye follows the fall of the string, its sway in the wind. Always with a Johns canvas, the eye is directed, across and around the planar surface, exploring the movement of the stenciled letters, objects, rulers, coat hangers, pieces of newspaper, string, and so on, as they dance around the expanse of the canvas. Objects are either painted or pasted onto the canvas, submerged in the density of the grey plane of representation, building up its texture in an effort to counteract the illusion of pictorial space. The objects, unlike paint, are in the realm of the everyday; they belong to the world we inhabit. And so, we study them as we would if they were objects in the world even when they are painted, curious as to their meaning in this new environment. We look at the canvas in the same way we would around a room filled with clutter, clutter that has nevertheless consciously been collected and deliberately placed. This dynamic perceptual experience is powered by objects whose use we don't fully understand, whose forms are usurped as the material dimension of Johns's painting. All of these formal questions, the motivation to an active inverted cinematic vision, is, for Johns, rendered on and in grey. Because in grey the eye is not weighed down or halted by the distractions of color and its association, thus leaving us free to follow the objects in the hope we might comprehend them, and in turn, the painting.

For example, before *Figure 5* (1960) in the Centre Pompidou, we stand back and watch our eyes in motion. It could be any other of the number paintings (*0–9*); the response is not specific to *Figure 5* or the Centre Pompidou. There is so much to see on this busy canvas, so much to look at, it is a veritable delight for the senses. We are immediately taken with the movement of the curve of the circular lower half of the number, the convergence of its top half, the multiple lines hatched into the surface, the newsprint underneath, the violet in the bottom left. Is grey an afterthought, or is it the designated surface color? We watch and follow the stopping and starting of the brushstrokes; they are never very long, always seemingly truncated, perhaps determined by the amount of paint left on the brush. There is no attempt at continuity of grey or white or black. The fragmentation of color and brushstrokes keeps us fascinated with the surface of the canvas. We approach this canvas with the mind and the body—the tension Johns creates between the rigid structure of the figure 5, outlined by its stencil, and the arbitrary, yet sometimes stilted, strokes that surround it in a kind of chaos, appearing to be in no given order, and yet, always meticulously organized into a disciplined pattern. It's all on the surface of the image.

Johns talks about Duchamp's final unfinished *The Large Glass* (1915–23) as a " 'painting of precision and beauty of indifference'; allowing the changing focus of the eye, of the mind, to place the viewer where he is, not elsewhere."[38] The requirement of the viewer's presence before the painting is the distinction of Johns's encaustics. They never flirt with the spiritual, emotional, ethereal world of dreams, fantasies, and desire. And the specific type of vision they call on is the same: it is physical. As is the experience of standing before the number paintings, in which the subject matter is finite in meaning, the paintings always place the viewer where she is not; the eye always in motion assumes the role of "meaning." It is perceptual, physical, motor, never contemplative. And thus, to the extent that the viewer is engaged in a process of reading, looking at objects, devices, newspaper fragments attached to the surface of a Johns painting, so are these objects no more than representation, one with the illusory, fictive quality of the framed image. It is also usual for Johns to paint over the objects, in grey. Flags, targets, maps, newspapers, other colors, words, and numbers are negated, erased, rendered one with the picture plane. It is as if, in a work such as *Newspaper* (1957), or any number of other paintings, we are pulled toward the canvas to read the newsprint, only to be confronted with the grey layer of paint that, in turn, forces recognition of the processes of our own perception. We recognize we have been deceived; what we see cannot be examined.

There are moments when Johns makes us laugh, moments that have fueled discussions of the irony of Johns's paintings.[39] For example, in *Ventriloquist* (1983) at the Museum of Fine Arts, Houston, cups, bowls, jars, and other containers float through the air. Accompanying them are a Newman lithograph, a Johns flag painting, an image of Moby-Dick, the great white whale, all within the frame of the painting, which is apparently a self-portrait. The scene is watched by Johns from the bathtub, the fixtures of which jut into the bottom right corner of the painting. Is Johns really watching himself, his life, and his art? Is he the ventriloquist who manipulates images and voices from the bathtub? Or are his paintings the ventriloquist, creating sounds, not images, visual riddles that confuse our eye, and disorient our senses? Who is watching, and what is it that we, the viewer, are looking at? How are we being asked to look at painting? This painting? The paintings depicted within *Ventriloquist*? Memory is also bound up with seeing on a Johns canvas, looking at a Johns canvas. We look at *Ventriloquist* and remember having seen the painting of flags before. And yet, in reality, we have not. A single orange, black, and green flag exists as a print (*Flag*, 1969) and another from 1968 depicts the orange, black, and green flag repeated in grey and white (*Flag*, 1968). However, the double orange, black, and green flags only exist here in *Ventriloquist.* If seeing has depth, it is misconceived in memory, the picture having no relationship to reality, or any other picture we may have seen in that reality. Yet again, it is deliberately designed to deceive the eye of the viewer.

On this canvas, grey is accentuated through its relationship with and between other colors as the relationship between different realities. Johns's painting of flags within *Ventriloquist* is in full color, the Newman zip image is a reproduction, the wicker stand, vase, and bath fixtures appear to be in color, the other objects floating through the hinged left-hand side of the painting are veiled behind grey streaks. Where does one plane of the image begin and the other end? What is the significance of the grey in relation to other colors? All of these questions are left unresolved by Johns, creating an ambiguity that gives visual and hermeneutic complexity to the painting. It is an ambiguity that becomes further complicated by grey, because grey unsettles the relationship between colors, confusing the hierarchy of which is the ground and which the figure. Grey is the veil that obscures clarity in *Ventriloquist.*

Land's End (1964) in San Francisco Museum of Modern Art offers a different experience of looking. Initially, the eye is caught up in the dizzying speed of the rotating disc, and simultaneously, tempted to join the upward-reaching hand in whatever it grasps for, the same hand we have seen in other paintings, such as *Periscope (Hart Crane)* (1963). In *Periscope,* however, the hand reaches into the painting as if to stop the spinning disc in the upper right corner; in *Land's End* it reaches upward, thereby ensuring that the disc's speed is dizzying, overwhelming, and needs to be halted if we are to concentrate on the painting. Then the dilemma begins: we want to respect *Land's End* and to follow the arrow down to the wall beneath the canvas, to move as it suggests. Our eyes are all over the place.

In the overload of visual stimuli, when standing before this Johns encaustic, we see the peculiar vision as it is represented through modernist abstract art. Johns's very medium is a medium of tactility and hapticality. He uses encaustic because with it he can mold and massage, manipulate it, push it around the canvas, bringing precision to the chaos that will confront the viewer's eyes. The encaustics are thus sensuous in a different way: they are sculptural, they motion toward the limitations of paint on a canvas, they create a dexterous eye and the need for a hand to reach into the depths of what Johns has to say, to slow it down and to understand it. The objects and corresponding subject matter can be touched, felt, seen, and true to Johns often lighthearted images, they are never mysterious, or of another world. Grey itself becomes tactile in a work such as *Near the Lagoon* when the color is used to direct visual attention away from paint toward movement of the catenary string as it sways on the canvas.

Of course, Johns's paintings do not end with the relationship between the eye, the paint on the canvas, and the objects depicted and placed thereon. It's not simply a relationship of physical presence, perception, and tactility. Especially when this relationship is explored in grey. Something magical happens in this interaction—in the exploration of color as light, color as opacity, impenetrability. I examine this magic later, but for the moment, it is important to underline that in these paintings there is no invitation to fall into this discovery, to become the wanderer and the wonderer. Johns's interest is consistently in the representation of the three-dimensional world, in which painting is a three-dimensional object, before which the viewer experiences her own three-dimensional body. The mind is kept occupied, preoccupied to ensure that we experience the body and the self as active and in motion, as we negotiate the physicality of the painting. We stand on the tips of our toes to see the upper reaches of the canvas, and we bend and turn to read the stencils in the bottom corners. For example, the body must be contorted to follow the U that falls off the canvas in *Land's End.* Or as we watch the grey letters of BLUE get pushed off by their lighter-shaded siblings in *Periscope (Hart Crane).* The physicality of the painting draws attention to our own senses, our own physicality as the eyes and body are summoned to the vitality of the canvas.

Critics often label Johns an intellectual artist, or an artist who produces paintings that engage us on an intellectual at the exclusion of the emotional level.[40] However, as I demonstrate, they are not simply intellectual: Johns's encaustic canvases capture the corporeality of vision.[41] Indeed, this makes Johns's grey encaustics radical for their time. The presence of the body on the canvas, and our own experiences of our bodies through a physical perception, together approach the kind of tactile visuality that claims a new definition of painting. At the time Johns paints these pictures, in the 1960s and 1970s, even the 1980s and 1990s, a tactile vision had only previously been talked about in relationship to the cinema. It is from the perspective of forty years and an understanding of the regimes of vision enabled by early cinema in particular that it is possible to give language to the visuality generated by Johns's encaustics. They offer a haptic visuality.[42] Nevertheless, with or without the language to describe it, Johns's engagement with the viewer's visual perception is exciting and breaks new ground in its time.

The corporealization of vision elicited by a Johns grey encaustic painting takes another form, in addition to the animation of the eye across the surface. In *Painting Bitten by a Man* we see the triumph of the performance and process of "painting" where paint is no longer the subject of a brush, but of a body. Johns's body and the (aggressive) traces it leaves take the place of the reality before the canvas that a different painting might represent. In *Painting Bitten by a Man* we see, smell, taste, and touch the one-time presence of Johns's body in action. Our sensuous experience of Johns biting the canvas thus corporealizes the process of looking at what is, effectively, a corporealized image, a painting bitten by a man. The painting thus poses challenges to our senses, invites us to see with our taste buds, to smell the wax we see with our eyes, to touch the painting as a desecrated object, if only in our minds. Here, vision is expanded to involve multiple senses and physical responses.

Vision and visuality as they are played out across Johns's paintings can be encapsulated by the experience itself, to create a viewing process that has never been so variegated as it is in grey paint. Vision is uncomfortable, tantalizing, laced with desire, confusion, and sometimes clarity. It is the territory of the hands, the nose, the taste buds. That said, whether we fall into a Rothko or our eyes dash around the canvas of a Johns painting, if we are curtailed and frustrated by a Scully or rest quietly in defeat before an Agnes Martin painting, all of these experiences begin with that of visual perception. Which isn't to say that these works exhibit some kind of shameless iconophilia. On the contrary, their deep ambivalence toward visual perception as well as visual experience, expressed through an embrace of all the other senses as well as the imagination, can only instill an uncertainty in the spectator who cautiously, yet expectantly, wants to form a connection to the paintings. In grey, the paintings accentuate this ambivalence, refusing a sense of closure, denying full access to their revelations. This process is perhaps best encapsulated by Johns's curtains, window frames, drawers, objects that open out into space, but are nevertheless opaque and lead nowhere. All of their troubled insights, their hazy perspectives on painting and its materials consciously depart from traditional modes of representation and perspective. As always, grey allows them to strip away all distractions and focus solely on the level at which they engage their viewer. In short, if only when the viewer makes meaning, these paintings in grey take on a historical significance outside of their frame.

In the Interstice: Painting and Other Media

Once again, it is in Rauschenberg's distinctive art that we see the lines between painting and other media, painting and other art forms, to use Michael Fried's word, "corroded."[43] In Rauschenberg's Combines, the distinctions between painting and drawing, painting and collage, painting and sculpture, are dissolved.[44] While artists working in grey paint are not overtly concerned to rupture the two-dimensional flat surface of the painted canvas, and unlike Rauschenberg, they do not always collapse the boundaries between art forms, they do expose and explore this interstice.[45] Even though grey paintings retain their status as paintings, they still radicalize the medium of painting, pushing it beyond its boundaries, from within the four sides of the frame. By extension, they witness the possibility of painting to continue, at a historical moment in the mid-twentieth century, when painting apparently no longer has anything left to do. I shall argue that this gesture of defiance gives the grey paintings discussed a cultural and historical charge.

Even in what have become known as his "device" paintings, Johns stays firmly within the four sides of the frame. While Rauschenberg pushes painting into the realm of sculpture, the constraints of the canvas remain central to Johns's work. Johns still paints. Even when objects, letters, devices transgress the two dimensions of the painted canvas, the end product is always a painting. What about the sculptures in grey, the paint tins, the flashlights, the cast of his own face, all of which are more than found objects and clearly in relationship with representations of the same in his paintings? When he is working in other art forms, most notably with Sculp-metal because it is consciously three-dimensional, consciously sculptural, Johns creates objects as sculptures, not paintings. Of course, there is an analogy, a relationship that is always present, a relationship between painting and cast iron, painting and objects in the world. The thick, glutinous encaustic paint on a canvas is also itself a form of sculpture, and the hand-made, artisanal, and sensuous objects are likewise erotic and filled with an awkward desire. Similarly, the objects that Johns sculpts over have appeared before, as found objects, attached to his canvases. *Souvenir* (1962) has a flashlight attached to the right-hand side of the canvas, a mirror to the top such that it will reflect the light when turned on and illuminate the "souvenir" of the painting's title. We understand the souvenir to be a plate on which Johns's own face is photographically reproduced. Around the edges of the plate, he has stenciled the three words "blue," "red," "yellow," again in grey. In this and other works, across art forms and different media, Johns explores similar questions, about the body, about his place in the artwork through the placement of his portrait, about the relationship of art to the everyday through attachment of household objects, to art history through obvious references to Duchamp's readymades. Nevertheless, in spite of the attachment of objects that clearly carry memories of the personal and historical past, the work remains within the framed canvas. They are objects attached to a painted canvas. For this reason, even though it incorporates different forms and media, painting and sculpture remain identifiable and distinct in Johns's oeuvre. And yet, as is the case with Richter, when Johns explores other media or art forms, they are always vehicles for the exploration of painting.

CY TWOMBLY

In paintings that incorporate other media, while always remaining on the canvas and within the frame, Twombly's grey works are illustrative of the use of a grey interstice to push painting beyond its existing limits in a manner different from Johns's. Twombly's cataloger Bastian argues that the grey-ground paintings in particular are scientific or mathematical treatises, that they shift from paintings with white scrawls to mathematical formulas on a so-called blackboard. Bastian sees the two *Treatise on the Veil* (Plates 12 and 13) paintings as Twombly's reference to the "philosophical hyperbole of gradations of the void wherein night, silence and isolation are as exquisitely calibrated as an algebraic formula."[46] This mention of algebraic formula and calibrations references the numbers, measurements, and calculations along the horizon line that segments both paintings. Bastian may be correct, but he also suggests that the paintings envision a mathematical precision. There may be a *quest* for precision and regulation, but there is no precision on Twombly's canvases. Indeed, the numbers and markings appear to be completely random. At least their logic is not immediately obvious. Such is the consistency with the works that come before and after both the 1968 and the 1970 versions of *Treatise on the Veil*. In spite of the pursuit of logic and meaning across the surface of almost every one of Twombly's works, the goal is never reached. The markings in "chalk" continue the theme of other works when they relate the scratchings, sketchings, and note taking, the thinking mind in process, as they are realized in different colors on white canvases, not only grey. Science and painting, the "blackboard" as ground and the canvas might come together, but they also remain distinct. As I argue in chapter 3, the white markings are in dynamic interaction with the grey ground, an interaction that is the single medium of painting in *Treatise on the Veil* and *Treatise on the Veil (Second Version)*. And still, the two media create the uncertainty of representation in Twombly's universe.

The difference of the two *Treatise on the Veil* canvases is the suggestion of order and rationalization through measurement. But this is an illusion. This is Twombly's representation of what is ultimately inexpressible and ineffable, as it is represented in his lifelong search for a language with which to make sense of the world. As I have suggested, painting and writing are placed in a dynamic struggle on Twombly's canvases, their worth measured against each other as they both refute the possibility of representing the essence of the world. On Twombly's canvases, painting and writing, sketching and scribbling are always in conflict. In this conflict lies the definition of painting, as it does battle with another medium. It is, in turn, important that writing and painting remain distinct for this conflict to remain in suspension, for painting to continue the search, for painting to have an identity.

Twombly's commentators and critics are always confident in their claim that these works pursue scientific rationality.[47] In the Museum für Moderne Kunst, Frankfurt, Twombly's 1966 triptych *Problem I, II, III* is illustrative of the problem with this thesis about rationality. It is true what critics say about these three identically sized paintings: they are about line, its creation of volume, the science of geometry, and the working through of mathematical questions on a grey canvas. The three drawn trapezoids are of different shapes, entirely different in their composition. What is most striking about the triptych is the irresolvable contradictions of what it represents. Unlike the conventional triptych—a structured and very precise form of presentation—*Problem I, II, III* is not to be read as a central panel with two side panels. Rather, like drawings in a book or mathematical problems, we "read" the three panels from left to right. This re-formation of the triptych is typical of Twombly. Always, when his works are in a series, they read like a narrative or, as others have remarked, poems.[48] And at the very same time that the second panel is a transformation of the first and the third a transformation of the second, we recognize that this cannot be so. The narrative is impossible. Like poetry. It is as though the second trapezoid erases the lines of the first to create a more complete, a bigger form, and the frenetic erasures of the third indicate the frustrations and tensions of not being able to arrive at the perfectly balanced form that, seen together, they indicate was the goal of the triptych. Similarly, it is almost impossible to focus on the trapezoid shape, its progression from *Problem I* to *II*, and on to *III*. Because in their characteristic state of being "under erasure," the figures are so fragile, and every line so fleeting, that the line and its affect are wiped away on and by grey. It is this so-called wiping away that captivates the viewer's attention. Ultimately, as is always the case with Twombly's paintings, the mathematics and scientific reason are overwhelmed by the impossibility of the same. On a grey canvas, the line is always under erasure. Moreover, the undererasure by and on grey becomes the subject of the *Problem I, II, III* triptych.

The search for a mathematical formula as the pursuit of abstract painting, of course, has a history. It is the project of early modernist abstraction: Malevich, El Lissitzky, Mondrian, and Robert Delauney all believed in the equation of scientific truth and abstract painting; hence the geometry of the shapes that cover their canvases. And for all of these artists, color led to these truths. For Twombly, however, the truth is more ambiguous; it is not scientific. Scientific rationality might be the goal, but the truth is grey. Painting has none of the alliances with science that were imagined at the beginning of the twentieth century. And Twombly convinces us of this through the enactment of the struggle between line and form, color as abstraction and figuration, the expressions of the soul and the reality of language that are the ongoing concern of those who write about art and aesthetics.[49] Line on Twombly's canvas is, as Bastian remarks, often devoted to organization and rationalization, the intrusion of the world of reality onto the spiritual terrain of the painted canvas. Perhaps Johns is doing the same in the catenary works. Then the string left swaying on the surface of images such as *Bridge* (1997) and *Near the Lagoon* are not extensions of the canvas, as Rondeau claims, but rather, they are the language of reality, a reality that struggles against the "monochrome" of grey.[50]

If we approach Twombly's paintings from a different perspective, beginning with the grey ground, there is much more than a struggle between science and writing taking place on their surface. Always, when in the company of Twombly's grey canvases, photography and the cinema are imminent. *Treatise on the Veil* and *Treatise on the Veil (Second Version)* illustrate how the grey-ground works do more than echo the forms and rhythms of the cinematic as it is envisioned in modernist painting. In their continued pursuit of Twombly's specific process of painting, his belief in painting as a form of being, a presence, and with it his role, the one who realizes that presence, the twin works are imbued with the forms, meanings, and medium specifics of the photograph and the cinema themselves.[51] If the other small- and large-scale grey-ground works as I discuss them are stages for the performance of an interaction between the variegated palette of greys and the obsessive, repeated forms of white writing, the two *Treatise on the Veil* works stage the engagement between painting, photography, and the cinematic. For Twombly, the disintegration, the ultimate search to solve the problem of painting, to find what he calls an essence in and of painting, is played out in the traces of his own process of thinking in these two works. Once again, the search takes place in the struggle between surface and ground, between grey and white line, across the repetitions of the two paintings.

First, it must be noted that *Treatise on the Veil* and *Treatise on the Veil (Second Version)* have been most intelligently analyzed for their references to music, another medium that everywhere influences the rhythmical and tonal qualities of Twombly's paintings. The two paintings are said to be inspired by Pierre Henry's 1951–53 French *musique concrète* composition: *The Veil of Orpheus.*[52] Henry's recording is iconoclastic: a recording of electronic sounds, voices for magnetic tape. Originally belonging to the ballet, *Orpheus 53, Treatise on the Veil* must, somehow be about Orpheus's descent into hell. It might also refer, as the catalog for Tate Modern's 2008 retrospective *Cycles and Seasons* suggests, to the lifting of the veil of Eurydice, or to the tearing of Orpheus to pieces.[53] Albeit from a different perspective to the ballet narrative, these paintings might be understood as caught in the middle of violent acts.

Twombly is said to have been struck by the musical fluidity and temporal duration of Henry's piece. Nicholas Serota has described the two paintings' broad horizontal extension with inscribed mathematical measurements as akin to a musical score, the "representation of a timeline without time."[54] This explanation corresponds to another: the markings tear the grey fabric of the veil, the fabric of the canvas, and thus, the time of cause-and-effect narrative. Seen through this lens, grey is the subject, the fabric, the fluid movement, while the white lines search for rationalization across the grey subject. In addition, Twombly's use of the figure of the veil, if only by allusion, might be understood as the return of one of the most common uses of grey paint since medieval times.[55] In particular, it might refer to the fabrics, cloths, veils, and linens discussed in chapter 2 that have been meticulously studied by painters since the Middle Ages.[56] Surely, therefore, the power of variegated grey paint in *Treatise on the Veil* and *Treatise on the Veil (Second Version)* has a place in the history of art's long preoccupation with the veil.

Accordingly, Twombly continues to interrogate painting and what is painting, especially because in *Treatise on the Veil* and *Treatise on the Veil (Second Version)*, the material on which and with which the work is executed becomes indistinguishable. Twombly's paintings also create an abstract and poetic form, just as draperies and fabrics did in the Renaissance, draperies and fabrics that assumed the role as subject of the image, rather than defining the figure they covered. When the grey abstract surface becomes the subject of painting, the push to abstraction is complete. Nevertheless, the fabrics, folds, breaks, textures of Twombly's grey in *Treatise on the Veil I* and *Treatise on the Veil (Second Version)* are preoccupied with movements of a different kind: they replicate the movements, undulations, cessations, and restartings in the narrative that is the treatise of the title. Twombly's two paintings might, accordingly, be anchored by centuries of painting in grey. And yet, they also extend this history: they realize the push toward abstraction begun in the studies of fabrics and linens centuries ago, as well as imagine a whole new subject matter.

To reiterate, perhaps the most fertile of the relationships played out across the six panels of each instance of *Treatise on the Veil* is that of photography and cinema. Bastian writes that Twombly told him *Treatise on the Veil* and *Treatise on the Veil (Second Version)* were inspired by a Muybridge photograph given to Twombly by Rauschenberg.[57] The photograph apparently depicts a veiled bride passing before a train, an object in motion. Bastian does not elaborate on the influence of Muybridge's photograph on the paintings, and it's difficult to recognize this story in the images themselves. Moreover, there is no apparent image of a veiled bride crossing in front of a train in Muybridge's oeuvre. Therefore, rather than seeing a specific Muybridge photograph in the two paintings, there is another of Muybridge's images that enables us to see a relationship to photography more broadly in Twombly's grey paintings.

Twombly was no stranger to photography. Ironically, his photographs are closer to paintings, exploring and discovering, not reproducing, the world he sees.[58] The photographs are always blurred, as if in the ultimate gesture of negation: the objectivity of the medium is questioned. The blur is also a distancing device, an insurance against the viewer's desire to become immersed in the photograph. In Twombly's photographs, it is as though photography is another medium through which to explore painting's eternal search for a visual language to understand, to reiterate nature, or at least to attempt such a vision. Seen in this way, these photographs tell more about painting than about photography. And for Twombly, painting is grey, always in motion, always in a search of definition.

Muybridge, in contradistinction, used photography as a scientific tool, to make sense of the world, for its truth and authentic representation of the world. Thus, in an image, or series of images, of which he made countless examples, the movement of animals and people are frozen in time through the use of stop-motion photography. Muybridge discovered that, for example, when a horse runs, there is a point in the sequence at which all four hooves leave the ground at the same time. Muybridge is a scientist who uses a camera as a scientific tool. And through the photographic camera's ability to see with a precision not available to the naked human eye, Muybridge becomes the physiologist who develops an understanding of perception. For Muybridge, stop-motion photography is always a scientific pursuit, an attempt to document and to create new forms of vision.[59]

Given Twombly's apparent belief in the inability of painting and representation to arrive at an end point, to realize itself fully, even in spite of its innate completion and perfection, it is unlikely he would attach importance to the truth of photography, to its scientific pursuit of absolute knowledge. Given the blurring and abstraction of his own photographs, their reduction to a play of light and shadow on a nonexistent surface, it seems unlikely that Twombly would turn to Muybridge in the belief that photography might articulate a precision that painting cannot. This is pure speculation, however, it is a speculation that I evidence in the role of representation, its relationship to truth, to absolutes, to other media on Twombly's canvases. Accordingly, it's neither an individual photograph nor photography per se that interests Twombly, but the relationship between painting and photography. And of course, grey is the only color to imagine the space between the two.

The relationship between painting in grey and photography, particularly, photography of Muybridge's era, is more convincing if Twombly's sibling *Treatise on the Veil* paintings are placed in conversation with a different set of Muybridge images: the photographs of Bridal Veil Falls in the Yosemite Valley in California. Muybridge photographed Bridal Veil in 1872, on a number of occasions, at different times of the year, different times of day, from different places. There is no agreement on how many times he photographed Bridal Veil, but he published hundreds of examples.[60] The most readily available and often reproduced of these is *Bridal Veil #6.*[61] Curiously, Twombly's two *Treatise on the Veil* paintings each comprise six linked panels. The serial placement of six still images (or frames) might be seen to mimic the illusion of moving images for which Muybridge is better known. Or perhaps Twombly's six frames with the horizontal line striating them one-third of the way up the canvas mimic the movement of the waterfall from which Muybridge takes the title of his photographs.

At the same time, Twombly's two *Treatise on the Veil* paintings are contrary to Muybridge's photographs, particularly, his representation of motion, change, and the passing of time. The six static Twombly panels are, in fact, discrete canvases marking a physical rift, a discontinuity that severs the continuity of the wax crayon made to look like a chalk horizon line, a line that, in turn, dissects shifting and multifarious grey fields. The five seams in the treatises remind of the distinction of painting as static and the kineticism that Muybridge made it his life's work to capture on film. In addition, the Yosemite Valley Bridal Veil is characterized by its verticality. The granite walls of the soaring rock faces are vertical, thereby making the natural formation and the waterfall, vertical. This verticality, which Muybridge captures in a number of the photographs, is both replicated in Twombly's six juxtaposed panels and canceled out by the horizontal chalk line that awkwardly dissects them. There is motion across each work, between the two, and yet there is a stasis reinforced by their two-dimensionality. The relationship is one of contradiction; it is grey.

It is said that a unique feature of Bridal Veil Falls, what draws Muybridge back again and again, is the extraordinary effect of the light on the geological formation. On the north side, the granite is yellow, and on the south, it is grey. Richard Lehman, another leading Twombly scholar, claims the grey of Twombly's monumental paintings is a representation of the screens against which Muybridge photographed his subjects in motion. This could well be the case, but there is another possible interpretation: Twombly's varying, moving greys, the washes and vibrations of grey, represent the changing face of the mountain as the sun moves across the Yosemite Valley in the course of a day. The two radically different greys of the respective *Treatise on the Veil* paintings are notable in this context: the dark, dense green-grey of the 1968 version are in direct contrast and conversation with the luminescent, light- and air-filled greys of the 1970 version. The two works, facing each other at Tate Modern's exhibition in 2008, are like night and day, darkness and light, the natural cycles of day. As the sun moves across the Yosemite Valley, as day passes into night, Bridal Veil also changes its tone, temperature, and density when it is captured in Muybridge's photographs. This reading of the two paintings makes sense within Twombly's larger fascination with the representation of the unfathomable, sublime, and mammoth natural formation, a formation that resists rationalization (and eventual representation).[62]

When the two *Treatise on the Veil* works came face-to-face for the first time at Tate Modern, the communication between painting and nature, painting and photography, was played out in the space between the two canvases, in the space of the room. Like Muybridge's still photographs, Twombly's paintings never make meaning on their own. Like Muybridge's, Twombly's search within the unsurpassable beauty of nature is carried by means of a repetition of images, a strategy he borrows from the technologically reproducible image in the middle of the nineteenth century. Twombly always paints in series and cycles, and with the *Treatise on the Veil* paintings there are two: they are a repetition. As if to establish a dialogue with Muybridge, Twombly journeys into the wilderness of nature and has no expectations about its possible taming, its rationalization. He is compelled to repeat, to re-present, to reproduce as if in a quest to find a definitive viewing position for an ultimately ungraspable natural phenomenon. The search must continue, but ultimately the destination will never be reached because like nature, the essence of painting is contained within itself, removed from its viewer. The same might be said of the wondrous and sublime geological formations in the Yosemite Valley, and the repeated attempts to "capture" their magnificence, to understand their logic in 1872.[63] And so, nature, photography, grey painting are all repeating and mirroring each other in Twombly's articulation of the process of painting across the two *Treatise of the Veil* paintings.[64]

It is important here to note that these paintings' reference to the cinema or a so-called cinematic form and meaning does not equate with a claim that the paintings should be seen as cinematic. Painting is static; the cinema is in motion. And yet, paintings such as Twombly's are executed in the twentieth century, the century of the cinema. They also involve motion, somewhere in their production of meaning. The cinema, whose silent images were once cast in grey, is the screen, so to speak, against which all of the paintings are conceived, imagined, and realized. As the grey color of the oils and synthetic paints is made possible by the turn of the twentieth century, so is the conversation with the cinema that takes place through the narrative progression and movement through time, the flow of line in conflict with the fracture of those lines in Twombly's works on grey canvas from the late 1960s and early 1970s.

As Kirk Varnedoe points out, Twombly's fascination for flowing, yet always agitated, lateral movement recalls the decomposition of form in motion explored by Italian futurists such as Giacomo Balla.[65] We see this in works such as *Cold Stream* (1966), with its endless horizontally spiraling lines in motion laterally across the canvas. This and other paintings echo cinematic motion without character or narrative development, and there is none of the emotional engagement that was the province of the cinema. The endless white, rolling loops have an energy and a purpose driven by a force much greater than the artist whose hand drives the inscriptions. They are powered by an energy that is surely monotonous, mechanical. The moving image, the photographic image in motion like the works of Italian futurism, are being driven, if not literally, then influentially, by the cinema. Indeed, the removal of emotion, the cool, self-conscious removal of a psychic identity, the push toward meaninglessness, are all reinforced—reflected and absorbed—in and by grey paint.

Painting in Struggle at the Interface with the Media

I have shown how the paintings of Johns and Twombly, for example, rest resolutely within the frame of painting. They are also in the service of validating and questioning the work of paint on a canvas, and simultaneously, exploring what it means to paint in a postwar, image-saturated consumer culture. Though the temptation might be to claim they are cut off from the world that produces them, to see them as referring only to themselves and, at best, the history of painting, is a limiting vision. Their form, concerns, and effect on the viewer make them all about the media that surround them as well: particularly, they engage in a discourse on the overwhelming, overbearing presence of the cinema and the mass media in the twentieth century. And like the cinema that hovers over and around their realization, when these paintings are in grey they find their purest, most painterly vision. It is as though the assertion of the importance of painting in a historical era when painting is supposedly no longer possible, is itself a struggle against the powers that be.

ANDY WARHOL

Perhaps more than any other postwar American artist, Warhol used painting (and other media) to engage with the political world in which art is made. In obvious and often quoted examples, the black figures against a silver background in Warhol's screen-printed versions of Elvis, electric chairs, car crashes, race riots, and Chairman Mao have everything to do with the world beyond the frame, an engagement with social or cultural, even reified politics.[66] We will also remember the storm created by Warhol, the Factory, and the plethora of works produced there in the 1960s, a radical project that redefined art, film, advertising, photography, and their place in the world. Warhol's screen prints are representational; they are a long way from Twombly's scrawls on grey, Rothko's painted forms, even Johns's painted poems about daily life. Nevertheless, Warhol, and later artists such as Mark Tansey continued the search, after modernism, for a "democratic" art in grey painting. Warhol, of all the postwar artists, is the one who brings the politics of content together with the intermedia created by references to the popular press on grey canvases. If Johns takes the project by Manet into the twentieth century, Warhol does the same to Picasso's in the postwar period.

Warhol's print on paper *Birmingham Race Riot* (1964) is a small print made from a photograph by Charles Moore published in *Life* magazine. Warhol, like Johns, uses grey as a way to challenge the viewer's numbness to the representation of death and disaster as it is splattered across the contemporary press. *Birmingham Race Riot* is designed to have us come away and see the world differently, to shock us with its unreadable violence. Warhol was seriously interested in color, the significance of color, its metaphorical and iconographical use. He printed the original *Birmingham Race Riot* in three colors: red, white, and blue. In the "white" version, which is in fact grey, on display in the Menil Collection, Warhol charges the image with a political responsibility through its appropriation from the press. The absence of any enhancement of the color, the refusal to introduce the glaring colors of sensationalism, give the painting a realism that makes it more frightening. Grey connects it directly and unmistakably to the printed press at the time, as well as with television. In 1964, television enjoyed its most provocative effects in the United States.[67] Its elements come together to convince viewers of the realities of what we know to be the injustice that swept the American south especially at that time. The policeman in the front of Warhol's image, his baton ready to strike, the dog rearing on the right-hand side as the man whose arm he will ravage tries to break away, the space given to the law officers and their dominance over the black men in the image, make for a devastating reality. Grey might be open minded and open ended, here used by Warhol to demonstrate from the margins, but it is also resolute in its indictment of the violent culture of racism.

Another image, *Crowd* (1963), captures the level of outrage in the death-and-disaster prints from the early 1960s. *Crowd* is significantly painted in 1963 and although the image does not explicitly reference the crowds of protest and rallies against racial injustice, the date does. *Crowd* is presented as an optical illusion. From a distance, at first glance, *Crowd* looks like it is one painting. But then as we move closer and study it, the image transforms into a filmic image—in the image we see the wear and tear on a filmstrip that has been run through the projector too many times—or the blackening of a screen-printed image, again, an image that has been printed on multiple occasions. And we see that *Crowd* is four separate frames, four repetitions of the same image, each with a different degree of "wear and tear." Recognizing that it is four images, we are drawn to decipher the order in which the four images were printed—but of course this is impossible. That is the point, the enigma of reproduction and appropriation, its original, its order, the relay of signification cut short by the various literal and metaphorical frames that enable it to be published, exhibited, seen.

Warhol's commentary on the reproduction of media, the multiplicity of media, and the appropriation of images from one medium to another is integrated into the cultural politics of America in the 1960s. For it is in the media that crimes are committed, it is in the media that lives are ravaged and voices are silenced, and it is in the media that these events become politically charged. After Warhol, such claims have become commonplace, obvious, even trite. But we must remember that in the 1960s, Warhol was radical and laid out many challenges to the art world establishment.

Warhol's screen prints and paintings might seem out of place here in a book motivated by the sensuousness of paint, particularly in its most abstract realizations. It is true that Warhol's attention to color and surface was often in the production of a lack of substance and depth, but up close, in person, today Warhol's images are beautiful, sensuous, steeped in history. Moreover, even as they approach abstraction in their repetition of the processes of mechanical production, they are figurative. However, in spite of their sensuousness, the surfaces are empty, an emptiness that is the very point of Warhol's painted work: endless repetition has worn down the painted surface to no more than the sheen of reproduction.[68] Lastly, it must be said that Warhol didn't paint a lot in grey, but nevertheless, those works he did execute in grey, and in particular, the screen prints, are among the most politically charged paintings of the postwar period. They encompass all of the concerns explored elsewhere in grey by other artists. In addition, Warhol's grey works add a new dimension to grey painting when they extend Picasso's discourse to develop a unique relationship to the printed press, a medium that was at the center of the politics of the public sphere in the 1960s and 1970s.

Today, there are other painters who use grey to explore related ends. Chuck Close is an obvious example, with his portraits that occupy the interstice of photography and painting. There they examine the influence of the one on the other in the interests of capturing the impossible division between reality and illusion. Nevertheless, I would argue that the themes and concerns of grey in the work of an artist such as Close are addressed by the abstract paintings of Johns, Twombly, and Warhol. All the ways grey is used to push the problems of painting to the fore of critical concern in postwar America are set in motion by these artists. Therefore, rather than reiterating how the same themes and concerns are explored by other painters—albeit in different ways—I shall reflect on another dimension of painting at the end of the twentieth century: how the relationship to everyday objects engages with the politics that surrounds them.

Political in Grey

In what might be the most political gesture of postwar American grey painting, Johns extends the canvas into the everyday world in unique ways. I discussed earlier in this chapter how hands reach in from the side of the frame and body fragments fall off the canvas. But even more powerful is when the United States is transposed to a chaotic *Map* (1960) in which brushstrokes confound the geography of the country and its relationship to the Atlantic Ocean. When the borders of the United States bleed into the ocean, or the *New York Times* can be seen underneath a brushstroke, something more than an uncertain national identity is brought to the fore. Johns elevates the level of critique of American icons, thus identity, by painting flags and maps and pasting press clippings from the *New York Times.* Johns's extension or continuation of the canvas to include these icons is an extension of his attachment of familiar household objects to the canvas.[69] All of them challenge the relationship of painting to the world on many different levels, but the intensity is increased when those objects are flags, maps, or the printed press.

Johns's encaustics are arguably the most radical grey paintings of postwar American art because of their unrelenting materiality. He critiques representation through an iconoclasm that allows for little confidence in the representation of the external world, and the impossibility of truth in the displacement of that world onto the canvas. In the conventional conception of art in the service of spiritual contemplation, the materiality of painting is left behind, or becomes transcended. Johns, however, does something different. Where Duchamp made things in the world into artworks by placing them in the context of the museum, Johns makes artworks into things. Johns's paintings are not only determined by the material forces of everyday life, they are also, in many ways, the ultimate iconoclastic gesture because of his insistence on their objectness, their status as things. This, while still being paintings.

Johns's re-presentation over and over and over again of the American flag and the map of the United States are his most political statements. As Moira Roth points out, in the very same years as Senator Joseph McCarthy's sensational pursuit of supposedly unpatriotic political opponents, Johns's decision to paint the American flag repeatedly cannot be accidental.[70] Like Warhol's reproduction and representation of images from the newspaper, Johns's encaustic, fragmented flags are not involved in reified politics, but they are, by default, commenting on American beliefs during the Cold War. Two paintings such as *Grey Flag* (1957) or *Two Flags* (1959) may not be a painting over of a familiar red, white, and blue American flag, but the use of grey encaustic and acrylic is, as Roth asserts, a strategy that plays with the viewer's expectations and perception, as well as engages discourses of concealment, secrecy, deception, and critique. Grey cannot, in these images, be dismissed as a natural or a neutral color. Grey challenges the political context in which these paintings are created.[71] Simply, in this instance, grey is not the color of the object in dispute in the world. To make the American flag in grey is thus an act of counterpatriotism.

While some critics want to argue that Johns's interest is in the surface of the painting only, in the veil that is thrown over the colors and contents underneath, I want to keep alive the prominence of newspapers, for example, in his work, if for no other reason than the fact that they are always strategically made visible, they are never fully concealed. The newspaper is everywhere the ground and abstraction of Johns's grey, even the colored paintings. The newspaper does not lead to the truth, ever. Because it is painted over, screwed up (*4 the News,* 1962), and made into a collage on the surface, there is little trust in the newspaper. The newspaper is dipped into molten, pigmented wax, and then attached to the surface, a technique Johns adapted from Rauschenberg.[72] In a work such as *Newspaper*, it is impossible to decide which is the artwork, which the primary element: is it the double page of the newspaper that is the not-fully concealed ground, or the statement announced by the thick, short, grey-and-white encaustic that follows the shape and motion of the pages underneath? Here, art is the everyday ephemeral object, and simultaneously, a disposable everyday object that is typically endowed with immense power, is transformed in a perceptual game with paint. In an era when art apparently had a tenuous relationship with politics, it's difficult to see Johns's constant use of newspaper, mixed together with grey paint, as a politically neutral statement.

Yau claims that the inclusion of the newspaper is in keeping with Johns's placement of his work in narratives of time. The newspapers are old, discolored, their text no longer relevant to the present moment of the painting or its viewing.[73] We might add that the newspapers adhered to Johns's canvas, even if they reported the most up-to-date events, are not to be taken as reflecting truth or reality in the first place. If Warhol repeats the sensational images of the press in his silk screens, Johns takes the text, magnifies it, borrows its typeface, and reduces the text to a pictorial element on the surface. By the time Johns has finished with this narrative of appropriation and manipulation, the newspaper is hardly a reliable source for news. When the masthead of the *New York Post* from a Friday in October is placed sideways, falling off the canvas of *Map* in 1963, we are not led to believe that there is anything worth reading in this newspaper. And yet, it has become an integral component of Johns's painting, which, thanks to its ambivalence and Johns's characteristic materiality, is something at which we look. Thus, Johns further complicates his act of disrespect to the nation shown through a map in which various states fall into the Atlantic Ocean, when he layers it over a newspaper that is seen but does not allow reading or comprehension of what it says.

The Postmodern Critique of Modernism

I close this chapter with a discussion of the grey paintings of Mark Tansey, an artist whose work is at the cutting edge of contemporary painting's use of satire and humor to explore the philosophy of picture making in the 1980s. Tansey belongs to a generation of Americans that returns painting to representation, but whose images can be as intellectually abstract and aesthetically elusive as any that come before, or are contemporary with, them. Tansey's work both encapsulates much of what has been seen in grey in earlier decades through critiquing it and opens up the use of grey painting to new questions and new possibilities. Tansey's painting amounts to a searing critique of the way that modernist painting has been written about, how it is displayed, bought, sold, and most obviously, how it is painted. Tansey's works might be understood as the paradoxical result of, as well as a brilliant riposte to, the debate about American abstract painting at the end of the twentieth century. Tansey uses grey paint as a way to challenge the limits of modernist, and in particular, abstract painting, as well as to essay against the assumptions of art historical criticism that came to dominate the debate from the 1960s into the 1980s. In grey paintings that develop a unique relationship to photography, cinema, the history of art, and especially, the media, Tansey's humorous, often impossible scenes draw on the history of art and the institutions that surround them in order to critique the very same. Tansey's position in relationship to modernist art both ties together and unravels all that is imagined before him in grey, as I have argued earlier.

In a painting such as the celebrated *The Innocent Eye Test* (1981), a cow is brought face-to-face with Paulus Potter's *The Young Bull* (1647), a painting applauded for its luminous grey skies and, in retrospect, its early Romantic vision (Plate 15). Tansey's grey painting sits in the Metropolitan Museum of Art, New York, making a mockery of the claims of painting, the truth claims attached to it, and the reverence shown it by the museum. We laugh at the claim to truth depicted by a real cow being introduced to Potter's painted cow. In another layer of irony, the painting was sold in 2009 by Gagosian Gallery on behalf of Charles Cowles.[74] It was revealed, however, that it was not Cowles's painting to sell, and that in fact 31 percent of the painting was owned by the Metropolitan Museum of Art. It's difficult not to see the squabbling over the painting that ended in a lawsuit, reflected in the irony of the very serious "experts" standing within *The Innocent Eye Test,* taking notes as they await the cow's response to her seventeenth-century painted relations.

The use of grey in *The Innocent Eye Test* is not unusual for Tansey, but it has a particularly potent significance. Like other of Tansey's work, the grey tones of *The Innocent Eye Test* underline the appearance of photo-realism. And this realism is further substantiated by the fact that the museum workers are looking on the meeting between cows as if they are observing a scientific experiment. A worker on the right wears a laboratory coat and holds a clipboard, while one on the left waits with a mop in anticipation of the cow's excitement at finding her mate in the picture. And in another layer that marks the further collapse between reality and representation within Tansey's painting, one of Monet's *Haystack* paintings from the 1880s or 1890s hangs to the right of Paulus Potter's *The Young Bull.* The cow in Tansey's painting is both given context for us and made comfortable by the presence of friends and food in paintings presented to her as the thing itself. It is not the painterly or art historical significance of these paintings within Tansey's painting that brings meaning for the cow: for the animal, it is the realism of the objects depicted in the paintings. In the guise of photographic press illustrations, grey reinforces the rhetoric of mechanical reproduction for us, and in turn, this accuracy removes all distinction between reality and representation for the cow. The layers of illusion are as complex as those of the testimony to authenticity. Typical of Tansey's paintings, and in another confusing layer of fiction, the scene did not really take place; it is simply given the aesthetic markers of photographic representation.

Mark Taylor briefly discusses Tansey's use of grey, or, as he calls it, "monochrome." He quotes Arthur C. Danto, who claims that the paintings are "old-fashioned, resembling plates of rotogravure of the kind I remember looking at in heavy volumes at my grandparents' house."[75] As Taylor remarks, this is Tansey's way of introducing temporality into his paintings in a gesture of defiance of the modernist prescription for temporal and spatial flatness. Tansey's expansion of temporality is underlined, according to Taylor, by the apparent age of the images that is, in turn, communicated by their unusual monochromes. Taylor's identification of the narrative longevity (which is rarely linear) only partly accounts for the ramifications of Tansey's multiple and expansive grey canvases.[76] The grey palette also contributes to the cynicism of images in which a peculiar form of photorealism is, at first glance, seen as journalistic realism. The journalistic realism depicts events both taking place and reproduced within the images. Similarly, the painting within the painting, itself an echo of an event also taking place in Tansey's painting, but an event that never took place anywhere else, is both in the process of being painted by an artist within the image and is completed simultaneously with the event it depicts. It is as though what is visually identifiable and coded as a painting is in fact a photographic image.

The instantaneity and immediacy of the completed paintings within paintings of *Action Painting* (1981) and *Action Painting II* (1984), for example, are underwritten by the fact that they are in grey. The painting within the painting is both critical of painting's photorealism—thanks to being in grey, which is not "photo-realist"—and suggesting a black-and-white photograph in its place. Moreover, the improbable *mise-en-abîme,* as well as our inability to grasp and, subsequently, articulate the logic of what we see, is underlined by the contradiction inherent in the fact that the surface of the painting is flat. The copies of copies, which are really copies of illusory events in the images, have an unlikeliness about them that makes the representation also an illusion, and a mockery of representation. The grey "photo-realism" both questions the principles of painting by invoking the instantaneity of photography and repeats them by making a temporally and spatially deceptive image on a flat canvas. As an extension of this critique, modernist representation and, particularly, abstract expressionism and post–abstract expressionism are simultaneously quoted and critiqued. We see events become two-dimensional paintings; thus, the flattening out of the modernist aesthetic is everywhere defining Tansey's images. And yet, the impossibility, the riddles reminiscent of Velázquez's *Las meninas,* as they are represented through a contemporary, yet historical, figuration, give substance, depth, and an interpretive dimension that is both a departure from and a critique of abstract modernist art. In his discussion of Tansey's philosophical pictures, Taylor says:

> Instead of turning away from painting and the questions raised about it, Tansey transforms painting into a questioning. . . . Tansey repeatedly seems to ask: "What is a picture?" Picture making, he concludes, is an inquiry or a process of questioning. Every solution he proposes dissolves as much as it resolves.[77]

In a further clarification of the relationship to modernist painting and its Greenbergian conception, Tansey complicates the temporality and history as represented on the canvas. In his constant references to centuries of art history, writing, critical theory, philosophy, even science, Tansey draws on the world outside painting both to answer the question "what is a picture?" as well as to critique the modernist solutions to the same question. Tansey's solutions "dissolve" modernist beliefs, without resolution of his own. This dissolution is most appropriately painted in grey in Tansey's images. He explains why:

> Because this simple but versatile syntax was shared by art, fiction, and photographic reality, it made possible another level of pictorial fiction where aspects of each could commune. That a painted picture no longer had to pretend to non-fiction, no longer had to be a cage for the real, made it possible to think in terms of a

> conjectural field or a place of inquiry. The picture could work as a hybrid form equidistant between the functions of painting, illustration, and photography.[78]

Tansey's painting *A Short History of Modernist Painting* (1982) depicts fifty-two panels in a grid structure that can, in turn, be seen as further summation, as well as refutation, of all I have said in these past two chapters. The work summarizes and simultaneously makes fun of how American painting engages with all that has gone before it, and all that influences it. Moreover, Tansey's critique is executed in greys that underline the pictorial fiction of this history. In this painting, or multiple paintings, Tansey has copied photographs, figures in motion, frozen in a moment in time, that remind us of the stills of a filmstrip. Windows are everywhere here: windows break, doors open, they reflect light, are transparent, opaque, a backdrop for action that takes place in them, in front of them, because of them. The vignettes encapsulate narratives about sight, sighting, insight, and, ultimately, blindness; as well as engaging with discourses on the picture plane, the grid, surface and depth, exteriority and interiority. The longer we look at *A Short History of Modernist Painting*, the clearer it becomes that it is more likely a different history: art is here understood as windows out of which it's not possible to see, mirrors that don't reflect, doors that don't open, fences that can't be climbed, black holes that lead nowhere. In short, art is a deceptive, illusory fiction that takes its viewer into a labyrinth of contradictions and disappointments.

Put another way, Tansey paints the history of the critical conception of art from the early Renaissance onward, in the style of 1950s print commercials, in 1979–80, and then savagely critiques it. Thus, he paints a history of the concerns of painting, not the history of modernist painting itself, and then reveals its insincerity. In another layer of complexity, the lower rows of images represent bodies: bodies break barriers, are contorted, blinded, work futilely, and then by means of the play with surface and depth that we find in Tansey's other works, the illusion and deception of the image in the guise of realism are brought to the fore. The artist, his works of art, single-color palettes, art history, fragmentation, and frustrated bodies and identities, all of these issues as the concerns of painting well before modernism, are summarized, critiqued, and pushed forward across otherwise impenetrable and unsurpassable boundaries.

Taylor argues that Tansey pushes the concerns of modernist painting forward by making it tactile. He says this because the brushstrokes are loose, and though from a distance they are photo-realist, up close, the thick, sensuous strokes refuse all thoughts of artifice. Questions are allowed to linger in the grey, in the gaps that are everywhere represented in Tansey's work: truth takes place between a here and a there, between a then and a now, times and spaces that are literally translated into demarcations created in water, nature, spaces that are only spaces when they are not windows and doors. Most significantly, meaning arises in the gap between illusion and reality, between photographic realism and its undoing through the materiality of paint, so cleverly executed in grey. In keeping with the double-sidedness of abstract grey painting, throughout his oeuvre, Tansey also does the very opposite: he pushes at the boundaries of modernist art by giving flat images an illusory, impossible depth and tactility. All of this said, I am not convinced that this result of the so-called tactility of Tansey's paintings is what makes them unique. Rather, as I have argued, it's the *mise-en-abîme* circularity of the exchange between opposites, the refutation of every trace of certainty, within the illusion of realist aesthetic that contains Tansey's unique contribution. It is in the limen created by opposites, exchanges, and refutations that modernist (abstract) painting is pushed beyond its own terms of existence that Tansey makes his most radical gestures.

Even his use of grey underlines the technique and resultant aesthetic of Tansey's paintings. It is significant that Tansey redraws and redefines the boundaries of American postwar abstraction in grey paintings that are, ultimately, illusory representations. Danto explains how Tansey's technique is almost that used in fresco painting:

> He begins with a layer of monochrome pigment that will dry in about six hours, after which it can only be modified with great pains. . . . The images are produced by wiping or pulling the paint away, and Tansey has various instruments for achieving the repertoire of textures this pulling away of pigment leaves behind. . . .

> Working from . . . a middle tone, adding darks and wiping away to the lights constituted by the tone of the ground of the original canvas, the result has the quality of old master paintings, which worked in and out of the middle tones in this manner.[79]

Thus, the use of so-called monochrome paint is the imperative not only of the paintings' conceptual register but also of the artist's technique. The technique itself, this wearing away of layers of paint before they dry, is a process that becomes visible on the surface of the image, in the grey appearances. Even when they are not grey—the images can be sepia or brown—the technique points to the creation of a one-dimensional image, a one-dimensionality that perfectly accords with the use of what Tansey calls black and white, what I call grey. His technique is always about creating a one-dimensional image, the dimension that will, in turn, conceal the distinction between reality and representation.

Tansey's simultaneous redoing and undoing of the concerns of modernist painting, particularly in the photo-realist grey works, summarize both its continuation and its death, long ago. Tansey's journey into representation, and simultaneous indulgence in the irony of this journey, is a postmodernist performance of the limitations of the modernist project. Moreover, this ironic performance realizes a critique that itself is the cultural politics of grey painting at the end of the twenty-first century. The confusion created by and on the surface of Tansey's paintings, their leading of the spectator (and the art market) on a chase around the painting, as well as on a tour of centuries of painting, is a culmination of sorts. Tansey's paintings entice the same spectator, the same market, that never quite knows where she is, never quite knows how to place itself. But as has been discovered in the other paintings I have discussed, all those that precede Tansey on the walls of the world's great museums, Tansey invites and allows us to sit for a while. Before we can get comfortable, however, we are shaken into a critically aware disillusionment. But this disillusionment does not incite us to turn away. Rather, after the irony, we believe in the possibility and return to our relationship with American modernism to find its cultural politics of engagement. In Tansey's paintings, this playful, yet highly critical, engagement with the institutions of American and European art raises the discourse and meaning to a level of public concern. We may look back through the lens of Tansey's visual riddles to identify the politics of painting as defined by its interaction with the institution, and at the very least, through the spectator that enables those institutions.

5

REINVENTION AND PERPETUATION

THE POSSIBILITY OF GREY FOR GERHARD RICHTER

In the Gray pictures it's lack of differentiation, nothing, nil, the beginning and the end, in the panes of glass it's the analogy with attitudes and possibilities, in the color charts it's chance, anything is correct, or rather, form is non-sense.
—**Gerhard Richter,** *Gerhard Richter: The Daily Practice of Painting*

I'm . . . fundamentally sceptical towards myself, hence towards others as well. And that's why I'm never sure if what I do is right or whether it's any good.
—**Gerhard Richter,** *Gerhard Richter: Texts*

GERHARD RICHTER'S GREY PAINTINGS touch all aspects and concerns of modernist painting. Richter has used grey in its many temperatures and tones for over fifty years. There are periods—the late 1960s and early 1970s, for example—when grey features more prominently. However, Richter has continued to reinvent the materiality and significance of grey paint across his oeuvre. He has interrogated and pushed at the limits of the formal, compositional, and medium-specific concerns that were the preoccupation of American postwar painting as I have discussed them. His work has always had political and historical dimensions, even as it has refused to engage with the events of German history that surround it. Moreover, the work has, most uniquely, reinvented thematic concerns such as the relationship between looking and knowing, between memory and identity, the body and the canvas. Accordingly, it simultaneously engages with all the issues of postwar European painting in grey, as if through the lens of American abstraction. Lastly, perhaps more than any other artist working in grey paint, Richter has continued to reinvent the medium of painting into the twenty-first century. This is achieved in an oeuvre in which, as others have noted, at least one-third of the paintings have been executed in grey, somewhere between black and white.[1]

All of the ways that grey paint has been envisioned, applied, conceived, and interpreted on the twentieth-century canvas are brought to life in Richter's oeuvre. His work extends from figuration to abstraction, the industrial to the Romantic, through the sculptural, architectural, photographic, cinematic, and theatrical dimensions of and at the interface with painting. Though Richter himself would challenge an ascription of "modernist" to his work, the materiality and immateriality of paint, the constant negotiation and renegotiation of the relationship between figure and ground, the intimacy and distinction of painting and photography, reproduction and originality, the contours and perspicacity of perception, the elusive quest to know reality through the illusions of pictorial representation—the concerns of what is understood as modernist art—are all taken up in Richter's work.[2] Although positioned quite differently, like Martin's grey works, Richter's stand outside modernism, and yet they offer one of the most acute visions of the limits of modernist painting. As a result of the breadth and depth, as well as the perpetual dissolution of the possibilities of modernist painting in the concerns of Richter's grey works, I place them as the summation of what can be done in grey.

I structure my discussion of Richter's use of grey with an exhibition that might seem removed from the subject of this book: *Acht Grau / Eight Grey* at the Deutsche Guggenheim in 2002 (see the frontispiece). This is a series of works that are apparently not concerned with paint on canvas. And yet, the works in the exhibition embrace all of the primary concerns of Richter's oeuvre in grey paint, as well as modernist painting of the twentieth century, and thus, *The Truth Is Always Grey.* For this reason, I place Richter's *Acht Grau* as the scaffolding for understanding his grey paintings on canvas, a vision that, in turn, leaves open many of the questions asked by (grey) painting more generally as I address them in *The Truth Is Always Grey.*

True to its unique characteristics, such as simultaneous absorption and reflection of light, ineffability and opacity, neutrality, warmth, and coolness, Richter uses grey to envision the task of painting in the twentieth and twenty-first centuries. Richter's work sees the purpose, meaning, flaws, and failures of painting in grey. In grey, Richter also reflects on what is inconsistent, contradictory, what goes unsaid, the opposite of what is claimed about modernism, about painting, and about grey. In a gesture that follows the often paradoxical nature of the paintings, as well as Richter's relationship to them, I read everything he writes about grey both with and against the grain. Richter often contradicts himself in different statements, thus leading to the possibility of multiple contradictory interpretations. This is also the irony of grey. For example, Richter claims:

> To me, grey is the welcome and only possible equivalent for indifference, noncommitment, absence of opinion, absence of shape. But grey, like formlessness and the rest, can be real only as an idea, and so all I can do is create a colour nuance that means grey but is not it. The painting is then a mixture of grey as a fiction and grey as a visible, designated area of color.[3]

With the persistent irony of grey in mind, I understand that, thanks to its "indifference, noncommitment, absence of opinion, absence of shape," grey paint has the potential to reveal the truth about painting, and about painting in (post) modernity, and eventually, about modernist art. To make this claim, I understand "absence" as deficiency, but it is also an absence that holds within it the possibility of fulfillment. Benjamin Buchloh writes of Richter's "deadening elimination of color in its reduction to the non-color of gray."[4] I also complicate this assertion. When he paints in grey, Richter does not engage with the loss of color, but rather with an intensification of the processes and possibilities of color. If Richter embraces and departs from all the concerns of modernist painting, then grey provides a space of great productivity. Grey is the way forward, rather than the void, or the noncolor of a medium that has nowhere else to go.

Therefore, in this chapter, I juxtapose Richter's writing with his painting to offer an interpretation of his use of grey that takes issue with the artist's words about grey. When Richter writes about grey (as opposed to paints in grey), he is not as optimistic about its possibilities:

> Grey. It makes no statement whatever; it evokes neither feelings nor associations; it is really neither visible nor invisible. Its inconspicuousness gives it the capacity to mediate, to make visible, in a positively illusionistic way, like a photograph. It has the capacity that no other colour has, to make "nothing" visible.[5]

I believe that the absence of statement he finds in grey is what makes Richter's use of the color exciting. On Richter's grey paintings, "nonstatement" is an articulation of the interstitial world of possibility.[6] Similarly, Richter's claim that grey paint is neither visible nor invisible is typical of his tendency to confound the perception and understanding of his paintings. For him, despite the most immediate impression of his claim, grey is the color through which as a painter he can most easily access reality, a painted reality. Grey is the color that expresses what cannot otherwise be visualized: "the states of being and situations that affect one."[7] As I shall demonstrate, grey fits very well with the contradiction and ambiguity of both Richter's oeuvre and modernist art in general. Grey is a nothingness that is pregnant with the gestatory phases of meaning and insight, as well as, a nothingness that signals negativity and death, a mourning from which there is no escape.[8]

Acht Grau (Eight Grey)

In 2002 Richter produced eight massive grey glass plates for the Deutsche Guggenheim—specially commissioned as one of its ongoing exhibitions that aimed to express the museum's intimate space on Unter den Linden in Berlin.[9] In *Acht Grau,* paint and support become indistinguishable.[10] Paint and support come together in what is, effectively, no more than a surface. The eight mirrored panels engage and rearticulate the changing nature of vision and perception; they engage the city streets outside and its history. They are simultaneously abstract and figurative, sitting as they do at the interstice of meaning and nihilistic vision, in the limen between painting and architecture, painting and performance, painting and sculpture, painting and cinema. The panels of *Acht Grau* are not necessarily Richter's greatest works, but they can be held up like a mirror to all that he claims about grey painting at this historical moment: 2002. These eight panels are an accumulation and culmination of everything that has concerned Richter across his fifty years of painting. And yet, so typical of Richter's wont to confound, nothing in these panels allows us to trace their history, to link them to the dense overpainting of later abstract works such as *St. Gallen* (1989), the *Wald* series (2005), and *Cage I–VI* (2006), to name just a few. Because, in its complete merging with the glass support through an industrial process, the paint in *Acht Grau* is no longer visible on the surface of the work.[11] And together with this play with visibility, the tactility, texture, movement, transparency, and opacity, the tone and rhythm of paint, are all banished from *Acht Grau.* All of the defining features of painting have been removed from the flat, grey, reflective surfaces. Thus, some might want to argue that the *Acht Grau* pieces have nothing to do with painting. Of course, this flattening out of the painted surface such that it is no longer separable from its support, and thus, no longer paint, is the point of *Acht Grau.* In the act of stretching the substance of paint, painting, and the painted surface seemingly beyond their own limits, the medium reaches a telos of sorts. Painting reaches its limit in 2002. Accordingly, in the same way Richter's paintings are an exposition of twentieth-century grey, so I understand *Acht Grau* as a summary of all his work in paint.[12]

Buchloh cites *4 Glasscheiben / 4 Panes of Glass* (1967) as the precursor to the 2002 installation at the Deutsche Guggenheim.[13] Indeed, the four sheets of 190-by-100-centimeter glass have, like all of Richter's works in glass, had all the intimacy, gesture, and dynamism of paint removed from them. They are, perhaps after Duchamp's *The Bride Stripped Bare by Her Bachelors, Even (The Large Glass)* of 1915–23, enigmatic, with reference to nothing other than their own meaninglessness. As with transparent glass, the surface has been made insubstantial such that it is the antithesis of painting. The meaning of *4 Glasscheiben* becomes determined by the reflection on their surface, a gesture or technique that recurs over the course of Richter's oeuvre, though it takes different colors, shapes, and forms. Like *Acht Grau,* the glass of *4 Glasscheiben* is transparent: in both series we look through and at the glass surface at one and the same time. Again, in a tendency that gathers momentum as Richter's career in painting progresses, in the 1967 work, the sheet of glass becomes a mirror and all meaning and representation are restored, made coherent, once the viewer stands before it. In recent years, Richter has taken this confounding use of glass to another level in works such as *11 Scheiben / 11 Panes* (2004).[14] In these works, stacked sheets of glass absorb and reflect all of these contradictions and conundrums, as well as create new ones. Now, with eleven sheets of glass, the mirrored image is refracted, broken, repeated in *mise-en-abîme.* All previous coherence given by the unity of the viewer's reflection in the sheet of glass is shattered. In certain displays, the installation further complicates the sheets when one or more of Richter's paintings placed on the walls of the same space can be seen "in fragments" behind or through the multiple glass sheets.[15] This undoing through further layering of the meaning of his earlier works is a typical creative gesture in Richter's practice: the destruction of the image is as important as the establishment of order and meaning in the first place. The paintings seen through the glass sheets are destroyed, and simultaneously created in a new fractured form. The grey surface of each *Acht Grau* panel is interrupted by the reflection of the visitor, the images and activities of all that fills the space of exhibition. In turn, these images in reflection are a proliferation of the painted images, the perpetual recreation of the substance and meaning of painting.

Following this infinitely twisting and turning narrative, anything in Richter's oeuvre that marks an antithesis or antagonism necessarily means the presence of the opposite. His *4 Glasscheiben* marks the evacuation, thus the antithesis, of painting, and painting simultaneously becomes the very substance of these transparent surfaces.[16] Because in their removal of all traces of paint, they discourse on its absence, thus, by default, they reference the significance of its presence. In contrast, the grey surfaces of *Acht Grau* do not need the evacuation of paint to embrace the presence of painting (and other media). There is no doubt that painting is the very substance of the eight grey, mirrored surfaces. This, despite the fact that the paint itself has been transformed through its fusion with glass, and, as Buchloh argues, the panes are in every way related to the earlier work in glass. That is, they are both painting become glass and glass from which painting has been removed.

There is another genre of Richter's work that infuses the grey reflective panels in the Deutsche Guggenheim that Buchloh mentions only in passing. Namely, the more than 130 *Grau* paintings produced from the 1960s onward can be seen and understood as the precursor to the quietly monumental, or even antimonumental, grey works on display at the Deutsche Guggenheim in 2002.[17] The eight grey panels of simultaneously mirrored and opaque glass might be the culmination of a lifetime's fascination with grey, grey paint, painting in grey. We might even go so far as to claim that these "mirror images" are the "Atlas" and compass of Richter's oeuvre: they are his way of seeing the world through the eyes of a painter. Fused together with these glass plates is a catalog of all Richter has done, and also, they offer a way of seeing the world, a way of relating to the world, in 2002. To put it another way, beyond their substance as grey paint fused with glass, the panels of *Acht Grau* look inward at their own density of meaning and association, as well as outward to the significance of the world that produces and sustains them.

Like the photographs in *Atlas, Acht Grau*'s panels are another repetition (embracing difference) of Richter's concern in paint of the relationship between art and politics, art and history as it has been visualized over the past fifty years.[18] The image of the spectator reflected back to herself, the building of the Deutsche Bank of which the Guggenheim occupies the ground floor, the world outside on Unter den Linden, all become visible on the glass surface, literally. The reflection of this world outside the artwork marks the historical or contextual engagement of *Acht Grau.* At the same time, the panels nevertheless celebrate the abstraction of color-field painting, albeit played out across industrially painted sheets of glass. It is a complex, multilayered historical world, approaching the labyrinthine, that exists on and through the surfaces of these panels as images, sculptures, screens, stage sets, architectural walls, and windows. It is a world in which history and art of all kinds coexist in the pursuit of a redefinition of both. I examine these themes and concerns of Richter's grey paintings in this chapter, but first, I begin with a discussion of Richter's grey.

Gerhard Richter Grey

If Klein's name is synonymous with the electric blue of IKB, why is Richter's not synonymous with grey? Perhaps because he has not promoted his grey paintings in the same way? But it is probably also because the connotations and dimensions of grey do not lend themselves to such publicity. While it might be argued that grey is everything that electric blue is not, for Richter, grey reaches far and wide. It is, like everything else that touches his paintings, fraught with ambiguities and ambivalences, double meanings and impossibilities, multiplicity and nothingness. Robert Storr identifies this in his discussion of Richter's nonlinear trajectory toward a "murky"—indeed, he uses the word "*gray*"—abstraction. Storr cites the priority that Richter gives to ambiguity in the image from early on. He quotes Richter to support his argument: "All that interests me is the gray areas, the passages and tonal sequences, the pictorial spaces, overlaps and interlockings," to posit that grey is the visual equivalent of uncertainty for the artist.[19] And then, Storr argues that grey is the genesis of color on this same trajectory. According to Storr, the turn to grey was a gesture of departure from the culture of reductivism that surrounded Richter growing up. He quotes Richter:

> The gray monochromes were the most complete ones I could imagine. The welcome and only correspondence to indifference, to a lack of conviction, the negation of commitment, anomie. After the gray paintings, after the dogma of "fundamental painting" whose purist and moralizing aspects fascinated me to a degree bordering on self-denial, all I could do was start all over again. This was the beginning of the first color sketches.[20]

The multiple and conflicting roles for grey in the oeuvre are the extension of the inconsistency of Richter's conception of grey as well as its continual reconception on the canvas. I have written elsewhere about Richter's pursuit of ephemerality, his insistence on contradictions *en abîme,* and the embrace of impossibility as it is expressed in grey paint. I have discussed how in the figurative photo-paintings of *18. Oktober 1977* (1988) Richter's grey is the palette for an interstitial world, creating both intellectual and emotional spaces that invite the viewer to insert and reinsert her memory into the narrative of German history.[21]

Unlike IKB, Richter's grey is never a single color, tone, or temperature, and even the way he applies grey continues to change throughout his career. Richter's grey is never simply a step on the way from white to black. Rather, it is the mixture of all colors, all greys together on one canvas, a rainbow in grey that sometimes begins on the doctor knife, and at other times does not appear until paint is applied to the canvas. As I have reinforced to be the case with the work of other nineteenth- and twentieth-century artists, on Richter's canvas, grey is never monochromatic: it is always a multiplicity of indefinable colors, shifting in intensity, thickness, luminosity, viscosity, and affect. The most common approach to Richter's use of grey follows a somewhat superficial interpretation of the artist's own claim that grey is "nothing, nil," "noncommitment." He writes that "the grey paintings—a painted grey surface, completely monochromatic—they come from a motivation, or result from a state, that was very negative."[22] While this is indeed one aspect of Richter's grey, it is just the beginning. The vision of grey must "be turned on its head in the end, and has come to a form where these paintings possess beauty."[23] Like every other aspect of Richter's practice, grey is neither one-dimensional nor straightforward.

My claim that the grey paintings, even in their 1960s and 1970s editions, are not monochrome and that grey is not "other" to, but on a continuum with, other colors, marks my departure from the more usual approach to Richter's works in particular and grey painting in general.[24] Even exhibitions such as that in Burgdorf, Switzerland, in 2004, an exhibition devoted entirely to the grey paintings, insist that grey is "without color," that it is used as a monochrome by Richter, that in the grey paintings Richter has "relinquished color," and that this "absence of color" is a leitmotif.[25] Even as the paintings themselves would not support these descriptions, and even as Richter's writings are ambiguous and can be interpreted to refute the one-dimensionality of his use of grey, still critics do not see, let alone fully investigate, its complexity.

From the 1960s and 1970s grey canvases, through the photo-paintings of the 1980s to the abstract works of the late 1990s and 2000s, Richter's grey develops dramatically. In the earlier works, grey is the color of steel and industry. It is the color of the industrialization that both challenges and inspires the future of painting at the turn of the twentieth century, fifty years before Richter paints. In paintings such as the *Wellblech / Corrugated Iron* series from 1967 or even the multiple works titled *Grau* made in 1968, grey painting struggles with the industrial processes that enabled it.[26] The rich texture, fluidity, and simultaneous ethereality of grey paint as Richter applies it to the canvas of the *Grau* paintings are reminiscent of steel. Even more so, in works such as the window series or the corrugated iron paintings, in which the representation is mathematical, and for want of a better description, geometrical, there is always tension between rationalization and its opposite. We are reminded that the windows and sheets with their shadows and blurs are painted representations: however precise they may appear at first glance, they are fused with ambiguity, inexplicability, and confusion. Once again, we find the "grids" of modernist painting in the 1960s and 1970s to be anything but gridded. The optical illusion of the curtains, windows, corrugated iron, and doors creates images that oscillate between abstract vertical lines of light and dark grey and the imprecision, at times the indecipherability, of the objects claimed to be represented by the titles. Is the shadow before or behind the object that casts it? Is the curtain revealing or concealing what is behind or in front of it? The grey oil-based and acrylic paint is the grey of corrugated iron, of astronomy, doors, and tubes. These are also the objects that fill Richter's canvases in the early decades of his career. In distinction to Johns, Richter is not interested in painting as object. The grey in his paintings can appear thin, smooth, and even, with an opacity that results from the application of paint through spraying. Thus, in grey, not only are we confused by the deceptive logic of paint and what is painted, but objects are transformed into paint. It is as though these works from the late 1960s and early 1970s are the precursor to *Acht Grau*.

By 2002, in *Acht Grau* Richter does not paint with such obvious figurative or representational references. He extends the use of grey such that the doors, the sea, the sky, the windows, corrugated iron, which in the 1960s and 1970s were the illusion of represented objects, by 2002 become the material both of representation and represented. In early works that push at the limits of figuration toward illusion and abstraction, we glimpse the first indications of Richter's simultaneous experimenting with the use of paint to facilitate a visual experience that leads the viewer into a questioning of her own place, her own identity in relationship to the painting. As I will discuss, with Richter, as with the painters discussed in earlier chapters, his commitment to abstraction goes hand in hand with a challenge to the conditions and process of viewing.

Gerhard Richter grey always has, I would argue, a historical dimension. It is modulated and transformed in a reflection of the world that gives it context. In his early works, Richter not only uses an industrial grey paint; he also thematizes industrialization through the representations in that same grey. The alienation of art and painting in particular, the apparent reproducibility of the grey canvas, the engagement with photography, the repeated erasure of the image and use of the canvas as a palimpsest, together with the challenges to vision, are all found on Richter's grey canvases, as well as concerns I have identified in modernist painting. Thus, in a work such as *Ohne Titel (grau) / Untitled (Grey)* from 1968,[27] the circular motion of the brushstroke creates layers over the traces of movement beneath and simultaneously cancels out what came before it, extending the space of the painting into the recesses of depth and simultaneously spilling into the space of the viewer. This work explores the substance of paint at the same time that it erases what is underneath it (Plate 16). The grey of black-and-white photography, the thick, intense matter of paint as medium, here perform and engage with the concerns of modernist painting. Richter uses grey in the late 1960s and early 1970s as the medium and tool of his interrogation of what painting is.

In 2002, in *Acht Grau,* the engagement with questions of modernity, modernism, and other media of the twentieth century, such as cinema and photography, can be seen to continue into this next century. The historical moment of *Acht Grau* is that of a fin de siècle marked by postindustrial forms always in a narrative movement toward obsolescence: computer, television, telephone, and all the other screens that we stare at incessantly only to see our own image reflected back to us. And like these screens, the surfaces of *Acht Grau* are constantly shifting in accordance with the light that hits them, the viewer who stands before them, looks at, and sees them. Vision and perception become recalibrated, no longer contained by the frame of painting, unpredictable and in motion. Grey is the ideal color for these processes of perception as they are generated by post-medium screens of all kinds.

As *Acht Grau* thematizes the grey of multimedia beyond the frame of the painting, beyond the walls of the Deutsche Guggenheim, the postwar and post-Wall identity of Berlin, the same argument can be made retrospectively about the untitled works of the 1970s such as *Grau / Grey* (1970).[28] The steel grey paint merges the concerns of industry and art, just as it was in the world beyond the gallery walls in the 1970s. In other paintings, the buildings and city streets in particular, even when they are representations of Milan (*Domplatz, Mailand / Cathedral Square, Milan* [1968]) or Berlin, remind us of the sky in the city of Düsseldorf, gateway to the industrial region of the Ruhr Valley where Richter studied and was tenured as a professor from 1971 to 1983. Similarly, as I suggest earlier, works such as the corrugated iron paintings (*Wellblech*), tubes (*Röhren* [1967]), or curtains (*Vorhang* [1965]) are a possible depiction of the industrial world that surrounded him in Germany. This reflection is reiterated in Richter's application of paint as well as in the illusionary form that emerges on the canvas when he experiments. Richter's use of grey in these early works can be said to references the medium he uses. If Monet's smoke from the train in the *Gare Saint Lazare* mirrors the meaning of the very building whose walls support it today (the Musée d'Orsay), then Richter's use of grey in the late 1960s and early 1970s reflects the color of steel and industry that are both in his midst and that flourish, but are nevertheless in the process of disintegration, during these decades.[29] If grey is the color of industry, a color made possible by the advent of manufactured paint and acrylic pigments, then Richter celebrates it, questions it, interrogates it, and engages in an ongoing relationship with it over and over and over again in the 1960s and 1970s.

In these years, Richter often painted the canvas entirely in grey. The grey was nuanced and changing, often in keeping with the movement of the brushstroke. It was never a single grey, never monochromatic. In paintings such as *Ohne Titel / Untitled* (1970), grey watches the movement of the brushstroke on a canvas, and in *Ohne Titel / Untitled* (1968), it represents the movement of the sponge with which it is applied.[30] These are works in which grey is the material of paint. Moreover, in juxtaposition with the changing uses of grey after the 1970s, the way he applies it also develops, to the point where he continues to rearticulate the boundaries of painting through a commitment to constant experimentation with application techniques. Richter always explores the parameters and possibilities of painting, and grey continues to be central to this lifelong search to push its limits.

In the early works in grey, the viewer watches where Richter's hand once commenced and ended, its movement across a canvas. Even when the illusions are complicated by tension and an uncertainty as to what is represented, the use of a spectrum of grey underlines the motion and traces of different modes of paint application: with brushes, spatulas, squeegees, and various other tools. Depending on the way light falls on the surface of the painting, we will see evidence of the artist's hand in motion, his mind at work. These paintings in grey come to be about light and the creation of shadow through the application of paint, about determining the length of the brushstroke, about emotion, blindness, and insight as they are achieved through pushing, layering, wiping, scraping, and all the many other ways Richter moves paint across and around a canvas. In these first decades, Richter chose to explore in grey. As is the case with the American artists, Richter uses grey as a way of staying focused on painting in a search for what it is that painting can do, what happens when paint is applied differently to a canvas. To do the same in red or blue or yellow would recast the representation in any number of ways. The question of paint and painting would be lost in the tangle of emotions and meanings that are pointed up by red, blue, yellow, even black. Painting in these early works is stripped to its barest elements: the movement of paint, as the trace of a brush, knife, sponge, or one of his various other tools across a canvas. Forty years later, with *Acht Grau,* Richter comes to see movement as redundant to the exploration of what painting is, what painting can do, its effect on the viewer. In *Acht Grau,* movement is transposed to our own movement as it is reflected in the mirrored surface of the panels. And yet, these panels continue to explore the possibilities of paint, even as it is fused with glass as support. Because it is ultimately paint that gives viewers reason to look at themselves in the mirrored glass that has become the surface of painting.

If the early grey canvases are all about paint, its texture, density, materiality, and the movement of the device of application on the canvas, in the 1980s the investigation of painting branches out to include the direct confrontation with photography and other media. In the 1980s Richter develops his signature style of the photo-paintings. If Richter chooses grey in the early works because it enables him to play with paint without distraction, in the photo-paintings twenty years later, the turn to grey enables him to distinguish painting from photography, a medium that moves between black and white in distinct, yet indistinguishable, gradations. Grey paint achieves a physical, perceptual blur that photography never does. At least photography cannot reproduce the kind of blur that Richter paints. Also, paint attains the rainbow of greys that photography cannot, but that photography inspires it to discover. In the early works, light and shadow are in constant play across the surface, depending on variables such as the direction and length of the brushstroke, the tool of application, the thickness of the paint, the distribution of white within the grey. By the 1980s, the photo-paintings are flat, even, with the sole movement of the medium being caught in the blur. In these images, grey paint has a presence, a truth and reality that photography can only aspire to: the grey blur captures the grey areas of knowing and seeing, those in-between places on the color spectrum not available to the mechanically precise photographic lens. And grey paint, when it is used to imitate black-and-white photography can simultaneously draw attention to its own artifice as representation and the lie of photography as an imitation of reality, blurred.

Richter's grey paint is much more than a reflection on paint. Unlike the more conventional conception of grey, it is not automatically melancholic or nostalgic—although it can be—but it is usually about time, and the relationship of the present to the past, of painting to other media. I have argued that grey is used to depict the passing of time, in the guise of improbable instantaneity, or the history of painting, in Tansey's work, for example. Richter's grey adds another narrative of time to the surface and meaning of painting. Memories and identities, both personal, of Richter's family, and political as they are raised in, for example, the 1960s portraits of politicians and poets, army commanders and capitalists, are always veiled with a blur, rendered in grey. This grey blur of the photo-painted portraits is the image's attempt to reflect on a past that can no longer be recaptured, or more likely, a past that was never very clear in the first place. And because it is forever out of reach, Richter both tries to recapture it and confirms the impossibility of such an exercise. Richter would not and does not use red, green, or yellow to achieve the effect that results from this backward-and-forward motion, ever. Grey depicts time, the past, the once was, the distortions of memory and history being returned to the surface in the form of an ambiguous blur. And grey signifies that the past ultimately stays in the past, that it is not reproducible.

This evocation of the past through the grey blur is variously used depending on the desired effect or a given phase of his career. In the 1980s everything changes, everything in grey, that is, and the blur is no longer his preoccupation. Whereas in the 1970s, the grey paint, the trace of the tool, and the object of representation are fused on the surface of the canvas, in the 1980s, Richter starts to "overpaint." In the overpaintings as well as images such as *Uran (1)* (1989), *Uran (2)* (1989), *Abstraktes Bild / Abstract Painting* (1992) or *Abstraktes Bild / Abstract Painting* (1999), indeed, any of those paintings where we can see what is underneath, he takes up the discourse of memory and simultaneous forgetting via the oscillation between revelation and concealment as others have discussed it.[31] Perhaps in these works, grey is an afterthought? Although it is rare, unusual, sometimes grey is applied as the ground on which another color is painted. That said, in the later paintings, grey is always the color of the overpainting, the veil that is drawn over the colorful world beneath the surface of the painting. And thus, questions of the past and of memory become more prominent in the 1980s onward, or at least they take a different turn, when layering with grey becomes a common strategy.

This said, however, Richter creates endlessly and impossibly contradictory dilemmas: instances of curtains, windows, paint as a veil also dominate the earlier works, if in a different guise as objects of "realist" representation.

Surface Representations: The Figure–Ground Tension

Following the characterization of modernist painting already discussed, Richter's more recent grey overpainted abstract works embrace and complicate the tension between figure and ground, surface and depth. *Acht Grau* is exemplary of this: its representation of the surface is both a formal construction as well as a conceptual field. Formally, *Acht Grau* is a series of glass panels in which paint and support are irreversibly fused: at high temperatures, the paint is melted and transformed into colored glass. Richter reduces, and simultaneously inflates, everything that has to do with painting onto the reflective surfaces of *Acht Grau.* Even though paint and painting as we know them have been removed from the surface, *Acht Grau* is painting in 2002 stretched to its limits. In its fusion of paint, support, technique, process, and the glass usually used to protect the surface of the painting, *Acht Grau* takes painting to another level. Richter will push painting even further in the digital manipulation and representations of *Strip* (2011), in tapestries, inkjet prints, and photocopies, but in 2002, *Acht Grau* is the new precipice.

What marked modernist painting's break with tradition was the way it drew attention to the surface as a single plane across which painting and representation unfolded. Gone were the perspectival renderings of a scene in a three-dimensional space. In their stead, artists such as Manet and Picasso introduced a painted surface that was uncertain of itself, and what it might represent, often taking the form of a blur, a fragmentation, or a transgression of the picture plane. Even if Richter himself resists the label of modernist, I am not the first to note Richter's affinity with Manet, whose works are among the earliest examples of modernist painting.[32] Storr cites Manet as the precursor to Richter, the history painter of *Oktober 18, 1977.* Storr traces the uneven lines between Manet and Richter, claiming that the nineteenth-century French painter not only prefaces Richter's focus on perpetrators doing their jobs, but also the aesthetic and political depiction of events based on documentary evidence, evidence supplied by photographic realism. I am also not the first to claim that for Richter it is no longer a question of what is represented by the blur (as it was for Manet), but rather, the blur itself has become the subject of the painting.[33] *Acht Grau* simply expands that blur—which is effectively a brushstroke in close-up—so that it covers the entire two-dimensional panel. The surface becomes, quite simply, one large grey blur.

In *Acht Grau,* the confusion in the corner of Manet's *Vue de l'exposition universelle de Paris* reaches an extreme conclusion when it comes to cover the mirrored surface, a paint surface that exists as a support for our own image.[34] On the planes of *Acht Grau,* ambiguity and confusion reign as we are made to look back on our own place in the gallery, the gallery's place in Berlin, in a post-reunification cultural moment.[35] These panels become a vision of the viewer in motion, in relationship to the shifting dynamics of the space occupied by both paintings and viewer, and to the others who move through and around this grey world.[36] The removal—or extension—of the blur to the entirety of the painted surface enables a shift to a form that privileges the image of the viewer on the glass support.

As I have indicated, Richter's preoccupation with the surface of the image began a long time before *Acht Grau.* I have discussed the use of grey paint to depict the cloth of Titian's aristocratic sitter, and Goya's attraction to grey walls, skies, and abstract backgrounds, as well as the sumptuous grey cloth in Renaissance painting. Similarly, I have demonstrated how twentieth-century painting has returned these luxurious fabrics to the representational field of the image. In Johns's paintings we saw curtains, drawers, fabrics of various kinds attached to the canvas in grey, as if to appropriate, or bring up to date, the cloth and grey surfaces of painting in previous centuries. Richter spends much of the earlier part of his career concerned with such objects. Curtains, covers, sheets, walls and other fabric, metal and architectural surfaces recur as the subject of his grey paintings. This strategy connects Richter's paintings to those of Johns, if only inductively. Richter uses these "objects" or better, surfaces, to draw attention to the surface of the image as no more than an image. Unlike Johns's, however, Richter's fabrics involve optical illusion in some form. And yet, as if in kinship with Johns, the various doors in paintings from 1967, such as *Kleine Tür / Small Door,* open into an indeterminate universe above the line of the clouds, as if seen from an airplane. The awkwardly open door, as though it is about to fall off its hinges that we do not see, also links the paintings to the surrealist depictions of discontinuous times and spaces. In Richter's later works, particularly after the 1980s, the surface conceals and reveals, the surface that creates optical illusions is transformed into abstract layers of paint with no apparent figurative dimension. However, Richter's early surfaces also share the value of the surface, if not the meaning given by the surrealists and other avant-garde French artists in the first half of the twentieth century. Like the surrealists'—and later Johns's—Richter's is not a surface that oscillates between materiality and immateriality. In Richter's early grey paintings from the 1960s and 1970s, the surface stymies all possible opening up to immateriality, indeed to anywhere other than what lies inside the frame. For Richter, the surface is either caught in the play of an optical illusion or it comes as a thick grey paint that is worked over and around the canvas in the interests of exploring its own resolute materiality. This, however, will change as Richter's relationship to painting develops in the decades to come. The early works, however, are in and about grey paint; even if they remind us of other images—steel, corrugated iron, curtains, windows and doors—they are insistent on the presence of paint. But first, it is productive to examine some of the later examples of Richter's curtains, blankets, covers, and walls.

In 1988 Richter painted *Decke / Cover.* As Götz Adriani informs us in his catalog essay for an exhibition of paintings from private collections, this image—apparently, just another abstract grey painting—in fact has a history.[37] The work was the second version of *Erhängte* made for the *October 18, 1977* cycle, an image that was itself a painted version of a press photograph of the corpse of Gudrun Ensslin in her cell in Stammheim Prison.[38] Nothing in *Decke* enables identification of what lies underneath the overpainting. But with Adriani's information, we can see the painting of a *Decke,* or cover, over a repainting of a press photograph. This is a repetition of the covering over of reality by a representation, whether photographed or painted, a strategy Richter often used in the 1960s and 1970s. Where twenty years earlier the surface was marked as an illusion by the tension created through shadows, open doors, or corrugated iron made abstract, in 1988 Richter goes one step further. He overlays his own (blurred) painted representation of a police photograph that has been republished in the press.[39] Thus, this gesture of concealing through paint of an already obscure vision (Richter's blurred, painted rendition of the photograph) realizes paint as the medium and subject matter of the grey palette of *Decke.* Paint has taken over as the subject and object, at one and the same time, the veil and the veiled. There is nothing beyond the surface; at most, paint is just another surface.

I have shown how *Erhängte* represents the violence of the official image of Ensslin in her cell. Ensslin's hanging body was discovered sequestered behind the blanket taken from her bed, in German, the *Decke.*[40] The police moved the blanket to photograph her hanging, thereby pulling back the curtain on her most private and intimate moment: her dead body. In *Erhängte* Richter repaints the image as it was published in *Der Stern*: the blanket pulled back, drawing attention to its status as a curtain revealing a performance played on a stage behind it. However, as I have argued, in *Erhängte,* through the blur of his brushstroke, Richter removes Ensslin's image from the spotlight of the press. Through the refusal of the clarity of perception, Richter's painted representation of a press photograph originally taken by the police as "evidence," asks the spectator to reflect on the violence of representation, the violent transgression of the private and intimate world of death by a disputed historical narrative. *Erhängte* rehangs the curtain behind which Ensslin is given refuge. Representation, more precisely, grey paint, covers over the truth as it can never be known. *Decke,* a painting that came to light after the exhibition of *October 18, 1977,* takes this process of covering and protecting the body one step further. A blanket of white paint ensures the appropriate reshrouding of a corpse, a shrouding that already protects it from the ogling eye of the world in *Erhängte.*[41] Thus, the reality of the photographed, and the later painted image, is further silenced behind a veil of white-grey paint. And it is silenced never to be heard again as the history is nowhere visible within the frame of *Decke.* To the naked, unknowing eye, this is just another of Richter's abstract overpainted canvases.

Erhängte discourses on the false claim of photography—especially that of an investigative or scientific kind—to reveal the truth of what took place in the sensational historical moment of Ensslin's death. Similarly, together with the other paintings of the *18. Oktober 1977* series, the blur functions to question the veracity of painting in its claim to be anything more than representation. *Decke* moves this trajectory one step further when it sequesters all pretense of reality behind a never fully opaque layer of paint. This function of (grey) paint as a mask, or in this case, a protection, is used repeatedly throughout Richter's oeuvre. Reality might not be recognizable or knowable behind the grey of the surface made by a single sweeping brushstroke, but that is not the point. All we need to know is that reality is not available to us as viewers. And we are asked to recognize that it is paint that both denies access to the reality of the canvas and, because we can see the paint underneath, has a pretension to be the reality. In turn, it is because of this pretension to reality that all attempts at representation must be covered over. In characteristic Richter fashion, paint is given an impossible and contradictory task: paint is both the material that stakes its claim to objective reality, and the material with which this claim is negated.

As we now know to be typical of Richter's paintings, the opposite is also true. The inability to access the reality sequestered behind the grey curtain of *Decke* is, in itself, the reality. The reality is that there is nothing behind the curtain, nothing in the image other than the illusions and deceptions of representation. Prior to the 1990s, for Richter, this notion of paint as a substance and surface that conceals and reveals is often swept across a figurative representation. And then, in the abstract paintings of the late 1990s and early 2000s, grey paint is both an abstract surface and the veil behind which abstraction is hidden. In this sense, *Decke* might be seen as being at the crossroads of Richter's move from figuration to abstraction. It is both the epitome of the curtains and covers and screens, windows and doors that are always open, but appear to lead nowhere. This can be seen in early works such as *Vorhang IV / Curtain IV* (1965) and *Türen / Doors* (1967). And, simultaneously, *Decke* is a precursor to those images in which all that is visible beneath the layers of grey on the surface is other colors, other colors made invisible by grey.

Another quality of *Decke* that inspires its placement at a crossroads in Richter's oeuvre is the glazed effect that comes from the grey-white vertical of what we now know to be hanging fabric. The painting is somewhat difficult to look at because it leaves an afterimage when the eye shifts horizontally across the canvas. From the very beginning, in spite of Richter's interest in surfaces, there is usually a glimpse of something secreted behind the curtains, veils, covers, and turned sheets. Rather than simply withholding the identity of what is behind them, Richter complicates the frustration of the viewer: the painted surface has the appearance of two-dimensionality, thus reflecting our look back on ourselves.[42] Alternatively, there are those paintings such as *Ohne Titel / Untitled* (1988) or *Ohne Titel / Untitled* (1971), both of which appear to be painted on a glass surface.[43] The paint is translucent: white paint becomes light and illuminates the image as if from behind. These qualities of the painted surface are, one could argue, precursors to the reflective surfaces that develop on a trajectory culminating in *Acht Grau.* In addition, more like the untitled paintings of the 1960s and 1970s mentioned earlier, and less like *4 Glassschieben*, *Acht Grau* develops out of Richter's career-long concern with color and light as they behave, at times, unpredictably, on the surface of a canvas.

Color and light are, arguably, the grey painted surface in its most exciting instantiation. We will remember grey paint is synonymous with light: it has been used to reflect and to witness the light in its midst, to create translucence and warmth as well as shadow and uncertainty. All of these characteristics of grey paint to induce opacity, transparency, visual disorientation, and spatial negotiation are familiar from the early Renaissance onward.[44] The appearance of color and light as a series of dynamic interactions and relations brought to life through the substance of grey paint, reaches a moment of intensification when it is made palpable in Richter's work. Indeed, one could argue that Richter's use of grey paint to create a surface of color and light is his most powerful transformation of the painting's surface into nothing and everything.

CAGE I–VI

If the glass and mirrored plates reduce painting to an ephemeral and ambiguous status of pure visuality, the powerful, cool surface renderings of Richter's six *Cage* (2006) canvases achieve an ephemerality of a different kind. Namely, their surfaces that comprise layer upon layer upon layer of paint are simultaneously transparent, reflective, and dense (Plate 17). Even in their titles, the *Cage I–VI* paintings translate a purity of sound into abstract painting. It is significant that Richter brings music and paint together on the surface without remystifying the experience of representation. He maintains ambiguity and tension at the level of the surface, ensuring that it is more than just material, and in its transformation into luminosity, it is always palpable. If there is more than a gratuitous titling of the works after John Cage's lecture on silence and nothingness, then in spite of claims to the contrary, perhaps the musical analogy of painting is, for Richter, the correlative of this abstraction.[45] Perhaps the musical analogy is the only way to understand the ethereality of the grey painted surface as light in and on *Cage I–VI.* A turn to the six *Cage* paintings will illuminate another relationship to the grey surface, a relationship that is, indeed, one aspect of the ambiguity and multiplicity of surfaces in Richter's oeuvre.

The greys—bluish, reddish, greenish, streaked, stained, and stirred together with varying shades of white, less of black, but always with some degree of both—give each painting a different tonality, a different temperature, a different energy. Similarly, the differing widths and intensities of the vertical streaks where Richter has dragged grey paint across the surface ensures each painting arouses varied levels of differing emotions, and each appeals to something different within the viewer. In his discussion of the more recent abstractions in white (which are, in fact, grey in color), Buchloh claims that Richter's abstractions represent a "chromatic reductivism that . . . insists on the achrome as the only credible application of paint."[46] In distinction from what Buchloh says about the large abstractions, *Cage I–VI* are grey, a color that allows the others underneath to erupt onto the surface, a color that facilitates a painted truth still in the process of revelation. Simultaneously, we see and learn as we are invited into the process at work in what might be taken as studies of the behavior of paint being dragged and rolled across and around the surface of a canvas, movements that stop abruptly, out of nowhere, creating an interruption befitting a composition by John Cage. The overall temperature of the six canvases is cool and light: this is yet another characteristic that takes us into the depths of the minimalist "nothingness" of Cage's music. Related, but not identical, the nothing of

Cage's scores and Richter's canvases in their wake does not mean emptiness and absence, but rather, plenitude and possibility. Everything is here on the surface, beckoning our engagement, imploring us to fall into the mirage, but never allowing us to do so. We might say that the "non-statement" of grey, in fact, opens the space for the music to begin.

In the United States, in the early 1950s, there was much focus in modern art, music, and writing on silence and nothing. Rauschenberg, for example, struck up a dialogue with Cage's groundbreaking ideas on silence, nothingness, on hearing and seeing as he articulated them in "Lecture on Nothing."[47] Most obviously, Rauschenberg's "conversation" with Cage can be identified in the white paintings that he later authorized others to repaint, and the ensuing black paintings. Newman objected that Rauschenberg's white canvases completely negated the surface of the works. This made them controversial. Newman followed with his own white canvases as if trying to correct Rauschenberg. His insistence that white was not blank, but pure, powerful and vulnerable, was underlined through the interruption of white by white in paintings such as *The Voice* (1950).[48] Despite the differences, fifty years later across the Atlantic, this same point motivates what Richter sees in grey. All that painting has to see is seen on the surface. And the multiple greys for which there is only one single word have the capacity to envision the very silence and nothingness, what Cage called "the empty space" that enables human hearing and seeing of the most profound order. For Cage, silence was an empty space, an opening for the sights and sounds of the world around: breathing, coughing, and so on. This translates in Richter's paintings to the images we project onto the surfaces. In turn, these mental images form a tapestry that tells multiple narratives. If grey is empty in Richter's series of six soundless paintings, then it is an emptiness awaiting the charge of profound meaning. Grey, like light, enables us to see, thus to know, the spaces opened up by transparency and nothingness. Grey is Cage-like silence in visual form.

Richter's surface of grey does not seduce and envelop us in the same way that Newman's tries to. And the *Cage* paintings are not two shades or variations of grey; they are one grey whose vulnerability allows the colors underneath to penetrate the surface. As a result, grey becomes constantly shifting, indeed, rainbow-like. This is how

Richter draws attention to the surface; it's so radically different from the way Newman did in 1950. The differences between the two styles are instructive, for through them we see Richter's use of the painted surface as a material manifestation of color that resists any chance of falling back into mystification, the mystification so venerated by artists attached to art as a spiritual pursuit. *The Voice* has the zip on its right-hand side, a marking that refuses the viewer's headlong fall into the sumptuous canvas. The interaction of color and light on the oily surface of the *Cage paintings* illustrates Richter's ultimate exploration of the spatial illusions created through the planarity of painting. And they too stymie the viewer's reverie, but through different strategies.

Here we see the essence—the truth—of paint as color and light. Its vulnerability lies in the fact that Richter has scratched and scoured the surface with paint. Grey becomes indistinguishable from green. It is also layered, chipped, and simultaneously in a struggle with red, yellow, purple, as though it is pulling and pushing the other colors, fighting for dominance on the surface of the canvas. And this struggle, this dynamic interaction between colors, somehow reduces, maybe it's better to say elevates, the conversation between color as paint, color as light, to the very surface and substance of painting. Grey instigates and prolongs this conversation. Grey is the harmony that keeps these colors engaged with one another. As a result of this "conversation," fifty years after painting was declared dead by artists and art historians alike, Richter continues to push its limits, and to convince that painting still has the capacity to engage through the randomness and unpredictability of color. In this instance, the use of grey to create a surface on which color is simultaneously revealed and concealed is what challenges our assumptions about paint and painting.

Richter's abstract works covered in grey, bound by grey, reflecting through the use of grey might beckon us, but they never envelop us. The closer we get to the cool greys of *Cage I–VI,* the more reflective the surface, the more the paintings seem to push us away. As we approach each canvas, it reflects light back at us from its shining grey surface. There is nothing intimate about these huge and imposing canvases. While *Acht Grau* carries the reflection of the surface to an extreme when the viewer's body in reflection assumes the place of the subject of painting, here, the relatively even distribution of paint across a woven canvas ensures that the works are paintings conventionally conceived. Nevertheless, the lack of privilege given to both the compositional orientation and various layers of color, the scratching, streaking, stopping, and starting of grey paint on the surface creates a coolness to the six *Cage* paintings. This, in turn, reinforces the distance created between painting and viewer. While the light, the coolness, the nonchalance of these paintings are achieved in grey, it is not because of grey that they are unapproachable. Rather, it is because so much of these paintings takes place on their surface. They are not miserable or dreary; on the contrary, they are alive. But they are alive because they reflect and refract back to us through the perplexing shine of their surface, in preparation for the mirrors that Richter executes elsewhere, both in the past and still to come.

Richter's single paintings are often meant to be seen together, either as part of a series or simply in communication with each other. It is rare to see Richter's works exhibited individually, but it does happen. However, this is often an impoverished experience. After all, it is not like looking at a Veronese or a Géricault or a Rubens in which a hermetically sealed narrative unfolds from beginning to end within a single frame. Typical of modern art, Richter's paintings are open and unfinished, ambivalent, and usually ask more questions than they answer. As if in an attempt to prolong the conversation of a single painting, throughout his career, Richter has continued to paint and to exhibit in series, creating works that form a community of paintings that happily engage with, complement, and complete each other. To take them out of this community is to rob them of their raison d'être, or to give them a new one. However, the significance of each painting is deepened and dramatized through juxtaposition on a wall with another Richter painting. Despite the apparent disparity between works across his career, there is a constant interweaving of references to his previous (and forthcoming works) inside and between each frame. Similarly, when an image such as *Gehöft / Farm* (1999) is placed next to a large abstract painting, as it was in Tate Modern's version of *Panorama*, we recognize that for Richter, the depiction of a painting is not what is important.[49] Rather, in each of these works, no matter the disparity, the questions remain the same: How to resolve the relationship between artist and painting? How to envision painting's place in the world? What is the value of abstraction? Where does abstraction begin and figuration end?

When we stand surrounded by the *Cage* paintings in their temporary home institution of Tate Modern, we are immersed in a community of paintings, and we are drawn to watch them interact with each other, primarily on the level of their grey surfaces. We engage less with them individually than we watch them engage with each other. Together, they create the tone and temperature of the room—cool, refreshing, light. As an ensemble, they may exclude us from their shared secrets, but they leave us feeling light, bright, carefree.

By contrast, *Cage I–VI* were shown 18 October 2008–1 February 2009 in an exhibition of Richter's abstract works at Cologne's Museum Ludwig. Here, the paintings hung on a single wall opposite the fiery reds of *Bach I–IV* (1992), an arrangement that created an entirely different community of paintings. In Cologne, the paintings were a progression, from light to dark grey; they followed a trajectory with a goal, a goal that would appear to be contrary to the unpredictable and yet internally logical trajectory of Richter's oeuvre. In their opposition to the impassioned, pulsating *Bach I–IV*, the *Cage* canvases were quieter, more somber, somehow more intellectual in their progression from light to darkness. Their placement in line, on one wall, underlined their aloofness and their refusal to be understood. When they lined a single wall, the invitation to be experienced by the world they create was withdrawn; the symphonic rhythms and vibrations that arose between them gave way to a battle with their nemesis on the opposite wall.

Rather than taking this as a negative experience of *Cage I–VI,* the encounter with the paintings in different spaces, arranged differently, creates another layer to the already complex layers of these predominantly grey paintings. In Cologne, we experienced *Cage I–VI* anew, as a different series of paintings. They commanded that we walk along from one through six, to read them from left to right, like a book, to notice the spaces between each. The result was that they were more stoic and resolute when face-to-face with *Bach I–IV,* rather than symphonic and atonal as they are when they surround us on all four walls at Tate Modern.

When there is a special exhibition on display at Tate Modern, the crowds are drawn by the publicity given that occasion. Few people bother to wander the halls of the permanent collection. At such times *Cage I–VI* sit alone, without spectators, the room, appropriately, empty and silent. This strikes me as an ideal viewing circumstance. At Tate Modern, surrounded by *Cage I–VI,* we are reminded of the pregnant silences and emptiness of the paintings' namesake, and of the atonal sounds they produce when they come together. Even on a weekday morning at the Museum Ludwig, the exhibition of Richter's abstract paintings drew big crowds to see the local talent. Thus, their battle with the *Bach* series was—equally appropriately—interrupted by the movements, pauses, and comments of the other visitors. The viewer can easily become distracted altogether from the noiseless drama taking place on the surface of *Cage I–VI* that she experiences in their exhibition at Tate Modern.

Once again, the question persists: why are *Cage I–VI* overpainted with grey? The question is best answered by thinking about what grey is doing on these canvases. Grey is everywhere and nowhere in these paintings. Grey is impossible to comprehend. Other colors—yellow, red, blue, green—are quantifiable, or rather, can be qualified, seen, understood in their verticality, in their horizontality, in their definitiveness. They may change from one color to another, but we can identify and articulate each one individually. Grey is more difficult. On these six paintings, yellow is yellow, red is red, blue is blue, but grey is a whole spectrum of ever-shifting tones, temperatures, densities. Is it the background or the foreground? Is it horizontal or vertical? Does it erase, or is it erased? And then of course, the minute we arrive at their comprehension, the opposite reveals itself to be true. The vivacity of this contradiction is what gives a series such as *Cage I–VI* depth, and makes grey indispensable to this depth. Because grey is the one thing, the one color that remains the same. It may shift along a scale of hues and tones, densities and temperatures, but while blue becomes yellow, which takes over from green, grey, at least within each painting, remains grey. Even if we cannot grasp it, grey is always present. Up close, each of the six *Cage* paintings changes, shifts from what it was at a distance. Red becomes magenta, it becomes orange, and then in places, it is pink and even purple. Red is anything but trapped in these paintings. And grey moves with the other colors, underlining the ambiguity, uncertainty, and continuing contradiction. This makes grey the most exciting of all colors for

Richter. At least in the large abstract works, grey is lush, it is playful, filled with light, with air, with possibility and infinity. Grey on the canvases of *Cage I–VI* is what opens them upward and outward, lifting the viewer to a belief in the possibility of painting.

The surface coolness, emptiness, and silence of *Cage I–VI,* their behavior as though they are a secret society of which we will never be members, enable the possibility experienced in their midst. This surface behavior held together by the spectrum of grey is the "nothingness" of the painted surface on which everything is possible. The ambiguity and evasiveness of Richter's surfaces relieve them of all mystery. The relationship we cannot resist having with them is full of frustrations and problems. Because at the same time, the silence and emptiness they evoke is calming and liberating. Indeed, they create a space in grey paint that we want to be associated with; we want the self-assuredness they have. But they prohibit this because they relate primarily to each other, never letting us fully into their circle. And so, we fill that space with our own imagined narratives, narratives we project onto the paintings. In turn, these narratives are what Richter's paintings ask of us: they ask us to see, to know, and to be with them in this way.

Vision, Perception, and the Spectator

Like all of Richter's work, *Acht Grau* animates the crisis of vision in modernity as it has been philosophically and critically articulated, as well as visually represented, over the past twenty years. As I have suggested through analysis of *Cage I–VI,* though I have used a different language, Richter's paintings mark the shift in vision from a transcendental to a scientifically explicable, and culturally grounded spectator. Again, typical of Richter's tendency to suspend understanding, the paintings do not settle on either side of this transition, but rather are caught in the space in between. They both absorb and reflect the gaze of the spectator: we are transfixed by the grey and enchanted by our own reflection, and that of the world beyond: the walls of the Deutsche Guggenheim, other spectators, the world outside on the streets of Berlin. The eight panels are simultaneously opaque and reflective, like the grey that colors them. Within the context of Richter's oeuvre, this is not such a surprising result.[50] However, in *Acht Grau* this process is literalized; it takes place at the level of physical perception. The museum visitor literally sees the painted panel as well as his or her own body in the space it reflects. And from here, visitors are called on to reflect on their conceptual relations to the work of art, the museum, and by extension, the other institutions that claim to enable it. In this way, physical perception becomes the foundation of all that *Acht Grau* represents.

Again and again, Richter's work embraces the thorny issue of how he sees, how we see, how painting sees, and of course, because of his lifelong problematization of the relationship between painting and photography, how the photograph sees—as it is explored through the medium of paint—and vice versa. Because Richter is never finished with one dimension of any concept, his works also reflect on how he, we, painting, and photography do not see. All of us are blind to the reality we nevertheless imagine we see and know. And simultaneously, we are granted perspicacity in our inability to see what is before us. The panels of *Acht Grau* are everywhere and always engaged with this game of seeing and knowing. When I look at the huge glass panels, they are nothing but a surface, simultaneously emptied of an image to look at; there is nothing to see. I am drawn to move closer, and as I do, the surface becomes filled with my own image. At some point in the viewing process, there is a shift: at a distance, I see grey panels reflecting the world around them, and up close, I see myself. I cannot look away. I am drawn to the image of myself—does my hair look okay? I admire the outfit I am wearing; I feel empowered by my command over my own image. Until, sensing I might be being watched, my vanity exposed, I step back, and move to the safety of seeing *Acht Grau* as a series of painted objects, outside of myself. Of course, there are many obstructions and veils to the truth of who I am when I look at myself in one of the mirrored grey panels. And just like a painted canvas, there's no space for contemplation of my mirror image. As soon as I am drawn close, I am instantly uncomfortable, and I recoil. There is no possibility of falling into either the unfathomable beauty of Richter's grey glass or a narcissistic fascination with my own image. Through this oscillation of fascination for the grey panel that also throws my own image back on myself, I am pushed to recognize my own processes of looking at my own behavior before an image, and the relationship I develop with an artwork, a relationship that begins with my sense of sight. This performance, or enactment, of the process of perception before an artwork is the recognition that we are deep in the world of a self-conscious vision when face-to-face with Gerhard Richter grey.

If modernist painting under the influence of the new technologies of photography and cinema was concerned to bring the process of perception to the surface of the work, such that in the form of the image we saw the fragmentation and mobility of the process of looking within technological modernity, then *Acht Grau* engages this intention.[51] In its interaction with a viewer, the series performs the new contours of vision: vision is seen here as a continual process of omnipotent observation, self-censoring; it is both subjective and dependent on form. Vision here is, in short, the realization of what Alberti attributed to Narcissus nearly six centuries ago.[52] Before the mirrored panel of *Acht Grau,* like Narcissus at the pool, we see both our selves and the world around us. The paintings are both the record of what is objectively visible and a representation of what we see as our subjective selves. And in the presence of these mirrors, we are invited to see things from new perspectives while retaining, or better, returning to, representational realism.

The eight grey panels at the Deutsche Guggenheim are also an opportunity for Richter's preoccupation with the distortion of vision, as if a stone has been dropped into Narcissus's pool to create ripples on the surface, both in its literal and its cognitive sense. We see the distortion everywhere, in different forms, with different consequences, in the photo-paintings of the 1980s, the portraits, the overpainted photographs, and even in the abstract paintings of more recent years. At the most fundamental level, the early works' indulgence in the material of paint, their tendency to make visible paint as a substance, and consequently, its viscosity, tactility, and sensuous pleasures, draw our attention to their status as painted representation. As such, they ask us to question the veracity of what we see. The blur, or distortion, that takes so many different forms throughout Richter's fifty years of painting is always inviting, and simultaneously, denying our visual access to knowledge of what we see. The relationship between seeing and knowing is never clear on Richter's canvas. This tension between seeing and knowing is what others have identified as characteristic of painting in the twentieth century.[53] *Acht*

Grau is no different in that the panels reenvision Richter's creation of insight, and simultaneously, the frustration of that insight on the painted surface. The relationship between representation and the world, or the object in the image, is akin in *Acht Grau* to its realization in, for example, *18. Oktober 1977.* The truth of the painting in grey is its ultimate inaccessibility to that object, its opacity to the truth of the real world. The spectator is involved in the world represented, invited to look closer, and simultaneously cast at a distance.

It is significant that the blur is grey, not the rainbow of colors Richter began to use in the 1980s, or black and white. He chooses grey, I would argue, because, so often, "seeing" is a penetration of a past that will ultimately bring insight to the confusion of the present. The world of the past is not black and white; it is always shaded by the passing of time and memory. Storr says of Richter's use of grey:

> Richter has lopped off the top of his gray scale and sometimes the bottom as well, leaving himself a *grisaille* range of ashen, slate, or anthracite tones that in their variously warm shades, cool bluish tints, and occasionally white-streaked accents deflate rounded shapes, slow the darting eyes on the lookout for surprises, and dampen the pictorial ambiance like a low, hushed cello drone. Above all, Richter does the opposite of what we expect from chiaroscuro painting; rather than reveal the essence of the image, his dour palette further conceals it. Playing against our desire to trust our own eyes, he has given us reason to mistrust them.[54]

There is no reason to argue with Storr. If the grey blur is an invocation of the past, the hazy, veiled world that is present to memory, then grey is the most realistic color for its depiction. In all the historical works—*18. Oktober 1977, Onkel Rudi* (1965), *Tante Marianne* (1965), and the other images that evoke loss, trauma, guilt, and the imperative to reconsider our assumptions about both personal and public (particularly German) history—the painting is grey. The use of grey is key to Richter's insistence that we revisit and reassess our relationship to the past. Our vision is hazy when Richter returns to and represents the realm of memory.

And yet Storr does not allow for the perspicacity of grey, as the blur that is simultaneously a call to look again. Even when Richter denies access to the truth, the reality, the moment of enlightenment through his use of grey, there is always a gesture toward it, even if it disintegrates before we reach the truth. The opposite is always woven into the discourse of the blur. Simultaneously, as we approach the mirrored surface of the panels in *Acht Grau,* or stand back to admire the rhythms and resonances across the surfaces of *Cage I–VI,* there is a moment of clarity and insight. In these later works the revelation is usually about our selves, our relationship to painting, in contrast to the revelations of painting itself in the earlier works from the 1960s and 1970s.

In the photo-paintings of the Baader-Meinhof group, *18. Oktober 1977,* the blur of the surface and the grey of the blur ensure this bifurcated presence/absence of both painting and spectator. When we look at Ensslin in *Gegenüberstellung* or Andreas Baader in *Erschossener I & II / Man Shot Down I & II* (1988) we strain to identify the person, then to pinpoint the facial expressions, to "see" the image and bring it into focus. At some point in the viewing process, we see and know who and what we are looking at, its place in German history. This is the process of looking at the *18. Oktober 1977* cycle. But ultimately, we cannot clarify what we see, we can never fully grasp the knowledge that the paintings impart, because it is gone, in the past, and thus signaled as absent on and to the image itself. This unknown, the daring to leave open and unimagined what might have taken place in the depicted events, is the clouding of vision that has come to characterize both our memories of the past and the modern moment more generally.

The clouding of vision is the inevitable residue of the much applauded precision of vision, the clarity that supposedly came with the introduction of the photographic camera, and the mechanization of everyday life, the authority of a voyeuristic gaze. Richter's use of grey draws attention to what is effectively the complexity and ambiguity of processes of looking, and looking at painting in particular. For him, grey visualizes a way of looking at the past and the relationship to the present via painting.

The uncertainty of seeing and processes of perception, both of and in representation-infused modern art from the turn of the nineteenth century onward, pervaded art history and later, visual and

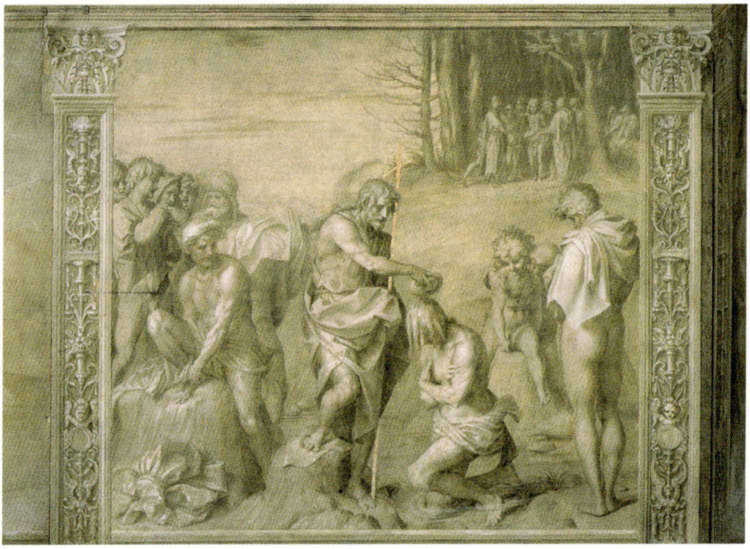

Plate 1. Andrea del Sarto (ca. 1487–1530), *Saint John the Baptist Baptizing,* 1509–26. Grisaille fresco. Chiostro dello Scalzo. Copyright Scala / Art Resource, NY.

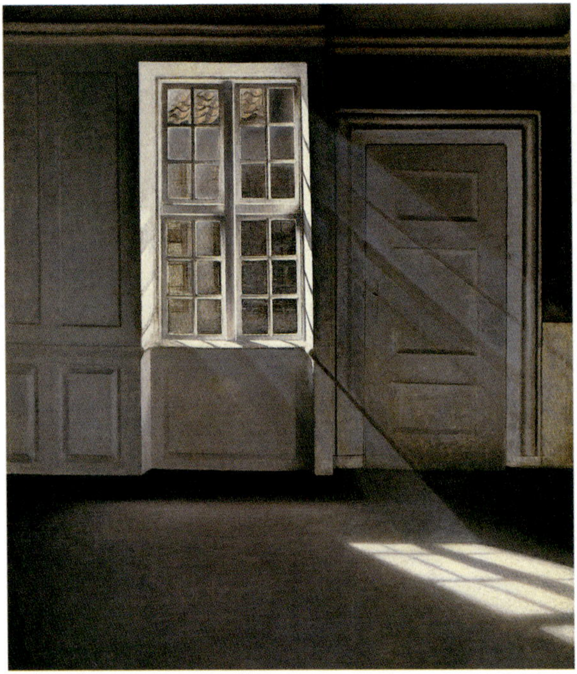

Plate 2. Vilhelm Hammershøi (1864–1916), *Sunbeams or Sunshine. Dust Motes Dancing in the Sunbeams,* 1900. Oil on canvas, 59 × 70 cm. Courtesy of Allan T. Kohl Minneapolis College of Art and Design Collection.

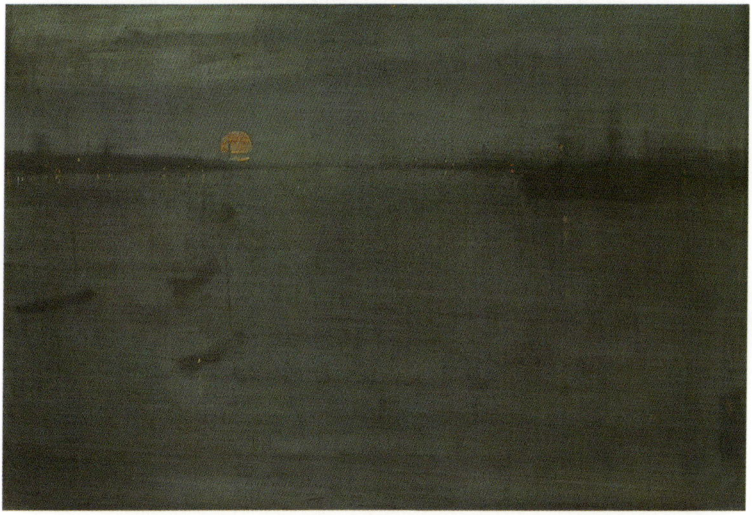

Plate 3. James McNeill Whistler, American (1834–1903), *Nocturne: Blue and Gold—Southampton Water,* 1872. Oil on canvas, 19⅞ × 29 15⁄16 inches (50.5 × 76 cm). Stickney Fund, 1900.52. Copyright The Art Institute of Chicago.

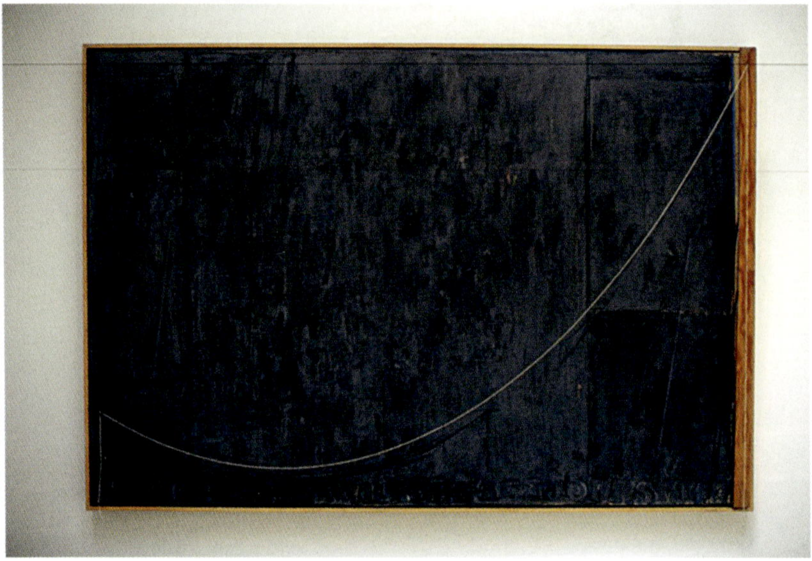

Plate 4. Jasper Johns (b. 1930), *Catenary (Manet–Degas),* 1999. Encaustic and sand on canvas with objects, 38 × 57 ¼ × 6 inches. Copyright Jasper Johns. Licensed by VAGA, New York, NY.

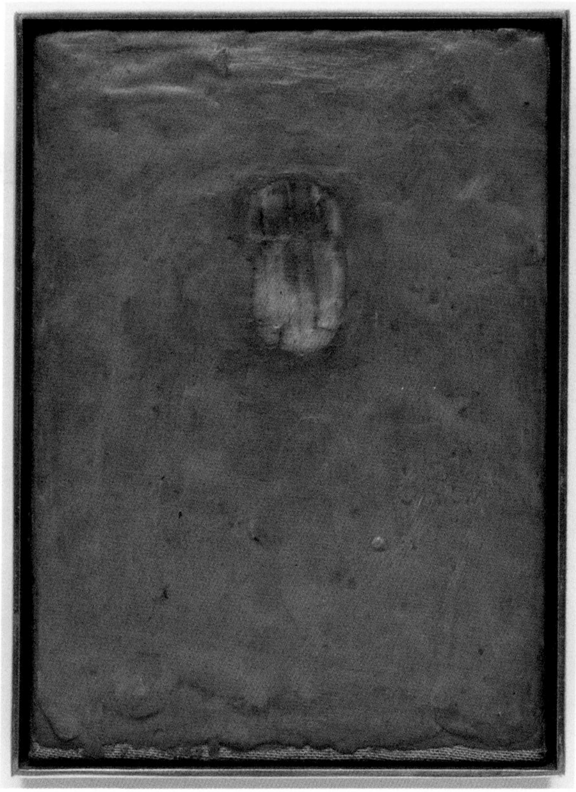

Plate 5. Jasper Johns (b. 1930), *Painting Bitten by a Man,* 1961. Encaustic on canvas mounted on type plate, 9½ × 6 ⅞ inches (24.1 × 17.5 cm). Gift of Jasper Johns in memory of Kirk Varnedoe, chief curator of the Department of Painting and Sculpture, 1989–2001. Copyright VAGA, New York, NY. The Museum of Modern Art digital image copyright The Museum of Modern Art. Licensed by SCALA / Art Resource, NY.

Plate 6. Mark Rothko (1903–1970), *Untitled,* 1969. Acrylic on canvas, 92 × 78⅞ inches. Catalogue Raisonné no. 814, Estate Number 5208.69.

Plate 7. Brice Marden (b. 1938), *The Seasons,* 1974–75. Oil and wax on canvas, 96 × 249 inches (243.8 × 632.5 cm), each panel 96 × 60 inches (243.8 × 152.4 cm). Accession number 1975-11 DJ. Photograph by Bill Jacobson Studio, New York. Courtesy The Menil Collection, Houston. Copyright 2016 Brice Marden / Artists Rights Society (ARS), New York.

Plate 8. Agnes Martin (1912–2004), *Untitled, #3,* 1989. Acrylic and graphite on canvas, 72 × 72 inches (182.9 × 182.9 cm). Photograph by Kerry Ryan McFate. Courtesy Pace Gallery. Copyright 2016 Agnes Martin / Artists Rights Society (ARS), New York.

Plate 9. Agnes Martin (1912–2004), *White Flower,* 1960. Oil on canvas, 72 × 72 inches (182 × 182 cm). Courtesy The Solomon R. Guggenheim Museum, New York. Copyright 2016 Agnes Martin / Artists Rights Society (ARS), New York.

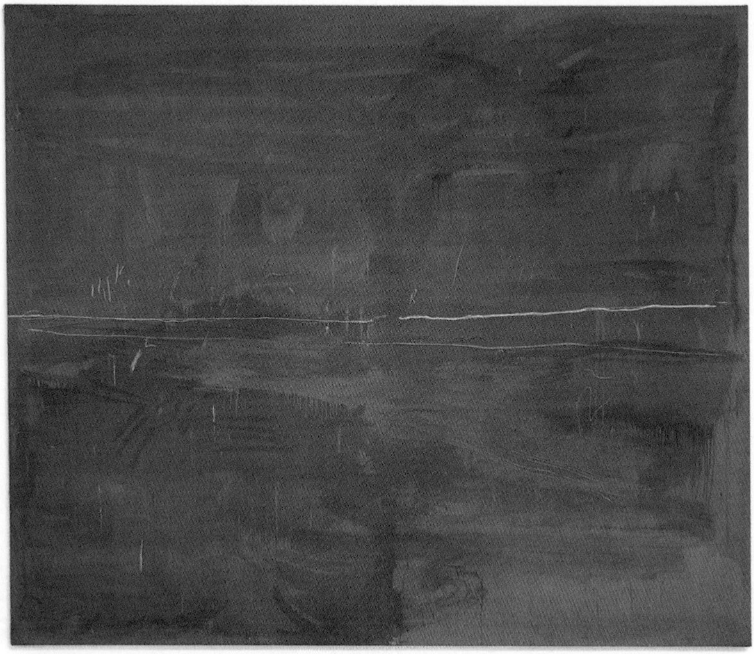

Plate 10. Cy Twombly (1928–2011), *Untitled (Bolsena),* 1969. Oil-based house paint, wax crayon, and pencil on canvas, 79 × 94⅔ inches (200.7 × 240.5 cm). Catalogue raisonné Bastian III, #79. Digital image courtesy Galerie Karsten Greve, St. Moritz/Paris/Cologne. Copyright Cy Twombly Foundation.

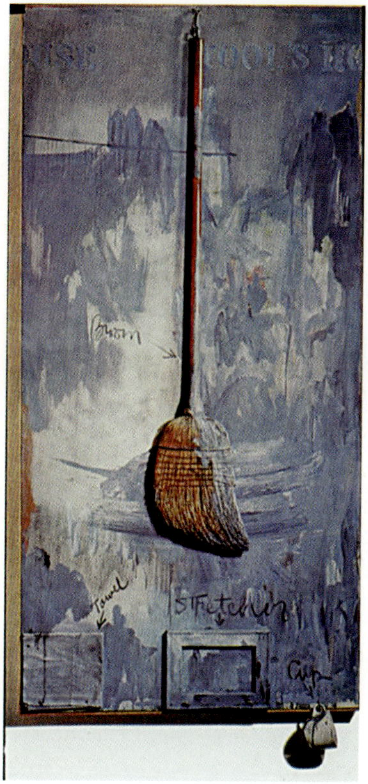

Plate 11. Jasper Johns (b. 1930), *Fool's House,* 1962. Oil on canvas with objects, 72 × 36 inches (182.9 × 91.4 cm). Courtesy University of California, San Diego. Copyright Jasper Johns. Licensed by VAGA, New York, NY.

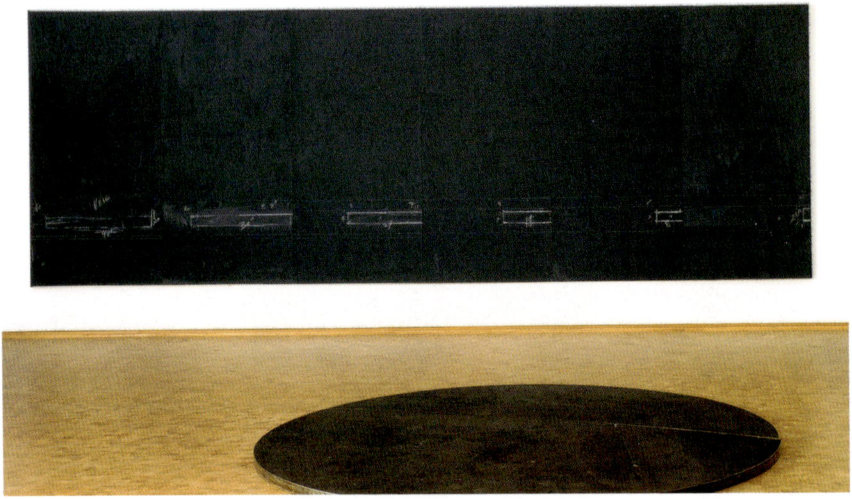

Plate 12. Cy Twombly (1928–2011), *Treatise on the Veil*, 1968. Oil and chalk on canvas, 254.5 × 750 cm. Photograph by Rheinisches Bildarchiv Köln. Copyright Cy Twombly Foundation.

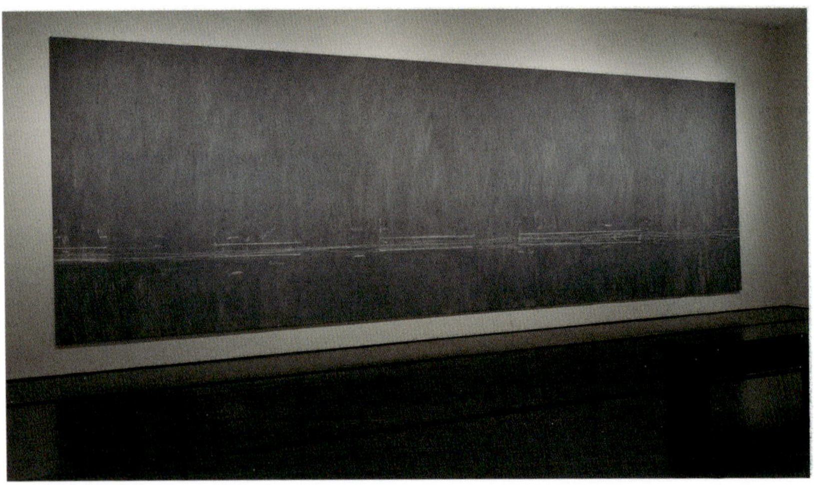

Plate 13. Cy Twombly (1928–2011), *Treatise on the Veil (Second Version)*, 1970. House paint and crayon on canvas, 118$\frac{1}{8}$ × 393$\frac{3}{8}$ inches (300 × 999.8 cm). Accession number 1998–009 DJ. Photograph by Paul Hester. Courtesy The Menil Collection, Houston. Copyright Cy Twombly Foundation.

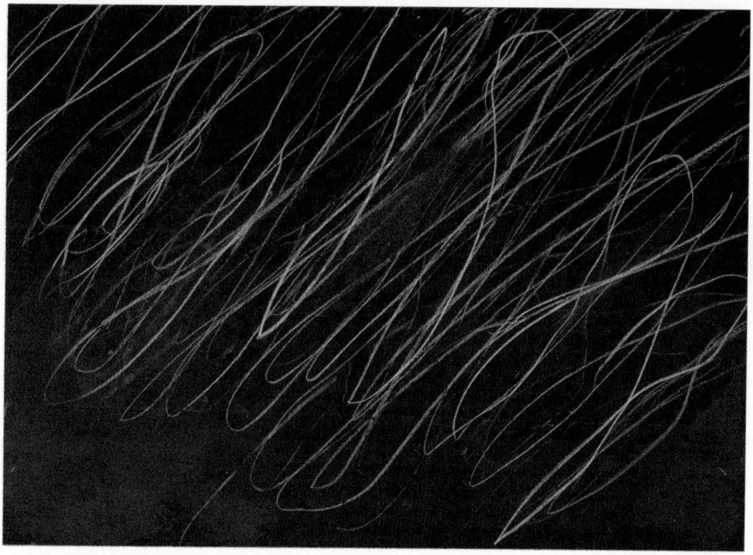

Plate 14. Cy Twombly (1928–2011), *Untitled*, 1970. Oil paint and wax crayon on paper, 27¾ × 39⅜ inches. Copyright Cy Twombly Foundation.

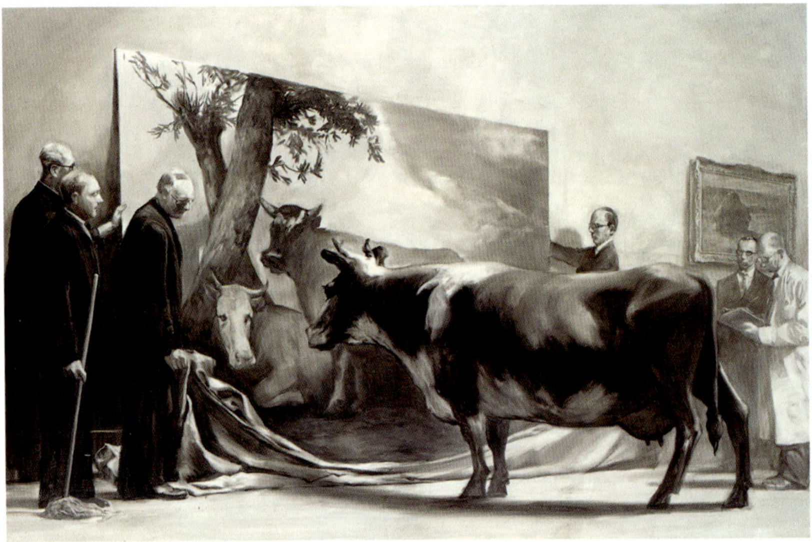

Plate 15. Mark Tansey (b. 1949), *The Innocent Eye Test,* 1981. Oil on canvas, 78 × 120 inches (198.1 × 304.8 cm). Gift of Jan Cowles and Charles Cowles in honor of William S. Lieberman, 1988 (1988.183), The Metropolitan Museum of Art. Copyright Mark Tansey. Collection of The Metropolitan Museum of Art. Courtesy Art Resource, NY.

Plate 16. Gerhard Richter (b. 1932), *Untitled (Grey)*, 1968. Oil on canvas, 50 × 50 cm. Catalogue Raisonné 194-6. Copyright 2016 Gerhard Richter.

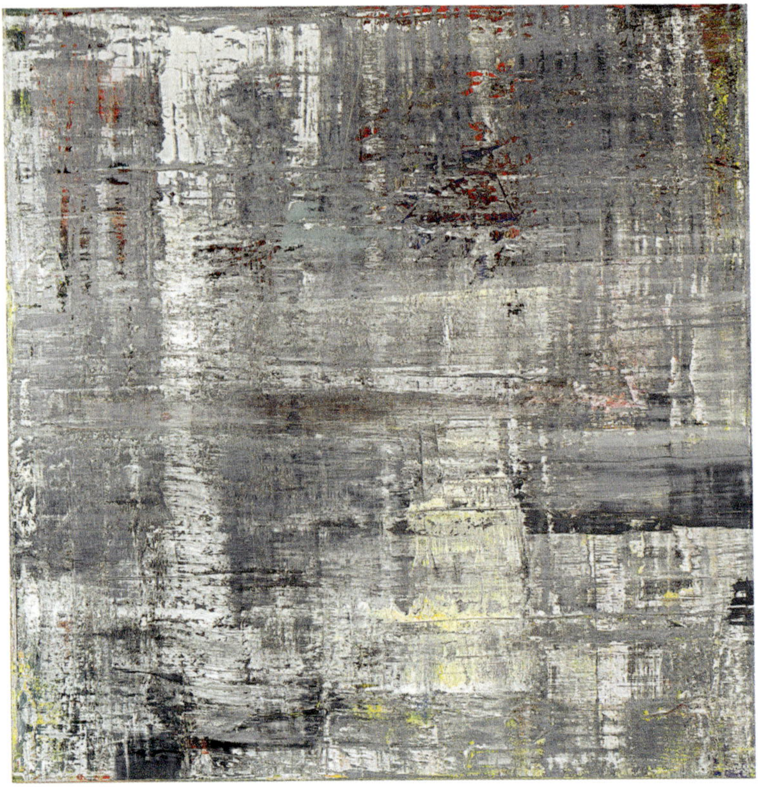

Plate 17. Gerhard Richter (b. 1932), *Cage V,* 2006. Oil on canvas, 300 × 300 cm. Catalogue Raisonné 897-5. Copyright 2016 Gerhard Richter.

image studies, until approximately twenty years ago.[55] In particular, the dominance of monocular theories of perception, specifically those based on a perspectival system where a viewer is disinterested, static, and omnipotent, were questioned at the turn of the century most forcefully by Monet and the impressionists. For Monet, the rendering visible of brushstrokes in the depiction of light and color is the representation of human vision: active, changing, never fixed, always in the process of transformation. As we know, Monet's canvases can be hazy, not necessarily blurred, but flirting with perceptual blindness of different kinds.

Richter's use of the grey blur is likewise the mark of modernism.[56] To give one example, on Richter's most political canvases, vision as physical perception is exposed as a veil behind which a truth, or at times, reality, resides. Even when the truth of that reality cannot be trusted, or remains subjective, it is a truth nevertheless. Richter has come to know this truth because he has lived and painted in a century overtaken by visual cultures and visual media that claim an ever dependable, ever more reliable form of realism, closer and closer to absolute truth. For Richter, that truth is ineffable. It is always grey. Because grey comes closest to the expression of the possibility of the nevertheless unattainable ideal. And through the relationship between painting and these other media as they are explored in Richter's paintings, photographic-based media are no more accurate than painting in their perception of the world about them. The blur in grey is the reality, the truth, of what visual representation has to offer. In Richter's paintings, this perception and vision is nonnegotiable, to the point where one might argue it has become a theoretical maxim. But, of course, for Richter, everything changes; nothing can remain static. That is the point.

It has been argued that Richter's most elegant and unique articulation of the crisis of vision that comes hand in hand with the transformations of modernity is the blur. However, this is only one of his multiple visions of the modernist project. For example, his wont to fracture and fragment the image is surely a replication of our tendency to see the world in pieces, from impossible angles. Perhaps most striking is the incompletion or fragmentation of those images that replicate the form and features of the mass media. In works such as *Tote / Dead* (1963), *Kuh / Cow* (1964), or those in which bodies are cut off, faces fragmented, buildings serrated, the figures are not only blurred but severed without concern, perhaps in reference to the fact that they must fit into the specifications of space in the press.[57] The incompletion can also be seen as a repetition of the one-dimensionality—an incompletion of another kind—that is, the world reproduced in and by the press. In all of these images, whether or not they include text, mastheads, or titles, the object of representation, the reality at two removes—one by the painting and another by the photograph it emulates—is left ambiguous because of its incompletion. And the paintings confront us with the limitations of practices of seeing and looking at the everyday world. Confined and conditioned by the press, we see, just like Richter's paintings, from unusual and impossible angles. And, of course, we are left with no other option but to see in fragments. The restless and unsuspecting viewer of this world might proceed with the illusion of omnipotence over reality. But according to Richter, the doing away with perspective, and all of these possibilities to see from on high, at an angle, in close up and on demand result in a subjective and complex processes of vision that can only be reflected in painting.

In *Acht Grau,* the blur and the multiple, fragmented perspectives shift to the surface reflection of the glass panel. I see myself in the reflection of the image, against a nondiscriminate, shapeless grey background. I have no access to anything other than my distorted and opaque image of myself. And this physical perception generates the conceptual distortions that are the inevitable consequences of a blindness of sorts. What I see in that mirror is so "blurred" by my own imagination that there is no objectivity to the image, especially when it is of myself. Thus, the blur is not only within the substance of paint but also within the substance or content of what I see when I look at these paintings, and by extension, the reality they represent. I am ultimately unable to separate truth from imagination, to distinguish what the painting sees from what I see. Such is the provenance of painting: it is both opaque and reflective, a reproduction of the world in mirror image as well as a transparent window onto the world, a world we also see in the buildings and streets outside as they are reflected in the surface.[58] For Richter, grey paint has the capacity to reveal all of this.

Painting and Other Visual Art and Media

In the 1980s, Richter began to explore consciously the relationship between painting and photography, a relationship that led to the multiplication and transformation of his own paintings. Then in the late 1990s and early 2000s, this process led to the manipulation and proliferation of his paintings through other media, and in reference to other media. Always, I would argue, the oeuvre is ultimately concerned to interrogate one medium—painting—through reference to multiple others. He repeatedly defines painting at the interface with photography, cinema, sculpture, theater, architecture, and, in recent years, the ancient media of carpet weaving together with the most contemporary, digital media. Always, the intermedia explorations are designed to push painting still further beyond its own boundaries, and usually in an attempt to disprove the truth of all visual representation.

Richter takes up the centuries-old question of "what is painting?" in many different ways. And his responses through reiterations in grey all challenge the identity of the medium. To do this, he takes painting into the world of photography, makes it cinematic, and then turns painting into a theater. His painting is never permanently traded with other media: painting more often falls in the cracks between it and other art forms and media, only to be pulled back again in an effort to reassert its uniqueness. Before I move to a discussion of how Richter's work in grey paint also courts the precarious boundaries between painting and cinema, painting and architecture, painting and theater, I want to pause briefly for a discussion of the grey overpainted photographs. In these, unlike the contemporaneous larger oil paintings, grey becomes interchangeable, or rather, almost interchangeable, with pink, baby blue, soft violet, and green.[59]

The exhibition in 2008 of five hundred overpainted photographs at the Museum Morsbroich, Leverkusen, Germany, showed all of Richter's lifelong concerns recur in the overpainted photographs.[60] These recurrences are, nevertheless, often in very different guises from the way they appear in the paintings. In these images—most of which are either untitled or minimally titled, and all of which are dated—painting and photography are placed in constant conversation. In many cases, the two art forms argue, vociferously. At times painting and photography belong to two different worlds; at times they are integrated and in complete unison with each other, a synergetic swell on the face of the photograph as it is transformed into a support for paint. And when grey paint appears to be falling out of the sky, it complements the desolate landscape across which it settles. In such instances, painting and photography are apparently of the same world. Similarly, in the delicate spray of pale pink or blue or grey paint on a photographed winter landscape, the paint becomes the softly falling snow in the foreground. In what Botho Strauss refers to as the "civil scenes," we see people, buildings, interior spaces, even the *Frankfurter Allgemeine Zeitung*, obscured by a swathe of muddy grey paint. At times the paint does not take to the surface of the photograph, shrinking like water escaping oil. In other paintings, *8. März 03*, for example, the grey paint is thick, solid, permanent, like the blanket of paint that now protects Gudrun Ensslin in *Erhängte*, and further in *Decke*. In these examples, people, places, and things are veiled, as if to prohibit us from seeing the reality we always want a photograph to represent. In the examples where a coat of grey paint slides across and recoils from the surface of the image, photographs are transformed into visions of a fantasy, an illusion, or if a reality, it is a reality that has become blurred. Sometimes, but not always, the paint transforms the photograph—from an infinitely reproducible image of an event that happened, into a unique, personal memory of which the viewer has no memory. The image is transformed from a Polaroid snapshot into an aesthetic jewel that creates a memory.

As one moves through the numerous rooms of the exhibition, there is little apparent clear development in the approach and handling of the paint or the photograph across the oeuvre. By the late 1990s and 2000s, however, patterns in paint on what now appears as a photograph-as-support come to mimic the same overpainting of the abstract paintings on canvas. Again, there is a strong suggestion that this eventuates because Richter privileges paint over photography as a way of seeing the world, of finding truth through representation, in representation. And yet, painting poses problems for Richter. Painting, we will remember, clouds vision, or clarifies its cloudedness. Thus, on the one hand, the overpainted photographs protest the idea that, with the invention of photography, there is no longer a need for painting, no place for painting in the world. In these examples, the work of painting, according to Richter, is not over. And on the other hand, according to Richter, the value and means of painting are only made visible when it is juxtaposed with photography. Likewise, photography's claims to truth and revelation are only made visible through putting it to the test of paint. Grey paint is, as these overpainted photographs insist, the medium through which as a painter, Richter can most easily access reality, a photographed and a painted reality, the reality of photography and painting, respectively. As Adriani points out, while critics and other artists wanted to doubt and dismiss, or at best, foretell the death of painting, Richter has quietly proved its sovereignty. Painting is the foremost means of seeing and knowing the world.[61] Because it is a seeing and knowing that is always self-consciously located in grey, a seeing and knowing that continues to clarify its lack of clarity. And as we have come to expect, painting itself creates its own occlusions to the truth. Painting is a thin veil that obscures the world; painting is an ambiguous messy medium in which nothing makes sense. Painting sits in the grey, in the interstice between concealment and revelation, between reality and representation, between now and then, between blindness and insight. This impossible contradiction is able to exist in the frames of Richter's paintings, or here, in the overpainted photographs, because it exists in grey, at the interface of two media. The photographs give the ultimate experience of modernist painting.

The overpainting of the photographs comes in a range of colors. In addition to grey, it is notably red, white, pink, green, blue, and, mostly, a mixture of at least two colors. Nevertheless, the palette is limited. Moreover, the palette is both limited and limitless because we know the colors come from the paint that is left over in the studio at the end of Richter's day. The overpainted photograph is a "serendipitous" creation: Richter explains in an interview with Markus Heinzelmann that the paint dripped onto the photographs as he was transferring the image to canvas.[62] In the 1990s, he deliberately "pulls" the photographs through the paint that is left over from the day's work on the large canvases. Richter uses paint on the large canvas that remains wet on the doctor blade for up to three days. This choice enables the paint and process of "overpainted photographs."[63] More importantly, because the beautiful colors from the day's work have run together on the doctor blade, it is not surprising that they often merge to make grey. Grey on the overpainted photographs is literally what is left over, unnoticed, interstitial, of an unfinished world. And it is also the result of other colors merging into a messy, obscured depiction. Thus, here, the paint used on the photographs becomes a metonym for all that Richter claims painting to be. This apparently simple, somewhat naive use of paint on photographs realizes an image that encapsulates all that it means to paint, all that paint can be. This is a truth that is painted in grey; even if for serendipitous reasons, it is literally and fundamentally grey. Grey thus offers a solution to the problem of, what is painting today?

As we know from *Acht Grau,* Richter does not stop at exploring the reality of painting through its relationship to photography. The truth in and of grey painting is also in the architectural and sculptural dimension of the panels of *Acht Grau.* This is not the only time Richter's mirrored glass panels have been designed and placed to articulate social spaces. All at once they define the spatial conditions in which they make sense, reach into a historical past and bring it into the present, and force us to question our own identities within this space, this history. The enormous window of 11,500 mouth-blown, antique glass panes in the Cologne Cathedral (2007) is a more recent example of this phenomenon. And before it, the 625 stained glass panes for the window of Haus Otte (1922) designed by Walter Gropius in Berlin-Zehlendorf.[64] However, the mirrored paintings in grey (and other colors) are different and exciting because they extend the space of the Guggenheim Museum, the Deutsche Bank, Richter's studio.[65]

As Buchloh says, works such as *Acht Grau* exist in a long line of German architectural and sculptural designs that place glass and light as their substance.[66] Like Mies van der Rohe's vision for the *Friedrichstrasse Skyscraper Project* in 1921, or the designs of the young Walter Gropius from the same interwar period, even the department stores designed for and built around the corner in Berlin's Mitte district, Richter's works in glass engage in a specifically German architectural conversation with glass, light, and steel.[67] Richter's work in glass shares few of the functional concerns of its predecessors but it does redefine space and our experience of it, and encourages us to negotiate our identity within it.[68] These works direct us where to stand, to walk, to move, and they encourage us to see the world from different perspectives. Moreover, as we go inside, as we are surrounded by Richter's glass panels, they open up space and our relationship to it, specifically the space of the Deutsche Guggenheim in a series of mirror reflections. We can become confused within these walls, because when mirrored surfaces are introduced, we lose our bearings, our reference points. The eight movable glass panels open up a mobile and uncertain place from which to command the space in which we stand. In effect, we lose orientation and the grey mirrors give us the experience of being in a maze. Or, put another way, *Acht Grau* creates a theatrical stage on which we are placed as the leading actors, only to find that we keep forgetting our parts at the moment our perspective changes.

Richter can be very specific about the architectural form and dimensions of the rooms in which his paintings are exhibited. He has even designed the spaces himself for some exhibitions. He is adamant that "a proper play needs a stage, and pictures need architecture. It's quite simple."[69] The relationship to architecture is, to be sure, very complex. In Berlin, he had the windows of the Deutsche Guggenheim unblocked, a strategy he had already implemented at the Städtische Kunsthalle Düsseldorf for his retrospective in that building in 1986.[70] In both these examples, windows and what can be seen through them, as well as what is reflected on the glass surface—both inside and outside—become integral to the artwork. Thanks to the windows, the world outside supplements that on the inside when it is reflected on Richter's grey surfaces. And so the viewer's experience of the work becomes linked to variables such as the weather, the time of the day, the events taking place on the street. This, then, merges with the drama of the gallery space as a stage, the drama of the visitors in the space at any given time as they interact with each other and the works. If, as Richter would have it, pictures need architecture, *Acht Grau* and the other mirrored works show the interdependence of the two forms: the panels are dependent on the architectural form and fittings that accommodate them for their meaning at any given moment.

The creation of uncertainty in relationship to space, and of constantly shifting spaces as they are forged by the artwork, reminds of the theater, particularly as it was developed in the early part of the twentieth century by dramaturges such as Erwin Piscator. Like

Piscator's use of the cinema onstage, the *Grauer Spiegel / Gray Mirror* (1991) opens out the space of the Saint Louis Art Museum such that several spaces come to coexist on the same plane—that of the artwork—simultaneously. And like a European art film from the 1970s, the narratives played out on this fractured plane are constantly in flux and are driven by an aleatory logic. People come and go, people walk in and out of the grey-mirrored frame, they sometimes pause, reflect on their own image, becoming actors being watched and an audience that watches. Strategically placed around the museum walls, on entering *Acht Grau* in the Deutsche Guggenheim on Unter den Linden, we are greeted with far more than grey paintings to look at, from a distance. We become involved in a complex narrative as we watch our reflection, that of other museum visitors, the panels' reflection of each other, the building walls, both inside and outside, on their glazed surfaces. Like another genre of architectural design in glass and light from early twentieth-century Germany, namely, the designs of Bruno Taut and Paul Scheerbart, and later, department stores at Chemnitz and Braunschweig in the 1920s, Richter's panels engage in discourses on the complicated relations of inside and outside, thus of the public and private, of space as it determines and accommodates our identities within the world.[71] Thus, in what is a unique achievement for painting, Richter's paintings take up the concerns of architecture and disorient us, make us reconsider our inhabitation of the museum space, our identity within that world.

Richter claims that works such as *Schwarz, Rot, Geld / Black, Red, Gold* (1999) at the Reichstag are site-specific, but that *Acht Grau* is not.[72] Because the grey panels are transportable, they can be, and indeed have been, exhibited in other spaces.[73] That said, however, it is possible to argue that each experience of the works is site-specific, because each is a performance dependent on the building, the street outside, the weather, the visitors who are or are not there on any particular day. This unique experience, as it touches upon the experience of architecture, performance, and other art forms, is perhaps something painting has always done. Nevertheless, what makes *Acht Grau* extraordinary is that the works perform what they also represent: they bring to the surface the true site-specificity of all painting. This task of painting—to make the role of art within the world conscious—is familiar from the end of the nineteenth century. Like the formation of painting at this time, throughout the twentieth century, Richter establishes a symphonic, but also atonal, relationship to the other arts. In this way, his *Acht Grau* become the sine qua non of painting in the twentieth century. They are paintings that tell us the truth of painting in its most distilled form as far as we know it, today.

Because *Acht Grau* is the result of Richter's imagination, the opposite is also true. The works have nothing in common with, or better, are doing something different from those of Picasso and Manet, or other artists working in grey. The architectural and three-dimensional spaces created by *Acht Grau* are like nothing else that has been done in painting. This is where Richter breaks the rules of all that painting can and is assumed to do. It is also where Richter breaks the rules of modernist painting: in its dimensionality and spatiality, Richter returns the theatrical to painting to make it more, not less, pure. Similarly, through the relationships across painting and other media, in a complete transgression of the modernist conception of painting, Richter explores the beginning and end of painting through an examination of its moment of confluence with—as opposed to its distinction from—other media.

Having experienced the multiple narratives of *Acht Grau,* when returning to other Richter series, we recognize the invocation of the cinema in the communities of paintings. And in the space between painting and cinema Richter, yet again, profoundly pushes the boundaries of painting as we know them. I have discussed how there are paintings, especially those with a surface wiped in glossy paint, in which the work is reduced (or elevated) to a play of light on the surface. This can also describe the cinema. In their communities, Richter's grey paintings can offer an experience that reminds of watching a film, a film in which time and space are constantly in motion. As Ensslin moves into the courtroom across the three grey photo-paintings of *Gegenüberstellung,* her facial expression changes, and thus, we find a different relationship to the cinema. Between and across these three images, Ensslin comes alive in time and space.[74] As the lighting changes across the triptych, so does the focus of her face and body. Her figure is placed in the center frame, just as it might be if she were shown entering the courtroom in a film sequence. And with these transitions of the image, we become drawn into her individual plight as we would be drawn into a film narrative if promised intimacy (as we are here) with a character. We become witness to her shifting emotions stirred up by the realization of her entrapment by political and social institutions. Together the three paintings do the work of the cinema. In particular, here it is the work of the silent cinema, in black and white, telling stories that were not always conclusive or designed to convince us of something we did not want to know about. Richter's historical and political images are, after all, always in grey. They are always blurred.

When the narrative does not unfold across multiple paintings, a drama is likely to develop in time and space within a single image. The shadowy figures of the artist in a series of overpainted photographs dated between 15 January 1990 and 26 January 1990 represent a self-realization in motion, on chairs with wheels, Richter's own paintings in the background, apparently a series, floating across a single wall. Before the image, we have the sense we are watching a movie.[75] The photographs are in motion, defined by their illusions, the specter of a figure, the artist who, like his paintings on the wall behind him, is an image whose only reality as a trace of something that once was before the camera. There is no original Gerhard Richter as subject of this overpainted photograph, only shadows on swivel chairs, reproductions of paintings in grey, traces of grey paint that seem to mimic the shadow of a lead that runs across the floor from one shadowy figure to an undefined space before the image.

Following six blurred photographs, made one each day between 15 January 1990 and 21 January 1990, Richter produced his self-portrait on the swivel chair in what we assume to be the studio five times, one each day between 22 January 1990 and 26 January 1990.[76] The form and color of the overpainting are different in each portrait, as are Richter's place and the density of his shadow within the frame. The replication of a portrait in which the self is an ever shifting and morphing shadow, with no body that might serve as the original of representation, further underlines the ephemerality of the artist, the image, the reality of what might be seen by a camera. This denial of the power of representation to imitate fully an object, or even to have any relationship to an object, as it is reiterated across Richter's whole oeuvre is the constant refrain of the cinema, at least those modernist cinematic images that best interrogate their own existence. The historical cinematic avant-garde of 1920s Europe with its play of light and shadow, its drama of appearance and disappearance, in time, through space might be identified as a precedent to these latter five repetitions of his self-portrait.[77]

Even more contemporary than the cinema, when Richter's painted glass panels come in grey and we find ourselves staring into and at the screen, narcissistically observing ourselves in our fragmented world, as well as watching other people, his painting strikes up a relationship with contemporary media. The surface of *Acht Grau* can remind of the computer screen in particular, but also the television and video surveillance monitors, all of which, ironically, are turned off in Richter's painted world. Even an image such as *Abstraktes Bild (Haut) / Abstract Painting (Skin)* (2004) that makes explicit reference to another surface in its title—that of the body—has its viewer staring. We stand before the painting as if an image is going to appear, as if the "static" of the surface is only a temporary painting, an interruption to the image. Accordingly, even when computer and other analog and digital image screens are not explicitly referenced, we behave toward the paintings as though they are. We stare fascinatedly, until we recognize (or don't) the dissolution of our selves, at a moment when we give in to the represented world. It could be that Richter is not interested in screens at all, and social conditioning finds the viewer looking to these paintings for images of a more everyday kind. Perhaps this is the only way to access the challenges of painting in the twenty-first century? Irrespective of how we look at Richter's grey canvases—both the paintings and the screens they appear to imitate—these images are always, ultimately, about painting and its concerns, concerns it might always have had over the centuries, but which Richter brings to our attention, on the grey surface of the image.

In all of these ways, Richter continues to push beyond the limits of painting. According to his paintings, and his grey paintings in particular, painting sits at the interface with many different visual media. In its relationship to sculpture, architecture, photography, and less obviously, but just as powerfully, the theatrical and cinematic, painting has as much to say and to do in the twenty-first century as it did in the twentieth. At least, the revelations of Richter's paintings are usually made possible through their embrace, their simultaneous differentiation from, and kinship with, the media that sit next to them.

They have become inseparable. In addition, through the conversations with other media, in Richter's images, we come to know the limits of painting, and to see it challenged in the very same moment. On Richter's canvas these limits are shown to us and challenged over and over again in grey paint.

Figuration into Abstraction and Back Again

Richter's world presents one of the most interesting examples of the modernist erasure of the line between figuration and abstraction. Like everything else in Richter's work, the conundrum of the distinction between figuration and abstraction takes place in the space between: between painting, photography, and other media, between the past and the present, for example, articulated in the overpainted photographs, the blur of the photo-paintings, or the fractures of the mirrored images. At the most obvious level, the figurative is restrained by the smears and blurring of paint until the object and the image become abstracted. As Richter has suggested, even the works that appear to be "of" a thing in the world are always abstracted. *Klorolle / Toilet Roll* (1964), *Familie / Family* (1964) and *Liegestuhl / Deck Chair* (1965) are good examples. They are unsettling because we lose sight—literally—of the reality at stake, the thing that is represented. As things, still life objects, animals, and humans can become ominous when everything gets blurred in grey. In works such as these or *Horst mit Hund / Horst with Dog* (1965) or *Telefonierender / Man on the Phone* (1965), the figures are distant, their actions uncertain, their facial expressions distorted, their characters made shady, threatening because of their amorphous grey depiction. Figures also acquire a sense of foreboding, their eyes blackened, mouths distorted, the background wiped away. Of course, like the distinction between painting and photography, there is always a clear definition between figurative and abstract elements of these images, often from the 1960s and 1970s. We can make out the shape of the chair; we are in no doubt as to what we are looking at in *Studentin / Student* (1967), to give another example. But the confrontational pose of the woman, the fact that the image has clearly been cut out from a newspaper and painted, the blacking out of the eyes, are Richter's way, in this and other of the portrait paintings in particular, to put pressure on the distinction between abstract and figurative. To reiterate, he employs this strategy to question the effectivity of painting in its representation of the world. The abstraction, the blurring in many different forms, appeals to his ongoing concern to underline the untenability of realism and realist painting. He claims, "All my work is non-realistic, only abstract paintings."[78] Even when the object of a still life or a sitter is identifiable, representation is abstracted. We might even go so far as to claim that this is the case for all representation, according to Richter. That is, the realism of painting has failed. The exposure of this "failure" of painting through making fragile the distinction between figuration and abstraction as well as the refusal to settle for one or the other is a strategy that confirms Richter's work as modernist.

Richter also paints images in grey that are fully abstract, ostensibly lacking in all figuration. They are seemingly, no more and no less than color. On Richter's canvas, however, what comes alive is an image, a narrative figuration in the mind of the spectator.[79] With Richter's paintings, no matter how apparently monochromatic or monocular the image in grey, we always become engaged in a process of imagining, and this image of imagination has a tactility and a reality to it. That is, despite all evidence to the contrary, we become convinced of the veracity of what we see, if only momentarily. What we see often takes shape in its narrative formation, whether that narrative is provided by us across the time we stand before the canvas, or by Richter through seriality to create a shifting temporality for painting. In the infinite grey canvases of the 1960s we become convinced by the recognition of an object, a story in the greyness. For example, in *Ohne Titel / Untitled* (1968), I am convinced I see some kind of excretion in motion against an air vent, probably industrial in kind. The gentle grey that ripples across the middle of *Ohne Titel / Untitled* (1968) is the sand in the desert, and in *Bunt auf Grau / Color on Grey* (1968) it is the sea, the sea as it leaves its impression on the sand at low tide.[80] If we spend time before many of these images in grey, they are only the very slightest of registers away from the photographs in *Atlas*, photographs of things, nature, and people. The images in *Atlas* are out of focus, "mistakes," photos of nothing in particular. And as we know, for Richter, "nothing" is possibility. The abstract works are captivating for this very reason: they are drenched in an aura of reference, always alluding to and suggesting the world, and yet, all reference to this world is removed. As Dave Hickey writes in a catalog for an exhibition of Richter's work at San Francisco Museum of Modern Art, the genius is in the paintings' dance at the indecipherable line between abstraction and figuration: "Richter's gestures reference the artist without expressing anything, reference the world without depicting anything, and, in doing so, the pictures maintain themselves, as Ellsworth Kelly's do, at the exact interface of the world and our knowing of it, alluding to both, bound to neither."[81]

Richter says as much when he acknowledges the presence of the spectator to his abstract paintings, and the power of the relationship that develops between person and painting: "We aren't capable of viewing paintings without searching for their inherent similarity with what we've experienced and what we know. To see what they offer us, whether they threaten us or whether they're nice to us, or whatever it might be."[82] With the image removed from the face of the painting, figuration takes place again and again in the mind of the viewer. This opening up to include the viewer in the hermeneutic moment of modern painting is Richter's announcement of the presence of a viewer as indispensable to the completion of a work of art. Thus, grey surfaces are given historical resonance. Their full meaning always unfolds in time, in a particular historical moment.

Hand in hand with this gesture outward, this is also the moment at which modernist painting becomes accessible to all. There is no need to be anxious before it, to feel ignorant of its iconic references, its historical traditions. Painting becomes accessible to all when it unfolds in the eyes and mind of the viewer, in the relationship between the canvas and viewer. The abstract paintings depend on this relationship for their raison d'être. Because, at their most fundamental level, meaning in Richter's paintings are built on the shifting and evasive relationship with their spectator.

If Richter's paintings say anything outside their own frame of reference, surely this is a bringing into focus and onto the canvas itself what was always at the center but remained obscured in modern painting: the spectator. For all of their ambiguities and uncertainties, Richter's works appear to place great confidence in the viewer's ability to find her way through the mire of disguises. These disguises are usually identified in the form of conceptual abstractions often said to distance and alienate the viewer of modern art. Richter's paintings and our experience of them appear to dispute these commonplaces. If we have the patience and the confidence to enter into the relationship with painting, then we will discover truths about modernist art. It is, as Richter would have it, in our relationship to painting, a relationship that begins with imagining, that we see objects and stories in the abstractions, that we become moved by painting.[83]

At the same time as we visually and intellectually experience the abstract paintings, standing before them, we become mesmerized by their ill-defined world. The sumptuous, thick, dense layers of paint pulled across, down, and around the canvas are seductive. In the series of untitled grey abstract paintings from the 1960s we fall into the maelstrom of a grey painted world as if it was a depiction of nature enraged: we are mesmerized by the movement of paint.[84] In later works in which grey is used to overpaint we become compelled to trace the patterns, looking for the logic of vertical, horizontal, and the layer upon layer of a spectrum of grey.[85] The movement of the brush, the drip of the paint, the hand and mind of the painter as he moves with purpose horizontally, vertically, at times unpredictably on a canvas are seductive. In these markings, we become enveloped by the beauty and abstraction, the illusory world of paint. Moving closer to the canvas, we get to feel, to smell, and to be touched by the paint.[86] As we experience the paint through other senses, the relationship between painting and viewer becomes haptic, motivated by the sensuous tactile element of paint. Richter thus holds the incompatibility of illusion and reality, abstraction and representation in balance.

The push toward abstraction and the simultaneous seduction of the painted surface reflect the romanticism of Richter's paintings in grey. The discourse of German Romanticism as it comes alive on Richter's canvases is neither a return to nor a complete break with the past as ideal. Take, for example, *Alpen II / Alps II* (1968/69). All of the turmoil and agitation of Turner's sea storms are stirred up as we stand before this image. The brushstrokes create a free and fluid movement of clouds, wind, and snow around the canvas. The world of an ill-at-ease nature has become the idol of this triptych formation. The flurry of the *Sternbild / Constellation* series (1969) has us mesmerized before it, and so by the time we reach paintings of the 1970s, such as *Grau / Grey* (1974), we are easily enticed into a sea in the midst of a storm.[87] We are defenseless, and we become totally caught up in the violent movement and danger of the natural world as it appears in these images. These variegated, mystical worlds of grey remind of the Romantic canvases of Turner. Even though Richter's paintings occupy a different place on the threshold between nature and painted abstraction, namely, that they are closer to abstraction than a representation of a storm at sea, they still seduce us into immersion in the world of nature at the interface with representation.

And yet, true to Richter's tendency to bind every possibility together with its opposite, the seduction is also the moment at which we recognize that the true object of painting is the painted image itself; it is the moment at which we see the density of these paintings as objects, not as representations. The natural world and its painted allusions are, in the end, a ruse to lead us to the realization that they are no more than material, painted representations. We are always brought back to the surface markings, the scrapings, the trace of paint left by the squeegee or the paintbrush.[88] At least, as I argue earlier, this is the case in the 1960s and early 1970s abstract works. Again, we see Richter's grey world oscillating uncomfortably between Romantic wandering and an enlightened habitation of the real world, a real world that is not accessible to the viewer of the great German Romantic paintings of Caspar David Friedrich. It is the real world as it is represented on the surface of the canvas.

A return to *Atlas* is critical if we are to recognize the materiality of representation, thus the frustration, and ultimate impossibility of falling into Richter's painted natural landscapes. When looking at the snowscapes of the early 1980s, even though the works such as *Davos* (1981) are oil on canvas, they look like enlarged versions of the photographs of the same from *Atlas*. Like each individual canvas in *18. Oktober 1977*, the snowscapes begin with images that have little to do with painting. In *Atlas* we find photographs, snapshots, images that might seem more suited to a family vacation album. The *Davos* series (1981) begins as a singled photograph.[89] In turn, the paintings belong to a series, and they sit next to each other on the gallery wall. Thus, the suggestion is that the image is cheap, dispensable, as Richter appears to mimic the practice of photographing the world in order to know it and to affirm self-identity as one does on vacation in the mountains. The photographs collected in *Atlas* on which the painted images are based are those that another person might throw away because they are over- or underexposed: the distinction between foreground and background is unclear (*Davos* [1973; *Atlas* Sheets: 336–340]). But in Richter's *Atlas,* the photograph of a winter landscape takes on a depth of meaning and consequence. And then when it is re-presented in paintings such as *Davos,* with its resonances of Friedrich's paintings of infinite landscapes, the works become even more complex. The lack of clarity, the haziness of the light, the sun creating different colors on the spectrum of grey, contribute to the mystery and possibility of a winter landscape at either end of the day. Through repetition, across different art forms, it's not possible to make definitive claims about the content, let alone the materiality of representation.

In paintings that remind of German Romantic landscape painting and, simultaneously, echo an ephemerality born of rationalization—through repetition, copying, blurring, and abstraction—Richter takes up all references to the use of paint as light, the luminescence of nature as it is repeated on the painted canvas. *Davos,* through its coupling with works such as Friedrich's *Mönch am Meer / Monk by the Sea* (1808–9), sees the possibility of hope and a clarity of vision at the edge of the world. Except that *Davos* also departs from Friedrich's landscapes of light expressed in soft grey paint because we are always brought back to *Atlas.* Thus, in the end, the imperfect photographs return us to the routine and technologically enabled world that Friedrich's lone wanderers transcend.

To return to Varnedoe's observation of the fundamental contradiction of abstract art: abstract art is always about nothing, and has a likeness, or is a figuration of something.[90] He goes on to say of Ryman's white canvases, "The less there is to look at, the more you have to look, the more you have to be *in* the picture."[91] The experience of standing before a picture of nothing and having something gradually revealed is familiar from looking at other colored canvases. Richter takes this irony one step further. Richter, we can argue, extends Ryman's white paintings as Varnedoe sees them. Richter invites us to see ourselves, our thoughts, our imaginations in the variegated grey paintings. And by the time Richter comes to *Acht Grau,* the vision is literal: we replace the nothingness with a picture of ourselves in a mirror and as a screen onto which we project our own image. In 2002, *Acht Grau* invites the viewer to become the subject and object of the abstract works, at the very same time that we step forward, if only in our thoughts, to see more deeply into the painting as subject and object. Thus, in this dramatic struggle between figuration and abstraction, in the relationship between painting and viewer, Richter's grey canvases especially reveal that the very substance of painting is in the contradictions and dilemmas of the relationship between us and the canvas.

The Politics of Grey

Modernist painting was subject to the criticism of elitism, nihilism, and narcissistic self-justification. Richter's grey paintings offer an opportunity to question the ongoing legitimacy of this claim in the late twentieth century.[92] For Richter, the blur, the abstraction, the layering through overpainting, the concealment and revelations of paint, refuse one-dimensionality and easy explanation. This is because these paintings are in the world; they have a social value. Even if the artist himself is adamant that his paintings are limited to the canvas, that they have neither political intention nor possibility, this does not mean we cannot see them as making important statements about the historical world.[93] Like Warhol's reproduction of the traumatic photographs from the newspaper that he transformed onto silk screens, Richter reaches for press images, primarily photographic, that he proceeds to abstract, in paint, and consequently, indict the truth claims of the original image. Richter makes it difficult to see, difficult to recognize what is being imagined. Even if Richter never provides an answer, not even an opinion on the historical and political figures and events he paints, the translation and blurring is a statement in itself.

In Richter's oeuvre, the sociohistorical dimension of painting begins with the conversation with other media and art forms, its capacity to mimic and be inspired by a whole range of visual practices that occupy our daily lives. And from here it takes on a growing complexity. In *Königsallee (grau)* (1969), the world, Königsallee, a shopping boulevard in wealthy Düsseldorf, is simultaneously painted over by and etched into the grey paint of the surface. The short, hatched brushstrokes of differing greys, in differing thicknesses, some with coagulations of paint left in their wake, might be hiding something beneath them. And then again, they might not. Perhaps the overpainting here is all there is to see and know about *Königsallee (grau)*. Although markedly different in technique and in purpose from earlier abstract paintings in grey, *Königsallee (grau)* makes a statement. To paint one of the wealthiest streets in Düsseldorf—the *Königsallee*—perhaps to cover an existing depiction with grey paint, is not without consequence. After all, we are fully aware of the charged significance of the images over which Richter painted as if to erase them (*Decke*). The painted negation of the image doubles as the grandeur of *Königsallee,* the transformation of a tree-lined street filled with wealthy businesses into a near abstract painting, calls attention to all of the pretensions of the location in reality. Richter is not an artist who is often concerned with the identity of place and its significance in a historical trajectory.[94] And so, when he is, it is intriguing that he paints a street in Düsseldorf with a history. And the very extension of this street into its monarchical history is a claim of socioeconomic significance. Even if he does not directly challenge the monarchical persuasion of the past, the very act of erasing this street through covering it with paint is far from neutral.

Returning once again to *Acht Grau* we see a series of paintings that would, at first glance, be considered anything but political. On a deeper level, within the walls of the gallery on the ground floor of the Deutsche Bank on Unter den Linden in post-Wall Berlin, before a series of mirrored panels in which the spectator sees only herself and her place in the physical space of the gallery and the world outside its walls, the grey mirrors are all about that viewer as she centers herself within the frame. And the subject inside that frame is in a spatial context charged by German history.

The creation of a politically and socially aware viewer in *Acht Grau* can be understood to be in the same vein as the viewer of *18. Oktober 1977.* In this series, a series before which we are called upon to revisit highly volatile events that had been problematically laid to rest because they were never adequately addressed in the first place, there is no question that we are expected to engage with the political dimensions of images in their multiple manifestations.[95] When I see myself and other spectators sharing the mirrored surfaces with the architecture of two (capitalist) institutions—the Deutsche Bank and the Solomon R. Guggenheim—against the backdrop of the traffic on Unter den Linden, there is no escaping a self-understanding within the deep and complex terrain of German history. Memories have to be reignited. Thus, even when Richter is not painting scenes from the past, works such as *Acht Grau,* like those in *18. Oktober 1977,* often stimulate Germany's historical narrative in the mind of the viewer.[96]

Richter's political claims, like the historical claims, are always, or nearly always, in grey. Few would question the political import of *Onkel Rudi* in his Luftwaffe coat, or even the series of *48 Portraits* (1971–72) in which artists and writers, not politicians, are held up as the authors of history.[97] Photographs of uncles and fathers just like the one in Richter's *Onkel Rudi* are all over Germany. At this time, in 1965, such images were on mantelpieces throughout both East and West in Cold War Germany. How does Germany come to terms with the role of its beloved fathers and the memory of what they did in World War II in the name of Germany? This is a question that few dared to ask in the 1960s, a question that could not begin to be answered publicly until the turn of the following century.[98] As if in a reminder that he has already asked this question, Richter photographs *Onkel Rudi* and produces eighty prints, each signed and dated, in 2000.

It is true that there existed artists and writers who addressed the issue of *Vergangenheitsbewältigung* from the 1970s onward in Germany. Richter, like them, was radical in his challenge to the German suppression of history and historical responsibility.[99] Thus, *Onkel Rudi* and the many other works, especially from this period of Richter's oeuvre, are recognizably political because of their overt content. And they are always in grey so as not to distract from the import of their claims, and simultaneously, to connect to and distance them from the proliferation of photographs in the press and on mantelpieces, in public and private spheres, that might have existed, but functioned as a way of forgetting rather than remembering the past. In *Onkel Rudi,* and later, in the figurative photo-paintings, such as those of the *18. Oktober 1977* cycle, Richter's grey palette creates both intellectual and emotional spaces that invite the visitor to insert and reinsert her memory into the narrative of German history.[100] And to be sure, this use of grey to represent the politics of German history,

German everyday life, and German politics, recurs throughout his oeuvre.

In 2005 Richter took on the traumatic subject of the attacks on the World Trade Center in *September* (2005).[101] He includes horizontal streaks that obscure the image of the towers underneath. The movement of the streaks from light to dark, white to grey, the horizontal paint in a tug-of-war with the vertical towers in the process of collapsing, are Richter trademarks. But the blue sky, the light, the clarity of the image are the traces of something other than Richter at work in this image. As we look closely, the ochre, grey, and eventually white smoke that clouds over the left tower, like the fire at the end of the executioners' guns in Manet's painting, and Goya's before his, speaks the violence and, here, silent trauma of the world-shattering event it depicts. As if to repeat history, the magnitude of this traumatic historical event is painted in the grey smoke that emits from the impact of the crime. Grey is Richter's stamp on the memory of the September 11 tragedy. And in memory of other historical tragedies, Richter's grey brings with it the scent of death, of the past, of the need to mourn and to remember. Even if these paintings appear ambivalent or ambiguous, rarely passing definitive judgment on the events and objects they depict, they are always engaged in a political discourse.

The image of the burning towers appeared ad infinitum on television, in magazines, in photo books, videos, on the World Wide Web, in every possible media. It was infinitely reproduced. It still is. This is, in many ways, Richter's concern. It's not the events themselves but, as always, the impossibility of representing them that Richter captures in a style that is at the crossroads of his photo-paintings and the overpainted photographs. The blurs, the horizontal lines that cancel the represented towers, the blur of the smoke, the doom of the encroaching grey sky, are the Richter vision of an image that ultimately, despite the concerted attempt to do so, could not be captured by a photograph. The *September* paintings, the first from 2005, and the digital print as a repetition made in 2009, are paintings over the top of the "photo-painting" of the twin towers.[102] In these two works, as reiterations of his representations elsewhere, Richter thus envisions the impossibility of the plight of painting, and all those images before, to represent the magnitude of such an event. In turn, the claim of the impossibility of painting, and the photographic image (in this case) before it, to picture reality becomes the polemic of Richter's oeuvre.

Buchloh comments on these two images thus: "The towers themselves . . . appear here as gray silhouettes that recall the painter's lifelong commitment to photographic grisaille as a medium of commemoration. They are formalized in alternating rectangular forms that approach the threshold of an abstract scansion of the pictorial plane."[103] Thus, Buchloh adds, Richter's "verge into abstraction" contributes to the impossibility of the painted project. To reiterate, the out-of-focus buildings define the trauma of the horrific event, thus its impossibility of being replicated. *September* represents a public history that, no matter how hard we try, cannot be obliterated. It must be negated through representation itself, because representation will always fall short of its coveted function. If the task of modernist representation is to depict itself, then the task of representing its failure is all that is left. And yet, the very existence of images such as *September* in 2005, together with its digital reiteration, pass on the responsibility to remember the past as we continue to define the present from representation. If nothing else, painting revivifies the need to remember where it no longer has the capacity to do so. And so, we look at *September* and we continue the process of witnessing these traumatic events. And again, like the repetitions of *Onkel Rudi* in 2000, Richter reinforces the necessity to remember in a reproduction of his own remembered image.

This leads back, once again, to the blur. Richter's blur carries with it perhaps the most disturbing political reality. It is not only members of the Baader-Meinhof group, *Onkel Rudi, Tante Marianne,* tourists eaten by lions from 1975, and the twin towers that we mourn. It is also the sense of loss, regret, separation, even nostalgia that comes in all of the portraits, and townscapes that look as though they are bombed out through their depiction in grey, through the presence of the blur. We mourn the places and people, even if they are alive, because their features are blurred; they no longer exist; their identities are always in the process of being wiped away by the painting, and thus, by the world. Or perhaps, as I suggest earlier, the blur signifies their process of revivification as opposed to their disappearance? Whether it is *Christiane und Kerstin* (1968), anonymous *Matrosen / Sailors* (1966) or the *Hannover Bahnhof / Hannover Station* (1967), the figures are no longer (or not yet) recognizable, but they are nevertheless present, and not forgotten. This mourning is the responsibility and politics of representation. It visualizes a use of the grey blur to demarcate the (ir)retrievable passing of time, not then or now, but a temporal sweep that simultaneously evokes an unnecessary, premature death, and the imperative to revivify and remember. This use of grey to remember, to mourn and memorialize, is the task of European painting in the postwar twentieth century. It is perhaps Richter's most profound statement.

The Artist Immersed in the Sea of Abstraction

In yet another contradiction that both fuels the meaning of his work and is intensified through his use of grey paint, Richter is always in the process of simultaneously annexing and erasing his presence on the canvas. For a painter of Richter's stature and reputation, it might seem hard to recognize or believe in his self-effacement as it is articulated in the epigraph to this chapter. But when we look closely, his identity and status as artist are constantly asserted only to disintegrate in grey paint. The very handing over of authority to the viewer as she comes to imagine her own history and identity in relationship to the work of art as I have described it is accompanied by an artist who steps aside. When we assume responsibility as the subject of a series such as *Acht Grau,* or even as our imaginations roam before *Cage I–VI,* Richter is no longer in control of meaning. This removal of the artist, always within the nevertheless very controlled structure and process of his paintings seems like a progression from what began as a self-effacement on the surface of the grey paintings from the 1960s and 1970s.

As early as the grey paintings of doors, windows, corrugated iron, and shadows in the 1960s, the hand of the artist is removed through the photographic quality of both (painted) visual grids and manufactured structures. It is subsequently reinstated through the introduction of the blur. The blur is, in Richter's oeuvre, the evidence of his hand on the canvas, his presence to the painting, his transformation of the photograph, his annotation to history. In these and the grey paintings into the 1980s and onward, Richter is the visionary who sees the conundrum of representation as well as the artist who effaces his own self-assertion in the face of this conundrum. He is an all-seeing and all-knowing artist, and through that omniscience, he reveals his observation of a history still unresolved. Put another way, within the structure of the painted canvas, controlled by the predictability of his daily practice, the aleatory can proliferate in Richter's paintings.

When in the presence of *Acht Grau,* the moment arrives when we no longer look for the trace of Richter's hand on the flat, mirrored surface. Rather, we approach the glass plate, drawn by admiration of our own image. As we are pulled away from the search to connect with the artist, out of the context of the gallery and Berlin outside, and as we assume our place at the center of performance in *Acht Grau,* the presence of the artist falls into the background. In the spirit of an architectural design, we think and see our own identity within a space that has nothing (and everything) to do with Richter, the one who designed it. This apparent handing over of the authority of his paintings to the space and the spectator is an enactment of Richter's lifelong act of humble self-examination and generosity.

And yet, this said, Richter has carefully placed the eight grey panels on the wall. He has tilted them at a precise angle, an angle the visitor has no authority to change, even though that is the implication of the hinged glass.[104] The artist carefully directs the viewer's experience before the grey panels. It is at the directive of the artist that we become involved in an examination of the painted surface, our own image, and its place in the spatial contexts. The conversation between works, the comment on the museum, all of these discourses Richter himself meticulously directs, if not dictates.

If so-called post-painterly American abstract painting sought to erase the self of the artist from the surface of the picture, literally, by removing the brushstroke and all other traces of identification, Richter goes one step further by effacing all gesture replacing it with the spectator's image in the frame. Thirty years after Donald Judd and Frank Stella claimed painting had become redundant in the pursuit of nonhieratic art, Richter shows us that it is still possible to create art that hands over its power to the spectator, and moreover, that this is indeed the task of painting. Buchloh insists that Richter becomes anonymous when he puts down his paintbrush in preference for a decorator's brush, a roller, or a squeegee, that is, when the trace of the artistic gesture is no longer apparent on the surface of the image. Buchloh refers to the big grey paintings in a 1986 interview and says, "Where the brushstrokes suddenly turn into a decorator's brushmarks, they take on a new dimension that I would describe as a quasi-mechanical or anonymous quality."[105] Richter disagrees in his response to Buchloh: he claims that there is no distinction in perception of painted marks executed with different instruments.[106] We still see painted marks, no matter the instrument. I agree with Richter: he remains present to the canvas irrespective of the instrument of paint application. The tactile layers, the material qualities of paint, left over from the early grey canvases, always remind that Richter has wiped and scraped, pushed and pulled paint around and across, up, down, over the surface. Thus, contrary to Buchloh's claim, it is not in the instrument that we locate the "anonymity" of Richter's practice.

Richter claims that anonymity comes in the painting of photographs. Nevertheless, standing before one of his photographs, especially as they are overpainted, in a series, or a photo-painting, we see and know it was made by Richter. In these photographs, Richter has made a process all his own; the style and choice of form are instantly recognizable. Nevertheless, there is an anonymity that comes in the guise of a self-effacement in Richter's images. Namely, in his humble gesture of inviting his spectator to finish the works, or better, to take over the creation of their meaning once they are on the wall of the gallery, Richter steps away from the images. The narratives we give the paintings, the objects we see in them, the references they make in our minds, mark the moments when the paintings no longer belong to Richter. Similarly, the fact that these works remain open and indecisive, always striving for something they will never reach, as well as the virtuosity of the application of paint that creates ambiguity and doubt, that is the point at which Richter concedes his lack of mastery over the process of painting. And it is in grey that all of this uncertainty becomes most certain.

In the five already discussed self-portraits (formerly titled *Selbst. 3-Faches / Self-Portrait. 3 Times*), Richter is everywhere present in and absent from the image. This is the quintessential vision of the indecisive artist, an artist who has given his authority to the illusions of photography (and cinema), to the gallery that exhibits the works, and, of course, to the viewer who sees them. Shadows of the artist, a shadow of the shadows, lean back in multiple swivel chairs. Richter's ghostlike figures even cast shadows on the walls behind them, walls devoted to the hanging of Richter's own grey paintings, paintings that are, in reproduction, themselves shadows of a kind. Richter haunts, or is watching over the gallery in which his images are exhibited, and yet, has no ultimate say in how they are perceived. And anyway, the photographic image that bears the trace of the man with his more resilient grey paintings in the background becomes erased by overpainting. In turn, the overpainting makes Richter's photograph, as well as the reproduced paintings on the walls, cheap, expendable, and simultaneously identifiably his. As if speaking or imagining the impossible authority of the modernist artist, Richter is both here and not here, photographed and deemed irrelevant. This impossible specter-like appearance permeates every canvas and every image in his oeuvre: These five overpainted photographs are a *mise-en-abîme* of shadows that happen to visualize the dilemmas and ambiguities that course through every work in the oeuvre.

There are other ways Richter effaces his own authority within the image—once again, the blur and the crisis of representation as he envisions it being the most obvious. The last five versions of the 1990 self-portraits are, as I have suggested, a visual crescendo of this concern.[107] They reiterate this inability to pin down the artist, literally. He, like his paintings, is always in motion, in transition, in more than three places at once, only ever a specter of what he might become on canvas. This elusiveness of both the paintings and the man who executes them is like an exposure of the unacknowledged deceit of modernist painting's authority. On the one hand, Richter places himself in the image and makes it identifiably his, claiming his stake as painter. On the other hand, this self is effaced in the interests of opening out the work to embrace the participation of the spectator. This might be understood to level the stakes of modernist painting: it is evidence of Richter's sense of the radicality and possibility of painting to break all the rules.

Richter engages with the impossibility of the artist to determine the reality of painting in a different way in overpainted photographs that depict his own paintings. It is also significant that the photographs over which Richter always paints are from his own collection. And they are predominantly of his family, friends, his house, vacations, in short, they are taken from his personal albums. Like the photos in any family album, the images in *Atlas*, which are also those that are overpainted, are the narratives through which Richter creates his identity, the images in which he envisions the narrative of his everyday life. Therefore, when he paints over photographs of his own paintings, the relationship to his identity as it is articulated in painting becomes compromised, and complicated. The application of left-over paint to a Polaroid photograph can be read as a kind of graffiti, a defacement of a photograph that can be reproduced, of a painting that cannot. This layer upon layer of reproduction and replication, only to find its eventual erasure, creates indecision, or perhaps an obsessive displacement, of the artist. The original painting—which as we know could well be taken from a photograph—is rendered anonymous through a Polaroid snapshot as it hangs on an unidentified wall. Subsequently, the *mise-en-abîme* continues as Richter defaces, or perhaps it is better to say he reworks, or re-presents, or reframes the snapshot in a painted gesture. However we define the process of replication, the result in paint is everything the Polaroid is not. The painting is unpredictable; it always bears the traces of the artist's complicated presence; it is textured and unique. But we also have a sense that for Richter, the reproduction on the way to infinity does not stop with the overpainting of a photograph of a painting probably based on a photograph. These works are all in a constant process of transformation, if only through the process of exhibition to different viewers. Richter's work is always subject to an endless movement between effacement and reassertion, the presence and absence of the artist.

Any one of Richter's series might be held up as illustration of this process. Among the exquisite works in the overpainted photograph exhibition at Leverkusen in 2008 were eight examples taken from the *128 Fotos von einem Bild / 128 Details from a Picture* taken in 1978. Richter says:

> In the summer of 1978 I took photographs of the surface of an oil sketch on canvas. These photographs were taken from various sides, from various angles, various distances and under different light conditions. The resulting 128 photographs were orga-

> nized in two versions: one, the sequential order that is presented here . . . and a second version presented pictorially in a grid form (now in the Kaiser Wilhelm Museum, Krefeld).[108]

The series sets photography and painting in tension in unique ways. On the surface of the series of 128 images, Richter stages a struggle between reproducibility and uniqueness. It is a struggle waged in grey. The original painting, *Halifax* (1978), is vibrantly colored, and in the photographic reproduction over which he paints, it is grey. Indeed, the grey photograph reduces, or elevates, the ambiguous patterns of the painting, predominantly red in the original, to what alternates between tracks in the sand, scratches on metal, landscape seen from above, even craters on the moon in the eye of the viewer. The in-close-up black-and-white Polaroid photos of *Halifax* transform the painting into a series of abstract lines and patterns, tactile and real, sensuous and intriguing.

The grey painted bands on the bottom of each photograph, varied in width, remind me of Rothko's *Untitled (Black on Grey)*, with one difference. Whereas Rothko, for example, uses grey paint as an opportunity to play with light and translucence, to lift the painting out of the obsolescence of black, for Richter, in this series, grey paint is not textured and nuanced, it is not tactile, and neither is it transparent or translucent. In a gesture that runs contrary to everything we have seen in Richter's paintings until this point, and everything about the paint in Richter's overpainted photographs, in *128 Fotos von einem Bild*, the medium of aesthetic beauty and auratic romanticism—paint—is flat and prohibitive. Grey paint shuts down the beauty of the photographs, photographs that revel in the richness of chiaroscuro, translucence, and illumination in all its other many visible manifestations. The grey paint is a blackened window being opened to reveal the mesmerizing landscape of the photographed painting underneath. This image alternates in the viewer's mind with its opposite: the grey paint as a mask, slowly obscuring the beautiful image beneath. This uncertainty that hovers over the image, where the photographic fragment is visually annexed and the ordinarily privileged painted gesture is flattened, expresses an ambivalence toward the value of painting. Perhaps, after all, it is painting that claims enlightenment but cannot substantiate that claim? In turn, when Richter questions the claims made by painting, by default, he questions who he is as a painter.

In an effort to reassert his authority that nevertheless simultaneously underlines its fragility, the *128 Fotos* were bound into a book of which 128 copies were made and sold in a grey cardboard box. Each box is signed and numbered in pencil, and each box contains a photograph that is signed and dated, this time, however, in felt-tip pen. This is so typical of Richter: the opposite is always written into an image, or in this case, a work, such that it cannot be pinned down. Here, the painted photograph is bound in a volume that is a unique collectible item, but whose uniqueness is always under the threat of erasure. Richter, the to-be-revered great artist thus fetishizes his work as a way of ensuring its iconicity, and nevertheless, insists on the inclusion of the gesture of effacement.[109] He signs and numbers the unique images in pencil. And, needless to add, when Richter is immersed in the *mise-en-abîme* of the relationship between painting and photography as he is here in *128 Fotos,* he is in a world of grey. Grey is the medium for his conviction regarding the uncertainty and unfinishedness of painting, the fragility of his role as a painter.

EPILOGUE

THE IRRESOLUTION OF GREY

GERHARD RICHTER IS NOT THE FIRST PAINTER, nor will he be the last, to perform the paradox of modernist painting in grey. Neither is Richter the only artist working with and simultaneously confronting painting today. Plenty of others have abandoned representation for the creation of sumptuous and seductive grey material surfaces. Similarly, these artists embrace grey as a challenge to the form, aesthetic, and significance of painting. Richter is only one of a number of contemporary artists who engage with the now urgent discussion on the mass reproduction and the banalization of images that accompanies it. However, Richter's painting in grey is a perspicacious embodiment of all that modernist painting repeats, and all that postmodernist painting moves beyond through its repetition of modernism. It is for this reason that I close this book with a discussion of Richter's grey paintings: they both inhabit and depart from all that I have argued grey painting achieves. Similarly, within *The Truth Is Always Grey,* Richter's work represents an end point of sorts.

To clarify: if we subscribe to Richter's refusal of the label of modernist, then his work draws attention to what it is not. It refers to and appropriates the tenets of modernism, and simultaneously departs from the concerns of earlier decades. Alternatively, we can approach Richter's refusal of the label as a challenge to modernism that becomes witnessed in his paintings. Accordingly, the relationship between grey and modernism is expanded through his contestation of modernism's claim on the color. In both cases, it's difficult to imagine modernist painting after Richter. Even without the historical shifts that have forced painting into new territory, abstract modernism reaches a culmination on Richter's grey canvases, remembering that within his oeuvre, the end point is always a springboard to what comes next. In this case, we might see him as the last painter to engage the concerns of modernism, even as he is not—apparently—using its visual language. To be sure, his work comes at the end of a generation of painters who can afford to paint grey abstract canvases that reflect on the cultural and political significance of painting.[1] And, in turn, his work is the launchpad for future generations who will negotiate painting and its relationship to the world in grey.

Today, the concerns of painting have shifted. Even when painting remains abstract, it makes sense within a different historical climate and, accordingly, assumes different responsibilities. For the generation of painters after Richter, the questions of painting in grey become ever more urgent. Contemporary artists are compelled to respond to the increasing iconoclasm that comes hand in hand with globalization, and the denigration of the image and visual representation that takes ever-greater hold thanks to the digital and ideological manipulation of images. In addition, the relations of politics and art, of history and art have changed to the extent that they demand an artist who analyzes and confronts this world head-on.

To give one example of this new generation of artists working in grey, Yan Pei-Ming is an artist who is both the descendant of a painter such as Richter and breaks away from this tradition altogether thanks to the political demands made on him and his art. Pei-Ming uses luminescent grey to put painting to its greatest test in his political paintings that nevertheless remain abstract. And because Pei-Ming engages with his historical moment, the paintings are not abstract from every perspective. In other words, he continues these ironies of grey, in grey. Pei-Ming draws on the history of Western art in grey to critique the distortions and lies of capitalism, and simultaneously to equate them with the violent dictatorships of communism. As Robert Fleck says in the catalog essay accompanying the exhibition *HELP!* at Thaddaeus Ropac's Paris gallery, Pei Ming's grey is about the momentary, the state of transience of the historical moment caught in the brushstroke and what it represents.[2] Although there is a lot of reference to grand-scale history painting in Pei-Ming's works—their size and subject matter, for example, give them an identity as history painting—they also sit comfortably within an avant-garde that dares to use grey to question. The artist claims his use of grey to confront the role of art is, in fact, an attack. Grey has the potency and the capacity to challenge, to sit on the margins of an art world in which colors sell. And for Pei-Ming, as for Picasso before him, the grey canvas is an attack on politics, the press, the media images that litter our contemporary environment. Even though grey is now all but extinct in the press, the movies, photographs, Pei-Ming reminds us that grey still has the power to represent. Moreover, for Pei-Ming, grey is the painted vocabulary of counternarrative.

The aggression of the brushstrokes in his paintings represents the violence and chaos of war. In the monumental paintings in the main ground floor gallery at Thaddaeus Ropac, *HELP!* (2011), *Quartier Chinois de Saigon / Chinese Section of Saigon* (2012), and *Char* (2013), dense, staccato-like brushstrokes in a spectrum of greys confront the spectator with the destruction and death promised by the content of the images: re-presented iconic media images of past and recent wars in Vietnam and the Middle East. The density of the paint, the sketchiness of the stroke, and thus, the painted form, create a style of painting that approaches the uncertainty of abstraction. Up close, luscious, thick paint loses all signification outside itself. And then as we move away from the canvas, the objects and shapes become more clearly defined, against an indefinable background; they become recognizable. At a distance, we are reminded that we have seen these objects as images before: in the press. We know well the image of an officer of the Vietnam National Police, his back turned to us, his gun against the head of a Viet Cong member, in a summary execution that came to stand for the horror of that war. When we move back from the canvas, the magnitude of the image also comes into view. The angry, abrupt brushstrokes transform into historical and political narratives that rail against the familiar events. However, unlike the history paintings he seems to reference, Pei-Ming's works simultaneously take on the warnings of the present: he paints memories made to show future generations the violence and destruction of war. This present that creates memories for the future is also in the very materiality of the grey brushstrokes. To give one more example, in *Char,* just as we are confronted by the tank that might fire in our direction at any moment, we are also confronted by a violence given energy by grey paint. Grey painting is turbulent and dangerous: on these canvases we discover that for Pei-Ming, grey paint is invested with the collaboration of the press, political power, and the history of art in the confrontational events that surround and await us. As visitors to the gallery, we feel that energy; we are in turn energized by the painting to question the forces that inspire Pei-Ming's counternarrative, what he calls the narrative of attack.

Thus, an artist such as Pei-Ming moves painting along a trajectory in which modernism as a concept continues to fuel a return to representation in grey. Like Richter and Johns, his work is tinged with irony, but it is caustic in kind. There is nothing playful about Pei-Ming's use of grey. Grey on these canvases might be luminescent, but it is deadly serious. All of which is to say that grey continues to be used to challenge the limits of painting, and to explore what painting can and must do. Pei-Ming's paintings exemplify how, after Richter, the most convincing search for the truth in grey painting is not to be found in modernist abstraction but rather, in the return to historical representation seen through the lens of paint as a medium of abstraction. And, returning to Richter, it is because of this contemporary redirection that Gerhard Richter grey demonstrates the possibility of an openness to painting's achievement of a truth, a truth in which the irony of modernism and the irony of grey are the primary vehicles. And because it is envisioned by Richter, the truth is still the "ongoing challenge"; it is "a model for . . . painting."[3] The truth has not yet arrived.

Pei-Ming is just one of a number of contemporary painters using grey, pushing grey paint to its limits in order to engage with the cultural and social urgency of painting in the twenty-first century. To name one more, Luc Tuymans's paintings represent and negotiate postwar history and memory, politics and culture on grey canvases that sit squarely within traditions of European painting in grey that I trace in earlier chapters. Tuymans doesn't simply use grey to depict dark or horrific moments in twentieth-century history, but in the process of representing history, he is always in the process of continuing the history of grey. His paintings create new histories for images in general, for painting, and grey painting in particular. To put it another way, a European painter such as Tuymans uses grey paint, often in its most superficial form, as a way of dealing with the traumas that were of and resulted from the twentieth century. His grey paint imagines events such as World War II, September 11, the ongoing violence of colonization. Even when he paints the depiction of history, and thus re-presents the representation of history, Tuymans gives depth and density to grey as well as to history in a nevertheless thin, ephemeral, grey paint. His paintings see how the twentieth century and its representation contaminate our present in ways that we were not previously been aware. Contamination, or historical longevity, is presented in grey: because grey is always irresolute, the questions of that which it represents, continue.

Tuymans uses a thin, fast, almost transparent array of greys to criticize the proliferation of images that create our political reality: images from the media, books, photographs, art history, and most recently, the digital images made by his cell phone. Tuymans uses the inherent ambiguity of grey—neither black nor white, both absorbent of and reflecting light, cool and warm, dark and light, luminescent and opaque—to reinforce the ambiguity of what he pictures, what his pictures remember. These may be superficial painted depictions, but they resonate with ambiguity, complexity, and historical depth.

For Tuymans, grey is the color best suited to creating the disquiet of contradictory images that resist all possibility of comprehension. In turn, the awkward dimensions and distortions of people's bodies and objects uncomfortably framed within Tuymans's paintings ensure their resistance to consumption. Grey figures, objects, landscapes, things of apparent importance, disappear off the side of the canvas, are eclipsed by an even darker grey shadow, or fade out of view. This ultimate inaccessibility within an unlocatable visual field is Tuymans's critique of visual representation today through the further complication of what is represented. The ever-shifting rainbow of greys in his palette repeats the impenetrability and frustration of the past, while all the time cloaking it in an ice coldness that isolates both us and the figures, places, spaces, and events either depicted within, or somewhere outside, the frame.

As if in a deliberate confusion and rebuttal of all that European painting has imagined in the postwar period, at the end of the twentieth century—I think here of the paintings of Antoni Tàpies,

Jean Fautrier, and even Anselm Kiefer's World War II paintings—Tuymans's paintings are marked by their transparency; it is as if they reduce their grey strokes to show a disdain for the violence and drama of the history that they witness. Tuyman's mottled grey paintings are replete with absence, creating empty spaces on cursory surfaces, that together lead to haunted depictions, with obscure meanings. To give one example from a series of paintings that references the Nazi Holocaust, *Der Architekt / The Architect* (1998) is a figure in the snow. We don't know if it looks forward or backward, thanks to a mask that could cover either the face or the back of the head. The image is, apparently, taken from the home movies of Albert Speer, the architect of Hitler's monumental cities.[4] The text that usually accompanies this series claims that the individual paintings echo the unrepresentability of the Holocaust. And yet, what makes *Der Architekt* compelling is that it exists beyond the context of German history. *Der Architekt* is an image of a man, or it could be a woman, who has fallen, or perhaps is just resting in the snow. He or she is vulnerable, but may be completely in control. In a landscape that is grey and luminous, there is a freshness and vivacity to an otherwise ambiguous painting. In distinction to the tendency of critics, I want to suggest that the ambiguity and inaccessibility of the image—as opposed to the unrepresentability of the Holocaust—are precisely the point. The particular grey of *Der Architekt* is the confirmation of the opacity of the image per se, and the mechanically reproduced image (from which it derives) in particular.

In Tuymans's works there is no painterliness, no noted aesthetic to hold on to, no texture to entice us or challenge us, no substance to confuse us. Rather Tuymans's paintings are flat, ephemeral visions that give the appearance of waiting for the real painting to begin. They are the reduction of painting to traces of grey on a canvas. As a result, they are political because they are a critique of all we have come to understand painting to be. And yet, they are still painting. However much grey painting is apparently no longer relevant, it is still the medium Tuymans chooses to use.

The Truth Is Always Grey is enabled by certain notions of abstraction, modernism, and painting. In turn, all of these are developed very specifically in postwar America. It is an American modernism that preoccupies my argument. In the two examples here, the work of Pei-Ming and Tuymans, abstraction is still the vehicle, sometimes the substance, of grey paint, but because these artists are of a different generation, working on different continents, the history of grey and the history of painting must be extended to remain relevant. Thus, Richter's works might be understood as somewhere between the grey abstraction of postwar American modernism, and postmodernist representations in grey of twenty-first century Europe. It is for this reason that I place their analysis at the close of *The Truth Is Always Grey* and, as such, at the beginning of a new line of inquiry. It is my intention that *The Truth Is Always Grey* opens up to this future of inquiry. The inconclusiveness of modernist grey painting, the uncertainty of painting, the continued work of grey as a legitimate color: these are the truths that grey and painting continue to explore in the twenty-first century, albeit through different approaches, forms, and aesthetics of abstraction.

ACKNOWLEDGMENTS

I am indebted to the many people who listened to me talk about grey painting over the years this book was being written. Most of all, I thank Joe McElhaney, John David Rhodes, and James Williams for reading multiple chapters and offering insights that stimulated significant revisions. Brian Price and Richard Allen gave readings that enabled me to strengthen the argument and focus the material. I am also grateful to James Polchin, whose enthusiasm for grey painting in the early phases of the book encouraged and inspired me.

Audiences at conferences at the University of Mainz and the University of East Anglia gave helpful feedback. I am grateful for the camaraderie of the small community of art historians working on grey painting whom I met at these conferences. I also thank my colleagues in the School of Arts, University of Kent for their support. A special thanks to Tom Henry, Michael Newall, and Ben Thomas for their willingness to engage in discussions of grey painting and for their bibliographic suggestions.

The book was generously funded by a Leverhulme Trust Research Fellowship. My thanks go to Jacqueline Aldridge for playing the devil's advocate on draft after draft of applications for funding that resulted in the Leverhulme Fellowship.

When Georgia Fee moved back to Paris in 2008, she not only shared my love of painting but also believed me when I insisted that grey was the most significant of all colors. Georgia's passion for art and her belief in me as a critic and writer, her willingness to trust that grey brought the world alive, fueled my fascination for grey during the years that followed. It is for me a great sadness that Georgia did not live to see this book published. I dedicate *The Truth Is Always Grey* to her memory.

Unless otherwise noted, all translations are my own.

NOTES

Introduction

1. Letter 521 from Vincent van Gogh to Theo van Gogh, Arles, 9 August 1888, *Letters of Vincent van Gogh,* ed. Mark Roskill (New York: Touchstone Books, 2008).

2. "Le tableau en est gris . . . gris comme la nature, gris comme l'atmosphère de l'été, quand le soleil étend comme un crepuscule de poussière tremblante sur chaque objet." Charles Baudelaire, "The Salon of 1845," in *Art in Paris, 1845–1862: Salons and Other Exhibitions,* trans. and ed. Jonathan Mayne (Ithaca, N.Y.: Cornell University Press, 1981), 19.

3. Theodor Adorno, "Society," in *Aesthetic Theory,* trans. and ed. Robert Hullot-Kentor (London: Continuum, 1997), 253.

4. Even Gerhard Richter is apparently disparaging of grey: "Grey is the epitome of non-statement. It does not trigger off feelings or associations, it is actually neither visible nor invisible." Gerhard Richter to Edy de Wilde, 23 February 1975, in *Gerhard Richter: Text; Writings, Interviews and Letters 1961–2007,* ed. Dietmar Elger and Hans Ulrich Obrist (London: Thames and Hudson, 2009), 92.

5. See *Gray Is the Color* (Houston: Institute for the Arts, Rice University, 1974); exhibition catalog. In 1974, Dominique de Menil's *Gray Is the Color* exhibition was the first of the handful of exhibitions devoted to the color grey. Other exhibitions devoted to grey are those on medieval manuscripts in grisaille in Paris (Ministère de la Culture et de la Communication, *La grisaille* [Paris: Musée d'Art et d'Essai, 1980]) and Brussels (Pierre Cockshaw, *Miniatures en grisaille* [Brussels: Bibliothèque Royale Albert 1er, 1986]), and the Jasper Johns exhibition at the Art Institute of Chicago. In 1974–75 there was an exhibition of Richter's grey paintings in Mönchengladbach, Germany. See Johannes Cladders, *Gerhard Richter. Graue Bilder*

(Mönchengladbach: Städtisches Museum Mönchengladbach, 4 December 1974–12 January 1975); exhibition catalog. The same exhibition traveled to Braunschweig: *Gerhard Richter. Graue Bilder* (Braunschweig: Kunstverein Braunschweig, Haus Salve Hospes, 9 February 1975–9 March 1975).

6. Druick's chapter in the catalog offers a history of the use of grey in painting, but it is brief and not sustained in the other analyses of Johns's work. Douglas W. Druick, "Jasper Johns: Gray Matters," in James Rondeau and Douglas W. Druick, *Jasper Johns: Gray* (New Haven, Conn.: Yale University Press, 2007), 80–107.

7. The major critics of Gerhard Richter's work are an exception here, though even then the attention to the use of grey paint is comparatively spare. See Julia Friedrich, *Grau ohne Grund: Richters Monochromen als Herausforderung der künstlerischen Avantgarde* (Cologne: Strzelecki Books, 2009); Dietmar Elger, *Gerhard Richter: A Life in Painting* (Chicago: University of Chicago Press, 2009). Elger, however, takes Richter's words about grey paint at face value, as I discuss later. This seems discordant with the way he uses grey paint throughout his career.

8. Beyond the visual arts, Italo Calvino, Milan Kundera, Ludwig Wittgenstein, and many others—writers, artists, philosophers, and critics of the twentieth century—believe grey is dull and empty, a noncolor, or colorless. However, each of these writers offers a perspective on grey that is potentially useful to a picture of its insights, and also its challenges to the conception of painting, and in turn, art history, and their relationship to industrial modernity.

9. These are all words used by Kandinsky to describe grey in Wassily Kandinsky, *Concerning the Spiritual in Art,* trans. M. T. H. Sadler (London: Dover, 1977), 37–39.

10. In chapter 1, I demonstrate how grey paintings from the fourteenth century through the Renaissance, baroque, and romanticism, carry the seeds of the modernist uses of the color in the nineteenth and twentieth centuries.

11. Philip Ball, *Bright Earth and the Invention of Colour* (London: Farrar, Straus and Giroux, 2002), 162–64.

12. Ibid., 163.

13. Ibid., 358. Ball explains how the grey scale was at the basis of his theory of the relationship between all other colors on the color wheel.

14. Again, it will be recalled that Rembrandt's paintings have been identified for their prefacing of the concerns of modern art, specifically their expression of an emotional inner life through the use of paint and color as light. See, for example, Alison McQueen, *The Rise of the Cult of Rembrandt: Reinventing an Old Master in Nineteenth-Century France* (Amsterdam: Amsterdam University Press, 2003).

15. Van Gogh, "On Shades of Grey" (1882), in *Art in Theory 1815–1900*, ed. Charles Harrison and Paul Wood (Oxford: Blackwell, 1998), 942–43.

16. This argument is made in Benjamin Buchloh's catalog essay, "Gerhard Richter's *Eight Gray:* Between *Vorschein* and *Glanz*," in *Gerhard Richter: Eight Gray* (Berlin: Deutsche Guggenheim and Hatje Cantz, 2002), 11–28; exhibition catalog.

17. In 2009 Richter produced four tapestries that were exhibited at Gagosian Gallery, London, 30 May 2013–27 July 2013. In a characteristic Richter strategy of replication, the tapestries were patterned from a reproduction of abstract paintings and then digitally designed before execution on the loom. See *Gerhard Richter: Tapestries* (London: Gagosian Gallery, 2013); exhibition catalog. In 2015, he collaborated with the composer Arvo Pärt for the Manchester International Festival, exhibiting oversized photographic reproductions of a single abstract painting. See Whitworth Art Gallery, University of Manchester, 9–19 July 2015. Accessed 8 December 2015. http://www.whitworth.manchester.ac.uk/whats-on/exhibitions/pastexhibitions/#.

18. These arguments can be found in the articles in Hal Foster, Rosalind Krauss, Yve-Alain Bois, and Benjamin H. D. Buchloh, *Art since 1900: Modernism Antimodernism Postmodernism* (London: Thames and Hudson, 2004).

19. Kazimir Malevich, *Essays on Art 1915–1933*, ed. Troels Andersen (London: Rapp and Whiting, 1969). See also Yve-Alain Bois, "Malevitch: Le carré, le degré zero," *Macula* 1 (1978): 35–36.

20. See Thierry de Duve, *Pictorial Nominalism: On Marcel Duchamp's Passage from Painting to the Readymade* (Minneapolis: University of Minnesota Press, 1991). De Duve explains the importance of the Duchamp readymade as a transition within modernist art to new conceptions of art. See also his essay "Why Was Modernism Born in France?," *Artforum* 52, no. 5 (January 2014): 190–97.

21. Three questions asked of painting resist its dethroning (which has a lot to do with photography and its displacement of painting as an art form): (1) How can paint as a medium of painting be analyzed and given new emphatic accents (impressionism)? (2) How can paint become independent, leave behind the law of colors, and receive its own absolute status? (3) How can paint as a material be replaced by other materials such as aluminum for white? See Peter Weibel, "An End to the 'End of Art'? / On the Iconoclasm of Modern Art," in *Iconoclash: Beyond the Image Wars in Science, Religion, and Art,* ed. Bruno Latour and Peter Weibel (Cambridge, Mass.: MIT Press, 2002), 611.

22. On minimalism's consciousness of its own emergence, see James Meyer, *Minimalism: Art and Politics* (New Haven, Conn.: Yale University Press, 2004).

23. These debates were carried out in the journal *Artforum* beginning in the early 1960s.

24. Here the most outstanding example is perhaps Yves Klein with his visionary paintings in blue. See Yves Klein, "The Evolution of Art towards the Immaterial," in *Yves Klein* (London: Gimpel Fils Gallery, London, 1973); exhibition catalog, unpaginated.

25. This is quoted so often that it no longer needs a reference.

26. Wassily Kandinsky, "Reminisences," in *Kandinsky: Complete Writings on Art,* vol. 1 (1901–21), ed. Kenneth C. Lindsay and Peter Vergo (London: Faber and Faber, 1982), 363.

27. Quoted by Hal Foster et al., *Art since 1900,* 178.

28. On the developments from natural to synthetic colors across the centuries, see Ball, "A Passion for Purple: Dyes and the Industrialization of Colour," in *Bright Earth,* 222–59.

29. On the production of color by artists, and particularly, the creation of ultramarine with lapis lazuli, see the catalog of the National Gallery, London's exhibition, *Making Colour,* 2014. Accessed 8 December 2015. http://www.nationalgallery.org.uk/making-colour. Yves Klein takes up all of the economic significance of lapis lazuli and creates International Klein Blue (IKB) as fetish object or commodity. See Sidra Sitch, *Yves Klein* (Ostfildern: Hatje Cantz, 1995). Similarly, Derek Jarman discusses this on the soundtrack of his film *Blue.* See Derek Jarman, *Blue: Text of a Film* (New York: Overlook Press, 1994). Also on the cultural and political significance, as well as the mystery, of color, see Michael Taussig, *What Color Is the Sacred?* (Chicago: University of Chicago Press, 2009).

30. See Michel Pastoureau, *Blue: The History of a Color* (Princeton, N.J.: Princeton University Press, 2001).

31. This is quoted by Michael Auping, Introduction to *Anselm Kiefer: Heaven and Earth* (Munich: Prestel, 2005), 39.

32. "The Spirit of Gray," Donald Kuspit's review of Kiefer's *Merkaba,* emphasizes a bleak vision of Kiefer's gray as what gives his work profundity. I, however, am not convinced there is absolutely no freedom in grey. Accessed 8 December 2015. http://www.artnet.com/magazine/features/kuspit/kuspit12–19–02.asp.

1. What Is Grey Painting?

1. Wassily Kandinsky, *Concerning the Spiritual in Art* (New York: Dover, 1977), 61.

2. Ludwig Wittgenstein, *Remarks on Colour,* ed. G. E. M. Anscombe; trans. Linda L. McAlister and Margarete Schättle (1950; Oxford: Blackwell, 1977), sec. III, paras. 68, 72.

3. Michael Taussig, *What Color Is the Sacred?* (Chicago: University of Chicago Press, 2009).

4. Wittgenstein, *Remarks on Colour,* sec. III, paras. 123, 127–29.

5. Ibid., e.g., sec. III, paras. 4, 128.

6. James Rondeau, "Jasper Johns: Gray," in Rondeau and Druick, *Jasper Johns: Gray,* 31.

7. Johann Wolfgang von Goethe, *Theory of Colours,* trans. Charles Lock Eastlake (London: John Murray, 1840), no. 556.

8. Ibid., no. 557.

9. Ibid., no. 36.

10. Ibid., no. 556.

11. Ibid., no. 61.

12. David Batchelor argues for the coexistence of the two, whereas Wittgenstein would maintain that everything that is grey marks the absence of light. "Grey, however," he says, "is not luminous." See David Batchelor, *The Luminous and the Grey* (London: Reaktion Books, 2014), 60–61. Wittgenstein is reproduced in Batchelor, *Colour* (Cambridge, Mass.: MIT Press, 2008), 107.

13. Goethe, *Theory of Colours,* no. 61.

14. Ibid., nos. 862–66.

15. Ibid., nos. 195–96.

16. Josef Albers, *Interaction of Color* (New Haven, Conn.: Yale University Press, 1963).

17. Josef Albers, "Gradation Studies—New Presentations," in ibid., 15–16.

18. Ibid., 20–21.

19. Ibid.,16.

20. Albers was born in Bottrop, deep in the industrial Ruhr Valley. This is somehow fitting for someone whose instructions on industrial modernism were facilitated through grey.

21. Albers, "Gradation Studies," 15.

22. Alan Shapiro, "Artists' Colors and Newton's Colors," *Iris* 85, no. 4 (December 1994): 600–30. See Leon Battista Alberti, *On Painting and On Sculpture: The Latin Texts of De Pictura and De Statua,* ed. and trans. Cecil Grayson (New York: Phaidon, 1972), 46–47.

23. Alberti, *On Painting and On Sculpture,* 46–47.

24. Ibid., 45.

25. Ibid., 46.

26. Baudelaire, "The Salon of 1845," in *Art in Paris, 1845–1862,* 31–32.

27. Wittgenstein, *Remarks on Colour,* sec. III, paras. 36–38, 40–41, 49.

28. See A. Maerz and M. Rea Paul, *A Dictionary of Color* (New York: McGraw-Hill, 1930), 201. Anthea Callen states in a discussion of grey in nineteenth-century impressionism: "The nineteenth-century artist's palette contained no 'pure' grey paints; by that I mean the neutral greys that only

became standard in the 1920s with the demand for exactly reproducible colours, as in industrial paints and finishes. The only grey paint sold in the ranges of Fine Artists' materials—Payne's grey—was itself a mixed 'coloured' tint. Payne's grey was variously described as pre-mixed from indigo, raw Siena and red lake, or Prussian blue, yellow ochre and crimson lake; there were probably other combinations, too. It was named after its inventor William Payne, a late 18th century water-colourist who came to fame through his innovative techniques and teaching of watercolour painting. The first dated usage of Payne's grey in England is from 1835—in watercolour rather than oil paint. Payne's grey in watercolour form is advertised in English colourmen's catalogues from the mid nineteenth century, for example in tin tubes from Winsor & Newton in 1857. In artists' painting treatises greys get short shrift: commentary usually has them described as not required among the painter's colours since they were readily mixed on the palette." Anthea Callen, "'Gris clair' and Coloured Greys," paper delivered at Association of Art Historians 2015 conference, University of East Anglia, Norwich, 10 April 2015. For more on the composition and use of manufactured greys, see Anthea Callen, *The Art of Impressionism: Painting Technique and the Making of Modernity*, 2nd ed. (New Haven, Conn.: Yale University Press, forthcoming).

29. Maerz and Paul, *A Dictionary of Color*, 201.

30. John Graham, "Pigments and Media," in *A Short History of Painting* (Los Angeles: CreateSpace, 2008), 13–17. It is curious that these developments in grey as a distinct ready-made color coincided with the invention of photography.

31. Taussig, *What Color Is the Sacred?*

32. This analysis of the structure of capital resonates throughout Taussig's *What Color Is the Sacred?* See, for example, "With a dash of sulfur, the sun that radiated out from van Gogh's sunflowers could revert to that other yellow, the yellow of hell and self-mutilation" (34).

33. Ibid., 22.

34. Taussig mentions grey a couple of times, once when quoting Richard Sasuly in a discussion of the concealment of German armaments factories in World War II, the other when quoting Goethe's description of the sky. See Taussig, *What Color Is the Sacred?*, 240.

35. Wittgenstein, *Remarks on Colour*, para. 63.

36. Pastoureau has written many works on color. See, e.g., Michel Pastoureau, *Figures et couleurs: Étude sur la symbolique et la sensibilité médiévales* (Paris: Le Léopard d'or, 1986); *Dictionnaire des couleurs de notre temps: Symbolique et société* (Paris: Bonneton, 1996); *Bleu: Histoire d'une couleur* (Paris: Seuil, 2000); *Les couleurs de nos souvenirs* (Paris: Seuil, 2010).

37. Michel Pastoureau, *Couleurs, images, symboles: Études d'histoire et d'anthropologie* (Paris: Le Léopard d'or, 1989), 16–18.

38. Ibid.

39. See Michel Pastoureau and Dominique Simonnet, *Couleurs: Le grand livre* (Paris: Panama, 2009), 124–25.

40. Ibid., 112–13, and 92, respectively.

41. “Il vit en bonne esperance, / Puisqu’il est vestu de gris, / Qu’il aura, à son advis, / Encore sa desirance; / Combien qu’il soit hors de France, / Par deca le mont Senis, / Il vit, etc. / Puisqu’il, etc. // Perdu a sa contenance, / Et tous ses jeux et ses ris, / Gaigner lui fault Paradis. / Par force de paciance. / Il vit, etc.” Accessed 17 May 2010. http://www.gutenberg.org/files/14343/14343-h/14343-h.htm.

42. Pastoureau, *Couleurs, images, symboles,* 116.

43. Michael Pastoureau, *Black: The History of a Color,* trans. Jody Gladding (Princeton, N.J.: Princeton University Press, 2009), 106–10.

44. Joseph Freiherr von Eichendorff, *Das Marmorbild* (The marble statue) (1819; Munich: Reclam, 1986). Novalis, *Hymns to the Night,* trans. Dick Higgins (Kingston, N.Y.: McPherson, 1988).

45. Michel Pastoureau, *Les couleurs de notre temps* (Paris: Bonneton, 2003), 153.

46. Druick, “Jasper Johns: Gray Matters,” 82.

47. These are discussed in chapter 2.

48. Michel Pastoureau, *Dictionnaire des couleurs de notre temps* (Paris: Bonneton, 2007), 137–39.

49. Michel Pastoureau and Dominique Simonnet, *Le petit livre des couleurs* (Paris: Panama, 2005), 91–92.

50. Richard Allen discusses Hitchcock’s grey within the context of color in his films. See Richard Allen, “‘The Lodger’ and the Origins of Hitchcock’s Aesthetic,” in *Hitchcock Annual* 10 (2001–2): 38–78.

51. Axel Hémery, “Un bref survol de la grisaille dans la peinture Européene,” in *Pas la couleur, rien que la nuance! Trompe-l’oeil et grisailles de Rubens à Toulouse-Lautrec,* ed. Axel Hémery (Toulouse: Musée des Augustins, 2008), 17–37. Hémery, like others who discuss the premodern period of artistic creation in grey, refers to the works as *grisaille.* This lack of distinction is common to art historians’ interchangeable use of “grey” and “grisaille.” See, for another example, *Gray Is the Color.*

52. In one of the earliest examples, Georges Méliès brings playing cards alive through stop motion in-camera editing in *Playing Cards* (1896). Perhaps the most famous examples are those of Sergei Eisenstein in *Strike* (1926). The industrialists, through the use of a dissolve, are transformed into a fox, an owl, a monkey, and a bulldog, respectively. The introduction of characters as moral qualities was also a common frame narrative of stage-based moral dramas in Germany in the 1910 into the 1920s. Filmmakers used the cinematic editing devices to bring characters alive to emphasize the specific

creativity of the cinema as well as to articulate the unfolding narrative. See Frances Guerin, "Legends of Light and Shadow," in *A Culture of Light: Cinema and Technology in 1920s Germany* (Minneapolis: University of Minnesota Press, 2005), 74–108.

53. Alexander Markschies, "Monochrome and Grisaille: An European Overview," in *Jan van Eyck Grisailles* (Madrid: Museo Thyssen-Bornemisza, 2009), 272; exhibition catalog.

54. Ibid.

55. It is said that Enrico Scrovegni built the chapel to make amends for his father's sin of usury, a necessary atonement for his father to obtain absolution so that his soul would be welcome to the Christian sacraments. There is debate as to whether or not Enrico Scrovegni himself was involved in usury. For arguments favoring a usury-and-penitence theme see Anne Derbes and Mark Sandona, *The Usurer's Heart: Giotto, Enrico Scrovegni, and the Arena Chapel in Padua* (University Park: Pennsylvania State University Press, 2008). For arguments against this idea, and highlighting Enrico's secular motivation for the lavish decoration, see Laura Jacobus, *Giotto and the Arena Chapel: Art, Architecture and Experience* (Turnhout, Belgium: Brepols/Harvey Miller Publications, 2008).

56. See Andrew Ladis for an elaboration on this argument. Ladis maintains that the frescoes should be approached as formal compositions that privilege a visual symmetry, not from the classical perspective as a narrative unfolding in time. The understanding of the dado figures as cinematic in their aesthetic and meaning accords with Ladis's analysis. See Andrew Ladis, *Giotto's O: Narrative, Figuration, and Pictorial Ingenuity in the Arena Chapel* (University Park: State University of Pennsylvania Press, 2008).

57. It became common practice to separate the dado and predella from the main commission. Although it was done, it wasn't a given that they were to be painted in grey. On the distinction of the Virtues and Vices from the main commission, see Andrew Ladis, ed., *Giotto and the World of Early Italian Art: An Anthology of Literature* (New York: Garland, 1998).

58. See Louise Bourdua and Anne Dunlop, eds., *Art and the Augustinian Order in Early Renaissance Italy* (Farnham, UK: Ashgate, 2007), 133.

59. See S. Pfeiffenberger, "The Iconology of Giotto's Virtues and Vices at Padua" (PhD diss., Bryn Mawr College, 1966). See also Douglas P. Lackey, "Giotto in Padua: A New Geography of the Human Soul," *Journal of Ethics* 9, nos. 3–4 (October 2005): 551–72; and Eva Frojmovic, "Giotto's Circumspection," *Art Bulletin* 89, no. 2 (June 2007): 195–210.

60. Giuseppe Basile, *Giotto: La Chapelle des Scrovegni,* trans. Françoise Liffran (Paris: Gallimard, 1993), 319.

61. As Andrew Ladis points out, their style resembles the external wings of High Renaissance altarpieces; Ladis, *Giotto and the World of Early Italian Art.*

62. Jill Bain, "Signifying Absence: Experiencing Monochrome in Medieval Painting," in *A Wider Trecento: Studies in 13th- and 14th-Century European Art Presented to Julian Gardner,* ed. Louise Bourdua and Robert Gibbs (Leiden: Brill, 2011), 8.

63. Frojmovic, "Giotto's Circumspection."

64. This same use of background colors is used in the ceiling decorations of the cartography room in the Vatican apartments. The figures are not as interesting as Giotto's because they are not infused with the same complexity of meaning and relevance. In addition, they do not have the kinetic, animated qualities of Giotto's figures. However, the juxtaposition alerts us to both the contemporary popularity of the technique, and the extraordinary usage by Giotto.

65. This is from the guidebook given out at the cloister. See Rosanna Caterina Proto Pisani, *Il Chiostro dello Scalzo a Firenze: Studio e scuola di pittura* (Florence: Sillabe, 2004).

66. For an account of what little information there is on the cloister and the confraternity, see ibid.

67. Giorgio Vasari, *The Lives of the Artists* (Oxford: Oxford University Press, 1998), 501.

68. Ibid. Vasari does not mention all of the scenes, but focuses on these. He also talks about Justice and Hope and the Baptism of Christ, because these are the ones he paints when he comes back from France. Similarly, these have a dimensionality that the others do not.

69. See Roger Fry, "An Unpublished Andrea del Sarto," *Burlington Magazine for Connoisseurs* 44, no. 255 (June 1924): 265.

70. See Antonio Natali and Alessandro Cecci, *Andrea del Sarto: Catalogue complet des peintures* (Florence: Cantini Editore, 1989), 143–52.

71. This has also been the evidence for some critics who find Andrea del Sarto's work derivative.

72. I think here of Masaccio's use of folds in fabric in *The Tribute Money* (1425) in the Brancacci Chapel in Florence.

73. Lorne Campbell, Miguel Falomire, Jennifer Fletcher, and Luke Syson, eds., *Renaissance Faces: Van Eyck to Titian* (New Haven, Conn.: Yale University Press, 2011).

74. The same painting can also be titled *Portrait of Girolamo Barbarigo,* as Vasari identified it in his 1568 biography of Titian. See Vasari, *The Lives of the Artists.*

75. On Titian's portraits as they are seen by his friend Pietro Aretino, see Luba Freedman, *Titian's Portraits through Aretino's Lens* (University Park: Penn State University Press, 1995).

76. I think here, for example, of the Portinari Altarpiece painted by Hugo van der Goes. When the side panels are closed, the frontispiece represents the Angel Gabriel in one panel and the Virgin in another, both painted in grisaille. *Annunciation,* by Hugo van der Goes (ca. 1473–78), is now in the Uffizi Gallery in Florence.

77. Fritz Grossmann, "Bruegel's 'Woman Taken in Adultery' and Other Grisailles," *Burlington Magazine* 94, no. 593 (August 1952): 218–27, 229.

78. Ibid.

79. Charles Dickens, *Bleak House* (London: Penguin, 1997).

80. In this and the other three scenes on the walls of the Museo de la Real Academia de Bellas Artes de San Fernando in Madrid (*A Scene of a Bullfight* [1812–14], *Procession of Flagellants* [ca. 1814–16], and *The Madhouse* [1812–14]), the viewer is equally struck by the richly textured walls and the tactility of their surface, a tactility and materiality envisioned in grey especially in *Procession of Flagellants* and *The Madhouse.* This use of grey as a stage is typical of Goya. See my review of the four paintings. Accessed 8 December 2015. https://www.artslant.com/ew/articles/show/9452-four-paintings-by-goya.

81. Although it is still a long way off, Goya's countryman Picasso will use a grey palette to meet political ends, to express the horrors of the war by which he is surrounded. See my discussion in chapter 2.

82. Anne Hollander, *Moving Pictures* (Cambridge, Mass.: Harvard University Press, 1991), 252–60. Fred Licht's book is the reference for the discussion of the public documentary aspect to Goya's paintings. See Fred Licht, *Goya* (New York: Abbeville Press, 2001).

83. See, e.g., the Prado's gallery guide, Valeriano Bozal, *Goya: Black Paintings* (Madrid: Fundación Amigos del Museo del Prado, 1999). See also Juan José Junqera, *The Black Paintings of Goya* (New York: Scala, 1999).

84. Junqera, *The Black Paintings of Goya.*

85. This curiosity is echoed in the National Gallery's guide to the painting.

86. Adam Lowe, "To See the World in a Square of Black," in Latour and Weibel, *Iconoclash,* 563.

87. This statement is perhaps referred to more as a convenience than as any kind of fact. Douglas Crimp, for example, uses it rhetorically in his landmark piece "The End of Painting," *October* 16 (Spring 1981): 75.

88. Ibid.

89. T. J. Clark, *Farewell to an Idea: Episodes from a History of Modernism* (New Haven, Conn.: Yale University Press, 1999).

90. Ibid., 173.

91. Interestingly, the other authors to whom I refer here, most notably, Krauss, take up the question of modernism as Clement Greenberg and Michael Fried initially theorized it. This is done primarily in the pages of *Artforum* in the 1960s and 1970s, and then later in the pages of *October.*

92. Foster, Krauss, Bois, and Buchloh, *Art Since 1900.*

93. Ibid.

94. Clement Greenberg, "Modernist Painting," in *The Collected Essays and Criticism,* vol. 4, *Modernism with a Vengeance, 1957–1969,* ed. John O'Brian (Chicago: University of Chicago Press, 1995), 85–93.

95. The critics writing in *Artforum* and *October* in the 1970s, '80s, and '90s were chief among those who departed from the rigidity and monocularity of Greenberg's theory of modern painting.

96. See Stefano Zuffi, *Color in Art* (New York: Harry Abrams, 2012), 310.

97. David Shapiro and Cecile Shapiro, "Abstract Expressionism: The Politics of Apolitical Painting," in Jack Salzman, ed., *Prospects* 3 (1978): 175–214. Reprinted in *Pollock and After: The Critical Debate,* ed. Francis Frascina (London: Routledge, 2000), 307–28. Other articles in this same anthology follow the link between abstract expressionism and American nationalism.

2. Visualizing Modern Life

1. The notion of the pictorial representation as a window is a legacy of the Renaissance, notoriously begun by Alberti in *De pictura* (1435). See Leon Battista Alberti, *On Painting,* trans. and ed. Rocco Sinisgalli (Cambridge: Cambridge University Press, 2011). It was taken up with particular verve by photography and film theorists looking to explain the ontology of the photographic image. Most significantly, it was developed by André Bazin in "Painting and Cinema," *What Is Cinema?* Vol. 1, 2nd ed., trans. Hugh Grey (Berkeley: University of California Press, 2004), 163–72.

2. In addition to Graham, "Pigments and Media," on the history of pigment production, see Ball, *Bright Earth,* and Victoria Finlay, *Color: A Natural History of the Palette* (London: Random House, 2003).

3. See Paloma Alarco, Michel Draguet, Thierry Dufrêne, and Jacques Taddei, *Monet et l'abstraction / Monet and Abstraction* (Paris: Hazan, 2010); exhibition catalog. The exhibition at the Musée Monet makes the argument that Monet is the father of postwar twentieth-century abstraction.

4. T. J. Clark, *The Painting of Modern Life: Paris in the Art of Manet and His Followers* (Princeton, N.J.: Princeton University Press, 1984), 62.

5. T. J. Clark, "Modernism, Postmodernism, and Steam," *October* 100 (Spring 2002): 159. Foucault refers to this painting also as evidence of his argument. We are given no access to what the woman watches because it

is in front of the painting in which she sits. Neither do we know what the little girl watches because it is obscured by smoke and steam. Michel Foucault, *Manet and the Object of Painting,* trans. Matthew Barr (London: Tate Publishing, 2009), 53–55.

6. As if to underline this synergy of paint and the goings-on of the train station, Monet's *Gare Saint Lazare* hangs in a train station cum museum, the Musée d'Orsay in Paris. In its very structure, the building marries industry and art in postwar Paris when it was transformed from train station to museum in order to house the nation's modern art.

7. Manet as "the first modernist painter" is a label that still holds sway today. It was first announced by Émile Zola in 1867, and then, nearly eighty years later Clement Greenberg equates modernism with Manet, and Manet with modernism. See Greenberg, "Modernist Painting," in *Collected Essays,* 4:86. See also Greenberg's writings from the 1940s such as "Abstract Art" (1944), in *The Collected Essays and Criticism,* vol. 1, *Perceptions and Judgments,* ed. John O'Brian (Chicago: University of Chicago Press, 1986), 93.

8. Carol Armstrong, *Manet Manette* (New Haven, Conn.: Yale University Press, 2002), 146.

9. Carol Armstrong, "Manet at the Intersection of Portraits and Personalities," in MaryAnne Stevens et al., *Manet: Portraying Life* (London: Royal Academy of Arts, 2013), 42–49.

10. While this double edge of photography as both recording and representing reality is not recognized by all writing at the time, it is most articulately expressed by Siegfried Kracauer in "Photography," *Theory of Film: The Redemption of Physical Reality,* ed. Miriam Bratu Hansen (Princeton, N.J.: Princeton University Press, 1997), 13–23.

11. T. J. Clark discusses Manet and his followers' representations of prostitution in the 1860s. See Clark, "Olympia's Choice," in *The Painting of Modern Life,* 79–146.

12. Michael Fried takes up this idea that was first explored by Gilles Deleuze in his larger argument about the end of the tradition of antitheatricality in painting. See Michael Fried, *Manet's Modernism; or, The Face of Painting in the 1860s* (Chicago: University of Chicago Press, 1996).

13. This argument began with Clement Greenberg in his writings from the 1940s on modernism. See Greenberg, "Modernist Painting."

14. This belief is maintained everywhere in this history of art. Even Oswald Spengler in "The Decline of the West" saw in Manet's work the end of an era in painting. See Arthur C. Danto, *After the End of Art: Contemporary Art and the Pale of History* (Princeton, N.J.: Princeton University Press, 1998), 61–80.

15. Armstrong, "Modernity according to Manet: Impressionism at the Salon, 1874 to 1879," in *Manet Manette*, 201–26.

16. Armstrong, "Mlle. Victorine in the Costume of an 'Espada': Painting and Exhibiting Victorine between 1862 and 1868," in *Manet Manette*, 168.

17. This painting is used by Jonathan Crary as a metonym for his theory of the transformations in vision in the nineteenth century. He focuses on the transformation of the liquid soap from an opaque white substance in a glass at the boy's right elbow to the transparent bubble at the end of the straw. This transformation from opacity to transparency effected through the cooperation of vision and touch, idea and matter, constitutes an "indivisible mode of knowledge." As such, Chardin's *Boy Blowing Bubbles* demonstrates the tactility embedded in vision, as well as the privileging of the optical, at this time. Jonathan Crary, *Techniques of the Observer: On Vision and Modernity in the Nineteenth Century* (Cambridge, Mass.: MIT Press, 1990), 62–66.

18. See, for example, Alexi Worth, "The Lost Photographs of Edouard Manet," in *Art in America* 95, no. 1 (January 2007): 59–65. Worth relies heavily on Beatrice Farwell, *Manet and the Nude: A Study of Iconography in the Second Empire* (New York: Garland, 1981). Farwell's was one of the first works to develop the notion of the relationship between Manet's painting and photography.

19. Greenberg sees Manet's paintings as the birth of modern art on the basis of their flatness, their address to the eye. For Greenberg, this flatness finds its telos in the work of Morris Louis and Kenneth Noland. See Greenberg, "Modernist Painting."

20. This is so eloquently exposed in Foucault's lecture on thirteen paintings by Éduoard Manet in Tunisia in 1971. See Michel Foucault, *Manet and the Object of Painting, trans. Matthew Barr* (London: Tate Publishing, 2013).

21. Manet and Whistler are often placed in the same tradition of realist painting, not only because they shared circles in Paris prior to Whistler's move to London in 1860, but also because of their admiration for Velázquez, their commitment to realism and the everyday, and, together with Gustave Courbet, their flouting of artistic tradition in the treatment of paint and its objects. See Fried, *Manet's Modernism,* on the roots and genesis of pictorial modernism, particularly, in relationship to those (including Whistler) on whom Manet was dependent for his visions.

22. The rawest and most vociferous criticism of Whistler's *Nocturne* paintings came from John Ruskin, the leading art critic of the time. Ruskin famously accused Whistler of "flinging a pot of paint in the public's face," in response to *Nocturne in Black and Gold: The Falling Rocket* when it was exhibited in 1878 at the Grosvenor Gallery in London. Whistler then sued Ruskin for libel. For an account of the trial, see Linda Merrill, *A Pot of*

Paint: Aesthetics on Trial in Whistler v Ruskin (Washington, D.C.: Smithsonian Institution Press, 1992).

23. Although Tate Britain owns four of the *Nocturnes,* only two were on display when I visited in summer 2013.

24. In the room, "1840," in Tate Britain, the *Nocturnes* are placed side by side with works such as James Tissot's *Holyday* (1876), Théodore Roussel's *The Reading Girl* (1886–87), and Philip Wilson Steer's *Girls Running, Walberswick Pier* (1889–94). For all of the innovation of these works, they are still a long way from the flat, horizontally composed, sketch-like *Nocturnes.*

25. For Whistler's version of the scandal caused by the *Nocturnes,* see his own account in James Whistler, *The Gentle Art of Making Enemies* (New York: Putnam, 1890).

26. This is a technique shared by other symbolist painters, but is pronounced in Hammershøi's work.

27. "Je suis intimement convaincu que moins un tableau est coloré, plus il est réussi du point de vue chromatique." Quoted in Felix Krämer, Naoki Sato, and Anne-Birgitte Fonsmark, *Hammershøi* (Paris: Hazan, 2008), 21.

28. For a perspective on Danish cinema from the period, particularly as it is connected to the development of modernist aesthetics, see Julie Allen, *Icons of Danish Modernity* (Seattle: University of Washington Press, 2012). On the penetration of outside public worlds into the home, see Guerin, *A Culture of Light,* especially chapter 5, "Reformulations of Space through Light in *Die Straße, Jenseits der Straße,* and *Am Rande der Welt,*" 154–92.

29. On the transformations to daily life in modernity, see, for example, Georg Simmel, "The Metropolis and Mental Life," in *The Sociology of Georg Simmel,* ed. and trans. K. Wolff (New York: Simon and Schuster, 1950), 409–24. Originally published 1902–3.

30. Foucault, "The Space of the Canvas," in *Manet and the Object of Painting,* 33–55.

31. On this notion of modernist art as a declaration of its own self-referential time and space, see Rosalind Krauss, "Grids," *October* 4 (Autumn 1977): 50–67.

32. Ibid., 49–55.

33. Clark, *Farewell to an Idea,* 205.

34. See Alan Trachtenberg, ed., *Classic Essays on Photography* (New Haven, Conn.: Leete's Island Books, 1980).

35. Of particular interest here are painters who turn to photography for radical new solutions to representation and documentation. See Elizabeth W. Easton, ed., *Snapshot: Painters and Photography, Bonnard to Vuillard* (New Haven, Conn.: Yale University Press, 2012).

36. *Picasso Black and White,* ed. Carmen Giménez (New York: Solomon R. Guggenheim Museum, with Prestel, 2012); exhibition catalog.

37. See Carmen Giménez, "Picasso Black and White," in ibid., 19–31.

38. See Caroline Brothers, *War and Photography: A Cultural History* (Oxford: Routledge, 1997), 212–16.

39. T. J. Clark, "Cubism and Collectivity," in *Farewell to an Idea,* 169–223.

40. Ibid.

41. Olivier Berggruen, "Picasso Monochrome," in Giménez, *Picasso Black and White,* 67.

42. On the extent to which Picasso was influenced by the events unfolding in modern European culture all around him, and his struggle to represent them, see T. J. Clark, *Picasso and Truth: From Cubism to Guernica* (Princeton, N.J.: Princeton University Press, 2013).

43. Kirk Varnedoe, "Why Abstract Art?," in *Pictures of Nothing: Abstract Art since Pollock* (Princeton, N.J.: Princeton University Press, 2006), 1.

44. The sea is the stage for emotion and dramas that continue on beyond the frame of the canvas. In Turner's stormy seas such as *Calais Pier* (1803) that echo the vigor and tenacity of his brushwork, we observe the buildup of paint as well as the welling up of emotion of the sea that is, effectively, the protagonist of this painting. It is the voluminous grey waves, and the heavy grey clouds, made more dynamic by the light of the sun that breaks through them, that draw our attention to this painting, and hold on to it once we are there. Even the boats at the compositional center appear to give voice to the magnificence and power of the sea. Courbet's sky in *Beach Scene* (1874), which sits in a room adjacent to Turner's *Snow Storm—Steam-Boat off a Harbour's Mouth* (1842) at Tate Britain, is painted with a palette knife, giving us another nineteenth-century vision of emotions and aspirations. The painting is, in short, the soul as it is reflected in the sea. In Courbet's painting, the pent-up grey sky consumes over two-thirds of the canvas. Here and in the Turner painting it is as though figuration is merely a ruse to enable the painter to indulge in the drama of the natural world of the sea, the sky in which it is reflected, and its painterly possibilities. For artists such as Turner and Courbet, the natural world is at its most dramatic and alive, its most ambiguous and emotional, when it is in painted in grey. Similar to the Whistler *Nocturnes,* the horizon line is not only present to *Beach Scene,* it also is emphasized by what looks to be the setting sun, but might be the rising sun, creating a slither of brilliant orange that simultaneously demarcates the horizon line. Nevertheless, Courbet's indulgence in the energy and emotion of the sky about to burst, and the fact that it consumes so much of the painting, the water the same steel grey tinged with the orange sun, creates

painting that verges into abstraction well before abstraction is a possibility in paint.

45. Pierre Borhan, "Adventure on the High Seas: Modernity and Capturing the Moment," in *The Sea: A Celebration in Photographs* (Paris: Flammarion, 2011), 71–101.

46. See, for example, the Lumière brothers, *La Mer* (1895); R. W. Paul and Brit Acres, *Rough Sea at Dover* (1895); R. W. Paul, *Rocky Shore* (1896); R. W. Paul and Henry Short, *Sea Cave Near Lisbon* (1896).

47. See George Lawrence's image titled *San Francisco Bay in Ruins from Lawrence Captive Airship, 200 Feet above San Francisco Bay Overlooking Waterfront* (1906). In Borhan, "Adventure on the High Seas," 74–75.

48. See, for example, the writings of Laszlo Moholy-Nagy, *Moholy-Nagy: An Anthology,* ed. Richard Kostelanetz (Boston: Da Capo Press, 1970), and the essays in Trachtenberg, *Classic Essays on Photography,* especially 109–90.

49. Roland Barthes brought this discourse on the photograph as a freezing of life, a progenitor of death, into widespread popular discourse. See Roland Barthes, *Camera Lucida: Reflections on Photography,* trans. Richard Howard (New York: Farrar, Straus and Giroux, 1981).

50. Krauss, "Grids," 64.

51. Clement Greenberg, "'American-Type' Painting," in *Art and Culture: Critical Essays* (Boston: Beacon Press, 1961), 208–29.

52. Clark identifies the near identicality of Picasso and Braque's works from this period as the shift to a "collective" creation. See Clark, "Cubism and Collectivity," in *Farewell to an Idea,* 169–223.

53. I am thinking here, for example, of Hans Richter, René Clair, and the post-Revolutionary Russian directors such as Dziga Vertov and Sergei Eisenstein.

54. For an interesting argument that weighs the tension between the mechanical production of the image and the individuality of the artist's hand that guides its organization, see Franz Roh, "Mechanism and Expression," in Trachtenberg, *Classic Essays on Photography,* 154–63.

55. Leading thoughts on these questions are from Michel Foucault, "What Is an Author?," in *Language, Counter-Memory, Practice: Selected Essays and Interviews,* ed. Donald Bouchard (Ithaca, N.Y.: Cornell University Press, 1980), 113–38. Otherwise, there is a proliferation of material on this topic.

56. The philosophical thinking is characteristic of Karl Marx found in, for example, Karl Marx, *Grundrisse: Foundations of the Critique of Political Economy,* trans. Martin Nicolaus (New York: Penguin, 1973), and becomes most articulately thematized by thinkers throughout the twentieth century.

57. John Berger, "Giacometti," in *About Looking* (London: Vintage, 1991), 178–83.

58. Ibid., 182.

59. Reinhold Hohl, *Alberto Giacometti* (New York: Harry N. Abrams, 1971), 225.

60. Valerie Fletcher, "The Paintings," in *The Studio of Alberto Giacometti* (Paris: Centre Pompidou, 2007), 200.

61. Giacometti's sculpted figures are equally trapped, framed, isolated by the alienation of modern life. They are cold, distant, and distanced. And they are cold because, among other reasons, they are grey, disproportionate, always isolated, never in conversation with each other, always at a literal and metaphorical distance from whatever it is that is next to them.

62. On the Holocaust as modernity gone awry, see Zygmunt Bauman, *Modernity and the Holocaust* (Cambridge: Polity, 1989).

63. Eadweard Muybridge, *The Human Figure in Motion* (New York: Dover, 1887).

64. David Sylvester, *Looking Back at Francis Bacon* (London: Thames and Hudson, 2000).

65. No specific photograph has been identified as the inspiration of Bacon's painting, but as Jan Cox suggests, the image of the female nude with her back turned toward the camera was found in Bacon's studio. See Jan Cox, "Wyndham Lewis and Francis Bacon." Accessed 8 December 2015. www.unirioja.es/listenerartcriticism/essays/essay-Wyndham-Lewis-and-Francis-Bacon.htm.

66. Marshall Berman, "All That Is Solid Melts into Air: Marx, Modernism and Modernization," in *All That Is Solid Melts into Air: The Experience of Modernity* (1982; repr., London: Penguin, 1988), 87–130.

67. Ibid.

68. See William Rubin, ed., *Pablo Picasso: A Retrospective* (New York: Museum of Modern Art, 1980); exhibition catalog.

69. Stephen A. Nash, "Picasso, War, and Art," in Stephen A. Nash, ed., *Picasso and the War Years, 1937–1945* (New York: Thames and Hudson, 1998), 17; exhibition catalog.

70. See Rudolf Arnheim, *The Genesis of a Painting: Picasso's Guernica* (Berkeley: University of California Press, 1962).

71. On the use of photography to report on the Spanish Civil War, and for a theoretical analysis of the relationship between war photography and the press, see Brothers, *War and Photography.* On the many different ways that photography and war have developed hand in hand, see Will Michels et al., *War / Photography Images of Armed Conflict and Its Aftermath* (New Haven, Conn.: Yale University Press, 2012).

72. Berggruen, "Picasso Monochrome."

73. Quoted in Herschell B. Chipp, *Theories of Modern Art* (Berkeley: University of California Press, 1984), 487.

74. This use of grey paint for the visual representation of the horrors of war, its magnitude, and its memory is reiterated throughout the century on the canvases of painters across Europe.

75. We will remember that Mantegna went back to antiquity and the importance of stone and marble in his painted representations of early biblical narratives. Barbara Rose also mentions the use of monochrome by radical painters from Malevich to Rauschenberg in theater sets as a way to challenge the overt expression of emotion in representation. See Barbara Rose, *Monochromes: From Malevich to the Present* (Berkeley: University of California Press, 2004), 60.

76. For more on the development of color in early film see Kim Tomadjoglou, ed., "Early Color," special issue, *Film History: An International Journal* 21, no. 1 (June 2009).

3. Grey Abstraction

1. Readers may question the limited choice of artists for discussion. However, while other painters, for example, Stella, de Kooning, Pollock, and Barnett Newman have all painted important single works in grey; grey is not at the heart of abstract expressionism, and neither do these artists spend a period of time working through their ideas in grey paint.

2. See Greenberg, "Modernist Painting." Greenberg's claim about the surface of the painting has been often critiqued and is now generally accepted as misleading.

3. This shift from a transcendent viewer in reverie to an embodied spectator who, at times, experiences a haptic vision, is discussed by critics such as T. J. Clark and Jonathan Crary. See Clark, *Farewell to an Idea*; Crary, *Techniques of the Observer.*

4. For a discussion of this tension between surface and objects in Johns's paintings, see Rosalind Krauss, "Jasper Johns: The Functions of Irony," *October* 2 (Summer 1976): 91–99.

5. For more on this painting, see Marco Livingstone, "Jasper Johns," in Richard Morphet, *Encounters: New Art from Old* (London: National Gallery, 2000), 176–89; exhibition catalog. The painting was commissioned by the National Gallery in London, which invited twelve contemporary artists to respond to pieces in its collection. Johns attributes the smaller size of the left margin of his catenary fragments to the fact that he was working from a photograph. See Scott Rothkopf, "Suspended Animation," in *Jasper Johns. Catenary* (Göttingen: Steidl, 2005), unpaginated, footnote 33; exhibition catalog.

6. On the catenary and its curve as the ideal of a hung chain or cable

that assumes its own weight when supported only at its ends, see Rothkopf, "Suspended Animation."

7. For a recent work on the objectness of Johns's paintings, see Barbara Hess, *Johns* (Cologne: Taschen, 2007).

8. See Leo Steinberg, "Jasper Johns: The First Seven Years of His Art," *Metro* 4/5 (1962); reprinted in Steinberg, *Other Criteria: Confrontations with Twentieth-Century Art* (New York: Oxford University Press, 1972), 17. See also John Yau, *A Thing among Things: The Art of Jasper Johns* (New York: Distributed Art Publishers, 2008).

9. Kelly Keegan and Kristin Lister, "Construction and Color: *Near the Lagoon*," in Rondeau and Druick, *Jasper Johns: Gray*, 165.

10. Ibid.

11. Rothkopf, *Jasper Johns. Catenary.* See also Mark Rosenthal, "The Crosshatch Series," and John Yau, "Bridge and Catenary Works," in *Jasper Johns: Seeing with the Mind's Eye*, ed. Gary Garrels (New Haven, Conn.: Yale University Press, 2013), 116–25 and 138–45, respectively.

12. This cycle is discussed in chapter 1.

13. Rondeau and Druick, *Jasper Johns: Gray*, 168.

14. This is not specific to Johns's paintings, and indeed could be said to define twentieth-century abstraction, at least as it is pursued in grey.

15. This was derived by Gottfried Wilhelm Leibniz, Christiaan Huygens, and Johann Bernoulli in 1691. See David Griffin, "Catenaries, Parabolas and Suspension Bridges." Accessed 7 October 2013. http://www.wokinghamu3a.org.uk/Maths_Catenaries,%20Parabolas%20and%20Suspension%20Bridges.pdf.

16. These images can be seen in Rothkopf, *Jasper Johns. Catenary.*

17. Jasper Johns, "A Conversation with Jasper Johns," in Rondeau and Druick, *Jasper Johns: Gray*, 161.

18. On the identification of the tactile or haptic quality of vision within the "scopic regimes of modernity," see Martin Jay, "Scopic Regimes of Modernity," in *Vision and Visuality*, ed. Hal Foster (Seattle: Bay Press, 1988), 3–23. I would argue that this characteristic of vision, which Jay identifies in twentieth-century French thought and writing on vision and modernity, is brought to the fore of painting by postwar American artists such as Rauschenberg and Johns.

19. Max Kozloff, "Johns and Duchamp," *Art International* 8, no. 2 (March 1964): 42–45. Reprinted in *Dancing Around the Bride: Cage, Cunningham, Johns, Rauschenberg, and Duchamp* (Philadelphia: Philadelphia Museum of Art, 2013), 93; exhibition catalog.

20. David Sylvester, *About Modern Art: Critical Essays, 1948–1996* (New York: Henry Holt, 1997), 228.

21. Rosalind Krauss, "Grids," in *The Originality of the Avant-Garde and Other Modernist Myths* (Cambridge, Mass.: MIT Press, 1985), 16.

22. The painting is said to be about the end of Johns's personal relationship with Rauschenberg. The controversial exhibition at the Smithsonian's National Portrait Gallery, *Hide/Seek,* explored the relationship between the two, while other critics are more interested in the mutual influence they had on each other's painting. However it is approached, the relationship is one of creativity and productive influence over many years. See Jonathan Katz and David Ward, *Hide/Seek* (Washington, D.C: Smithsonian Books, 2010); exhibition catalog.

23. On the role of viewer desire as it is translated by Johns's paintings, see Yau, *A Thing among Things.*

24. I discuss the radicality of this kind of vision as it is incited by twentieth-century abstraction in grey in chapter 4.

25. Florence Ingleby, ed., *Sean Scully: Resistance and Persistence: Selected Writings* (London: Merrell, 2006).

26. Ibid., 87.

27. Ibid., 88.

28. Brad Prager, *Aesthetic Vision and German Romanticism: Writing Images* (Berlin: BOYE6, 2010).

29. Jay, "Scopic Regimes of Modernity."

30. This brings to mind the significance of James Turrell's *Laar* (1976), which is color as light that has the illusory perception of paint. See Craig Adcock and James Turrell, *The Art of Light and Space* (Berkeley: University of California Press, 1990).

31. The face of an early Rembrandt portrait and the entrance of Christ to summon Matthew in Caravaggio's *The Calling of Saint Matthew* (1599) are obvious examples of this tendency.

32. Roland Barthes, "Cy Twombly: Works on Paper (1979)," in *The Responsibility of Forms: Critical Essays on Music, Art, and Representation,* trans. Richard Howard (Berkeley: University of California Press, 1985), 166.

33. I am thinking here again of the work of artists such as Turrell, Robert Irwin, and Doug Wheeler. See Robin Clark et al., *Phenomenal: California Light, Space, Surface* (Berkeley: University of California Press, 2011).

34. Walter Benjamin, *Walter Benjamin: Selected Writings,* vol. 1, *1913–1926,* ed. Marcus Bullock and Michael Jennings (Cambridge, Mass.: Harvard University Press, 2004).

35. Norman Bryson, *Vision and Painting: The Logic of the Gaze* (New Haven, Conn.: Yale University Press, 1983), 94.

36. Walter Benjamin, "A Child's View of Colour // 1914–15," in Batchelor, ed., *Colour,* 63–64. See also Walter Benjamin, "Aphorisms on Imagination and Colour // 1914–15," in ibid., 65.

37. For a detailed discussion of Rothko's process, see Carol Mancusi-Ungaro, "Material and Immaterial Surface: The Paintings of Rothko," in *Mark Rothko,* ed. Jeffrey Weiss (Washington, D.C.: National Gallery of Art, 1998), 283–300; exhibition catalog. For a detailed examination of the process of the Seagram Murals, see also Leslie Carlyle et al., "The Substance of Things," *Rothko: The Late Series,* ed. Achim Borchardt-Hume (London: Tate Modern, 2008), 75–85; exhibition catalog.

38. Achim Boarchardt-Hume, "Shadows of Light: Mark Rothko's Late Series," in Borchardt-Hume, *Rothko: The Late Series,* 27.

39. This layering of paint, in a process that results in revealing and concealing, might be seen as engaging with some of the same concerns as Gerhard Richter's *128 Fotos von einem Bild / 128 Details from a Picture,* a series of images in which he overpaints a photograph of a painting in 128 different variations. See my discussion of this series in chapter 5.

40. On the border left around the edge of the painting when Rothko removed the tape used to attach his works to the easel, see David Anfam, "The World in a Frame," in Borchardt-Hume, *Rothko: The Late Series,* especially 235, footnote 30.

41. Robert Goldwater, "Rothko's Black Paintings," *Art in America* 59 (March–April 1971): 62.

42. Briony Fer, "Seeing in the Dark," in Borchardt-Hume, *Rothko: The Late Series,* 43.

43. Barbara Novak and Brian O'Doherty, "Rothko's Dark Paintings: Tragedy and Void," in Weiss, *Mark Rothko,* 266.

44. See "Brice Marden: Selected Statements, Notes and Interviews," in *Brice Marden: Paintings, Drawings, and Prints, 1975–80, ed. Nicholas Serota* (London: Whitechapel Art Gallery, 1981), 57; exhibition catalog.

45. Quoted in Carol Mancusi-Ungaro, "Marden's Materiality: The Monochromes," in *Plane Image: A Brice Marden Retrospective,* ed. Gary Garrels (New York: Museum of Modern Art, 2006), 112; exhibition catalog.

46. Francesco Clemente, "A Private Rebel: Brice Marden," *Res: Anthropology and Aesthetics* 51 (Spring 2007): 250.

47. See Richard Shiff, "Force of Myself Looking," in Garrels, *Plane Image,* especially 29–32.

48. Marden is quoted by Mancusi-Ungaro as saying that when *The Seasons* were first exhibited in Houston at Rice Institute for the Arts in 1975, he considered them unfinished. When he went ahead and finished them, the uncertainty of the bottom edges was painted over. See Mancusi-Ungaro, "Marden's Materiality," 115.

49. Yve-Alain Bois, "Marden's Doubt," in *Brice Marden: Paintings 1985–1993,* ed. Ulrich Loock and Yve-Alain Bois (Bern: Kunsthalle Bern, 1993), 12–66; exhibition catalog.

50. Quotation from Christine Mehring, "Brice Marden: *Muses Drawing 5 (Mnemosyne)*, 1989–91," in *Drawing Is Another Kind of Language: Recent American Drawings from a New York Private Collection* (Boston: Harvard University Art Museums, 1997), 1; exhibition catalog.

51. See chapter 2 for more on Giacometti's portraits in grey.

52. David Anfam, *Brice Marden: Ru Ware, Marbles, Polke* (New York: Matthew Marks Gallery, 2012), 17; exhibition catalog.

53. Ibid.

54. Briony Fer, "Infinity," in *The Infinite Line: Re-making Art after Modernism* (New Haven, Conn.: Yale University Press, 2004), 48–49.

55. Ibid. See also Kasha Linville, "Agnes Martin: An Appreciation," *Artforum International* 9, no. 10 (June 1971): 72–73; Rosalind Krauss, in the title essay of *The Originality of the Avant-Garde and Other Modernist Myths* (Cambridge, Mass.: MIT Press, 1985), 155–70. See also Rosalind Krauss, her later essay on Martin and the grid in the Whitney catalog, Barbara Haskell et al., *Agnes Martin* (New York: Whitney Museum of American Art, 1992), 155–65; exhibition catalog. Reprinted in Rosalind Krauss, "Agnes Martin: The / Cloud/," in *Bachelors* (Cambridge, Mass.: MIT Press, 1999), 75–90. See also Brendan Prendeville, "The Meaning of Acts: Agnes Martin and the Making of Americans," *Oxford Art Journal* 31, no. 1 (2008): 51–73.

56. Lynne Cooke, Karen Kelly, and Barbara Schröder, eds., *Agnes Martin*, Dia Art Foundation, New York (New Haven, Conn.: Yale University Press, 2011), 11.

57. Arne Glimcher says this in his introduction to *Agnes Martin: Paintings, Writings, Remembrances* (London and New York: Phaidon, 2012), unpaginated.

58. See the reproduced handwritten notes in Glimcher, *Agnes Martin*, unpaginated.

59. Jonathan Katz succinctly articulates the contradictions that arise in her work. Jonathan Katz, "Agnes Martin and the Sexuality of Abstraction," in Cooke, Kelly, and Schröder, *Agnes Martin*, 171–73.

60. Kasha Linville, "Agnes Martin: An Appreciation," *Artforum* 9, no. 10 (June 1971): 73.

61. See Krauss, "Agnes Martin: The /Cloud/."

62. See Lynne Cooke, ". . . in the classical tradition . . . ," in Cooke, Kelly, and Schröder, *Agnes Martin*, especially 11–16

63. Kasha Linville's early review of Martin's works describes this experience slightly differently, but nevertheless, as bifurcated across seeing it in close up and at a distance. Linville, "Agnes Martin: An Appreciation," 72.

64. Heiner Bastian, ed., *Cy Twombly. Catalogue Raisonné of the Paintings*, vol. 3, *1966–1971* (Munich: Schirmer/Mosel, 1994).

65. Foster, Krauss, Bois, and Buchloh, *Art since 1900,* 372.

66. Rosalind Krauss, "Cy Was Here; Cy's Up," *Artforum International* 33, no. 1 (September 1994): 74, 118.

67. Ibid., 118.

68. See Martha Cooper and Henry Chalfant, *Subway Art* (New York: Thames and Hudson, 1984).

69. Krauss also refers to *Panorama* to argue for the scatological implications of the supposed graffiti markings. See Rosalind Krauss, *The Optical Unconscious* (Cambridge, Mass.: MIT Press, 1994), 243–308.

70. Clark, *Farewell to an Idea,* especially the chapter on Pollock, "The Unhappy Consciousness," 299–369.

71. Sean Scully, "Landline," in Ingleby, *Sean Scully,* 125.

72. Marden, "Brice Marden: Selected Statements, Notes and Interviews."

73. Clemente, "A Private Rebel," 250.

74. This notion of the in-forme was conceived by Georges Bataille in 1929 to characterize the formlessness of modern art. I use it here, however, with reference to its instantiation by Krauss and Bois in their exhibition, *Formless: A User's Guide* at the Centre Pompidou in 1996. The two critics appropriated the term as the driving force to identify the everydayness, which includes the mess, even the waste of modern art in the twentieth century. See Yve-Alain Bois and Rosalind E. Krauss, *Formless: A User's Guide* (London and New York: Zone Books, 2000).

75. Up close, the mystery of the lines as the perfect grid evaporates when we recognize that the lines are never perfect because they are always hand drawn.

76. Douglas Crimp, "Opaque Surfaces," *Arte come arte* (Milan: Centro Comunitario di Brera, 1973), unpaginated.

77. Juliet Wilson Bareau and David C. Degener, eds., *Manet and the Sea* (Chicago: Art Institute of Chicago, 2004); exhibition catalog.

78. Jeffrey Weiss, "Painting Bitten by a Man," in *Jasper Johns: An Allegory of Painting, 1955–1965* (Washington, D.C.: National Gallery of Art; New Haven, Conn.: Yale University Press, 2007), 10; exhibition catalog.

79. It could also be argued that Scully, as an artist, creates an uncertain space as his work captures his own Irish American identity. Scully was born in Ireland and educated in the United States in the 1970s, and his work always has the impression of not belonging. I therefore discuss it here somewhat cautiously as it is more in the service of my argument regarding the erasure of all distinction between figuration and abstraction than it is in any identification of a particularly American aesthetic.

80. Scully's lecture at the Phillips Collection in 2005 is particularly indicative of the way that landscapes, things, and people rest as a layer of inspira-

tion for his paintings, rather than as subjections of representation. See Sean Scully, "The Phillips Collection Lecture," Washington, D.C., 2005, in Ingleby, *Sean Scully*, 163–85.

81. Ibid.

82. David Carrier, *Sean Scully* (London: Thames and Hudson, 2006), 166.

4. Beyond Modernist Abstraction

1. See, for example, Clement Greenberg, "'American-Type' Painting."

2. Quoted in Bruce Glaser, "Questions to Stella and Judd," in *Minimal Art: A Critical Anthology*, ed. Gregory Battcock (New York: E. P. Dutton, 1968), 158.

3. This is Varnedoe's argument in *Pictures of Nothing*.

4. T. J. Clark, "The Unhappy Consciousness," in *Farewell to an Idea*, 299–369.

5. Boris Groys, *Art Power* (Cambridge, Mass.: MIT Press, 2008). See especially "On the New" and "Iconoclasm as an Artistic Device," 23–42 and 67–81, respectively.

6. As Mark Taylor argues, this vein of iconoclasm runs deeply through Jewish monotheism, Protestant puritanism, and Western thought. However, it can be traced back to book 10 of Plato's *Republic*. See Mark C. Taylor, *The Picture in Question: Mark Tansey and the Ends of Representation* (Chicago: University of Chicago Press, 1999), 7–9.

7. Groys's work is, like the modernism he characterizes and critiques, driven by a Hegelian Marxist logic.

8. I take this term from the important essays by Max Kozloff, "American Painting during the Cold War," and Eva Crockcroft, "Abstract Expressionism, Weapon of the Cold War," in *Pollock and After: The Critical Debate*, ed. Francis Franscina (New York: Harper and Row, 1985), 130–54.

9. The centrality of authors and artists as having a privileged vision of a world in crisis was brought to the United States through the writing of Roland Barthes, then Michel Foucault, and was continued by post-structuralism.

10. I am thinking here of Roland Barthes, "The Death of the Author," in *Image-Music-Text*, trans. Stephen Heath (New York: Hill and Wang, 1980), 142–47; and Michel Foucault, "What Is an Author?" These ideas were translated into the minimalist sculptural work of artists such as Robert Morris and Donald Judd, sculptors who eschewed every trace of their presence from depersonalized and manufactured structures and objects.

11. Robert Rauschenberg was one of the first artists to explore this idea

in the early 1950s. With his connection to John Cage, Rauschenberg sought to erase the unique traces of his individual genius and to focus on the connections of painting to the mass market and the commodity status of art within it. Rauschenberg, like Warhol after him, was increasingly interested in the influence of the mechanical on artistic agency, in reaction to what they perceived as the excess of abstract expressionism. In particular, Rauschenberg was preoccupied by the omnipresence of media images woven into the fabric of American life. This would thus become the subject and medium of his work. Of course, today, Rauschenberg's collages are anything but anonymous and mass produced, even if they are made from found objects, mass media images; even if they reject or remove the artist's gesture of identification, the indexical traces of the artist's body, Rauschenberg is everywhere present to his Combines. I have never walked past a Rauschenberg in a museum not recognizing it as being the work of Robert Rauschenberg.

12. Rosalind Krauss identifies the ruler as also canceling out. See Rosalind Krauss, "Jasper Johns," *Lugano Review* 1, no. 2 (II / 1965): 93–97.

13. There is no shortage of literature on the biographical, the personal, the artist's body and identity in Johns's paintings. See, for example, Fred Orton, *Figuring Jasper Johns* (London: Reaktion Books, 1994); Jill Johnston, *Jasper Johns: Privileged Information* (London: Thames and Hudson, 1996).

14. Much has been written on Johns's body and its presence on his canvases. For one of the best examples, see Yau, *A Thing among Things.*

15. Ibid.

16. Florence Berkman, "Pop Art on Exhibition Free, Far Out," *Hartford Times,* June 11, 1964, 26.

17. Wagstaff is quoted here by Berkman, ibid.

18. Foster, Krauss, Bois, and Buchloh, *Art since 1900,* 372.

19. See Bastian, *Cy Twombly: Catalogue Raisonné,* vol. 3, *1961–1971.*

20. Kiefer is another artist who takes up the imperative to represent the problems of history in grey. However, the disintegration, the ultimate failure of art and painting in the work of an artist like Kiefer come in the impossibility of approaching the subject matter, or for Giacometti, Richter, and other modernist artists, the need to paint the same thing over and over again.

21. See Achim Borchardt-Hume, "Shadows of Light: Mark Rothko's Late Series," in Borchardt-Hume, *Rothko: The Late Series,* 13–30.

22. Thomas Crowe, "The Marginal Difference in Rothko's Abstraction," in *Seeing Rothko,* ed. Glenn Phillips and Thomas Crowe (Los Angeles: J. P. Getty Trust, 2005), 35.

23. In a statement made to Daniel Bell in the mid-1950s, Rothko stated that eighteen inches was the ideal viewing distance of his canvases. Quoted

in Teresa Hensick and Paul M. Whitmore, "Rothko's Harvard Murals," in *Mark Rothko's Harvard Murals*, ed. Marjorie B. Cohn (Cambridge, Mass.: Harvard University Art Museums, 1988), 15; exhibition catalog.

24. Krauss makes this argument in her discussion of the modernist use of the grid, a discussion that extends to the obsessive repetitions of modern art per se. See Rosalind E. Krauss, "The Originality of the Avant-Garde," in *The Originality of the Avant-Garde and Other Modernist Myths*, 160–61.

25. James Elkins, *Pictures and Tears: A History of People Who Have Cried in Front of Paintings; How Painting Can Make You Cry* (New York: Routledge, 2001).

26. Ibid., 211.

27. I think here of the Pace Gallery exhibition, *The 80's: Grey Paintings*, 16 September 2011–29 October 2011. Accessed 8 December 2015. http://www.pacegallery.com/newyork/exhibitions/11193/agnes-martin-the-80s-grey-paintings. See also Glimcher, *Agnes Martin.*

28. I discussed these shifts in perception of Martin's grey paintings such as *A Grey Stone* and *White Flower* in chapter 3.

29. I saw Martin's *Leaves* on display at DIA Art Foundation, New York in the early 2000s. It is rarely exhibited, however.

30. Krauss, "Grids."

31. Fer, *The Infinite Line*, 47–63.

32. Clark, "The Unhappy Consciousness," in *Farewell to an Idea*, 299–369.

33. Quoted in Philip Guston and Harold Rosenberg, "Philip Guston's Object: A Dialogue with Harold Rosenberg," in *Philip Guston: Recent Paintings and Drawings* (New York: Jewish Museum, 1966), 9–10; exhibition catalog.

34. Ibid.

35. Morton Feldman, "After Modernism," *Art in America* 59, no. 6 (November–December 1971): 71–72.

36. David Kaufmann, *Telling Stories: Philip Guston's Later Works* (Berkeley: University of California Press, 2010), 11.

37. Carrier, *Sean Scully*, 26.

38. Quoted in Jasper Johns, "The Green Box," in *Marcel Duchamp in Perspective*, ed. Joseph Masheck (Boston: Da Capo, 2002), 110.

39. Krauss, "The Functions of Irony."

40. Catherine Craft, "Being an Artist," in *Jasper Johns* (New York: Parkstone Press, 2012), 9–48.

41. This tendency for a tactile, corporeal vision reaches new levels with the video artwork of an artist such as Gary Hill in the 1990s.

42. Antonia Lant, "Haptical Cinema," *October* 74 (Fall 1995): 45–73. Laura Marks has developed Lant's early writings on the tactility of cinema, and both authors ground their discussions in art historical discourse. See

Laura Marks, *The Skin of the Film: Intercultural Cinema, Embodiment, and the Senses* (Durham, N.C.: Duke University Press, 2000).

43. Fried famously condemned Rauschenberg for his contribution to the "illusion that the barriers between the arts are in the process of crumbling . . . and that the arts themselves are at last sliding toward some kind of final, implosive, highly desirable synthesis." Michael Fried, "Art and Objecthood" (1967), reprinted in Michael Fried, *Art and Objecthood: Essays and Reviews* (University of Chicago Press, 1998), 148–72.

44. Again, this was pointed out in a well-known discussion on the breakdown of the barriers between media. See Allan Kaprow, "Experimental Art," in *Essays on the Blurring of Art and Life,* expanded ed. (Berkeley: University of California Press, 1993), 73. In several of the Combines Rauschenberg confronts and blurs the distinctions between depicted space and the illusory space of photography. We also see Rauschenberg move into the space of other media, stepping out of the frame of the two-dimensional image.

45. If Rauschenberg persistently explored other media as a way to interrogate the gap between art and life, the paintings in grey pursue the gap between painting and other media to meet similar ends. Rauschenberg expresses this in a conversation with John Cage. John Cage, *Conversing with Cage,* ed. Richard Kostelanetz (New York: Limelight Editions, 1994), 181. On Rauschenberg's habitation of the space between art and life, see Arthur Danto, preface to *Unnatural Wonders: Essays from the Gap between Art and Life* (New York: Columbia University Press, 2007).

46. Bastian, *Cy Twombly: Catalogue Raisonné of the Paintings,* vol. 3, *1966–1971,* 31.

47. Ibid.

48. See my discussion of *Untitled (Say Goodbye Catullus, to the Shores of Asia Minor)* (1994) in the Menil Collection. Accessed 8 December 2015. http://fxreflects.blogspot.com/2009/07/cy-twombly-menil-collection-houston.html.

49. See, for example, Yves Klein, "War between Line and Colour, or Towards the Monochrome Proposition" (1954). Reprinted in Batchelor, *Colour,* 118–19. See also Wassily Kandinsky, *Point and Line to Plane* (London: Dover Publications, 1979).

50. Rondeau, "Jasper Johns: Gray." Rondeau uses the word *monochrome* to describe these paintings.

51. This idea of painting as a realization of an "experience with its own innate history. It does not illustrate—it is the sensation of its own realization" was articulated in one of Twombly's rare texts about his work in 1957. Cited in Bastian, *Catalogue Raisonné of the Paintings,* vol. 3, *1966–1971,* 27.

52. See, for example, Richard Leeman, *Cy Twombly: A Monograph* (London: Thames and Hudson, 2005), 204–5.

53. See also Jeffrey Weiss's review of the exhibition, "Cy Twombly. Tate Modern, London," *Artforum International* 47, no. 2 (October 2008): 368, 370.

54. Nicholas Serota, *Cy Twombly: Cycles and Seasons* (London: Tate Publishing, 2008).

55. See Leonardo da Vinci's *Drapery for a Seated Figure* (1470). On the use of cloths, draperies, and veils in the Renaissance, see Paul Hills, *Veils and Drapery in Italian Renaissance Art: Material and Metaphor* (New Haven, Conn.: Yale University Press, 2016).

56. See the catalog for the exhibition titled *The Poetry of Draped Figures*, Christ Church, Oxford University, 2 November 2009–7 February 2010.

57. Bastian, *Cy Twombly: Catalogue Raisonné of the Paintings*, vol. 3, *1966–1971*.

58. Laszlo Glozer, *Cy Twombly: Photographs 1951–2007* (Munich: Schirmer/Mosel, 2008).

59. Marek Pytel, "Eadweard Muybridge: Inverted Modernism and the Stereoscopic Vision," *Early Popular Visual Culture* 11, no. 1 (2013): 71–82.

60. Rebecca Solnit, *River of Shadows: Eadweard Muybridge and the Technological Wild West* (New York: Penguin, 2003), 83.

61. Every Google search for Muybridge's *Bridal Veil* results in images of no. 6.

62. Solnit notes the unusual appearance of the Yosemite rock formations as they are represented in Muybridge's images due to the removal of the horizon line. See Solnit, *River of Shadows*, 86.

63. Muybridge was not the only photographer fascinated by Bridal Veil in his time. See, for example, the albumen prints of the falls by Carleton Watkins from 1870.

64. Martin also paints to explore the productivity of painting in its interface with other media, paintings in which this interstice is mirrored in and by grey. For Martin the tension is between writing, sketching, and paint. I refer to Fer's discussion of Martin's use of graphite pencil in concert with paint to replicate the relationship between painting and canvas, and indeed, the relationship between graphite and paint goes further than this. While Martin is always a painter of oil on canvas, she is equally devoted to drawing on paper. Critics have commented on the ambivalence between the drawing and the wash on Martin's canvases. It is this ambivalence between space (as demarcated by paint) and movement of the pencil, gesture, the line, the mark that creates the conflict and tension between media in Martin's work. Griselda Pollock, "Agnes Dreaming: Dreaming Agnes," in *3 × Abstraction: New Methods of Drawing; Hilma Af Klint, Emma Kunz, Agnes Martin*, ed. Catherine de Zegher and Hendel Teicher (New York: The Drawing Center, with Yale University Press, 2005), 159–84; exhibition catalog.

65. Kirk Varnedoe, "Inscriptions in Arcadia," in *Cy Twombly: A Retrospective* (New York: Museum of Modern Art, 1994), 40–41; exhibition catalog.

66. Warhol's Death and Disaster tabloid images are characteristically a single-color palette, though not always grey.

67. In particular, it was at this time that the television intervened in public life in the United States with its broadcasting of the violence of the war in Vietnam. For the first time in history, images of the battlefield were transmitted to the living room. In turn, television images of the destruction and violence of American soldiers in Vietnam ignited waves of public protest that would, eventually, lead to the pulling out of troops. See Andrew Hoskins, *Televising War: From Vietnam to Iraq* (London: Bloomsbury Academic, 2005).

68. This is also contrary to Rothko's, Johns's, and Marden's love affair with paint and the painted surface, but then, that's just the point: there is no single destiny for paint on a canvas.

69. See Yau, *A Thing among Things.*

70. Moira Roth, "The Aesthetic of Indifference," *Artforum International* 16, no. 3 (November 1977): 46–53.

71. Roth discusses Johns's flags as "neutral reproductions of the American flag." Her characterization of the paintings as "neutral" is in keeping with her argument about the apparent "Aesthetic of Indifference" of the post–abstract expressionist artists. Thus, the highly charged symbol of American patriotism is reimagined as neutral in works such as *Grey Flag.* I am taking her interpretation one step further by claiming that this supposed neutrality, is in fact, a highly political gesture.

72. Rondeau, "Jasper Johns: Gray," 29–30.

73. Yau, *A Thing among Things,* 86.

74. This information is common knowledge and is provided by the museum in the title card for the painting.

75. Taylor, *The Picture in Question,* 31.

76. On the question of historical anachronism in Tansey's paintings see Danto's discussion of the way French World War I soldiers meet US World War II soldiers in a contemporary style in *The Triumph of the New York School* (1984), or the impossible scene of American Indians coming upon Robert Smithson's *Spiral Jetty* in *Purity Test* (1982). Arthur C. Danto, "Mark Tansey: The Picture within the Picture," in *Mark Tansey: Visions and Revisions* (New York: Harry N. Abrams, 1992), 7–29.

77. Taylor, *The Picture in Question,* 35–36

78. Tansey, "Notes and Comments," *Mark Tansey: Visions and Revisions,* 128.

79. Danto, "Mark Tansey: The Picture within the Picture," 15.

5. Reinvention and Perpetuation

1. Reinhard Spieler, "Without Color," in *Gerhard Richter: Ohne Farbe / Without Color,* ed. Reinhard Spieler et al. (Ostfildern: Museum Franz Gertsch and Hatje Cantz Verlag, 2004), 9; exhibition catalog.

2. Gerhard Richter, "Interview with Robert Storr," in Elger and Obrist, *Gerhard Richter: Text,* 379.

3. From a letter to Edy de Wilde, 23 February 1975, in *Gerhard Richter: The Daily Practice of Painting; Writings and Interviews 1962–1993,* ed. Hans Ulrich Obrist; trans. David Britt (London: Thames and Hudson, 1995), 82–83.

4. Benjamin Buchloh, "Gerhard Richter's New Abstractions: Infinite and Infinitesimal," in *Gerhard Richter. Abstract Paintings* (Paris: Marian Goodman Gallery, 2008), 66; exhibition catalog.

5. From a letter to E. de Wilde, 23 February 1975, in Obrist, *Gerhard Richter: The Daily Practice of Painting,* 83.

6. The preceding quotation is also written as "Grey is the epitome of non-statement" in British translations.

7. "Interview with Jan Thorn-Prikker, 2004," in Elger and Obrist, *Gerhard Richter: Text,* 478.

8. Others have claimed that Richter is the exemplary modernist painter. See, for example, Gertrud Koch, "The Richter Scale of Blur," *October* 62 (Autumn 1992): 133–42. See also the other essays collected in Jean-Philippe Antoine, Gertrud Koch, and Luc Lang, *Gerhard Richter* (Paris: Dis Voir, 1995).

9. The Deutsche Guggenheim was open on Unter den Linden between 1997 and 2012.

10. Gerhard Richter and Benjamin H. D. Buchloh, *Gerhard Richter: Acht Grau/Gerhard Richter: Eight Grey* (Berlin: Deutsche Guggenheim, in association with Hatje Cantz Verlag, 2002); exhibition catalog, Deutsche Guggenheim, 11 October 2002–5 January 2003.

11. Buchloh describes how the panels are produced: "Pure pigment is dispersed on the backside of a glass pane and subsequently fused with the surface at considerable heat." Benjamin H. D. Buchloh, "Gerhard Richter's *Eight Gray:* Between *Vorschein* and *Glanz,*" in ibid., 19 note 6.

12. Of course, it is not the end point for Richter's vision of paint, as he goes on over the next decade to pursue painting beyond painting when he exhibits photocopies of his work, and makes tapestries of the abstract paintings. According to the paintings, the end has arrived and is simultaneously still to come.

13. Buchloh, "Gerhard Richter's *Eight Gray,*" 14.

14. CR 886-4. I identify each of the works that bear generic titles by the

catalogue raisonné entry as they are given on Richter's website: http://www.gerhard-richter.com.

15. Most recently, this was the effect created in the Centre Pompidou installation of *Panorama,* the Richter retrospective that traveled from Berlin to London to Paris. *Gerhard Richter. Panorama,* Musée National d'Art Moderne, Centre Georges Pompidou, Paris, France, 6 June 2012–24 September 2012.

16. One could also argue that they end up referring to everything outside themselves when they act as mirrors to reflect the world of Berlin outside the Deutsche Guggenheim.

17. Buchloh mentions Richter's "commitment to the non-color gray from the mid-1960s onward" and identifies gray monochrome paintings CR 143-1, CR143-2, and CR143-3 from the 1960s as being engaged with the issues of the contradiction between the purity of abstraction and the dynamics of referentiality, but there is little mention of the importance or significance of their color: grey. See Buchloh, "Gerhard Richter's *Eight Gray,*" 18.

18. Helmut Friedel, ed., *Gerhard Richter: Atlas* (New York: Distributed Art Publishers, 2007).

19. Quoted by Robert Storr, "Gerhard Richter: Forty Years of Painting," in *Gerhard Richter: Forty Years of Painting* (New York: Museum of Modern Art, 2002), 55; exhibition catalog.

20. Ibid., 68. Original text from Gérard Audinet, "L'age d'oeuvre: Early and Late," *Kanaleurope* 3 (1992): 45.

21. Frances Guerin, "The Grey Space Between: Gerhard Richter's *18. Oktober 1977,*" in *The Image and the Witness: Trauma, Memory and Visual Culture,* ed. Frances Guerin and Roger Hallas (London: Wallflower Press, 2007), 111–26.

22. Elger and Obrist, *Gerhard Richter: Text,* 191.

23. Ibid.

24. See, for example, Friedrich, *Grau ohne Grund.* Friedrich's book is one of a handful that specifically address the significance of grey as subject matter in twentieth-century painting. This is in addition to the publications that accompanied the exhibition of Richter's grey paintings in Mönchengladbach and Braunschweig in 1975: *Gerhard Richter. Graue Bilder,* as well as the *Ohne Farbe / Without Colour* exhibition in Burgdorf, Switzerland, in 2005. See Spieler et al., *Gerhard Richter: Ohne Farbe / Without Color.*

25. Spieler et al., *Gerhard Richter. Ohne Farbe / Without Color.*

26. CR 194-18.

27. CR 194-6.

28. CR 247-11.

29. A particularly interesting history of the rise and fall of German in-

dustry in the postwar period is Werner Abelshauser's as it puts it within the frame of the encroachment of American Fordism and its development. See Werner Abelshauser, *The Dynamics of German Industry: Germany's Path toward the New Economy and the American Challenge* (New York: Berghahn Books, 2005).

30. These three paintings are CR 247-1, CR 247-2, and CR 194-12, respectively.

31. The two *Abstraktes Bild* images from 1992 and 1999 are listed as CR 753-10 and CR 860-7, respectively. There are numerous sources for the discussion of memory in Richter's early works in particular. See, for example, Benjamin Buchloh, "Divided Memory and Post-Traditional Identity: Gerhard Richter's Work of Mourning," *October* 75 (Winter 1996): 61–82. Christian Lotz gives a good introduction to the claim for the materialization of memory in the blurred photo-paintings. See Christian Lotz, *The Art of Gerhard Richter: Hermeneutics, Images, Meaning* (London: Bloomsbury, 2015), especially chapter 2.

32. Robert Storr, "Painting History—Painting Tragedy," in *Gerhard Richter October 18, 1977* (New York: Museum of Modern Art, 2000), 123–28; exhibition catalog.

33. Koch, "The Richter Scale of Blur." See also Koch's more general work that is relevant here: Gertrud Koch, "The Open Secret: Gerhard Richter and the Surface of Modernity," in Antoine, Koch, and Lang, *Gerhard Richter*, 9–28.

34. This blur is discussed in the opening pages of Clark, *The Painting of Modern Life*.

35. Richter had the normally blacked-out windows of the Deutsche Guggenheim opened so that the street and its activities outside were visible on the panels, depending on the angle at which they were seen.

36. Each panel was mounted on a metal frame with fastenings that could be loosened so that the panel could be tilted, in theory to accommodate the needs of the individual spectator. But in practice, any adjustment could only be made by Richter himself or the curators.

37. Götz Adriani, "On the 'Desire to Paint Something Beautiful,'" in *Gerhard Richter: Paintings from Private Collections*, ed. Götz Adriani (Ostfildern: Hatje Cantz Verlag, 2008), 30.

38. Ibid. See CR 680-3. Gudrun Ensslin was an early member of the Baader-Meinhof group or Red Army Faction, a self-designated terrorist group committed to exposing the injustices of postwar German political and social institutions. Ensslin, Andreas Baader, and Jan-Carl Raspe committed suicide in Stammheim Prison, where they were being held following a number of murders.

39. See Guerin, "The Grey Space Between.."

40. Ibid.

41. The work was first exhibited at the Kunsthalle, Nuremberg, in a small exhibition: *Malerei: Gotthard Graubner, Johannes Grützke, Gerhard Richter. Beispiele au seiner Privatsammlung*, 28 July 1989–17 September 1989. The *18. Oktober 1977* cycle was first exhibited in the same year at Museum Haus Esters, Krefeld, 12 February 1989–9 April 1989.

42. Richter frustrates the viewer's expectations through the representation of curtains, fabrics of all sorts, doors and windows from his earliest works. See, for example, *Vorhang IV / Curtain IV* (1965; CR 57).

43. CR 684-2 and CR 319, respectively.

44. I discuss this relationship in chapters 3 and 4 when I demonstrate that grey is the luminescence on the canvas of a Rothko painting, the illumination of Scully's grey work, the soft and gently pulsating light of a Martin painting. Even the grey on Whistler's canvases in the dense night air that hangs over the Thames has, as I argue in chapter 2, a luminescence to it.

45. We see how Richter arrives at the title for the *Cage* series in *Gerhard Richter Painting*, when he says he was listening to Cage's music as he was painting the works. Directed by Corinna Belz (Berlin: Zero One Film, 2011), DVD.

46. Buchloh, "Gerhard Richter's New Abstractions," 67.

47. John Cage, *Silence: Lectures and Writings* (Middletown, Conn.: Wesleyan University Press, 1961).

48. The white Newman zip on a heavily layered and worked-up egg tempera-white ground insists on the variegated identity of white.

49. The three installations of *Panorama* in Berlin at the Neue Nationalegalerie, Tate Modern London, and Centre Pompidou Paris were very different. Not only were different works included; they also were curated as three different exhibitions.

50. I write at length about how the paintings in *18. Oktober 1977* ask that we both reflect on the events depicted and consider our responsibility for their memory. See Guerin, "The Grey Space Between."

51. Anne Friedberg, *Window Shopping: Cinema and the Postmodern* (Berkeley: University of California Press, 1994).

52. Alberti, *On Painting.*

53. Krauss, *The Optical Unconscious.*

54. Storr, "The Paintings," in *Gerhard Richter October 18, 1977*, 112–13.

55. Martin Jay is among those who point out that, since the Enlightenment, the omnipotence of and vision as epistemology have consistently been questioned and challenged in intellectual and artistic circles. Martin Jay, *Downcast Eyes: The Denigration of Vision in Twentieth-Century French Thought* (Berkeley: University of California Press, 1993).

56. Monet's images obscure for different reasons, notably in a search for

purity of vision, and not for the truth about the world. Koch makes the argument that the blur is Richter's vision of modernism. See Koch, "The Richter Scale of Blur."

57. *Tote / Dead* (CR 9); or *Kuh / Cow* (CR 15). Other examples are *Alfa Romeo* (1965; CR 68) and *Domecke / Cathedral Corner* (1987; CR 629-1).

58. For the first time ever, the windows of the Deutsche Guggenheim were opened so that inside and outside were able to be integrated, the one a continuation of the other on the surface of the eight grey mirrored surfaces. See Buchloh, *Gerhard Richter: Acht Grau.*

59. It may be tempting to argue that we could say the same about the *Cage* paintings, especially given what I say above. In these later works, however, grey remains distinct because it retains a mutability; other colors, yellow, red, blue, green, are quantifiable, or rather, can be qualified, seen, understood in their verticality, in their horizontality, in their definitiveness. Grey is more difficult. Yellow is yellow, red is red, blue is blue, but grey is a whole spectrum of ever shifting tones, temperatures, densities. Is it the background or the foreground? Is it horizontal or vertical? Does it erase, or is it erased?

60. Markus Heinzelmann, Uwe M. Schneede, Botho Strauss, and Siri Hustvedt, *Gerhard Richter. Overpainted Photographs* (Leverkusen: Museum Morsbroich, in association with Hatje Cantz Verlag, 2008); exhibition catalog.

61. Adriani, "On the 'Desire to Paint Something Beautiful,'" in Adriani, *Gerhard Richter. Paintings from Private Collections,* 11.

62. Markus Heinzelmann, "Blurring: Gerhard Richter's Overpainted Photographs as Objects of Contemplation," in Heinzelmann et al., *Gerhard Richter. Overpainted Photographs,* 87.

63. Uwe M. Schneede, "Reality, the Photograph, the Paint, and the Picture," in Heinzelmann et al., *Gerhard Richter. Overpainted Photographs,* 193.

64. Gerhard Richter, *Glassfenster, 625 Farben / Glass Window, 625 Colors* (1989)

65. See, for example, *Zwölf Spiegel für eine Bank / Twelve Mirrors for a Bank* (1991), and *Sechs Spiegel für eine Bank / Six Mirrors for a Bank* (1991). See also *Schwarz, Rot, Gold / Black, Red, Gold* (1999).

66. Buchloh, "Gerhard Richter's *Eight Gray,*" 20–24.

67. This also reminds of the architects working in glass who were interested in exploring the dynamic interaction between light and glass in the 1920s, especially Paul Scheerbart and others associated with the Gläserne Kette group. See Dennis Sharp, ed., *Glass Architecture by Paul Scheerbart and Alpine Architecture by Bruno Taut,* trans. James Palmes (New York: Praeger, 1972).

68. On Richter's use of glass, see Taisuke Edamura, "Vitreous Demeanor and Gerhard Richter's Moving Glass," *Wreck* 3, no. 1 (2010): 13–17.

69. "Interview with Hans Ulrich Obrist" (2006), in Elger and Obrist, *Gerhard Richter: Text,* 522.

70. Jürgen Harten, *Gerhard Richter. Bilder = Paintings 1962–1985* (Cologne: DuMont, 1986).

71. See Iain Boyd Whyte and Romana Schneider, eds., *Die gläserne Kette* (Berlin: Ernst & Sohn, 1986).

72. The piece, which resembles a German flag (its dimensions are 2072 × 317 cm), was made specifically to hang in the newly renovated Reichstag.

73. They were, for example, exhibited in Düsseldorf at the K20 Kunstsammlung Nordrhein-Westfalen in 2005, the Guggenheim Museum, Bilbao, Spain, in 2004.

74. See Guerin, "The Grey Space Between," for a more detailed analysis of the cinematic movement of the three *Gegenüberstellung* paintings as a series.

75. The titles for these images were changed on Richter's website. Until April 2017, they were titled *Selbst. 3-Faches / Self-Portrait. 3 Times,* followed by the date. However, the titles are now represented by dates only. As of the writing of this book, the catalogue raisonné of the overpainted photographs was not published, and therefore none of the works have corresponding numbers. Accessed 24 April 2017. www.gerhard-richter.com/en/art/overpainted-photographs/self-portraits-81.

76. More recently, Richter has been known to take pictures and paintings out of the catalogue raisonné. See Heiner Neuendorf, "Collectors Alarmed as Gerhard Richter Disowns Early Works from West German Period," *Artnews,* 21 July 2015. Accessed 8 December 2015. https://news.artnet.com/people/gerhard-richter-omits-art-from-catalogue-318665.

77. I am thinking here specifically of the light-in-motion studies of Viking Eggeling and Laszlo Moholy-Nagy from the 1920s.

78. Gerhard Richter, *Spiegel* interview conducted by Susanne Beyer and Ulrike Knöfel in 2005 in Elger and Obrist, *Gerhard Richter. Text,* 505.

79. I allude to this phenomenon in relation to *Cage I–VI.*

80. CR 194-10, CR194-2, and CR 194-8, respectively.

81. Dave Hickey, "Richter's Hope," in *Richter 858: Eight Abstract Pictures,* ed. David Breskin (San Francisco: San Francisco Museum of Modern Art and the Shifting Foundation, 2002); exhibition catalog.

82. "Interview with Hans Ulrich Obrist, 2007," in Elger and Obrist, *Gerhard Richter. Text,* 532.

83. He talks about this in Corinna Belz's film *Gerhard Richter: Painting.*

84. For examples see those mentioned earlier in the CR 194 series.

85. See, for example, *Abstraktes Bild / Abstract Painting* (2000; CR 867) and *Abstraktes Bild / Abstract Painting* (2000; CR 868).

86. *Abstraktes Bild / Abstract Painting* (2000; CR 867-1, 867-2, 867-3), *Abstraktes Bild / Abstract Painting* (2000; CR 868-1, 868-2, 868-3, 868-4), *Zweige / Branches* (2000; CR 870-2).

87. CR 224, 361-1, and 361-2, respectively.

88. This conscious density and materiality of paint are why these works are so different from those of abstract expressionism, even though they can often be coupled with them.

89. CR 468-1, 2, 3, and 469-1.

90. Varnedoe, "Why Abstract Art?," 1. I introduce this idea in chapter 2.

91. Varnedoe, *Pictures of Nothing*, 243.

92. This formed part of the criticism leveled at early European modernism, especially surrealism, futurism, and cubism. See Donald Kuspit, *The Cult of the Avant-Garde Artist* (Cambridge: Cambridge University Press, 2004).

93. "Interview with Benjamin Buchloh," in Elger and Obrist, *Gerhard Richter. Text*, 177–78.

94. Königsallee replaced the fortifications of the court in 1802. Today it is a shopping avenue of the magnitude of Avenue Montaigne in Paris or Fifth Avenue in New York. It is also a symbol of Düsseldorf as the capital of the most economically powerful state in Germany.

95. See Guerin, "The Grey Space Between."

96. I make this argument about the politics of works exhibited in this space of the Deutsche Guggenheim on Unter den Linden. See Frances Guerin, "The Placement of Shadows: What's Inside William Kentridge's *Black Box*?," in *Taking Place: Location and the Moving Image*, ed. Elena Gorfinkel and John David Rhodes (Minneapolis: University of Minnesota Press, 2011), 233–54.

97. See Benjamin Buchloh, "Divided Memory and Post-Traditional Identity: Gerhard Richter's Work of Mourning," *October* 75 (Winter 1996): 61–82.

98. "Coming to terms with the (Nazi) past" was most vigorously discussed in the Historians' Debate in Germany in 1986/87. See Richard J. Evans, *In Hitler's Shadow: West German Historians and the Attempt to Escape from the Nazi Past* (London: Pantheon Books, 1989).

99. The German term *Vergangenheitsbewältigung* has no equivalent in English. It can be translated, however, as "coming to terms with the past." A handful of German artists and filmmakers especially became engaged with these questions in the early 1960s. See, for example, the work of Anselm Kiefer, Alexander Kluge, and Rainer Werner Fassbinder, to name just a few.

100. Guerin, "The Grey Space Between."

101. *September* (2005; CR 891-5).

102. *September* (2009; Editions CR 139).

103. Buchloh, "Gerhard Richter's New Abstractions," 70.

104. See Buchloh, *Acht Grau.*

105. Elger and Obrist, *Gerhard Richter. Text,* 184.

106. Ibid.

107. Another of his haunting self-portraits (*Selbstporträt / Self-Portrait,* CR 836-2) also demonstrates this simultaneous presence and effacement of the artist: Richter's head is bowed, his image blurred; we cannot see him and he does not look at us. The image is painted after a photograph from *Atlas.* We recognize that there is no chance of finding the man in his paintings—the search for the identity of the artist is a search pursued in vain. But we must continue the search; otherwise we would never know of its fictions.

108. Gerhard Richter, *128 Fotos von einem Bild 1978* (Cologne: Verlag der Buchhandlung Walther König, 1999).

109. It is also interesting that, as of the writing of this book, the work has not yet sold. Some copies of the original 128 can still be found for sale on the internet.

Epilogue

1. I am not suggesting that this is what Richter would claim to be doing, but rather that as critics we are called to look at the works for the measure of their cultural value.

2. Robert Fleck, *Yan Pei-Ming. HELP!* (Paris: Galerie Thaddaeus Ropac, 2013); exhibition catalog.

3. Gerhard Richter, "Interview with Christiane Vielhaber" (1986), in Elger and Obrist, *Gerhard Richter. Text,* 192.

4. Madeleine Grynsztejn and Helen Molesworth, *Luc Tuymans* (New York: D.A.P., 2009).

INDEX

FRANCES GUERIN teaches in the School of Arts, University of Kent. She is the author of *A Culture of Light: Cinema and Technology in 1920s Germany* (Minnesota, 2005) and *Through Amateur Eyes: Film and Photography in Nazi Germany* (Minnesota, 2011), as well as editor of *The Image and the Witness: Trauma, Memory, and Visual Culture* (with Roger Hallas) and *On Not Looking: The Paradox of Contemporary Visual Culture.*